Key 키출판사

매3영

모의고사

기출 | 하프

교육 R&D에 앞서가는

왜 〈매3영 기출하프모의고사〉인가

수능 영어 독해는
시간 싸움입니다.

수능 영어는 총 45문항을 제한 시간 70분 안에 푸는 시험입니다. 이중 듣기 17문항을 위한 25분과 마킹 시간 5분을 빼면, 독해 28문항에 오롯이 투자할 수 있는 시간은 40분 정도에 불과합니다. 즉 산술적으로 독해 한 문제를 푸는 데 드는 시간이 1분 20~25초 사이여야 한다는 의미입니다. 영어 독해 문제를 푸는 과정은 단순히 단어나 문장의 표면적 의미를 이해하는 과정을 넘어, 깊은 사고 과정을 통해 단락의 핵심과 행간의 의미를 적극적으로 파악하고 추론해야 하는 활발한 정신 작용입니다. 수능에서 원칙적으로 속도보다 역량 측정을 중시함에도 불구하고, 많은 수험생들이 가장 큰 고민거리로 '시간 부족'을 호소하는 것이 바로 이 때문입니다.

시간 관리의 열쇠는
체계적인 실전 훈련에 있습니다.

시간 부족을 해결하려면 평소에 '시간 관리' 연습을 많이 해봐야 한다는 것은 당연한 결론입니다. 그렇다면 어떻게 훈련해야 할까요? 답은 가능하면 실전 모의고사 한 세트 단위로 전체적인 시간 흐름을 관리하는 연습을 꾸준히 해봐야 한다는 것입니다. 아무리 문항당 1분 20초가 평균 풀이 시간이라고 해도, 유형별로 시간이 더 들어가는 문제도, 덜 들어가는 문제도 있기 때문입니다. 예컨대 목적, 심경, 일치불일치처럼 정답의 단서 위주로 속독해 빠르게 해결할 수 있는 문제가 있는가 하면, 지문을 전체적으로 다 읽고도 중요한 한 문장을 여러 번 다시 읽으며 고민해야 하는 빈칸, 순서, 삽입과 같은 문제도 있습니다. 따라서 '진짜' 실전력을 기르려면, 한 문제 한 문제씩 시간을 정해 푸는 연습은 적합하지 않습니다. 여러 유형이 뒤섞여 있는 하나의 세트 안에서 강약 조절을 훈련하며, 시험장에서 그대로 활용할 나만의 풀이 흐름을 미리 준비해두는 과정이 꼭 필요합니다.

그래서, <매3영 기출하프모의고사>는 '진짜' 실전 훈련에 집중합니다.

하지만 이렇듯 세트별 실전 훈련의 중요성을 알더라도, 처음부터 매일 모의고사를 한 세트씩 풀기에는 큰 부담이 따릅니다. 수능은 장기전인 만큼 매일 모든 과목을 고르게 공부해야 하므로, 과목별로 적절한 하루 공부량을 설계해 꾸준히 실천하는 것이 무엇보다 중요합니다. 그래서 <매3영 기출하프모의고사>는 한 세트의 '절반' 분량부터 시작하는 단계적 실전 훈련을 제시합니다. 하루 20분 투자로 실전 감각을 극대화할 수 있는 공부법을 차근차근 안내합니다.

'분량은 절반, 효과는 2배' 되는 체계적인 문항 구성

수능 영어 독해 28문항은 무작위로 구성되지 않습니다. 유형별, 모듈별로 철저한 설계를 바탕으로 합니다. <매3영 기출하프모의고사>는 최신 5개년 문항별 출제 비중 분석을 토대로, 매일 수능을 '실전 느낌 그대로' 재현할 수 있는 <14문항 × 14회분>을 담았습니다.

실제 수능

번호	유형	분류
18	목적 파악	대의 파악
19	심경 파악	
20	주장 파악	
21	함축 의미	함의
22	요지 파악	대의 파악
23	주제 추론	
24	제목 추론	
25	도표 불일치	세부 내용
26	내용 불일치	
27	안내문 불일치	
28	안내문 일치	
29	어법성 판단	어법 어휘
30	어휘 추론	
31	빈칸 추론	빈칸
32	빈칸 추론	
33	빈칸 추론	
34	빈칸 추론	
35	무관한 문장	간접 쓰기
36	순서 배열	
37	순서 배열	
38	문장 삽입	
39	문장 삽입	
40	문단 요약	
41~42	장문 독해1	복합 문항
43~45	장문 독해2	

하프모의고사

번호	유형	분류
01	목적/심경 파악	대의 파악
02	주장/요지 파악	
03	함축 의미	함의
04	주제/제목 추론	대의 파악
05	도표/내용/안내문 일치불일치	세부 내용
06	어법성 판단 / 어휘 추론	어법 어휘
07	빈칸 추론	빈칸
08	빈칸 추론	
09	무관한 문장	간접 쓰기
10	순서 배열	
11	문장 삽입	
12	문단 요약	
13~14	장문 독해	복합 문항

⟨매3영 기출하프모의고사⟩, 이렇게 공부하세요

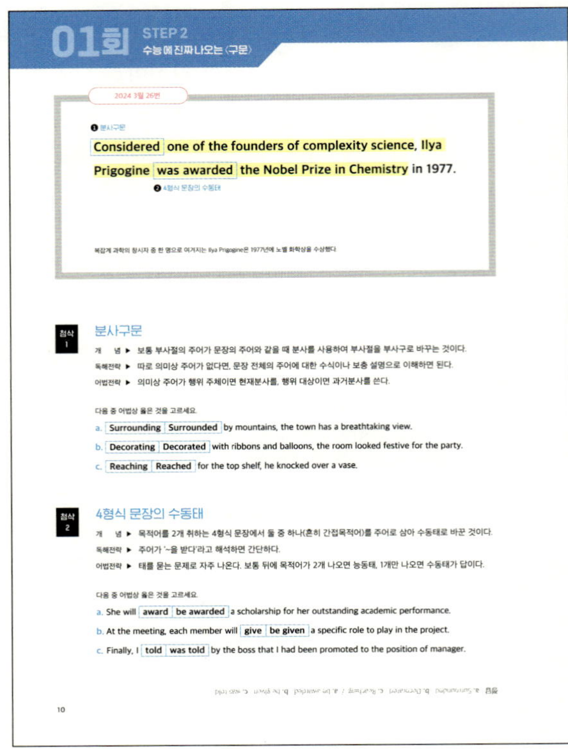

수능 필수 단어 학습

- 회차별로 꼭 알아야 하는 수능 필수 단어 목록을 확인하고, 몰랐던 단어는 문제풀이 전에 미리 암기하세요.

수능 필수 구문 학습

- 문제를 더욱 어렵게 만드는 수능 필수 구문을 실제 기출 문장으로 확인하세요.

- 구문별로 꼭 알아야 할 독해, 어법 전략을 체크하고, 기출과 비슷한 예문 속에서 전략이 어떻게 적용되는지 점검해 보세요.

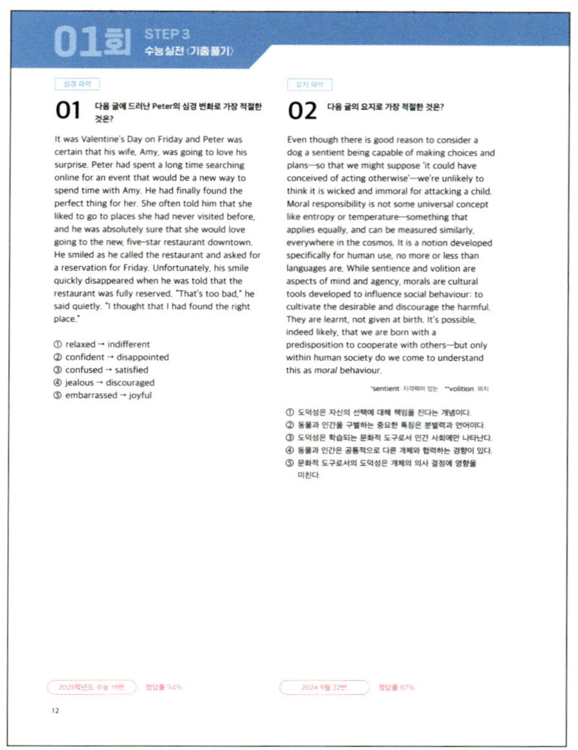

수능 기출 문제풀이

- 실전 느낌 그대로 구성한 '기출하프모의고사'를 제한 시간에 맞춰 풀어보세요. 문제마다 유형과 난이도에 따라 시간 안배를 달리하며 실전 감각을 길러 보세요.

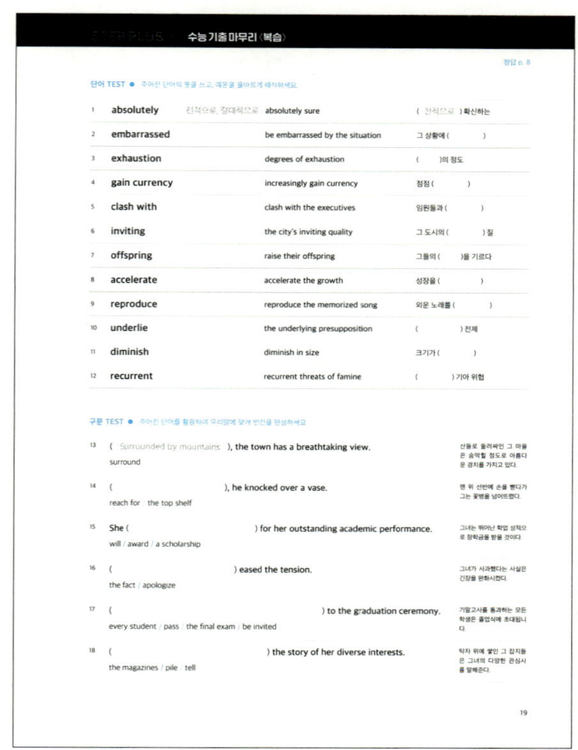

핵심 단어, 구문 복습

- 문제풀이 전 봤던 단어, 구문을 최종적으로 복습하며 '진짜' 내 것으로 만드세요.

정답 및 해설

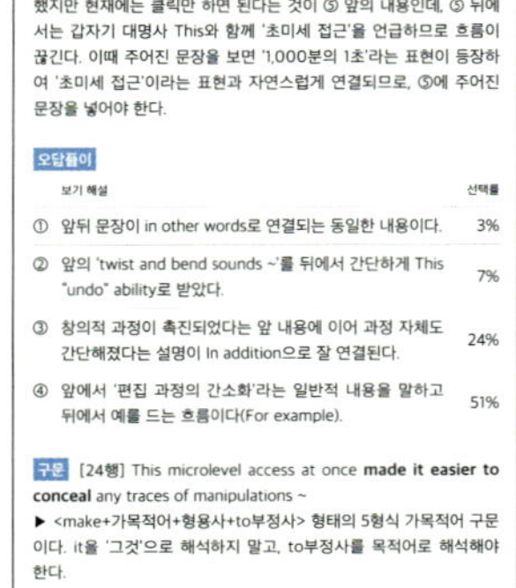

틀린 문제는 상세 해설 및 오답풀이를 통해 복습하며, 정답과 오답의 이유를 확인하세요.

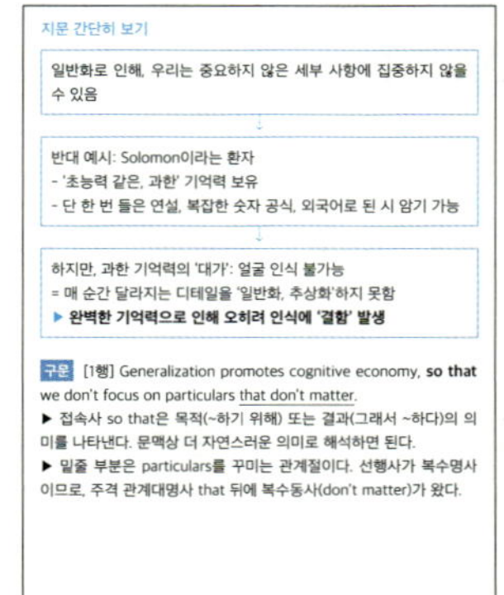

지문간단히보기는 복잡한 논리 구조도 쉽게 파악할 수 있도록, 글의 흐름을 간단한 표로 제시합니다. 정답을 맞혔더라도 핵심 파악이 어려웠다면 꼭 체크해 보세요.

차례

기출 하프 모의고사

● 문제에 나오는 단어들을 확인하세요.

☐ absolutely	ad. 전적으로, 절대적으로	☐ offspring	n. 자손
☐ disappear	v. 사라지다	☐ delicate	a. 정교한, 섬세한
☐ discouraged	a. 낙담한, 의욕이 꺾인	☐ curb	v. 억제하다, 제한하다
☐ embarrassed	a. 당황한, 난처한	☐ instructive	a. 유익한, 교육적인
☐ conceive of	~을 생각하다, 상상하다	☐ accelerate	v. 가속화하다
☐ wicked	a. 사악한	☐ memorize	v. 암기하다, 외우다
☐ cosmos	n. 우주	☐ overlap	v. 겹치다 n. 중복
☐ no more or less	별반 다르지 않은, 더도 덜도 아닌	☐ reproduce	v. 재현하다, 복제하다
☐ black and white	흑백 (논리)의, 이분법적인	☐ uneven	a. 고르지 않은
☐ competently	ad. 유능하게	☐ philosopher	n. 철학자
☐ severe	a. 심각한	☐ presupposition	n. 전제
☐ exhaustion	n. 소진, 탈진	☐ underlie	v. ~에 기초가 되다
☐ overcome	v. 극복하다	☐ figurative	a. 구상의, 조형의, 비유적인
☐ gain currency	유행하다, 통용되다	☐ represent	v. 나타내다, 표현하다, 대표하다
☐ threaten	v. 위협하다	☐ familiar with	~에 익숙한, 친숙한
☐ crucial	a. 아주 중요한	☐ diminish	v. 작아지다, 축소시키다
☐ circle back to	~로 다시 돌아오다, 회귀하다	☐ egocentric	a. 자기중심적인
☐ incorporate	v. 통합하다, 포함시키다	☐ diversification	n. 다각화, 다양화
☐ drop out of	~을 중퇴하다	☐ agricultural	a. 농업의
☐ founder	n. 창시자, 설립자	☐ recurrent	a. 반복되는
☐ inaccuracy	n. 부정확성	☐ literate	a. 글을 읽고 쓸 줄 아는
☐ assist with	~을 돕다	☐ compression	n. 압축
☐ clash with	~와 충돌하다	☐ regard A as B	A를 B라고 간주하다, 여기다
☐ measuring stick	측정의 잣대, 가늠자	☐ raw material	원료
☐ inviting	a. 매력적인, 솔깃한	☐ sensitive	a. 민감한

2024 3월 26번

❶ 분사구문

Considered one of the founders of complexity science, Ilya Prigogine **was awarded** the Nobel Prize in Chemistry in 1977.

❷ 4형식 문장의 수동태

복잡계 과학의 창시자 중 한 명으로 여겨지는 Ilya Prigogine은 1977년에 노벨 화학상을 수상했다.

첨삭 1 · 분사구문

개　념 ▶ 보통 부사절의 주어가 문장의 주어와 같을 때 분사를 사용하여 부사절을 부사구로 바꾸는 것이다.

독해전략 ▶ 따로 의미상 주어가 없다면, 문장 전체의 주어에 대한 수식이나 보충 설명으로 이해하면 된다.

어법전략 ▶ 의미상 주어가 행위 주체이면 현재분사를, 행위 대상이면 과거분사를 쓴다.

다음 중 어법상 옳은 것을 고르세요.

a. **Surrounding** **Surrounded** by mountains, the town has a breathtaking view.

b. **Decorating** **Decorated** with ribbons and balloons, the room looked festive for the party.

c. **Reaching** **Reached** for the top shelf, he knocked over a vase.

첨삭 2 · 4형식 문장의 수동태

개　념 ▶ 목적어를 2개 취하는 4형식 문장에서 둘 중 하나(흔히 간접목적어)를 주어로 삼아 수동태로 바꾼 것이다.

독해전략 ▶ 주어가 '~을 받다'라고 해석하면 간단하다.

어법전략 ▶ 태를 묻는 문제로 자주 나온다. 보통 뒤에 목적어가 2개 나오면 능동태, 1개만 나오면 수동태가 답이다.

다음 중 어법상 옳은 것을 고르세요.

a. She will **award** **be awarded** a scholarship for her outstanding academic performance.

b. At the meeting, each member will **give** **be given** a specific role to play in the project.

c. Finally, I **told** **was told** by the boss that I had been promoted to the position of manager.

2024 3월 39번

❸ 동격 접속사 that

The fact **that** perspective and information about spatial layout go together **reveals** something important about *seeing*.

❹ 주어-동사 수 일치

시점과 공간 배치 정보가 함께 어우러진다는 사실은 '본다는 것'에 관한 뭔가 중요한 것을 드러낸다.

첨삭 3 — 동격 접속사 that

개 념 ▶ fact, news, idea, rumor, evidence 등 추상명사 뒤로 그 내용을 설명하는 명사절을 연결할 때 쓴다.

독해전략 ▶ that절의 내용을 정확하게 파악해야 '사실, 뉴스, 개념, 소문, 증거'의 의미를 제대로 아는 것이다.

어법전략 ▶ 동격의 that절은 명사절이므로, 접속사 that 뒤에는 완전한 문장이 온다.

다음 중 어법상 옳은 것을 고르세요.

a. The fact | that | what | she immediately apologized eased the tension.

b. He was thrilled by the news | that | what | his manuscript had been accepted for publication.

c. The rumor | that | which | Mr. Kim would resign was met with mixed reactions from students.

첨삭 4 — 주어-동사 수 일치

개 념 ▶ 긴 주어 속 핵심이 되는 명사를 찾아 동사의 단수/복수 여부를 결정하는 것이다.

독해전략 ▶ 핵심 주어와 동사를 중심으로 문장의 대략적 의미를 먼저 파악하고, 수식어를 덧붙여 나간다.

어법전략 ▶ 주어에 형용사구, 분사구, 관계절 등이 붙어 길어질 때 문장 전체의 동사를 정확히 찾아야 한다.

다음 중 어법상 옳은 것을 고르세요.

a. Anyone eager to improve their skills | is | are | welcome to join the workshop.

b. Every student who passes the final exam | is | are | invited to the graduation ceremony.

c. The books and magazines piled on the table | tell | tells | the story of her diverse interests.

01 다음 글에 드러난 Peter의 심경 변화로 가장 적절한 것은?

It was Valentine's Day on Friday and Peter was certain that his wife, Amy, was going to love his surprise. Peter had spent a long time searching online for an event that would be a new way to spend time with Amy. He had finally found the perfect thing for her. She often told him that she liked to go to places she had never visited before, and he was absolutely sure that she would love going to the new, five-star restaurant downtown. He smiled as he called the restaurant and asked for a reservation for Friday. Unfortunately, his smile quickly disappeared when he was told that the restaurant was fully reserved. "That's too bad," he said quietly. "I thought that I had found the right place."

① relaxed → indifferent
② confident → disappointed
③ confused → satisfied
④ jealous → discouraged
⑤ embarrassed → joyful

02 다음 글의 요지로 가장 적절한 것은?

Even though there is good reason to consider a dog a sentient being capable of making choices and plans—so that we might suppose 'it could have conceived of acting otherwise'—we're unlikely to think it is wicked and immoral for attacking a child. Moral responsibility is not some universal concept like entropy or temperature—something that applies equally, and can be measured similarly, everywhere in the cosmos. It is a notion developed specifically for human use, no more or less than languages are. While sentience and volition are aspects of mind and agency, morals are cultural tools developed to influence social behaviour: to cultivate the desirable and discourage the harmful. They are learnt, not given at birth. It's possible, indeed likely, that we are born with a predisposition to cooperate with others—but only within human society do we come to understand this as *moral* behaviour.

*sentient: 지각력이 있는   **volition: 의지

① 도덕성은 자신의 선택에 대해 책임을 진다는 개념이다.
② 동물과 인간을 구별하는 중요한 특징은 분별력과 언어이다.
③ 도덕성은 학습되는 문화적 도구로서 인간 사회에만 나타난다.
④ 동물과 인간은 공통적으로 다른 개체와 협력하는 경향이 있다.
⑤ 문화적 도구로서의 도덕성은 개체의 의사 결정에 영향을 미친다.

2025학년도 수능 19번   정답률 94%

2024 9월 22번   정답률 87%

03 밑줄 친 Burnout hasn't had the last word.가 다음 글에서 의미하는 바로 가장 적절한 것은?

To balance the need for breadth (everyone feels a bit burned out) and depth (some are so burned out, they can no longer do their jobs), we ought to think of burnout not as a *state* but as a *spectrum*. In most public discussion of burnout, we talk about workers who "are burned out," as if that status were black and white. A black-and-white view cannot account for the variety of burnout experience, though. If there is a clear line between burned out and not, as there is with a lightbulb, then we have no good way to categorize people who say they are burned out but still manage to do their work competently. Thinking about burnout as a spectrum solves this problem; those who claim burnout but are not debilitated by it are simply dealing with a partial or less-severe form of it. They are experiencing burnout without *being* burned out. Burnout hasn't had the last word.

*debilitate: 쇠약하게 하다

① Public discussion of burnout has not reached an end.
② There still exists room for a greater degree of exhaustion.
③ All-or-nothing criteria are applicable to burnout symptoms.
④ Exhaustion is overcome in different ways based on its severity.
⑤ Degrees of exhaustion are shaped by individuals' perceptions.

04 다음 글의 제목으로 가장 적절한 것은?

There are good reasons why open-office plans have gained currency, but open offices may not be the plan of choice for *all* times. Instead, the right plan seems to be building a culture of change. Overly rigid habits and conventions, no matter how well-considered or well-intentioned, threaten innovation. The crucial take-away from analyzing office plans over time is that the answers keep changing. It might seem that there is a straight line of progress, but it's a myth. Surveying office spaces from the past eighty years, one can see a cycle that repeats. Comparing the offices of the 1940s with contemporary office spaces shows that they have circled back around to essentially the same style, via a period in the 1980s when partitions and cubicles were more the norm. The technologies and colors may differ, but the 1940s and 2000s plans are alike, right down to the pillars running down the middle.

*rigid: 굳은 **pillar: 기둥

① Why Are Open-office Plans So Cost-efficient?
② How to Incorporate Retro Styles into Office Spaces
③ An Office Divided: Why Partitions Limit Productivity
④ Office Designs: What Goes Around Comes Around
⑤ Tips for Managing Contemporary Office Spaces

2024 6월 21번   정답률 25%

2024 9월 24번   정답률 76%

05 Ilya Prigogine에 관한 다음 글의 내용과 일치하지 <u>않는</u> 것은?

Ilya Prigogine was born into a Jewish family in Moscow. In 1921, he and his family left Russia, eventually settling in Belgium. His parents encouraged him to become a lawyer, and he first studied law at the Free University of Brussels. It was then that he became interested in psychology and behavioral research. In turn, reading about these subjects sparked his interest in chemistry since chemical processes affect the mind and body. He eventually dropped out of law school. Prigogine then studied chemistry and physics at the same time at the Free University of Brussels. He obtained the equivalent of a master's degree in both fields in 1939, and he obtained a PhD in chemistry in 1941 at the Free University of Brussels, where he accepted the position of professor in 1947. Considered one of the founders of complexity science, Ilya Prigogine was awarded the Nobel Prize in Chemistry in 1977.

*equivalent: 상응하는 것

① 1921년에 그와 그의 가족은 러시아를 떠났다.
② 부모님은 그가 변호사가 되기를 권했다.
③ Free University of Brussels에서 화학과 물리학을 동시에 공부했다.
④ 1941년에 Free University of Brussels의 교수직을 수락했다.
⑤ 1977년에 노벨 화학상을 수상했다.

06 다음 글의 밑줄 친 부분 중, 문맥상 낱말의 쓰임이 적절하지 <u>않은</u> 것은?

Memory is shaped by emotions connected to an experience. For this reason, inaccuracies often ① <u>hide</u> the full picture of what happened. For example, a company might decide to hire a consultant to assist with a major project. During this project, the consultant demonstrated some personality traits that clashed with a couple of the executives involved. Through the course of the project, they were able to put aside the personality ② <u>conflicts</u> in order to see their vision become a reality. Ultimately, the project was a success, enabling the company to move forward and profit. At a later date, the company, remembering the previous success, expressed an ③ <u>interest</u> in hiring the same consultant for another large project. The executives who struggled with his personality last time may most vividly remember their difficulty in overcoming his personality and related emotions. In this case, the success of the project fades into the background as they focus on their previous experience, colored by their feelings of ④ <u>discomfort</u>. As a result, they convince the company to ⑤ <u>rehire</u> the consultant, making project completion more difficult.

2024 3월 26번   정답률 86%

2024 5월 30번   정답률 27%

07 다음 빈칸에 들어갈 말로 가장 적절한 것은?

City quality is so crucial for optional activities that the extent of staying activities can often be used as a measuring stick for the quality of the city as well as of its space. Many pedestrians in a city are not necessarily an indication of good city quality —many people walking around can often be a sign of insufficient transit options or long distances between the various functions in the city. Conversely, it can be claimed that a city in which many people are not walking often indicates good city quality. In a city like Rome, it is the large number of people standing or sitting in squares rather than walking that is conspicuous. And it's not due to necessity but rather that _______________________________________. It is hard to keep moving in city space with so many temptations to stay. In contrast are many new quarters and complexes that many people walk through but rarely stop or stay in.

*pedestrian: 보행자 **conspicuous: 눈에 띄는

① the city quality is so inviting
② public spaces are already occupied
③ public transportation is not available
④ major tourist spots are within walking distance
⑤ the city's administrative buildings are concentrated

빈칸 추론

08 다음 빈칸에 들어갈 말로 가장 적절한 것은?

The term *Mother Tree* comes from forestry. It has been clear for centuries that tree parents play such an important role in raising their offspring that they can be compared to human parents. A mother tree identifies which neighboring seedlings are hers using her roots. She then, via delicate connections, supports the seedlings with a solution of sugar, a process similar to a human mother nursing her child. Shade provided by parents is another form of care, as it curbs the growth of youngsters living under their crowns. Without the shade and exposed to full sunlight, the young trees would shoot up and expand the width of their trunks so quickly they'd be exhausted after just a century or two. If, however, the young trees stand strong in the shadows for decades—or even centuries—they can live to a great age. Shade means less sunlight and therefore considerably less sugar. _______________________________________, as generations of foresters have observed. To this day, they talk of what is known in German as *erzieherischer Schatten* or "instructive shade."

*crown: 수관(나무의 가지와 잎이 있는 부분)

① One can pleasantly cool down under the shade of large trees
② The trees manage to extend their roots towards the water source
③ The attempts to outgrow neighboring seedlings are likely to succeed
④ Mother trees provide shade to accelerate the growth of their offspring
⑤ The slow pace of life gently imposed by the mother tree is no accident

09 다음 글에서 전체 흐름과 관계 <u>없는</u> 문장은?

Avian song learning occurs in two stages: first, songs must be memorized and, second, they must be practiced. In some species these two events overlap, but in others memorization can occur before practice by several months, providing an impressive example of long-term memory storage. ① The young bird's initial efforts to reproduce the memorized song are usually not successful. ② These early songs may have uneven pitch, irregular tempo, and notes that are out of order or poorly reproduced. ③ However, sound graphs of songs recorded over several weeks or months reveal that during this practice period the bird fine-tunes his efforts until he produces an accurate copy of the memorized template. ④ An important idea to emerge from the study of birdsong is that song learning is shaped by preferences and limitations. ⑤ This process requires hearing oneself sing; birds are unable to reproduce memorized songs if they are deafened after memorization but before the practice period.

*avian: 조류의

10 주어진 글 다음에 이어질 글의 순서로 가장 적절한 것은?

Philosophers who seek to understand the nature of time might consider the possibility of time travel. But there are no real-life cases of time travel.

(A) It seems that something must happen to prevent you from doing this, because if you were to succeed, you would not exist and so you would not have been able to go back in time. As a result of thinking through these sorts of cases, some philosophers claim that the very notion of time travel makes no sense.

(B) In situations such as this, philosophers often construct thought experiments—imagined scenarios that bring out the thoughts and presuppositions underlying people's judgments. Sometimes these scenarios are drawn from books, movies, and television. Other times, philosophers just make up their own scenarios.

(C) Either way, the point is to put such concepts to the test. In the case of time travel, for example, a common thought experiment is to imagine what would happen if you went back in time and found yourself in a position to interfere in such a way that you were never born.

① (A) – (C) – (B)
② (B) – (A) – (C)
③ (B) – (C) – (A)
④ (C) – (A) – (B)
⑤ (C) – (B) – (A)

11

글의 흐름으로 보아, 주어진 문장이 들어가기에 가장 적절한 곳은?

> This stands in contrast to earlier figurative art, which had been as focused on representing what the artist *knew* about the objects and the space he or she was painting as on how they *looked*.

Almost all the figurative paintings we are familiar with now are in perspective. They present foreshortened figures and objects that diminish as they move away from the focal point of the painting. (①) A painting in perspective represents how the world *looks* to a person seeing the scene from a particular position in space. (②) These pictures are beautiful in their own right, but they do not represent scenes as we might see them if we were looking at them. (③) They are also less informative as to the layout of the space they represent. (④) The fact that perspective and information about spatial layout go together reveals something important about *seeing*. (⑤) Not only do we see the world through an egocentric frame but we also see it in a way that allows us to extract information about distances to, and sizes of, objects relative to us, and relative to one another.

*perspective: 원근법, 시점
**foreshorten: (회화·사진에서 대상을) 축소하다

12

다음 글의 내용을 한 문장으로 요약하고자 한다. 빈칸 (A), (B)에 들어갈 말로 가장 적절한 것은?

There is a tendency, once the dust of an emergency has settled down, to seek the reduction of famine vulnerability primarily in enhanced economic growth, or the revival of the rural economy, or the diversification of economic activities. The potential contribution of greater economic success, if it involves vulnerable groups, cannot be denied. At the same time, it is important to recognize that, no matter how fast they grow, countries where a large part of the population derive their livelihood from uncertain sources cannot hope to prevent famines without specialized entitlement protection mechanisms involving direct public intervention. Rapid growth of the economy in Botswana, or of the agricultural sector in Kenya, or of food production in Zimbabwe, explains at best only a small part of their success in preventing recurrent threats of famine. The real achievements of these countries lie in having provided direct public support to their populations in times of crisis.

*famine: 기아 **vulnerability: 취약

↓

Although economic growth can be somewhat ___(A)___ in diminishing a country's risk of famine, direct approaches to helping the affected people play a(n) ___(B)___ role in this process.

	(A)		(B)
①	productive	……	complicated
②	fruitful	……	critical
③	dominant	……	comprehensive
④	restrictive	……	appropriate
⑤	desirable	……	cost-effective

13~14 다음 글을 읽고, 물음에 답하시오.

People are correct when they feel that the written poetry of literate societies and the oral poetry of non-literate ones differ considerably from the everyday language spoken in the community. Listeners not only accept the (a) strange use of words, rearrangement of word order, assonance, alliteration, rhythm, rhyme, compression of thought, and so on —they actually expect to find these things in poetry and they are disappointed when poetry does not sound "poetic." But those who regard poetry as a (b) different category of language altogether are deaf to the true achievements of the poet. Rather, the poet artfully manipulates the same raw materials of his language as are used in everyday speech; his skill is to find new possibilities in the resources already in the language. In much the same way that people living at the seashore become so accustomed to the sound of waves that they no longer hear it, most of us have become (c) sensitive to the flood tide of words, millions of them every day, that hit our eardrums. One function of poetry is to depict the world with a (d) fresh perception—to make it strange—so that we will listen to language once again. But the successful poet never departs so far into the strange world of language that none of his listeners can (e) follow him. He still remains the communicator, the man of speech.

*assonance: 유운(類韻) **alliteration: 두운(頭韻)
***depict: 묘사하다

제목 추론

13 윗글의 제목으로 가장 적절한 것은?

① Make It New: How Poetry Refreshes Everyday Language
② Why Do Poets No Longer Seek Inspiration from Nature?
③ The Influence of Natural Sounds on Poetic Expression
④ Ways to Cite Poetic Expressions in Everyday Speech
⑤ Beauty Rediscovered: The Return of Oral Poetry

어휘 추론

14 밑줄 친 (a)~(e) 중에서 문맥상 낱말의 쓰임이 적절하지 <u>않은</u> 것은?

① (a)
② (b)
③ (c)
④ (d)
⑤ (e)

2024 9월 41~42번

13 정답률 55%　　14 정답률 42%

정답 p. 8

단어 TEST ● 주어진 단어의 뜻을 쓰고, 예문을 올바르게 해석하세요.

1	**absolutely**	전적으로, 절대적으로	absolutely sure	(전적으로) 확신하는
2	**embarrassed**		be embarrassed by the situation	그 상황에 ( )
3	**exhaustion**		degrees of exhaustion	( )의 정도
4	**gain currency**		increasingly gain currency	점점 ( )
5	**clash with**		clash with the executives	임원들과 ( )
6	**inviting**		the city's inviting quality	그 도시의 ( ) 질
7	**offspring**		raise their offspring	그들의 ( )을 기르다
8	**accelerate**		accelerate the growth	성장을 ( )
9	**reproduce**		reproduce the memorized song	외운 노래를 ( )
10	**underlie**		the underlying presupposition	( ) 전제
11	**diminish**		diminish in size	크기가 ( )
12	**recurrent**		recurrent threats of famine	( ) 기아 위협

구문 TEST ● 주어진 단어를 활용하여 우리말에 맞게 빈칸을 완성하세요.

13 (Surrounded by mountains), **the town has a breathtaking view.**
surround

산들로 둘러싸인 그 마을은 숨막힐 정도로 아름다운 경치를 가지고 있다.

14 (   ), **he knocked over a vase.**
reach for / the top shelf

맨 위 선반에 손을 뻗다가 그는 꽃병을 넘어뜨렸다.

15 **She** (   ) **for her outstanding academic performance.**
will / award / a scholarship

그녀는 뛰어난 학업 성적으로 장학금을 받을 것이다.

16 (   ) **eased the tension.**
the fact / apologize

그녀가 사과했다는 사실은 긴장을 완화시켰다.

17 (   ) **to the graduation ceremony.**
every student / pass / the final exam / be invited

기말고사를 통과하는 모든 학생은 졸업식에 초대됩니다.

18 (   ) **the story of her diverse interests.**
the magazines / pile / tell

탁자 위에 쌓인 그 잡지들은 그녀의 다양한 관심사를 말해준다.

기출 하프 모의고사

● 문제에 나오는 단어들을 확인하세요.

☐ **deposit**	v. 입금하다, 맡기다	☐ **optimistically**	ad. 낙관적으로
☐ **withdraw**	v. 인출하다, 철수하다	☐ **cling to**	~에 매달리다
☐ **valid**	a. 유효한, 타당한	☐ **overestimate**	v. 과대평가하다
☐ **account**	n. 계좌, 계정, 설명	☐ **well-intentioned**	a. 선의의
☐ **trade-off**	n. (상충·대립되는 요소 간의) 균형	☐ **intensely**	ad. 지극히, 강렬하게
☐ **inaccessible**	a. 접근할 수 없는	☐ **objection**	n. 반대
☐ **marginalize**	v. ~을 소외시키다, 하찮게 대하다	☐ **be rooted in**	~에 뿌리를 두다, 원인을 두다
☐ **obstacle**	n. 장애물	☐ **bottom line**	(최종 결산 후) 순익[손실], 핵심, 요점
☐ **flexibility**	n. 유연성	☐ **arise**	v. 생기다, 발생하다
☐ **gold plating**	금도금(값비싸고 불필요한 부속품을 더하기)	☐ **tie in with**	~와 관련 있다, 일치하다, 병행되다
☐ **characteristic**	n. 특성	☐ **authority**	n. 권위
☐ **justification**	n. 명분, 정당화	☐ **formulate**	v. 정립하다, 체계적으로 구성하다
☐ **marked**	a. 뚜렷한, 두드러진	☐ **proclamation**	n. 선언, 선포
☐ **temptation**	n. 유혹	☐ **superiority**	n. 우위, 우월성
☐ **contagion**	n. 전염(병), 오염	☐ **abundance**	n. 풍부함
☐ **intervention**	n. 개입	☐ **risk averse**	위험을 회피하려 하는
☐ **mounting**	a. 커지는, 증가하는	☐ **unevenness**	n. 불균형
☐ **evoke**	v. (감정을) 불러일으키다	☐ **supplemental**	a. 보충하는, 보완하는
☐ **despair**	n. 절망	☐ **proliferate**	v. 증식시키다
☐ **priceless**	a. 대단히 귀중한	☐ **manipulation**	n. 조작
☐ **ultimately**	ad. 궁극적으로	☐ **sacrifice**	v. 희생하다
☐ **constitute**	v. ~을 구성하다	☐ **momentous**	a. 중대한
☐ **ambiguity**	n. 모호함, 애매함	☐ **audible**	a. 잘 들리는, 들을 수 있는
☐ **eyes-on-the-prize**	a. 목표에 몰두하는	☐ **feat**	n. 재주, 기량
☐ **self-disciplined**	a. 자기 통제적인, 자기 수양의	☐ **distinct**	a. 별개의, 구별되는, 뚜렷한

❶ 접속사+분사구문 ❷ 가목적어 it

Clothes can be inexpensively purchased **while making** **it** **easy to convey** notions of wealth, intellectual stature, relaxation or environmental consciousness.

옷은 부, 지적 능력, 휴식 또는 환경 의식의 개념을 전달하는 것을 쉽게 만드는 한편, 저렴하게 구매될 수 있다.

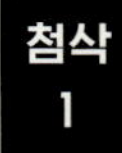

접속사 + 분사구문

개　　념 ▶ 현재분사 또는 과거분사로 시작되는 분사구문 앞에 접속사를 남겨둔 형태이다.

독해전략 ▶ 문장의 의미를 구체화해주는 접속사에 유의하면서 읽는다.

어법전략 ▶ 별도의 의미상 주어가 없는 한, 문장의 주어를 기준으로 능동(V-ing)과 수동(p.p.)을 판단한다.

다음 중 어법상 옳은 것을 고르세요.

a. While | **worked** | **working** | on the project, they encountered unforeseen challenges.

b. When | **informed** | **informing** | about the delay, the passengers patiently waited at the gate.

c. Once | **reached** | **reaching** | the summit, the girls celebrated their achievement.

가목적어 it

개　　념 ▶ make, find, leave 등이 쓰인 5형식 문장에서 to부정사 또는 that절 목적어를 대신하는 의미 없는 it을 말한다.

독해전략 ▶ 목적격보어 뒷부분을 잘 읽는 것이 문장의 의미를 정확히 파악하는 데 중요하다.

어법전략 ▶ 진목적어인 to부정사를 원형부정사로 잘못 쓰거나, 목적격보어 자리에 부사를 잘못 쓰지 않도록 한다.

다음 중 어법상 옳은 것을 고르세요.

a. Breaking down the steps makes it easy | **understand** | **to understand** | the process.

b. It is common for beginners to find it | **difficult** | **difficultly** | to play the guitar at first.

c. Advanced technology makes it possible | **automate** | **to automate** | repetitive tasks efficiently.

2022 4월 35번

❸ what이 이끄는 명사절 주어

What **characterizes philosophy and science in early modern Europe and marks a break from earlier traditions** is the concern to tailor theories to **evidence** **rather than** **authority or tradition.**

❹ A rather than B

초기 근대 유럽에서 철학과 과학을 특징짓고 이전 전통과의 분리를 나타내는 것은 이론을 권위나 전통보다는 증거에 맞추려는 관심이다.

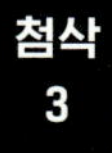

what이 이끄는 명사절 주어

개　　념 ▶ 선행사를 포함한 관계대명사 what은 문장의 주어 역할을 하는 명사절을 이끌 수 있다.

독해전략 ▶ <what S V + be …>의 구조라면, be동사 뒤가 의미의 핵심이 된다. '~한 것은 (바로) …이다'라고 해석되기 때문이다.

어법전략 ▶ what절 주어는 단수 취급하며, what 뒤에는 불완전한 문장이 연결된다.

다음 중 어법상 옳은 것을 고르세요.

a. What I find astonishing | is | to be | his dedication to helping others.

b. What she lacks, despite her talent and skills, | is | are | the confidence needed to pursue her dreams.

c. What they discovered fundamentally | altered | altering | our understanding of the natural world.

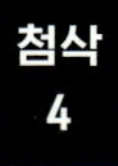

A rather than B

개　　념 ▶ 'B보다 (오히려, 차라리) A'라는 의미를 나타낸다.

독해전략 ▶ 주제와 대비되는 B를 이용해 주제인 A를 강조하는 표현이다. 즉, 의미의 핵심은 A에 있다.

어법전략 ▶ A, B는 병렬구조를 이룬다. 즉 A와 B의 문법적 성격이 같다.

다음 중 어법상 옳은 것을 고르세요.

a. Teaching and mentoring, rather than | dictate | dictating |, define Irene's leadership style.

b. The team aimed to collaborate closely rather than | work | working | independently on the project.

c. He chose to take time and reflect rather than | rushes | rush | to make hasty decisions.

정답 a. is b. is c. altered / a. dictating b. work c. rush

01 다음 글에 드러난 Jerry의 심경 변화로 가장 적절한 것은?

"5,000 dollars has been deposited? Thank you. I'll check it out now." Jerry Shaw hung up with a smile on his face. Humming, he headed to the bank to withdraw some cash. He stopped at the ATM, inserted the card and entered his PIN. The screen flashed the message, "Card not valid—please see a teller." *What? My bonus was deposited just now!* Entering the bank, Jerry told the teller what had happened. She studied the screen and frowned. "Mr. Shaw, your account was closed. All your funds were withdrawn when you closed it," she said. "What do you mean? I never did! It must be identity theft!" yelled Jerry, his voice barely under control.

① delighted → panicked
② anxious → envious
③ sympathetic → exhausted
④ grateful → indifferent
⑤ confused → enthusiastic

02 다음 글의 요지로 가장 적절한 것은?

In order to be successful and equitable, ecosystem management must be linked to poverty reduction. Urban infrastructure projects need to address the trade-offs between conservation, livelihoods, and equitable distribution of resources. Historically there has been tension when conservation models that create protected areas are perceived as inaccessible to communities. Often, these models are implemented at the expense of poor and marginalized residents and users of resources from the areas. Social, economic, and environmental development programs have become obstacles to sustainable development because there is no balance between the need to protect ecosystem services and the desire to use resources to address community needs. Communities need to be allowed to identify and negotiate their own options and to increase their flexibility to cope with unexpected change.

*equitable: 공평한

① 무분별한 도시 개발은 사회적 양극화를 심화한다.
② 도시 기반 시설 확충 시 안정적인 재정 지원이 중요하다.
③ 인근 지역 간의 긴밀한 협력은 생태계 보존의 기반이 된다.
④ 자원의 순환과 공정한 배분은 지속가능한 발전의 필수조건이다.
⑤ 생태계 관리 시 빈곤층을 포함한 지역사회의 요구를 고려할 필요가 있다.

2023 4월 19번   정답률 93%

2023 7월 22번   정답률 43%

함축 의미

03 밑줄 친 "The best is the enemy of the good."이 다음 글에서 의미하는 바로 가장 적절한 것은?

Gold plating in the project means needlessly enhancing the expected results, namely, adding characteristics that are costly, not required, and that have low added value with respect to the targets—in other words, giving more with no real justification other than to demonstrate one's own talent. Gold plating is especially interesting for project team members, as it is typical of projects with a marked professional component—in other words, projects that involve specialists with proven experience and extensive professional autonomy. In these environments specialists often see the project as an opportunity to test and enrich their skill sets. There is therefore a strong temptation, in all good faith, to engage in gold plating, namely, to achieve more or higher-quality work that gratifies the professional but does not add value to the client's requests, and at the same time removes valuable resources from the project. As the saying goes, "The best is the enemy of the good."

*autonomy: 자율성 **gratify: 만족시키다

① Pursuing perfection at work causes conflicts among team members.
② Raising work quality only to prove oneself is not desirable.
③ Inviting overqualified specialists to a project leads to bad ends.
④ Responding to the changing needs of clients is unnecessary.
⑤ Acquiring a range of skills for a project does not ensure success.

주제 추론

04 다음 글의 주제로 가장 적절한 것은?

Facing large-scale, long-term change can seem overwhelming. Problems like global contagion or economic inequality are so complex that it can be hard to believe any intervention might make a difference. Working through fears of what could be depends on connecting with the abstract. Linking issues like climate change, for example, with the realities of our own neighborhoods, jobs, and relationships, translates conceptual ideas into concrete emotions. Thinking of how the beaches we love might disappear, how more frequent floods might destroy our homes, or how we might have to move to flee mounting wildfire risk, evokes feelings like anger, sadness, or guilt—feelings that inspire us to act. A recent study found that when people feel personally affected by potential climatic change, they are more likely to support carbon reduction efforts and push for proactive policies. Forming emotional connections to potential futures helps us move from denial and despair to action.

① effectiveness of making remote problems personal
② impacts of negative tone in news on problem solving
③ contribution of experts to solving large-scale problems
④ limits of personal intervention in minimizing climate change
⑤ risks of attempting to predict events with limited information

05 Charles H. Townes에 관한 다음 글의 내용과 일치하지 <u>않는</u> 것은?

Charles H. Townes, one of the most influential American physicists, was born in South Carolina. In his childhood, he grew up on a farm, studying the stars in the sky. He earned his doctoral degree from the California Institute of Technology in 1939, and then he took a job at Bell Labs in New York City. After World War II, he became an associate professor of physics at Columbia University. In 1958, Townes and his co-researcher proposed the concept of the laser. Laser technology won quick acceptance in industry and research. He received the Nobel Prize in Physics in 1964. He was also involved in Project Apollo, the moon landing project. His contribution is priceless because the Internet and all digital media would be unimaginable without the laser.

① 어린 시절에 농장에서 성장하였다.
② 박사 학위를 받기 전에 Bell Labs에서 일했다.
③ 1958년에 레이저의 개념을 제안하였다.
④ 1964년에 노벨 물리학상을 수상하였다.
⑤ 달 착륙 프로젝트에 관여하였다.

06 다음 글의 밑줄 친 부분 중, 어법상 <u>틀린</u> 것은?

Trends constantly suggest new opportunities for individuals to restage themselves, representing occasions for change. To understand how trends can ultimately give individuals power and freedom, one must first discuss fashion's importance as a basis for change. The most common explanation offered by my informants as to why fashion is so appealing is ① <u>that</u> it constitutes a kind of theatrical costumery. Clothes are part of how people present ② <u>them</u> to the world, and fashion locates them in the present, relative to what is happening in society and to fashion's own history. As a form of expression, fashion contains a host of ambiguities, enabling individuals to recreate the meanings ③ <u>associated</u> with specific pieces of clothing. Fashion is among the simplest and cheapest methods of self-expression: clothes can be ④ <u>inexpensively</u> purchased while making it easy to convey notions of wealth, intellectual stature, relaxation or environmental consciousness, even if none of these is true. Fashion can also strengthen agency in various ways, ⑤ <u>opening</u> up space for action.

*stature: 능력

07 다음 빈칸에 들어갈 말로 가장 적절한 것은?

There's reason to worry that an eyes-on-the-prize mentality could be a mistake. Lots of research shows that we tend to be over-confident about how easy it is to be self-disciplined. This is why so many of us optimistically buy expensive gym memberships when paying per-visit fees would be cheaper, register for online classes we'll never complete, and purchase family-size chips on discount to trim our monthly snack budget, only to consume every last crumb in a single sitting. We think "future me" will be able to make good choices, but too often "present me" gives in to temptation. People have a remarkable ability to ________________ their own failures. Even when we flounder again and again, many of us manage to maintain a rosy optimism about our ability to do better next time rather than learning from our past mistakes. We cling to fresh starts and other reasons to stay upbeat, which may help us get out of bed in the morning but can prevent us from approaching change in the smartest possible way.

*crumb: 부스러기   **flounder: 실패하다   ***upbeat: 낙관적인

① criticize
② remind
③ ignore
④ detect
⑤ overestimate

08 다음 빈칸에 들어갈 말로 가장 적절한 것은?

Everyone who drives, walks, or swipes a transit card in a city views herself as a transportation expert from the moment she walks out the front door. And how she views the street ____. That's why we find so many well-intentioned and civic-minded citizens arguing past one another. At neighborhood meetings in school auditoriums, and in back rooms at libraries and churches, local residents across the nation gather for often-contentious discussions about transportation proposals that would change a city's streets. And like all politics, all transportation is local and intensely personal. A transit project that could speed travel for tens of thousands of people can be stopped by objections to the loss of a few parking spaces or by the simple fear that the project won't work. It's not a challenge of the data or the traffic engineering or the planning. Public debates about streets are typically rooted in emotional assumptions about how a change will affect a person's commute, ability to park, belief about what is safe and what isn't, or the bottom line of a local business.

*swipe: 판독기에 통과시키다   **contentious: 논쟁적인
***commute: 통근

① relies heavily on how others see her city's streets
② updates itself with each new public transit policy
③ arises independently of the streets she travels on
④ tracks pretty closely with how she gets around
⑤ ties firmly in with how her city operates

09 다음 글에서 전체 흐름과 관계 없는 문장은?

What characterizes philosophy and science in early modern Europe and marks a break from earlier traditions is the concern to tailor theories to evidence rather than authority or tradition. ① Galileo Galilei, Francis Bacon, René Descartes, and others formulated explanations of the heavens, of the natural world around them, and of human nature and society not by appealing to the proclamations of earlier thinkers. ② Nor were religious principles and ecclesiastic dogma their guiding lights. ③ Rather, they took their lead from reason—what some thinkers called "the light of nature"—and experience. ④ The fierce debates on the superiority of reason or experience continued, but all serious thinkers ultimately abandoned experience in the development of modern science and philosophy. ⑤ Whether they proceeded according to the logic of deduction or through the analysis of empirical data, the modern scientific method they developed consists in testing theories according to reason and in light of the available evidence.

*ecclesiastic dogma: 교회의 교리   **deduction: 연역

10 주어진 글 다음에 이어질 글의 순서로 가장 적절한 것은?

Plants show finely tuned adaptive responses when nutrients are limiting. Gardeners may recognize yellow leaves as a sign of poor nutrition and the need for fertilizer.

(A) In contrast, plants with a history of nutrient abundance are risk averse and save energy. At all developmental stages, plants respond to environmental changes or unevenness so as to be able to use their energy for growth, survival, and reproduction, while limiting damage and non-productive uses of their valuable energy.

(B) Research in this area has shown that plants are constantly aware of their position in the environment, in terms of both space and time. Plants that have experienced variable nutrient availability in the past tend to exhibit risk-taking behaviors, such as spending energy on root lengthening instead of leaf production.

(C) But if a plant does not have a caretaker to provide supplemental minerals, it can proliferate or lengthen its roots and develop root hairs to allow foraging in more distant soil patches. Plants can also use their memory to respond to histories of temporal or spatial variation in nutrient or resource availability.

*nutrient: 영양소   **fertilizer: 비료   ***forage: 구하러 다니다

① (A) – (C) – (B)　　② (B) – (A) – (C)
③ (B) – (C) – (A)　　④ (C) – (A) – (B)
⑤ (C) – (B) – (A)

11 글의 흐름으로 보아, 주어진 문장이 들어가기에 가장 적절한 곳은?

Because the manipulation of digitally converted sounds meant the reprogramming of binary information, editing operations could be performed with millisecond precision.

The shift from analog to digital technology significantly influenced how music was produced. First and foremost, the digitization of sounds—that is, their conversion into numbers—enabled music makers to undo what was done. (①) One could, in other words, twist and bend sounds toward something new without sacrificing the original version. (②) This "undo" ability made mistakes considerably less momentous, sparking the creative process and encouraging a generally more experimental mindset. (③) In addition, digitally converted sounds could be manipulated simply by programming digital messages rather than using physical tools, simplifying the editing process significantly. (④) For example, while editing once involved razor blades to physically cut and splice audiotapes, it now involved the cursor and mouse-click of the computer-based sequencer program, which was obviously less time consuming. (⑤) This microlevel access at once made it easier to conceal any traces of manipulations (such as joining tracks in silent spots) and introduced new possibilities for manipulating sounds in audible and experimental ways.

*binary: 2진법의 **splice: 합쳐 잇다

12 다음 글의 내용을 한 문장으로 요약하고자 한다. 빈칸 (A), (B)에 들어갈 말로 가장 적절한 것은?

Put a hamster on a wheel, and it will start running. Give the hamster a treat, and it will run even longer. Stop dispensing the treats, and the hamster will stop running—completely. The original motivation has thereby become extinguished. The school system has been taking advantage of this psychological feature by replacing young children's natural curiosity and joy of discovery with praise, grades, and other short-term performance boosters. As the story goes, there once was an old man who enjoyed watching sunsets from his porch. One day, a bunch of kids came over and started playing loudly in front of his house. The man asked the kids to move over, but they ignored him. Next day, the children came again. The man called them over, gave each one a nickel, and asked them to make as much noise as they possibly could—to which they happily obliged. The man kept regularly handing out coins, until one day he told the kids that he was no longer paying them. "Then we aren't going to make noise for you," the children announced—and left.

↓

It is possible to ____(A)____ an individual's willingness to do something by consistently providing ____(B)____ for the action for some time and then withholding them.

	(A)		(B)
①	remove	……	rewards
②	remove	……	punishments
③	boost	……	explanations
④	evaluate	……	punishments
⑤	boost	……	rewards

13~14 다음 글을 읽고, 물음에 답하시오.

Generalization promotes cognitive economy, so that we don't focus on particulars that don't matter. The great Russian neuropsychologist Alexander Luria studied a patient, Solomon Shereshevsky, with a memory impairment that was the (a) opposite of what we usually hear about—Solomon didn't have amnesia, the loss of memories; he had what Luria called hypermnesia (we might say that his superpower was superior memory). His supercharged memory allowed him to perform amazing feats, such as repeating speeches word for word that he had heard only once, or complex mathematical formulas, long sequences of numbers, and poems in foreign languages he didn't even speak. Before you think that having such a fantastic memory would be great, it came with a (b) cost: Solomon wasn't able to form abstractions because he remembered every detail as distinct. He had particular trouble identifying people. From a neurocognitive standpoint, every time you see a face, it is (c) unlikely that it looks at least slightly different from the last time—you're viewing it at a different angle and distance than before, and you might be encountering a different expression. While you're interacting with a person, their face goes through a parade of expressions. Because your brain can (d) generalize, you see all of these different manifestations of the face as belonging to the same person. Solomon couldn't do that. As he explained to Luria, (e) recognizing his friends and colleagues was nearly impossible because "everyone has so many faces."

*impairment: 장애

13 윗글의 제목으로 가장 적절한 것은?

① Face Recognition Technologies: Blessing or Not?
② The Faster You Memorize, the Faster You Forget
③ Generalization Can Be Both a Shortcut and a Trap!
④ The Flaw in Cognition Caused by Flawless Memory
⑤ Why It Gets Difficult to Remember Details As You Age

14 밑줄 친 (a)~(e) 중에서 문맥상 낱말의 쓰임이 적절하지 <u>않은</u> 것은?

① (a)
② (b)
③ (c)
④ (d)
⑤ (e)

2023 7월 41~42번

13 정답률 43%   **14** 정답률 69%

정답 p. 15

단어 TEST ● 주어진 단어의 뜻을 쓰고, 예문을 올바르게 해석하세요.

1	**withdraw**	인출하다, 철수하다	withdraw some cash	약간의 현금을 (인출하다)
2	**valid**		card not valid	( ) 않은 카드
3	**marked**		a marked professional component	( ) 전문적 요소
4	**evoke**		evoke feelings like guilt	죄책감 같은 감정을 ( )
5	**ambiguity**		a host of ambiguities	다수의 ( )
6	**overestimate**		overestimate their failures	그들의 실패를 ( )
7	**intensely**		intensely personal	( ) 개인적인
8	**arise**		arise independently	별개로 ( )
9	**superiority**		the superiority of reason	이성의 ( )
10	**abundance**		nutrient abundance	영양분의 ( )
11	**sacrifice**		without sacrificing the original version	원본을 ( ) 않고
12	**feat**		amazing feats	놀라운 ( )

구문 TEST ● 주어진 단어를 활용하여 우리말에 맞게 빈칸을 완성하세요.

13 **When (** informed about the delay **), the passengers patiently waited at the gate.**
inform about / the delay

지연에 관해 안내받자, 승객들은 참을성 있게 게이트에서 대기했다.

14 **(** **), the girls celebrated their achievement.**
once / reach / the summit

정상에 오르자, 소녀들은 성취를 축하했다.

15 **It is common for beginners (** **) the guitar at first.**
find / difficult / play

초보자들이 처음에 기타를 연주하기가 어렵다고 생각하는 것은 흔하다.

16 **(** **) the concern to tailor theories to evidence.**
characterize / modern science / be

근대 과학을 특징짓는 것은 이론을 증거에 맞추려는 관심이다.

17 **(** **) is his dedication to helping others.**
find / astonishing

내가 놀랍다고 여기는 것은 타인을 돕는 것에 대한 그의 헌신이다.

18 **He chose to (** **) to make hasty decisions.**
take time / rush

그는 성급한 결정을 내리려고 서두르느니 시간을 갖기로 했다.

기출 하프 모의고사

● 문제에 나오는 단어들을 확인하세요.

☐ seasoned	a. 노련한, 경험 많은		☐ reportedly	ad. 전하는 바에 따르면
☐ article	n. 기사		☐ contemporary	a. 당대의, 동시대의, 현대의
☐ paralyzed	a. 마비된		☐ astronomical	a. 천문학의
☐ scold	v. 꾸짖다		☐ hemisphere	n. (지구나 뇌의) 반구
☐ tolerate	v. 견디다, 참다		☐ misperception	n. 오해
☐ corrective	a. 바로잡는, 교정하는		☐ emerge	v. 떠오르다, 생겨나다, 부상하다
☐ consequence	n. 결과, 영향		☐ be suited for	~에 적합하다
☐ productively	ad. 생산적으로		☐ expansion	n. 확대, 확장
☐ flick a switch	스위치를 (켜거나 끄려고) 탁 누르다		☐ implication	n. 영향, 결과, 함축, 연루
☐ stand in the way	방해하다		☐ with regard to	~에 관해
☐ out of the loop	(소외되어) 상황을 잘 모르는		☐ sturdy	a. 튼튼한, 강건한
☐ periodically	ad. 주기적으로		☐ assign	v. 부여하다, 할당하다, (일을) 맡기다
☐ enforce	v. 시행하다		☐ subconsciously	ad. 무의식적으로
☐ massive	a. 거대한		☐ affordability	n. (가격의) 경제성, 적정성
☐ authorities	n. 관계자, 당국		☐ segment	n. 부문, 분야
☐ unappreciative	a. 인정하지 않는		☐ end up V-ing	결국 ~하다
☐ garment	n. 의복, 의상		☐ solidify	v. 확고히 하다, 굳히다
☐ tailor	v. (특정 대상에) 맞추다, 재단하다		☐ feed on	~ 때문에 더 강해지다, ~을 먹고 살다
☐ ill equipped	준비가 안 된, (장비를 제대로) 갖추지 않은		☐ be conditioned to	~하도록 조건화되다
☐ exploitation	n. 이용, 착취		☐ variant	n. 변형, 변이
☐ manufacturing	n. 제조(업)		☐ subtle	a. 미묘한
☐ dismiss	v. 무시하다, 묵살하다		☐ crisis	n. 위기
☐ authorship	n. (원)저자, 출처		☐ improbable	a. 있을 법하지 않은, 사실 같지 않은
☐ adjustment	n. 수정, 적응		☐ imperceptible	a. (너무 작아서) 감지할 수 없는
☐ commission	v. 의뢰하다, 위탁하다		☐ gradually	ad. 점진적으로, 점점

2021 9월 21번

❶ 동명사의 수동태

For one thing, **the fear of** being left out of the loop can keep them glued to their enterprise social media.

❷ keep+목적어+형용사/분사

우선, 상황을 잘 모르고 혼자 남겨진다는 두려움은 이들이 자신들의 기업 소셜미디어에 계속 매달리게 할 수 있다.

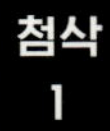

동명사의 수동태

개　념 ▶ 동명사(V-ing)가 being p.p. 형태로 쓰이면 수동의 의미를 나타낼 수 있다.

독해전략 ▶ 동명사의 의미상 주어가 행위를 '당하는' 대상임을 고려해 '~되는 것'이라고 해석한다.

어법전략 ▶ 동명사의 의미상 주어가 행위를 행하는지(V-ing), 당하는지(being p.p.)를 잘 판단해서 쓴다.

다음 중 어법상 옳은 것을 고르세요.

a. His love for music led to him selecting / being selected for the band.

b. Supporting / Being supported by friends during tough times makes a huge difference.

c. The honor of recognizing / being recognized for her achievements boosted her confidence.

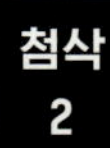

keep+목적어+형용사/분사

개　념 ▶ keep은 주로 형용사/분사를 목적격보어로 취해 '~이 계속 …하게 하다'의 의미를 나타낸다.

독해전략 ▶ 목적어와 목적격보어 사이에 be동사가 숨어 있다고 생각하면 의미를 파악하기 쉽다.

어법전략 ▶ keep뿐 아니라 make, leave, find 또한 <동사+목적어+형용사/분사>의 구조로 흔히 쓴다.

다음 중 어법상 옳은 것을 고르세요.

a. The gentleman kept his promises fulfilling / fulfilled without any compromise.

b. He keeps his presence feeling / felt in the competitive business world.

c. She made her voice hearing / heard in the crowded meeting room.

정답 **a.** being selected **b.** Being supported **c.** being recognized / **a.** fulfilled **b.** felt **c.** heard

2022 9월 41~42번

❸ 계속적 용법의 which

It cannot be observed in "human time," which is why documentary filmmaker Jeff Orlowski, who tracks climate change effects on glaciers and coral reefs, uses "before and after" photographs to highlight changes that occurred gradually.

❹ 삽입구문

그것은 '인간의 시간' 동안에는 관찰될 수 없는데, 이것은 빙하와 산호초에 미치는 기후 변화의 영향을 추적하는 다큐멘터리 영화 제작자 Jeff Orlowski 가 점진적으로 일어난 변화를 강조하고자 '전후' 사진을 이용하는 이유이다.

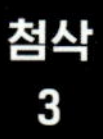

계속적 용법의 which

개　념 ▶ 콤마 뒤의 관계대명사 which는 단어뿐 아니라 구나 절을 선행사로 받아 보충 설명한다.

독해전략 ▶ which를 뒤에서부터 해석하지 말고, '그리고 이것은(= and it/this)'이라고 해석하면 간단하다.

어법전략 ▶ 관계대명사 that 또는 what은 which처럼 계속적 용법으로 쓰일 수 없음을 비교해 둔다.

다음 중 어법상 옳은 것을 고르세요.

a. He completed the marathon, that | which was an incredible feat considering his injury.

b. The garden bloomed beautifully in spring, which | it delighted all the residents.

c. They traveled to Italy for their vacation, which | what had always been their dream destination.

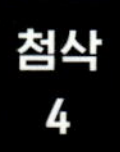

삽입구문

개　념 ▶ 2개의 콤마(,)나 줄표(—) 사이에 앞말에 대한 추가적인 정보를 끼워 넣는 것이다.

독해전략 ▶ 필수적인 정보보다는 그야말로 '부가적인' 정보를 주는 경우가 많으므로 가볍게 읽는다.

어법전략 ▶ 문장구조를 파악할 때는 삽입구문을 건너뛰고 읽으면 문장의 주요 성분이 더 쉽게 눈에 보인다.

다음 중 어법상 옳은 것을 고르세요.

a. The concert, which lasted for hours, were | was truly spectacular.

b. The painting, created by a famous landscape artist, capture | captures everyone's attention.

c. The decision, made | was made after extensive research, was praised as groundbreaking.

정답 a. which b. which c. which / a. was b. captures c. made

목적 파악

01 다음 글의 목적으로 가장 적절한 것은?

Morganic Corporation, located in the heart of Arkansas, spent the past decade providing great organic crops at a competitive price, growing into the ninth leading organic farming operation in the country. As a seasoned writer with access to Richard Taylor, the founder and president of Morganic, I propose writing a profile piece on Taylor for your magazine. I believe the time has come to cover Morganic's rise in the organic farming industry. The piece would run in the normal 800–1,200 word range with photographs available of Taylor and Morganic's operation. Thank you for your consideration of this article. I hope to hear from you soon.

① 잡지사에 기사 기고를 하겠다고 제안하려고
② 기사 지면을 늘려줄 것을 요청하려고
③ 새로 나온 유기농 제품을 소개하려고
④ 기사에 대한 피드백에 감사하려고
⑤ 창업에 관한 조언을 구하려고

주장 파악

02 다음 글에서 필자가 주장하는 바로 가장 적절한 것은?

More often than not, modern parents are paralyzed by the fear that they will no longer be liked or even loved by their children if they scold them for any reason. They want their children's friendship above all, and are willing to sacrifice respect to get it. This is not good. A child will have many friends, but only two parents—if that—and parents are more, not less, than friends. Friends have very limited authority to correct. Every parent therefore needs to learn to tolerate the momentary anger or even hatred directed toward them by their children, after necessary corrective action has been taken, as the capacity of children to perceive or care about long-term consequences is very limited. Parents are the judges of society. They teach children how to behave so that other people will be able to interact meaningfully and productively with them.

① 부모는 두려워 말고 자녀의 잘못된 행동을 바로잡아 주어야 한다.
② 부모는 자녀의 신뢰를 얻기 위해 일관된 태도로 양육해야 한다.
③ 부모는 다양한 경험을 제공하여 자녀의 사회화를 도와야 한다.
④ 부모는 자녀의 친구 관계에 지나치게 개입하지 말아야 한다.
⑤ 부모는 자녀와 유대감을 쌓으며 친구의 역할을 해야 한다.

2023 3월 18번   정답률 77%

2021 4월 20번   정답률 60%

03 밑줄 친 Flicking the collaboration light switch가 다음 글에서 의미하는 바로 가장 적절한 것은?

Flicking the collaboration light switch is something that leaders are uniquely positioned to do, because several obstacles stand in the way of people voluntarily working alone. For one thing, the fear of being left out of the loop can keep them glued to their enterprise social media. Individuals don't want to be—or appear to be—isolated. For another, knowing what their teammates are doing provides a sense of comfort and security, because people can adjust their own behavior to be in harmony with the group. It's risky to go off on their own to try something new that will probably not be successful right from the start. But even though it feels reassuring for individuals to be hyperconnected, it's better for the organization if they periodically go off and think for themselves and generate diverse—if not quite mature—ideas. Thus, it becomes the leader's job to create conditions that are good for the whole by enforcing intermittent interaction even when people wouldn't choose it for themselves, without making it seem like a punishment.

*intermittent: 간헐적인

① breaking physical barriers and group norms that prohibit cooperation
② having people stop working together and start working individually
③ encouraging people to devote more time to online collaboration
④ shaping environments where higher productivity is required
⑤ requiring workers to focus their attention on group projects

04 다음 글의 제목으로 가장 적절한 것은?

There is a story about F. Yates, a prominent UK statistician. During his student years at St. John's College, Cambridge, Yates had been keen on a form of sport. It consisted of climbing about the roofs and towers of the college buildings at night. In particular, the chapel of St. John's College has a massive neo-Gothic tower adorned with statues of saints, and to Yates it appeared obvious that it would be more decorous if these saints were properly attired in surplices. One night he climbed up and did the job; next morning the result was generally much admired. But the College authorities were unappreciative and began to consider means of divesting the saints of their newly acquired garments. This was not easy, since they were well out of reach of any ordinary ladder. An attempt to lift the surplices off from above, using ropes with hooks attached, was unsuccessful. No progress was being made and eventually Yates came forward and volunteered to climb up in the daylight and bring them down. This he did to the admiration of the crowd that assembled.

*decorous: 품위 있는 **surplice: 흰 가운
***divest: 벗기다

① A Scary Legend About the Statues at St. John's College
② A Student Who Solved a Problem of His Own Making
③ Standards of Beauty Varying from Person to Person
④ A Smart Professor Who Identified a Criminal
⑤ A Success Story of a Mysterious Architect

05 다음 도표의 내용과 일치하지 <u>않는</u> 것은?

Percentages of Respondents Who Sometimes or Often Actively Avoided News in Five Countries in 2017, 2019, and 2022

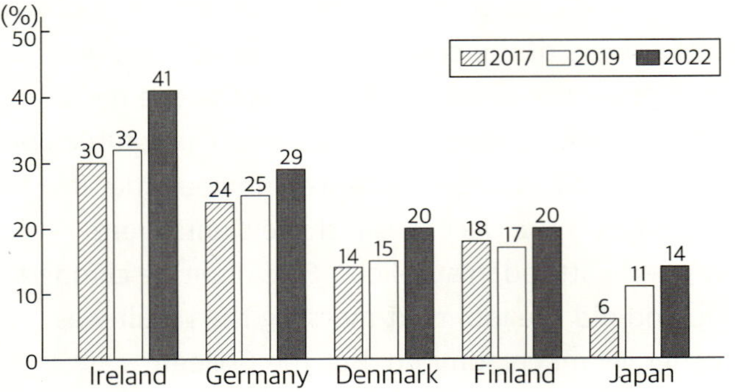

The above graph shows the percentages of the respondents in five countries who sometimes or often actively avoided news in 2017, 2019, and 2022. ① For each of the three years, Ireland showed the highest percentage of the respondents who sometimes or often actively avoided news, among the countries in the graph. ② In Germany, the percentage of the respondents who sometimes or often actively avoided news was less than 30% in each of the three years. ③ In Denmark, the percentage of the respondents who sometimes or often actively avoided news in 2019 was higher than that in 2017 but lower than that in 2022. ④ In Finland, the percentage of the respondents who sometimes or often actively avoided news in 2019 was lower than that in 2017, which was also true for Japan. ⑤ In Japan, the percentage of the respondents who sometimes or often actively avoided news did not exceed 15% in each of the three years.

06 다음 글의 밑줄 친 부분 중, 문맥상 낱말의 쓰임이 적절하지 <u>않은</u> 것은?

In poorer countries many years of fast growth may be necessary to bring living standards up to acceptable levels. But growth is the means to achieve desired goals, not the ① <u>end</u> in itself. In the richer world the whole idea of growth—at least as conventionally measured—may need to be ② <u>maintained</u>. In economies where services dominate, goods and services tailored to our ③ <u>individual</u> needs will be what determine the advance of our societies. These could be anything from genome-specific medicines to personalized care or tailored suits. That is different from more and more stuff, an arms race of growth. Instead, it means improvements in ④ <u>quality</u>, something that GDP is ill equipped to measure. Some fifty years ago one US economist contrasted what he called the "cowboy" economy, bent on production, exploitation of resources, and pollution, with the "spaceman" economy, in which quality and complexity replaced "throughput" as the measure of success. The ⑤ <u>move</u> from manufacturing to services and from analog to digital is the shift from cowboy to spaceman. But we are still measuring the size of the lasso.

*throughput: (일정 시간 내에 해야 할) 처리량
**lasso: (카우보이가 야생마를 잡는 데 사용하는) 올가미 밧줄

07 다음 빈칸에 들어갈 말로 가장 적절한 것은?

One of the criticisms of Stoicism by modern translators and teachers is the amount of repetition. Marcus Aurelius, for example, has been dismissed by academics as not being original because his writing resembles that of other, earlier Stoics. This criticism misses the point. Even before Marcus's time, Seneca was well aware that there was a lot of borrowing and overlap among the philosophers. That's because real philosophers weren't concerned with authorship, but only what worked. More important, they believed that what was said mattered less than what was done. And this is true now as it was then. You're welcome to take all of the words of the great philosophers and use them to your own liking (they're dead; they don't mind). Feel free to make adjustments and improvements as you like. Adapt them to the real conditions of the real world. The way to prove that you truly understand what you speak and write, that you truly are original, is to

____.

*Stoicism: 스토아 철학

① put them into practice
② keep your writings to yourself
③ combine oral and written traditions
④ compare philosophical theories
⑤ avoid borrowing them

08 다음 빈칸에 들어갈 말로 가장 적절한 것은?

When trying to understand the role of the sun in ancient journeys, the sources become fewer and the journeys less well known. Herodotus writes about an exploratory voyage commissioned by the ancient Egyptian King Necho II in about 600 BC. Necho II reportedly ordered a Phoenician expedition to sail clockwise around Africa, starting at the Red Sea and returning to the mouth of the Nile. They were gone for three years. Herodotus writes that the Phoenicians, upon returning from their heroic expedition, reported that after sailing south and then turning west, they found the sun was on their right, the opposite direction to where they were used to seeing it or expecting it to be. Contemporary astronomical science was simply not strong enough to fabricate such an accurate, fundamental and yet prosaic detail of where the sun would be after sailing past the equator and into the southern hemisphere. It is this that leads many of today's historians to conclude that the journey ____.

*fabricate: 꾸며 내다, 만들어 내다   **prosaic: 평범한

① must have taken place
② was not reported at all
③ was not worth the time
④ should have been planned better
⑤ could be stopped at any moment

09 다음 글에서 전체 흐름과 관계 없는 문장은?

Although organizations are offering telecommuting programs in greater numbers than ever before, acceptance and use of these programs are still limited by a number of factors. ① These factors include manager reliance on face-to-face management practices, lack of telecommuting training within an organization, misperceptions of and discomfort with flexible workplace programs, and a lack of information about the effects of telecommuting on an organization's bottom line. ② Despite these limitations, at the beginning of the 21st century, a new "anytime, anywhere" work culture is emerging. ③ Care must be taken to select employees whose personal and working characteristics are best suited for telecommuting. ④ Continuing advances in information technology, the expansion of a global workforce, and increased desire to balance work and family are only three of the many factors that will gradually reduce the current barriers to telecommuting as a dominant workforce development. ⑤ With implications for organizational cost savings, especially with regard to lower facility costs, increased employee flexibility, and productivity, telecommuting is increasingly of interest to many organizations.

*telecommute: (컴퓨터로) 집에서 근무하다

10 주어진 글 다음에 이어질 글의 순서로 가장 적절한 것은?

Shakespeare wrote, "What's in a name? That which we call a rose by any other name would smell as sweet."

(A) Take the word *bridge*. In German, *bridge* (die brücke) is a feminine noun; in Spanish, *bridge* (el puente) is a masculine noun. Boroditsky found that when asked to describe a bridge, native German speakers used words like *beautiful, elegant, slender*. When native Spanish speakers were asked the same question, they used words like *strong, sturdy, towering*.

(B) According to Stanford University psychology professor Lera Boroditsky, that's not necessarily so. Focusing on the grammatical gender differences between German and Spanish, Boroditsky's work indicates that the gender our language assigns to a given noun influences us to subconsciously give that noun characteristics of the grammatical gender.

(C) This worked the other way around as well. The word *key* is masculine in German and feminine in Spanish. When asked to describe a key, native German speakers used words like *jagged, heavy, hard, metal*. Spanish speakers used words like *intricate, golden, lovely*.

*jagged: 뾰족뾰족한 **intricate: 정교한

① (A) – (C) – (B)　　② (B) – (A) – (C)
③ (B) – (C) – (A)　　④ (C) – (A) – (B)
⑤ (C) – (B) – (A)

11 글의 흐름으로 보아, 주어진 문장이 들어가기에 가장 적절한 곳은?

Personal stories connect with larger narratives to generate new identities.

The growing complexity of the social dynamics determining food choices makes the job of marketers and advertisers increasingly more difficult. (①) In the past, mass production allowed for accessibility and affordability of products, as well as their wide distribution, and was accepted as a sign of progress. (②) Nowadays it is increasingly replaced by the fragmentation of consumers among smaller and smaller segments that are supposed to reflect personal preferences. (③) Everybody feels different and special and expects products serving his or her inclinations. (④) In reality, these supposedly individual preferences end up overlapping with emerging, temporary, always changing, almost tribal formations solidifying around cultural sensibilities, social identifications, political sensibilities, and dietary and health concerns. (⑤) These consumer communities go beyond national boundaries, feeding on global and widely shared repositories of ideas, images, and practices.

*fragmentation: 파편화 **repository: 저장소

12 다음 글의 내용을 한 문장으로 요약하고자 한다. 빈칸 (A), (B)에 들어갈 말로 가장 적절한 것은?

Experiments suggest that animals, just like humans, tend to prefer exaggerated, supernormal stimuli, and that a preference can rapidly propel itself to extreme levels (*peak shift effect*). In one experiment, through food rewards rats were conditioned to prefer squares to other geometric forms. In the next step, a non-square rectangle was introduced and associated with an even larger reward than the square. As expected, the rats learned to reliably prefer the rectangle. Less predictable was the third part of the experiment. The rats were offered the opportunity to choose between the rectangle they already knew and associated with large rewards and another rectangle, the proportions of which were even more different from those of a square. Interestingly, rats picked this novel variant, without undergoing any reward-based conditioning in favor of it. A possible explanation is thus that they chose the larger difference from the original square (i.e., the exaggeration of *non-squareness*).

↓

In an experiment, after first establishing an ____(A)____ to squares, and then to non-square rectangles, rats were seen to pursue ____(B)____ rectangularity even without any additional reward.

	(A)		(B)
①	inclination	……	severe
②	opposition	……	familiar
③	inclination	……	vague
④	opposition	……	unexpected
⑤	attachment	……	subtle

13~14 다음 글을 읽고, 물음에 답하시오.

Climate change experts and environmental humanists alike agree that the climate crisis is, at its core, a crisis of the imagination and much of the popular imagination is shaped by fiction. In his 2016 book *The Great Derangement*, anthropologist and novelist Amitav Ghosh takes on this relationship between imagination and environmental management, arguing that humans have failed to respond to climate change at least in part because fiction (a) <u>fails</u> to believably represent it. Ghosh explains that climate change is largely absent from contemporary fiction because the cyclones, floods, and other catastrophes it brings to mind simply seem too "improbable" to belong in stories about everyday life. But climate change does not only reveal itself as a series of (b) <u>extraordinary</u> events. In fact, as environmentalists and ecocritics from Rachel Carson to Rob Nixon have pointed out, environmental change can be "imperceptible"; it proceeds (c) <u>rapidly</u>, only occasionally producing "explosive and spectacular" events. Most climate change impacts cannot be observed day-to-day, but they become (d) <u>visible</u> when we are confronted with their accumulated impacts.

Climate change evades our imagination because it poses significant representational challenges. It cannot be observed in "human time," which is why documentary filmmaker Jeff Orlowski, who tracks climate change effects on glaciers and coral reefs, uses "before and after" photographs taken several months apart in the same place to (e) <u>highlight</u> changes that occurred gradually.

*anthropologist: 인류학자
**catastrophe: 큰 재해   ***evade: 피하다

제목 추론

13 윗글의 제목으로 가장 적절한 것은?

① Differing Attitudes Towards Current Climate Issues
② Slow but Significant: The History of Ecological Movements
③ The Silence of Imagination in Representing Climate Change
④ Vivid Threats: Climate Disasters Spreading in Local Areas
⑤ The Rise and Fall of Environmentalism and Ecocriticism

어휘 추론

14 밑줄 친 (a)~(e) 중에서 문맥상 낱말의 쓰임이 적절하지 <u>않은</u> 것은?

① (a)
② (b)
③ (c)
④ (d)
⑤ (e)

13 정답률 57%   14 정답률 44%

정답 p. 22

단어 TEST ● 주어진 단어의 뜻을 쓰고, 예문을 올바르게 해석하세요.

1	**seasoned**	노련한, 경험 많은	a seasoned writer	(노련한) 작가
2	**paralyzed**		paralyzed by fear	두려움으로 ( )
3	**tolerate**		tolerate the momentary anger	순간적인 분노를 ( )
4	**periodically**		periodically go off	( ) 자리를 뜨다
5	**authorities**		the college authorities	대학 ( )
6	**dismiss**		be dismissed by academics	학자들에 의해 ( )
7	**astronomical**		astronomical science	( ) 과학
8	**misperception**		misperceptions of telecommuting	재택근무에 대한 ( )
9	**sturdy**		a sturdy bridge	( ) 다리
10	**segment**		smaller and smaller segments	점점 더 작은 ( )
11	**improbable**		improbable catastrophes	( ) 큰 재해들
12	**gradually**		occur gradually	( ) 일어나다

구문 TEST ● 주어진 단어를 활용하여 우리말에 맞게 빈칸을 완성하세요.

13 (The fear of being left out) **keeps them glued to their social media.**
the fear / leave out

소외되는 것에 관한 두려움은 그들이 소셜 미디어에 계속 매달리게 한다.

14 **His love for music led to him (**).
select / for the band

음악에 대한 그의 사랑은 그가 밴드에 선택되도록 만들었다.

15 **She (**) **in the crowded meeting room.**
make / voice / hear

그녀는 사람 가득한 회의실에서 자기 목소리가 들리게 만들었다.

16 **He completed the marathon, (**) **considering his injury.**
an incredible feat

그는 마라톤을 마쳤는데, 이것은 그의 부상을 고려하면 대단한 성과였다.

17 **The garden bloomed beautifully in spring, (**).
delight / all the residents

그 정원은 봄에 꽃이 아름답게 피었고, 이것은 모든 주민을 기쁘게 했다.

18 **The concert, which lasted for hours, (**).
be / truly / spectacular

몇 시간 동안 계속된 그 콘서트는 정말 장관이었다.

기출 하프 모의고사

● 문제에 나오는 단어들을 확인하세요.

☐ shiver	v. 떨다	
☐ overjoyed	a. 매우 기쁜	
☐ walk on air	구름 위를 걷다, 몹시 기뻐하다	
☐ accountability	n. 책임(성)	
☐ confer	v. 주다, 부여하다	
☐ in proportion to	~에 비례해서	
☐ disposition	n. 성향, 기질	
☐ irreversibly	ad. 비가역적으로, 되돌릴 수 없게	
☐ glorify	v. 미화하다	
☐ wasteland	n. 황무지	
☐ cut down on	~을 줄이다	
☐ violation	n. 침해, 위반	
☐ spontaneously	ad. 자발적으로, 저절로	
☐ like-minded	a. 생각이 비슷한	
☐ executive	n. 관리자, 임원	
☐ improvise	v. 즉흥적으로 하다	
☐ conflicting	a. 상충하는, 모순되는	
☐ enroll at	~에 등록하다	
☐ pension	n. 연금	
☐ bulky	a. 부피가 큰	
☐ retiring	a. 내성적인, 남과 잘 어울리지 않는	
☐ limit A to B	A를 B에 국한시키다	
☐ quantify	v. 정량화하다	
☐ inferior	a. 열등한	
☐ rigid	a. 완고한, 엄격한	

☐ counter	v. (위협 등에) 대응하다, (주장 등에) 반대하다	
☐ physiological	a. 생리학의	
☐ unambiguously	ad. 분명히	
☐ strike down	~의 목숨을 앗아가다	
☐ promptly	ad. 신속히, 즉시	
☐ outcompete	v. 경쟁자보다 우세하다	
☐ accumulate	v. 축적되다	
☐ development	n. (음악) 전개부 (악상이 발전되는 부분)	
☐ automate	v. 자동화하다	
☐ finite	a. 유한한, 한정된	
☐ circumstance	n. 상황, 환경	
☐ shabby	a. 터무니없는	
☐ suspicion	n. 의심	
☐ unceasing	a. 끊임없는	
☐ emphasize	v. 강조하다	
☐ revelation	n. 뜻밖의 새로운 발견, 계시	
☐ displace	v. 대체하다, 대신하다	
☐ instinct	n. 직관, 직감, 본능	
☐ considerable	a. 상당한	
☐ unattainable	a. 얻을 수 없는	
☐ continuum	n. 연속체	
☐ formula	n. 공식, 제조법	
☐ irrelevant	a. 무관한	
☐ intensive care	중환자실, 집중치료실	
☐ infection	n. 감염	

2021 9월 22번

❶ 장소의 부사구 도치   ❷ between A and B

At the heart of this process is the tension between the professions' pursuit of autonomy and the public's demand for accountability.

이 과정의 핵심에는 전문직의 자율성 추구와 대중의 책임 요구 사이의 긴장이 있다.

첨삭 1 · 장소의 부사구 도치

개　념 ▶ 본래 동사 뒤에 오는 장소 부사구나 전치사구가 문장 맨 앞에 오면 〈동사+주어〉 어순이 된다.

독해전략 ▶ 주로 동사 뒤(주어)에 문맥이나 의미상 중요한 내용이 제시되므로 이에 주목해서 읽는다.

어법전략 ▶ 동사 뒤의 주어에 동사를 수 일치시키는 패턴으로 자주 출제된다.

다음 중 어법상 옳은 것을 고르세요.

a. In the vase │ is │ are │ flowers of vibrant colors, each carefully arranged.

b. Between the two towering mountains │ stand │ stands │ a solitary ancient castle.

c. Between the tall bookshelves │ lie │ lies │ a cozy couch, inviting visitors.

첨삭 2 · between A and B

개　념 ▶ 'A와 B 사이'라는 의미의 전치사구이다. A와 B는 명사구 병렬구조를 이룬다.

독해전략 ▶ A와 B를 명확하게 파악해야 한다. 수식어가 많으면 and로 연결되는 대상이 무엇인지 헷갈릴 수 있다.

어법전략 ▶ <between A and B>가 특히 주어 뒤에서 주어를 수식할 때 동사의 수 일치에 유의한다.

다음 중 어법상 옳은 것을 고르세요.

a. The harmonious collaboration between art and science │ fuel │ fuels │ creativity and innovation.

b. The difference between the busy city life and the simplicity of the countryside │ is │ are │ clear.

c. Choosing between a stable job in finance and my passion for music │ was │ were │ not easy.

❸ it's time 가정법   ❹ so that 부사절

It's time we changed our thinking so that there is no difference between the rights of humans and the rights of the rest of the environment.

인간의 권리와 나머지 환경의 권리 사이에 차이가 없도록, 우리가 생각을 바꿔야 할 때이다.

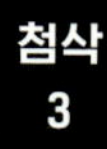

it's time 가정법

개　념 ▶ 현재 이뤄지지 않은 일에 대해 '~해야 할 때'라고 주장하는 표현으로, 가정법 과거의 일종이다.

독해전략 ▶ 주로 문제에 대한 해결이나 필자의 주장 등 핵심을 제시할 때 사용되므로 주의 깊게 읽어야 한다.

어법전략 ▶ 과거 동사 대신 <should+동사원형>을 쓰거나, 문장을 <it's time for A to-V>로 바꿔도 된다.

다음 중 어법상 옳은 것을 고르세요.

a. It's time she | visited | visits | her grandparents. They miss her.

b. It's time you | learned | to learn | to drive; it would make life easier.

c. It's time we resolved the issues and | move | moved | forward.

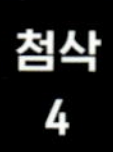

so that 부사절

개　념 ▶ so that이 이끄는 부사절은 목적(~하기 위해서) 또는 결과(~해서 …하다)의 의미를 나타낸다.

독해전략 ▶ 목적과 결과를 엄격히 구별하기보다, 결국 '주절'하는 이유가 so that 뒤의 내용임을 이해하면 된다.

어법전략 ▶ so that 뒤에는 완전한 문장이 온다. 다른 접속사와 의미상으로도 구별해두도록 한다.

다음 중 의미상 적절한 것을 고르세요.

a. He adjusted the heat dial | if | so that | the room would be warmer.

b. He studied diligently | so that | except that | he would excel in the upcoming exam.

c. I set an alarm so that I | would oversleep | would not oversleep | for the early meeting.

정답 a. visited   b. learned   c. moved / a. so that   b. so that   c. would not oversleep

01 다음 글에 드러난 'I'의 심경 변화로 가장 적절한 것은?

Finally, it came to my turn. I was supposed to walk backward off the cliff. Just looking down the cliff made my legs begin to shake. I knew there was a safety rope around me in case I should black out. I had an intellectual understanding of the whole situation and an intellectual sense of security. Nevertheless, my hair stood on end and I shivered all over. That first step off the cliff was the most difficult moment, but I made it—as did others. I arrived safely at the bottom, overjoyed by the success of meeting the challenge. I felt as though I was walking on air.

① relaxed → nervous
② angry → ashamed
③ terrified → delighted
④ envious → sympathetic
⑤ disappointed → hopeful

02 다음 글의 요지로 가장 적절한 것은?

Historically, the professions and society have engaged in a negotiating process intended to define the terms of their relationship. At the heart of this process is the tension between the professions' pursuit of autonomy and the public's demand for accountability. Society's granting of power and privilege to the professions is premised on their willingness and ability to contribute to social well-being and to conduct their affairs in a manner consistent with broader social values. It has long been recognized that the expertise and privileged position of professionals confer authority and power that could readily be used to advance their own interests at the expense of those they serve. As Edmund Burke observed two centuries ago, "Men are qualified for civil liberty in exact proportion to their disposition to put moral chains upon their own appetites." Autonomy has never been a one-way street and is never granted absolutely and irreversibly.

*autonomy: 자율성　**privilege: 특권
***premise: 전제로 말하다

① 전문직에 부여되는 자율성은 그에 상응하는 사회적 책임을 수반한다.
② 전문직의 권위는 해당 집단의 이익을 추구하는 데 이용되어 왔다.
③ 전문직의 사회적 책임을 규정할 수 있는 제도 정비가 필요하다.
④ 전문직이 되기 위한 자격 요건은 사회 경제적 요구에 따라 변화해 왔다.
⑤ 전문직의 업무 성과는 일정 수준의 자율성과 특권이 부여될 때 높아진다.

2022 3월 19번　　정답률 85%　　　2021 9월 22번　　정답률 46%

함축 의미

03 밑줄 친 the role of the 'lion's historians'가 다음 글에서 의미하는 바로 가장 적절한 것은?

There is an African proverb that says, 'Till the lions have their historians, tales of hunting will always glorify the hunter'. The proverb is about power, control and law making. Environmental journalists have to play the role of the 'lion's historians'. They have to put across the point of view of the environment to people who make the laws. They have to be the voice of wild India. The present rate of human consumption is completely unsustainable. Forest, wetlands, wastelands, coastal zones, eco-sensitive zones, they are all seen as disposable for the accelerating demands of human population. But to ask for any change in human behaviour—whether it be to cut down on consumption, alter lifestyles or decrease population growth—is seen as a violation of human rights. But at some point human rights become 'wrongs'. It's time we changed our thinking so that there is no difference between the rights of humans and the rights of the rest of the environment.

① uncovering the history of a species' biological evolution
② urging a shift to sustainable human behaviour for nature
③ fighting against widespread violations of human rights
④ rewriting history for more underrepresented people
⑤ restricting the power of environmental lawmakers

제목 추론

04 다음 글의 제목으로 가장 적절한 것은?

The most innovative teams are those that can restructure themselves in response to unexpected shifts in the environment; they don't need a strong leader to tell them what to do. Moreover, they tend to form spontaneously; when like-minded people find each other, a group emerges. The improvisational collaboration of the entire group translates moments of individual creativity into group innovation. Allowing the space for this self-organizing emergence to occur is difficult for many managers because the outcome isn't controlled by the management team's agenda and is therefore less predictable. Most business executives like to start with the big picture and then work out the details. That's why so many of the best examples of improvised innovation take place outside of formal organizations. In improvisational innovation, teams start with the details and then work up to the big picture. It's riskier and less efficient, but when a successful innovation emerges, it's often very surprising and imaginative.

① The Start of Innovation: A Leader's Big Picture
② Unpredictable Changes: Challenges to Innovation
③ Conflicting Ideas Lead to the Ultimate Innovation
④ Weakness of Improvisational Teams in Emergencies
⑤ Improvised Innovation Emerges from the Bottom Up

2021학년도 수능 21번   정답률 49%

2021 10월 24번   정답률 36%

05 Josef Sudek에 관한 다음 글의 내용과 일치하지 <u>않는</u> 것은?

Josef Sudek was born in the Czech Republic. Originally a bookbinder, Sudek was badly injured during World War I, resulting in the loss of his right arm. After the injury, he spent three years in various hospitals, and began to take photographs out of boredom. In 1922, he enrolled at the State School of Graphic Arts in Prague, where he studied photography for two years. His army disability pension allowed him to make art without worrying about an income. He photographed many night-scapes of Prague and the wooded landscapes of Bohemia. Sudek didn't let his disability get in the way and, despite having only one arm, he used very heavy and bulky equipment. Often known as the 'Poet of Prague,' Sudek never married, and was a shy and retiring person. He never appeared at his exhibition openings. He died on 15 September 1976, when he was 80 years old.

① 제1차 세계 대전 중 심한 부상으로 오른팔을 잃었다.
② Prague에 있는 학교에서 2년 동안 사진술을 공부했다.
③ 연금을 받아서 수입 걱정 없이 예술 창작을 할 수 있었다.
④ 매우 무겁고 부피가 큰 장비를 사용했다.
⑤ 자신의 전시회 개막식에 항상 참석했다.

06 다음 글의 밑줄 친 부분 중, 문맥상 낱말의 쓰임이 적절하지 <u>않은</u> 것은?

Those who limit themselves to Western scientific research have virtually ① <u>ignored</u> anything that cannot be perceived by the five senses and repeatedly measured or quantified. Research is dismissed as superstitious and invalid if it cannot be scientifically explained by cause and effect. Many continue to ② <u>object</u> with an almost religious passion to this cultural paradigm about the power of science—more specifically, the power that science gives them. By dismissing non-Western scientific paradigms as inferior at best and inaccurate at worst, the most rigid members of the conventional medical research community try to ③ <u>counter</u> the threat that alternative therapies and research pose to their work, their well-being, and their worldviews. And yet, biomedical research cannot explain many of the phenomena that ④ <u>concern</u> alternative practitioners regarding caring-healing processes. When therapies such as acupuncture or homeopathy are observed to result in a physiological or clinical response that cannot be explained by the biomedical model, many have tried to ⑤ <u>deny</u> the results rather than modify the scientific model.

*acupuncture: 침술   **homeopathy: 동종 요법

07 다음 빈칸에 들어갈 말로 가장 적절한 것은?

Imagine some mutation appears which makes animals spontaneously die at the age of 50. This is unambiguously disadvantageous—but only very slightly so. More than 99 per cent of animals carrying this mutation will never experience its ill effects because they will die before it has a chance to act. This means that it's pretty likely to remain in the population—not because it's good, but because the 'force of natural selection' at such advanced ages is not strong enough to get rid of it. Conversely, if a mutation killed the animals at two years, striking them down when many could reasonably expect to still be alive and producing children, evolution would get rid of it very promptly: animals with the mutation would soon be outcompeted by those fortunate enough not to have it, because the force of natural selection is powerful in the years up to and including reproductive age. Thus, problematic mutations can accumulate, just so long as ____________________ ____________________________________.

*mutation: 돌연변이

① the force of natural selection increases as animals get older
② their accumulation is largely due to their evolutionary benefits
③ evolution operates by suppressing reproductive success of animals
④ animals can promptly compensate for the decline in their abilities
⑤ they only affect animals after they're old enough to have reproduced

08 다음 빈칸에 들어갈 말로 가장 적절한 것은?

Development can get very complicated and fanciful. A fugue by Johann Sebastian Bach illustrates how far this process could go, when a single melodic line, sometimes just a handful of notes, was all that the composer needed to create a brilliant work containing lots of intricate development within a coherent structure. Ludwig van Beethoven's famous Fifth Symphony provides an exceptional example of how much mileage a classical composer can get out of a few notes and a simple rhythmic tapping. The opening da-da-da-DUM that everyone has heard somewhere or another ________________________________ throughout not only the opening movement, but the remaining three movements, like a kind of motto or a connective thread. Just as we don't always see the intricate brushwork that goes into the creation of a painting, we may not always notice how Beethoven keeps finding fresh uses for his motto or how he develops his material into a large, cohesive statement. But a lot of the enjoyment we get from that mighty symphony stems from the inventiveness behind it, the impressive development of musical ideas.

*intricate: 복잡한 **coherent: 통일성 있는

① makes the composer's musical ideas contradictory
② appears in an incredible variety of ways
③ provides extensive musical knowledge creatively
④ remains fairly calm within the structure
⑤ becomes deeply associated with one's own enjoyment

09 다음 글에서 전체 흐름과 관계 <u>없는</u> 문장은?

Interestingly, experts do not suffer as much as beginners when performing complex tasks or combining multiple tasks. Because experts have extensive practice within a limited domain, the key component skills in their domain tend to be highly practiced and more automated. ① Each of these highly practiced skills then demands relatively few cognitive resources, effectively lowering the total cognitive load that experts experience. ② Thus, experts can perform complex tasks and combine multiple tasks relatively easily. ③ Furthermore, beginners are excellent at processing the tasks when the tasks are divided and isolated. ④ This is not because they necessarily have more cognitive resources than beginners; rather, because of the high level of fluency they have achieved in performing key skills, they can do more with what they have. ⑤ Beginners, on the other hand, have not achieved the same degree of fluency and automaticity in each of the component skills, and thus they struggle to combine skills that experts combine with relative ease and efficiency.

10 주어진 글 다음에 이어질 글의 순서로 가장 적절한 것은?

> In the course of acquiring a language, children are exposed to only a finite set of utterances. Yet they come to use and understand an infinite set of sentences.

(A) Yet, they all arrive at pretty much the same grammar. The input that children get is haphazard in the sense that caretakers do not talk to their children to illustrate a particular point of grammar. Yet, all children develop systematic knowledge of a language.

(B) Thus, despite the severe limitations and variation in the input children receive, and also in their personal circumstances, they all develop a rich and uniform system of linguistic knowledge. The knowledge attained goes beyond the input in various ways.

(C) This has been referred to as the creative aspect of language use. This 'creativity' does not refer to the ability to write poetry or novels but rather the ability to produce and understand an unlimited set of new sentences never spoken or heard previously. The precise linguistic input children receive differs from child to child; no two children are exposed to exactly the same set of utterances.

*haphazard: 무작위적인, 되는 대로의

① (A) – (C) – (B)　　② (B) – (A) – (C)
③ (B) – (C) – (A)　　④ (C) – (A) – (B)
⑤ (C) – (B) – (A)

11 글의 흐름으로 보아, 주어진 문장이 들어가기에 가장 적절한 곳은?

> Indeed, in the Middle Ages in Europe, calculating by hand and eye was sometimes seen as producing a rather shabby sort of knowledge, inferior to that of abstract thought.

Babylonian astronomers created detailed records of celestial movements in the heavens, using the resulting tables to sieve out irregularities and, with them, the favour of the gods. (①) This was the seed of what we now call the scientific method—a demonstration that accurate observations of the world could be used to forecast its future. (②) The importance of measurement in this sort of cosmic comprehension did not develop smoothly over the centuries. (③) The suspicion was due to the influence of ancient Greeks in the era's scholasticism, particularly Plato and Aristotle, who stressed that the material world was one of unceasing change and instability. (④) They emphasized that reality was best understood by reference to immaterial qualities, be they Platonic forms or Aristotelian causes. (⑤) It would take the revelations of the scientific revolution to fully displace these instincts, with observations of the night sky once again proving decisive.

*celestial: 천체의 **sieve: 거르다

---

12 다음 글의 내용을 한 문장으로 요약하고자 한다. 빈칸 (A), (B)에 들어갈 말로 가장 적절한 것은?

The computer has, to a considerable extent, solved the problem of acquiring, preserving, and retrieving information. Data can be stored in effectively unlimited quantities and in manageable form. The computer makes available a range of data unattainable in the age of books. It packages it effectively; style is no longer needed to make it accessible, nor is memorization. In dealing with a single decision separated from its context, the computer supplies tools unimaginable even a decade ago. But it also diminishes perspective. Because information is so accessible and communication instantaneous, there is a diminution of focus on its significance, or even on the definition of what is significant. This dynamic may encourage policymakers to wait for an issue to arise rather than anticipate it, and to regard moments of decision as a series of isolated events rather than part of a historical continuum. When this happens, manipulation of information replaces reflection as the principal policy tool.

*retrieve: (정보를) 추출하다 **diminution: 감소

↓

> Although the computer is clearly ___(A)___ at handling information in a decontextualized way, it interferes with our making ___(B)___ judgments related to the broader context, as can be seen in policymaking processes.

	(A)		(B)
①	competent	……	comprehensive
②	dominant	……	biased
③	imperfect	……	informed
④	impressive	……	legal
⑤	inefficient	……	timely

13~14 다음 글을 읽고, 물음에 답하시오.

There is evidence that even very simple algorithms can outperform expert judgement on simple prediction problems. For example, algorithms have proved more (a) <u>accurate</u> than humans in predicting whether a prisoner released on parole will go on to commit another crime, or in predicting whether a potential candidate will perform well in a job in future. In over 100 studies across many different domains, half of all cases show simple formulas make (b) <u>better</u> significant predictions than human experts, and the remainder (except a very small handful), show a tie between the two. When there are a lot of different factors involved and a situation is very uncertain, simple formulas can win out by focusing on the most important factors and being consistent, while human judgement is too easily influenced by particularly salient and perhaps (c) <u>irrelevant</u> considerations. A similar idea is supported by further evidence that 'checklists' can improve the quality of expert decisions in a range of domains by ensuring that important steps or considerations aren't missed when people are feeling (d) <u>relaxed</u>. For example, treating patients in intensive care can require hundreds of small actions per day, and one small error could cost a life. Using checklists to ensure that no crucial steps are missed has proved to be remarkably (e) <u>effective</u> in a range of medical contexts, from preventing live infections to reducing pneumonia.

*parole: 가석방　**salient: 두드러진
***pneumonia: 폐렴

제목 추론

13　윗글의 제목으로 가장 적절한 것은?

① The Power of Simple Formulas in Decision Making
② Always Prioritise: Tips for Managing Big Data
③ Algorithms' Mistakes: The Myth of Simplicity
④ Be Prepared! Make a Checklist Just in Case
⑤ How Human Judgement Beats Algorithms

어휘 추론

14　밑줄 친 (a) ~ (e) 중에서 문맥상 낱말의 쓰임이 적절하지 <u>않은</u> 것은?

① (a)
② (b)
③ (c)
④ (d)
⑤ (e)

2023학년도 수능 41~42번

13 정답률 44%　　**14** 정답률 51%

정답 p. 29

단어 TEST ● 주어진 단어의 뜻을 쓰고, 예문을 올바르게 해석하세요.

1	**overjoyed**	매우 기쁜	overjoyed by the success	성공에 (매우 기쁜)
2	**accountability**		the public's demand for accountability	( )에 대한 대중의 요구
3	**cut down on**		cut down on consumption	소비를 ( )
4	**retiring**		a shy and retiring person	수줍음이 많고 ( ) 사람
5	**counter**		counter the threat	위협에 ( )
6	**strike down**		strike the animals down	그 동물들의 ( )
7	**promptly**		get rid of the mutation very promptly	그 돌연변이를 매우 ( ) 없애다
8	**finite**		a finite set of utterances	일련의 ( ) 발화
9	**shabby**		a shabby sort of knowledge	( ) 종류의 지식
10	**unceasing**		unceasing change	( ) 변화
11	**unattainable**		unattainable data	( ) 데이터
12	**infection**		prevent infections	( )을 예방하다

구문 TEST ● 주어진 단어를 활용하여 우리말에 맞게 빈칸을 완성하세요.

13 **At the heart of this process** (is a long-lasting tension).
a long-lasting tension
이 과정의 핵심에는 오래 지속된 긴장이 있다.

14 **Between the tall bookshelves** ( ), **inviting visitors.**
lie / a cozy couch
높은 책장 사이로 안락한 소파가 있어, 방문객들을 부른다.

15 ( ) **fuels innovation.**
the collaboration / art / science
예술과 과학 간의 협업은 혁신을 부추긴다.

16 **It's time** ( ); **it would make life easier.**
learn / drive
넌 운전하는 것을 배워야 할 때야. 그럼 생활이 더 편해질 거야.

17 **He adjusted the heat dial** ( ).
the room / will be / warm
그는 그 방이 더 따뜻해지도록 난방기 다이얼을 조절했다.

18 **I set an alarm** ( ) **for the early meeting.**
will / oversleep
나는 이른 회의에 늦잠을 자지 않도록 알람을 맞췄다.

기출 하프 모의고사

05

기출 하프 모의고사

● 문제에 나오는 단어들을 확인하세요.

☐ out of sight	시야에서 사라진, 보이지 않는		☐ fascinate	v. 매료시키다
☐ blush	v. (얼굴이) 빨개지다, 부끄러워하다		☐ tread(-trod-trodden)	v. 밟다, 걷다
☐ play out	전개되다		☐ inanimate	a. 무생물의
☐ once and for all	완전히, 최종적으로		☐ fool A into B	A를 속여 B하게 하다
☐ deliberately	ad. 의도적으로		☐ integration	n. 통합
☐ scatter	v. 분산시키다, 흩뜨리다		☐ take into account	~을 고려하다
☐ fixate on	~에 집착하다		☐ sufficiently	ad. 충분히
☐ put in perspective	균형 있게 바라보다		☐ reinforce	v. 강화하다
☐ nonstick	a. (프라이팬 등이 요리 도중) 눌어붙지 않는		☐ boil down to	결국 ~이 되다, ~로 요약하다
☐ demographic	a. 인구통계적인		☐ predominately	ad. 주로, 대체로
☐ profitable	a. 수익성 있는		☐ indication	n. 징후, 표시
☐ rely (up)on A to-V	A가 ~할 것이라 믿다		☐ manufacturer	n. 제조업자
☐ retention	n. 유지, 보유		☐ ready-to-wear	a. 기성복의
☐ mark out	~을 표시[구분]하다, 두드러지게 만들다		☐ hand down	~을 물려주다
☐ outbreak	n. 발발, 급증		☐ conceivably	ad. 아마도
☐ endure	v. 지속되다, 견디다		☐ allergic to	~에 알레르기가 있는, ~을 몹시 싫어하는
☐ measurement	n. 측정		☐ universal	n. 보편적인 것 a. 보편적인
☐ bias	n. 편향, 편견		☐ obsession	n. 강박
☐ emphasis	n. 강조, 역점		☐ loosen up	긴장을 풀다, 몸을 풀다
☐ put an end to	~을 없애다, 끝내다		☐ odd	n. 가능성, 확률 a. 이상한
☐ orientation	n. 성향, 방향, 지향		☐ starvation	n. 아사, 굶주림
☐ stimulating	a. 아주 흥미로운, 자극이 되는		☐ catastrophic	a. 재앙의, 파멸의, 비극적인
☐ sustenance	n. 생존, 생명 유지, 지속		☐ adaptive	a. 적응하는
☐ exotic	a. 이국적인		☐ inhibit	v. 억제하다
☐ invariable	a. 불변의		☐ absurd	a. 터무니없는, 불합리한

2024학년도 수능 21번

❶ 명사를 꾸미는 to부정사

Scattered attention harms **your ability** **to let go of** **stress,** because even though your attention is scattered, it is narrowly focused, ❷ 등위접속사 for **for** **you are able to fixate only on the stressful parts of your experience.**

분산된 주의는 스트레스를 해소하는 능력을 손상시키는데, 왜냐하면 여러분의 주의가 분산되더라도, 여러분은 경험 가운데 스트레스가 많은 부분에만 집착할 수 있기에 그것이 좁게 집중되기 때문이다.

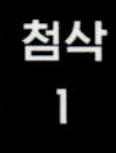

명사를 꾸미는 to부정사

개   념 ▶ to부정사는 명사 뒤에서 명사를 꾸미는 수식어구 역할을 할 수 있다.

독해전략 ▶ 보통 '~할, ~하려는'으로 해석하여 앞의 명사에 의미를 연결하면 된다.

어법전략 ▶ 수식받는 명사가 to부정사구의 의미상 목적어인 경우, to부정사구는 목적어가 빠진 불완전한 구조로 남는다.

다음 중 어법상 옳은 것을 고르세요.

a. Her ability | solves | **to solve** | complex problems makes her an invaluable member of our team.

b. He found a new way | **to organize** | organized | the files that saved everyone a lot of time.

c. He always brings something | **to read** | to read it | on long flights to pass the time.

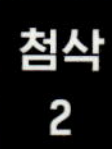

등위접속사 for

개   념 ▶ 등위접속사 for는 앞뒤로 문장을 연결할 수 있으며, '왜냐하면 ~이다'라는 의미로 해석된다.

독해전략 ▶ 뒷 내용이 앞에 대한 이유이므로, 앞 내용이 이해되지 않았을 때 주의 깊게 읽으면 도움이 된다.

어법전략 ▶ 전치사 for와 구별해 둔다. 전치사 for 뒤에는 명사구가, 접속사 for 뒤에는 <주어+동사>가 나온다.

다음 중 문맥상 올바른 접속사를 고르세요.

a. I was late for the meeting, | so | **for** | my car had broken down on the way.

b. She missed the early morning bus, | **so** | for | she had to walk to school in the cold weather.

c. They studied hard for the exam, | **for** | so that | they knew the material was challenging.

❸ 관계부사 where

This kind of error, where results are always on one side of the real value, is called "bias."

❹ 5형식 문장의 수동태

결과가 항상 실제 값의 어느 한쪽에 있는 이런 오류는 '편향'이라 불린다.

관계부사 where

개　　념 ▶　where는 물리적 장소뿐 아니라 상황(situation, case 등)을 나타내는 명사를 꾸미거나 보충 설명한다.

독해전략 ▶　선행사를 재진술 또는 구체화한 것이 where절의 내용이므로, where 뒤를 주의 깊게 읽는다.

어법전략 ▶　관계부사 where 뒤에는 완전한 문장이 온다. 뒤에 불완전한 문장이 오는 관계대명사 which와 구별해 둔다.

다음 중 어법상 옳은 것을 고르세요.

a. The restaurant 　which　 where 　we celebrated our anniversary has exquisite cuisine.

b. He told us about the situation 　which　 where 　his patience was tested to its limits.

c. I found the book very insightful, 　which　 where 　you recommended last week.

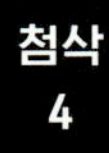

5형식 문장의 수동태

개　　념 ▶　<동사+목적어+목적격보어> 형태의 5형식 구조가 수동태로 바뀌면 <주어+be p.p.+보어> 구조가 된다.

독해전략 ▶　동사가 무엇이든, 결과적으로는 '주어 = 보어'의 의미가 성립하게 된다.

어법전략 ▶　<be p.p.> 뒤에 특히 형용사 보어가 올 때 부사 자리로 혼동하지 않도록 한다.

다음 중 어법상 옳은 것을 고르세요.

a. Due to the hardships he endured throughout his life, he 　calls　 is called 　"the man of tragedy."

b. The document is left 　incomplete　 incompletely 　because of missing information.

c. The success was made 　possibly　 possible 　by the collective effort of the team.

01 다음 글에 드러난 'I'의 심경 변화로 가장 적절한 것은?

The hotel lobby was elegant and well lit. Good, light brown woodwork and stainless steel. A short metro carriage runs through this place carrying executives. I am well dressed in a charcoal colour suit with a matching tie and black shoes. I feel great thinking I am fitted out to charm any crowd. But I forget where I've left my briefcase and laptop. I stop the metro and tell them that I need to check for my bag in their glass bag carriage. I find all sorts of bags except mine. I doubt whether I have brought it with me to this country at all. Mr nice guy that I am, I don't like to keep others waiting. I let the metro move which moves quickly and is almost out of sight when I realise that one of my expensive shoes is missing! I must have left it in the cabin while looking for the bag and the metro has left. I feel myself blushing.

① nervous → relieved
② delighted → bored
③ curious → disappointed
④ surprised → indifferent
⑤ satisfied → embarrassed

02 다음 글에서 필자가 주장하는 바로 가장 적절한 것은?

We try to avoid uncertainty by overanalyzing. But we don't have complete control over how the future will play out. You may feel that if you can just answer your "worry question" once and for all, you will be satisfied and you can finally drop your rumination, but has this ever actually happened to you? Has there ever been an answer that allowed you to stop worrying? There is only one way out of this spiral, and that is not to try to gain control, but to give it up. Instead of pushing back against uncertainty, embrace it. Instead of trying to answer your worry question, deliberately practice leaving it unanswered. Don't ask others and don't think about it. Tell yourself that analysis is *not* the solution, but really just more of the same problem.

*rumination: 반추(反芻) **spiral: 소용돌이

① 분석을 통해 미래의 불확실성을 통제하기보다 수용해야 한다.
② 타인에게 의존하기보다는 스스로 문제 해결력을 길러야 한다.
③ 걱정을 유발하는 문제 상황을 객관적으로 판단해야 한다.
④ 문제의 해결책을 찾기 전에 원인을 먼저 분석해야 한다.
⑤ 만일의 상황에 대비하여 꼼꼼하게 계획을 세워야 한다.

2020 7월 19번　　정답률 86%　　　　2022 4월 20번　　정답률 77%

03 밑줄 친 a nonstick frying pan이 다음 글에서 의미하는 바로 가장 적절한 것은?

How you focus your attention plays a critical role in how you deal with stress. Scattered attention harms your ability to let go of stress, because even though your attention is scattered, it is narrowly focused, for you are able to fixate only on the stressful parts of your experience. When your attentional spotlight is widened, you can more easily let go of stress. You can put in perspective many more aspects of any situation and not get locked into one part that ties you down to superficial and anxiety-provoking levels of attention. A narrow focus heightens the stress level of each experience, but a widened focus turns down the stress level because you're better able to put each situation into a broader perspective. One anxiety-provoking detail is less important than the bigger picture. It's like transforming yourself into a nonstick frying pan. You can still fry an egg, but the egg won't stick to the pan.

*provoke: 유발시키다

① never being confronted with any stressful experiences in daily life
② broadening one's perspective to identify the cause of stress
③ rarely confining one's attention to positive aspects of an experience
④ having a larger view of an experience beyond its stressful aspects
⑤ taking stress into account as the source of developing a wide view

04 다음 글의 주제로 가장 적절한 것은?

The primary purpose of commercial music radio broadcasting is to deliver an audience to a group of advertisers and sponsors. To achieve commercial success, that audience must be as large as possible. More than any other characteristics (such as demographic or psychographic profile, purchasing power, level of interest, degree of satisfaction, quality of attention or emotional state), the quantity of an audience aggregated as a mass is the most significant metric for broadcasters seeking to make music radio for profitable ends. As a result, broadcasters attempt to maximise their audience size by playing music that is popular, or—at the very least—music that can be relied upon not to cause audiences to switch off their radio or change the station. Audience retention is a key value (if not the key value) for many music programmers and for radio station management. In consequence, a high degree of risk aversion frequently marks out the 'successful' radio music programmer. Playlists are restricted, and often very small.

*aggregate: 모으다   **aversion: 싫어함

① features of music playlists appealing to international audiences
② influence of advertisers on radio audiences' musical preferences
③ difficulties of increasing audience size in radio music programmes
④ necessity of satisfying listeners' diverse needs in the radio business
⑤ outcome of music radio businesses' attempts to attract large audiences

2024학년도 수능 21번   정답률 51%

2023 9월 23번   정답률 44%

05 Jean Renoir에 관한 다음 글의 내용과 일치하지 <u>않는</u> 것은?

Jean Renoir (1894-1979), a French film director, was born in Paris, France. He was the son of the famous painter Pierre-Auguste Renoir. He and the rest of the Renoir family were the models of many of his father's paintings. At the outbreak of World War I, Jean Renoir was serving in the French army but was wounded in the leg. In 1937, he made *La Grande Illusion*, one of his better-known films. It was enormously successful but was not allowed to show in Germany. During World War II, when the Nazis invaded France in 1940, he went to Hollywood in the United States and continued his career there. He was awarded numerous honors and awards throughout his career, including the Academy Honorary Award in 1975 for his lifetime achievements in the film industry. Overall, Jean Renoir's influence as a film-maker and artist endures.

① 유명 화가의 아들이었다.
② 제1차 세계대전이 발발했을 때 프랑스 군에 복무 중이었다.
③ *La Grande Illusion*을 1937년에 만들었다.
④ 제2차 세계대전 내내 프랑스에 머물렀다.
⑤ Academy Honorary Award를 수상하였다.

06 다음 글의 밑줄 친 부분 중, 문맥상 낱말의 쓰임이 적절하지 <u>않은</u> 것은?

How the bandwagon effect occurs is demonstrated by the history of measurements of the speed of light. Because this speed is the basis of the theory of relativity, it's one of the most frequently and carefully measured ① <u>quantities</u> in science. As far as we know, the speed hasn't changed over time. However, from 1870 to 1900, all the experiments found speeds that were too high. Then, from 1900 to 1950, the ② <u>opposite</u> happened—all the experiments found speeds that were too low! This kind of error, where results are always on one side of the real value, is called "bias." It probably happened because over time, experimenters subconsciously adjusted their results to ③ <u>match</u> what they expected to find. If a result fit what they expected, they kept it. If a result didn't fit, they threw it out. They weren't being intentionally dishonest, just ④ <u>influenced</u> by the conventional wisdom. The pattern only changed when someone ⑤ <u>lacked</u> the courage to report what was actually measured instead of what was expected.

*bandwagon effect: 편승 효과

07 다음 빈칸에 들어갈 말로 가장 적절한 것은?

People have always needed to eat, and they always will. Rising emphasis on self-expression values does not put an end to material desires. But prevailing economic orientations are gradually being reshaped. People who work in the knowledge sector continue to seek high salaries, but they place equal or greater emphasis on doing stimulating work and being able to follow their own time schedules. Consumption is becoming progressively less determined by the need for sustenance and the practical use of the goods consumed. People still eat, but a growing component of food's value is determined by its ________________ aspects. People pay a premium to eat exotic cuisines that provide an interesting experience or that symbolize a distinctive life-style. The publics of postindustrial societies place growing emphasis on "political consumerism," such as boycotting goods whose production violates ecological or ethical standards. Consumption is less and less a matter of sustenance and more and more a question of life-style—and choice.

*prevail: 우세하다 **cuisine: 요리

① quantitative
② nonmaterial
③ nutritional
④ invariable
⑤ economic

08 다음 빈칸에 들어갈 말로 가장 적절한 것은?

Like faces, sometimes movement can ________________________________. For example, toys that seem to come alive fascinate children. In my day, one of the popular toys was a piece of finely coiled wire called a "Slinky." It could appear to walk by stretching and lifting up one end over another down an incline, a bit like an acrobatic caterpillar. The attraction of the Slinky on Christmas Day was the lifelike movement it had as it stepped down the stairs before someone trod on it or twisted the spring and ruined it for good. Toys that appear to be alive are curiosities because they challenge how we think inanimate objects and living things should behave. Many toys today exploit this principle to great effect, but be warned: not all babies enjoy objects that suddenly seem lifelike. This anxiety probably reflects their confusion over the question, "Is it alive or what?" Once babies decide that something is alive, they are inclined to see its movements as purposeful.

*incline: 경사면 **acrobatic: 곡예를 부리는

① fool us into thinking that something has a mind
② help us release and process certain feelings
③ shift our energy and protective mechanisms
④ secretly unlock emotions that words cannot
⑤ create a definite sense of achievement

09 다음 글에서 전체 흐름과 관계 <u>없는</u> 문장은?

Since their introduction, information systems have substantially changed the way business is conducted. ① This is particularly true for business in the shape and form of cooperation between firms that involves an integration of value chains across multiple units. ② The resulting networks do not only cover the business units of a single firm but typically also include multiple units from different firms. ③ As a consequence, firms do not only need to consider their internal organization in order to ensure sustainable business performance; they also need to take into account the entire ecosystem of units surrounding them. ④ Many major companies are fundamentally changing their business models by focusing on profitable units and cutting off less profitable ones. ⑤ In order to allow these different units to cooperate successfully, the existence of a common platform is crucial.

10 주어진 글 다음에 이어질 글의 순서로 가장 적절한 것은?

A firm is deciding whether to invest in shipbuilding. If it can produce at sufficiently large scale, it knows the venture will be profitable.

(A) There is a "good" outcome, in which both types of investments are made, and both the shipyard and the steelmakers end up profitable and happy. Equilibrium is reached. Then there is a "bad" outcome, in which neither type of investment is made. This second outcome also is an equilibrium because the decisions not to invest reinforce each other.

(B) Assume that shipyards are the only potential customers of steel. Steel producers figure they'll make money if there's a shipyard to buy their steel, but not otherwise. Now we have two possible outcomes—what economists call "multiple equilibria."

(C) But one key input is low-cost steel, and it must be produced nearby. The company's decision boils down to this: if there is a steel factory close by, invest in shipbuilding; otherwise, don't invest. Now consider the thinking of potential steel investors in the region.

*equilibrium: 균형

① (A) – (C) – (B)　　② (B) – (A) – (C)
③ (B) – (C) – (A)　　④ (C) – (A) – (B)
⑤ (C) – (B) – (A)

11

글의 흐름으로 보아, 주어진 문장이 들어가기에 가장 적절한 곳은?

By now designers worked predominately within factories and no longer designed for individuals but for mass markets.

Earliest indications of the need for inspiration for fashion direction are possibly evidenced by a number of British manufacturers visiting the United States in around 1825 where they were much inspired by lightweight wool blend fabrics produced for outerwear. The ready-to-wear sector was established much earlier in America than in Britain and with it came new challenges. (①) Previously garments were custom-made by skilled individuals who later became known as or recognized as being fashion designers. (②) These handmade garments that are now accepted as being the fashion garments of that time were only made for those with the means to pay for them. (③) The lesser-privileged mass market wore homemade and handed down garments. (④) Later, by the end of the industrial revolution, fashion was more readily available and affordable to all classes. (⑤) Thus the direct communication link between the designer and client no longer existed and designers had to rely on anticipating the needs and desires of the new fashion consumer.

12

다음 글의 내용을 한 문장으로 요약하고자 한다. 빈칸 (A), (B)에 들어갈 말로 가장 적절한 것은?

From a cross-cultural perspective the equation between public leadership and dominance is questionable. What does one mean by 'dominance'? Does it indicate coercion? Or control over 'the most valued'? 'Political' systems may be about both, either, or conceivably neither. The idea of 'control' would be a bothersome one for many peoples, as for instance among many native peoples of Amazonia where all members of a community are fond of their personal autonomy and notably allergic to any obvious expression of control or coercion. The conception of political power as a *coercive* force, while it may be a Western fixation, is not a universal. It is very unusual for an Amazonian leader to give an order. If many peoples do not view political power as a coercive force, *nor as the most valued domain*, then the leap from 'the political' to 'domination' (as coercion), *and from there* to 'domination of women', is a shaky one. As Marilyn Strathern has remarked, the notions of 'the political' and 'political personhood' are cultural obsessions of our own, a bias long reflected in anthropological constructs.

*coercion: 강제　**autonomy: 자율
***anthropological: 인류학의

↓

It is ___(A)___ to understand political power in other cultures through our own notion of it because ideas of political power are not ___(B)___ across cultures.

	(A)		(B)
①	rational	……	flexible
②	appropriate	……	commonplace
③	misguided	……	uniform
④	unreasonable	……	varied
⑤	effective	……	objective

13~14 다음 글을 읽고, 물음에 답하시오.

Clinical psychologists sometimes say that two kinds of people seek therapy: those who need tightening, and those who need loosening. But for every patient seeking help in becoming more organized, self-controlled, and responsible about her future, there is a waiting room full of people (a) <u>hoping</u> to loosen up, lighten up, and worry less about the stupid things they said at yesterday's staff meeting or about the rejection they are sure will follow tomorrow's lunch date. For most people, their subconscious sees too many things as bad and not enough as good. It makes sense. If you were designing the mind of a fish, would you have it respond as strongly to opportunities as to threats? No way. The cost of missing a cue that signals food is (b) <u>low</u>; odds are that there are other fish in the sea, and one mistake won't lead to starvation. The cost of missing the sign of a nearby (c) <u>predator</u>, however, can be catastrophic. Game over, end of the line for those genes. Of course, evolution has no designer, but minds created by natural selection end up looking (to us) as though they were (d) <u>designed</u> because they generally produce behavior that is flexibly adaptive in their ecological niches. Some commonalities of animal life even create similarities across species that we might call design principles. One such principle is that bad is (e) <u>weaker</u> than good. Responses to threats and unpleasantness are faster, stronger, and harder to inhibit than responses to opportunities and pleasures.

13 윗글의 제목으로 가장 적절한 것은?

① Concept of Evolutionary Design: A Biological Nonsense
② Pleasure-Seeking Instinct Propels Us to Adventure
③ Why Do We Cling to Absurd-Looking Promises?
④ Are We Programmed to Be Keener to Threats?
⑤ Worries: An Excuse for Persistent Inaction

14 밑줄 친 (a)~(e) 중에서 문맥상 낱말의 쓰임이 적절하지 <u>않은</u> 것은?

① (a)
② (b)
③ (c)
④ (d)
⑤ (e)

2020 3월 41~42번

13 정답률 42%   **14** 정답률 46%

정답 p. 36

단어 TEST ●　주어진 단어의 뜻을 쓰고, 예문을 올바르게 해석하세요.

1	**blush**	(얼굴이) 빨개지다, 부끄러워하다	feel myself blushing	내 얼굴이 (빨개지는) 것을 느끼다
2	**deliberately**		deliberately practice	( ) 연습하다
3	**scatter**		scattered attention	( ) 주의
4	**retention**		audience retention	청취자 ( )
5	**outbreak**		the outbreak of World War I	제 1차 세계대전의 ( )
6	**stimulating**		stimulating work	( ) 일
7	**fascinate**		fascinate children	아이들을 ( )
8	**reinforce**		reinforce each other	서로를 ( )
9	**ready-to-wear**		the ready-to-wear sector	( ) 부문
10	**allergic to**		allergic to any expression of control	그 어떤 통제의 표시든 ( )
11	**loosen up**		loosen up and worry less	( ) 덜 걱정하다
12	**absurd**		absurd-looking promises	( ) 보이는 약속

구문 TEST ●　주어진 단어를 활용하여 우리말에 맞게 빈칸을 완성하세요.

13　Scattered attention harms (your ability to let go of stress).
　　let go of
　　분산된 주의는 스트레스를 해소하는 여러분의 능력을 손상시킨다.

14　He always ( ) on long flights.
　　bring / read
　　그는 항상 긴 비행 때 뭔가 읽을 것을 가지고 다닌다.

15　I was late for the meeting, ( ) on the way.
　　break down
　　나는 미팅에 늦었는데, 내 차가 가는 도중 고장 났기 때문이었다.

16　The restaurant ( ) has exquisite cuisine.
　　celebrate / our anniversary
　　우리가 기념일을 축하했던 레스토랑은 요리가 훌륭하다.

17　He told us about the situation ( ).
　　his patience / test / to its limits
　　그는 그의 인내심이 한계까지 시험당했던 상황에 관해 우리에게 말해주었다.

18　( ) by their collective effort.
　　the success / make / possible
　　그 성공은 그들 공동의 노력에 의해 가능하게 만들어졌다(가능해졌다).

기출 하프 모의고사

● 문제에 나오는 단어들을 확인하세요.

☐	export	n. 수출 v. 수출하다	☐	elaboration	n. 정교함, 자세한 설명
☐	steady	a. 꾸준한	☐	in step with	~에 발맞춰, 보조를 맞춰
☐	overlook	v. 간과하다	☐	accustomed to	~에 익숙한
☐	bystander	n. 방관자	☐	resolution	n. 해상도
☐	generate	v. 창출하다, 만들어내다	☐	treaty	n. 조약
☐	inherently	ad. 본질적으로	☐	advocate	n. 옹호자 v. 옹호하다
☐	disrupt	v. 무너뜨리다	☐	alliance	n. 동맹
☐	status quo	현재 상태	☐	fall apart	무너지다, 허물어지다
☐	necessitate	v. ~을 필요로 하다	☐	sophisticated	a. 정교한, 세련된
☐	habituated to	~에 익숙한, 길들여진	☐	sweep away	완전히 없애다
☐	get rid of	~을 없애다, 제거하다	☐	misdirection	n. 잘못된 방향(으로 보냄)
☐	gravitation	n. 중력	☐	reflexive	a. 반사 (작용)의
☐	submission	n. 제출(물)	☐	malicious	a. 악의적인
☐	amazed	a. 신기해하는, (깜짝) 놀란	☐	tip off	(~에게) 귀띔해주다, 제보하다
☐	astonishing	a. 놀라운, 믿기 힘든	☐	amiss	a. 잘못된
☐	glance	v. 흘긋 보다	☐	ubiquitous	a. 어디에나 있는
☐	elementary	a. 아주 쉬운, 기본적인	☐	prone to	~에 취약한, ~하기 쉬운
☐	detective	n. 탐정, 형사	☐	intervention	n. 개입
☐	commonality	n. 공통점	☐	probabilistic	a. 확률적인
☐	decouple	v. 분리하다	☐	map out	짜다, 설계하다, 배치하다
☐	detached from	~로부터 분리된	☐	blunt	a. 직설적인, 무딘
☐	predetermined	a. 미리 정해진	☐	mystical	a. 신비스러운
☐	initiate	v. 창안하다, 개시하다	☐	ingrained	a. 깊이 스며든, 뿌리 깊은
☐	spontaneity	n. 자발성	☐	overvalue	v. 과대평가하다
☐	authenticity	n. 진정성, 진짜임	☐	embrace	v. 받아들이다

❶ 관계대명사 that

Habit design has rules that define and explain why some products change lives while others do not.

❷ 대동사 do

습관 설계는 어떤 제품들은 삶을 바꾸는 한편 다른 것들은 그렇지 않은 이유를 규정하고 설명하는 규칙을 지닌다.

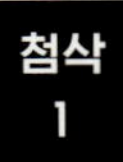

관계대명사 that

개　념 ▶ 선행사 뒤에서 선행사를 수식하는 불완전한 절을 연결할 때 쓴다.

독해전략 ▶ 선행사를 구체화하는 that 뒤의 내용에 유의하며 독해한다.

어법전략 ▶ what과 쓰임을 구별해야 한다. what은 선행사를 포함하고 있어서 that과 달리 선행사가 필요하지 않다.

다음 중 어법상 옳은 것을 고르세요.

a. The cat that | what roams the neighborhood often visits my house.

b. That | What roamed the neighborhood was actually just a small cat.

c. People applauded the movie that | what she filmed in the desert for its stunning scenery.

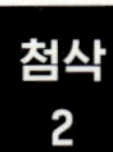

대동사 do

개　념 ▶ 앞에 나온 일반동사구를 반복하지 않고자 do/does/did로 대체하는 것이다.

독해전략 ▶ 어떤 동사구를 대신하는지 파악하려면 앞 문맥을 잘 봐야 한다.

어법전략 ▶ 앞에 조동사/be동사가 오면 do/does/did를 활용하지 않고, 조동사/be동사를 그대로 대동사로 활용한다.
이 조동사에는 완료시제의 have도 포함된다.

다음 중 어법상 옳은 것을 고르세요.

a. Mary works diligently to achieve her goals, as she is | does in every aspect of her life.

b. The athlete is more dedicated to training than all the other players do | are.

c. Julie has explored the city more extensively than any of us is | has.

2021 3월 41~42번

❸ 사역동사 5형식

If we stop trying to **make** computer creativity **look** human, not only **will computers teach** us new things about our own creative talents, but they might become creative in ways that we cannot begin to imagine.

❹ 부정어구의 도치

만약 우리가 컴퓨터 창의력을 인간적으로 보이게 만들려는 시도를 멈춘다면, 컴퓨터는 우리의 창의적 재능에 관한 새로운 것들을 우리에게 가르쳐 줄 뿐만 아니라, 또한 우리가 상상하기 시작하지도 못할 방식으로 창의적이 될지도 모른다.

첨삭 3

사역동사 5형식

개　　념 ▶　make/have/let 뒤에는 원형부정사(능동) 또는 과거분사(수동)가 목적격보어로 나올 수 있다.

독해전략 ▶　주어와 함께 읽으면, '(주어)로 인해 (목적어)가 ~하게 되다'의 의미로 볼 수 있다.

어법전략 ▶　목적어가 목적격보어의 행위 주체인지(능동), 대상인지(수동)에 따라 목적격보어의 형태가 결정된다.

다음 중 어법상 옳은 것을 고르세요.

a. The boss let them work | to work from home two days a week to improve work-life balance.

b. The court made him pay | paid a heavy fine as a consequence of the repeated violations.

c. John had the landscapers redesign | redesigned his entire backyard to include a small pond.

첨삭 4

부정어구의 도치

개　　념 ▶　부정어구가 문장 맨 앞에 오면, 주어와 동사는 의문문 어순(조동사+주어)으로 도치된다.

독해전략 ▶　도치는 '강조'를 목적으로 일어나는 만큼, 글의 핵심을 담고 있을 가능성이 크다.

어법전략 ▶　주어와 동사가 통째로 도치되는 것이 아니므로, 어순에 주의해야 한다.

다음 중 어법상 옳은 것을 고르세요.

a. Not only she finished | did she finish the marathon, but she also set a new record.

b. Little knew he | did he know that his small act of kindness would thoroughly change his life.

c. At no point we have | have we encountered such a challenging obstacle during our expedition.

01 다음 글의 목적으로 가장 적절한 것은?

Dear Lorenzo Romano,

I heard from Antonio Ricci of Rome that you are producing handmade gloves for export in a variety of natural leathers. I read about your business on your website. There is a steady demand in my country for high quality leather gloves, and I am able to charge good prices. Please let me know full details of the gloves you would recommend. It would also help if you could provide me with some samples of the gloves you produce. I hope to hear from you soon.

Sincerely yours,
Jonathan Turner

① 제품의 모든 세부 사항과 견본을 요청하려고
② 신제품의 가격 인상 요인에 대해 설명하려고
③ 수출할 제품에 대한 전수 검사를 의뢰하려고
④ 웹 사이트에 게시한 정보의 수정을 촉구하려고
⑤ 제조업체에 품질 개선을 위한 회의를 제안하려고

02 다음 글의 요지로 가장 적절한 것은?

Often overlooked, but just as important a stakeholder, is the consumer who plays a large role in the notion of the privacy paradox. Consumer engagement levels in all manner of digital experiences and communities have simply exploded—and they show little or no signs of slowing. There is an awareness among consumers, not only that their personal data helps to drive the rich experiences that these companies provide, but also that sharing this data is the price you pay for these experiences, in whole or in part. Without a better understanding of the what, when, and why of data collection and use, the consumer is often left feeling vulnerable and conflicted. "I love this restaurant-finder app on my phone, but what happens to my data if I press 'ok' when asked if that app can use my current location?" Armed with tools that can provide them options, the consumer moves from passive bystander to active participant.

*stakeholder: 이해관계자   **vulnerable: 상처를 입기 쉬운

① 개인정보 제공의 속성을 심층적으로 이해하면 주체적 소비자가 된다.
② 소비자는 디지털 시대에 유용한 앱을 적극 활용하는 자세가 필요하다.
③ 현명한 소비자가 되려면 다양한 디지털 데이터를 활용해야 한다.
④ 기업의 디지털 서비스를 이용하면 상응하는 대가가 뒤따른다.
⑤ 타인과의 정보 공유로 인해 개인정보가 유출되기도 한다.

2022 3월 18번   정답률 88%

2022 6월 22번   정답률 49%

03 밑줄 친 last in, first out이 다음 글에서 의미하는 바로 가장 적절한 것은?

While user habits are a boon to companies fortunate enough to generate them, their existence inherently makes success less likely for new innovations and startups trying to disrupt the *status quo*. The fact is, successfully changing long-term user habits is exceptionally rare. Altering behavior requires not only an understanding of how to persuade people to act but also necessitates getting them to repeat behaviors for long periods, ideally for the rest of their lives. Companies that succeed in building a habit-forming business are often associated with game-changing, wildly successful innovation. But like any discipline, habit design has rules that define and explain why some products change lives while others do not. For one, new behaviors have a short half-life, as our minds tend to return to our old ways of thinking and doing. Experiments show that lab animals habituated to new behaviors tend to regress to their first learned behaviors over time. To borrow a term from accounting, behaviors are LIFO—"last in, first out."

*boon: 요긴한 것   **regress: 되돌아가다

① The behavior witnessed first is forgotten first.
② Almost any behavior tends to change over time.
③ After an old habit breaks, a new one is formed.
④ The habit formed last is the hardest to get rid of.
⑤ The habit most recently acquired disappears soonest.

04 다음 글의 제목으로 가장 적절한 것은?

There was once a certain difficulty with the moons of Jupiter that is worth remarking on. These satellites were studied very carefully by Roemer, who noticed that the moons sometimes seemed to be ahead of schedule, and sometimes behind. They were *ahead* when Jupiter was particularly *close* to the earth and they were *behind* when Jupiter was *farther* from the earth. This would have been a very difficult thing to explain according to the law of gravitation. If a law does not work even in *one place* where it ought to, it is just wrong. But the reason for this discrepancy was very simple and beautiful: it takes a little while to *see* the moons of Jupiter because of the time it takes light to travel from Jupiter to the earth. When Jupiter is closer to the earth the time is a little less, and when it is farther from the earth, the time is more. This is why moons appear to be, on the average, a little ahead or a little behind, depending on whether they are closer to or farther from the earth.

*discrepancy: 불일치

① The Difficulty of Proving the Gravitational Law
② An Illusion Created by the Shadow of the Moon
③ Why Aren't Jupiter's Moons Observed Where They Should Be?
④ Obstacles in Measuring Light's Speed: Limits of Past Technology
⑤ Ahead and Behind: Moons Change Their Position by Themselves

05 WGHS Geography Photo Contest에 관한 다음 안내문의 내용과 일치하는 것은?

WGHS Geography Photo Contest

The event you've been waiting for all this year is finally here! Please join Wood Gate High School's 10th annual Geography Photo Contest.

Guidelines
- Participants should use the theme of the "Beauty of Rivers Crossing Our City."
- Submissions are limited to one photo per person.
- Files should not be larger than 50 MB.

Schedule

	When	Where
Submission	October 2 -October 8	Email: geography@ woodgate.edu
Voting	October 11 -October 13	School Website: https://www. woodgate.edu
Exhibition	October 16 -October 20	Main Lobby

Note
- The top 10 photos selected by students will be exhibited.
※ For more information, visit the geography teacher's room.

---

① 처음으로 개최되는 대회이다.
② 출품 사진 주제에 제한이 없다.
③ 100 MB 크기의 파일을 제출할 수 있다.
④ 투표는 일주일간 실시된다.
⑤ 학생들이 선정한 사진들이 전시될 것이다.

06 다음 글의 밑줄 친 부분 중, 어법상 틀린 것은?

Dr. Joseph Bell was a professor of medicine at the University of Edinburgh. His students were amazed by his astonishing powers of observation. He seemed able to determine what patients did for a living, or what illness ① they might have, simply by glancing in their direction. One time he concluded that a patient ② had walked across a golf course on the way to the doctor, simply by looking at his shoes. One of Bell's students was particularly impressed with his teacher's abilities. He filled up notebooks with examples of ③ what he called Bell's "eerie trick of spotting details." The student eventually went into practice himself outside London. When business was slow he filled his spare moments by writing stories. He took Dr. Bell's powers of perception, and gave them to a character of his own making—a character who made the young doctor, Arthur Conan Doyle, ④ famous around the world. And so the professor who made even the most complex diagnosis seem "elementary" ⑤ becoming the inspiration for fiction's greatest detective, Sherlock Holmes.

*eerie: 오싹한   **diagnosis: 진단

07 다음 빈칸에 들어갈 말로 가장 적절한 것은?

A commonality between conceptual and computer art was ______________________________. Conceptual artists decoupled the relationship between the art object and artist by mitigating all personal signs of invention. The artist became detached from the idea of personalized draftsmanship by installing a predetermined system—a type of instruction for another to follow. That way there was, as Sol LeWitt states, no "dependence on the skill of the artist as a craftsman." Effectively any person could carry out the instructions. The same process was at work in computer art, where artists devised a predetermined drawing algorithm for the computer automaton to carry out the instruction. The human agent initiated the conceptual form, and a machine actuated it. Likewise, the computer artwork lacked any autographic mark, trace of spontaneity, or artistic authenticity. The plotter arm would replace the human arm in the production process.

*mitigate: 완화하다 **actuate: 작동시키다
***plotter: 플로터(데이터를 도면화하는 출력 장치)

① the suppression of authorial presence
② the rejection of meaningless repetition
③ the elevation of ordinary objects to art
④ the preference of simplicity to elaboration
⑤ the tendency of artists to work in collaboration

08 다음 빈칸에 들어갈 말로 가장 적절한 것은?

The ideal sound quality varies a lot in step with technological and cultural changes. Consider, for instance, the development of new digital audio formats such as MP3 and AAC. Various media feed us daily with data-compressed audio, and some people rarely experience CD-quality (that is, *technical* quality) audio. This tendency could lead to a new generation of listeners with other sound quality preferences. Research by Stanford University professor Jonathan Berger adds fuel to this thesis. Berger tested first-year university students' preferences for MP3s annually for ten years. He reports that each year more and more students come to prefer MP3s to CD-quality audio. These findings indicate that listeners gradually become accustomed to data-compressed formats and change their listening preferences accordingly. The point is that while technical improvements strive toward increased sound quality in a technical sense (e.g., higher resolution and greater bit rate), listeners' expectations do not necessarily follow the same path. As a result, "improved" *technical* digital sound quality may in some cases lead to a(n) ______________________________.

*compress: 압축하다

① decrease in the perceptual worth of the sound
② failure to understand the original function of music
③ realization of more sophisticated musical inspiration
④ agreement on ideal sound quality across generations
⑤ revival of listeners' preference for CD-quality audio

09 다음 글에서 전체 흐름과 관계 <u>없는</u> 문장은?

A group of academics, mainly political scientists, assumed that human rights treaties did *not* have any effect on the behavior of countries. ① Indeed, these academics, who typically called themselves "realists," assumed that international law generally did not affect the behavior of states. ② They saw the international arena as a security competition among different states, a zero-sum game in which one state's gain was another state's loss. ③ International lawyers and human rights advocates assumed that human rights treaties caused countries to improve their treatment of their citizens. ④ In such conditions, states could gain little by cooperating with each other—except in temporary military alliances or security agreements that could fall apart at a moment's notice. ⑤ International law could play a minimal role or none at all, and was perhaps just an illusion, a sophisticated kind of propaganda—a set of rules that would be swept away whenever the balance of power changed.

10 주어진 글 다음에 이어질 글의 순서로 가장 적절한 것은?

One common strategy and use of passive misdirection in the digital world comes through the use of repetition.

(A) This action is repeated over and over to navigate their web browsers to the desired web page or action until it becomes an almost immediate, reflexive action. Malicious online actors take advantage of this behavior to distract the user from carefully examining the details of the web page that might tip off the user that there is something amiss about the website.

(B) The website is designed to focus the user's attention on the action the malicious actor wants them to take (e.g., click a link) and to draw their attention away from any details that might suggest to the user that the website is not what it appears to be on the surface.

(C) This digital misdirection strategy relies on the fact that online users utilizing web browsers to visit websites have quickly learned that the most basic ubiquitous navigational action is to click on a link or button presented to them on a website.

① (A) – (C) – (B)　　② (B) – (A) – (C)
③ (B) – (C) – (A)　　④ (C) – (A) – (B)
⑤ (C) – (B) – (A)

11

글의 흐름으로 보아, 주어진 문장이 들어가기에 가장 적절한 곳은?

> However, human reasoning is still notoriously prone to confusion and error when causal questions become sufficiently complex, such as when it comes to assessing the impact of policy interventions across society.

Going beyond very simple algorithms, some AI-based tools hold out the promise of supporting better causal and probabilistic reasoning in complex domains. (①) Humans have a natural ability to build causal models of the world—that is, to explain *why* things happen—that AI systems still largely lack. (②) For example, while a doctor can explain to a patient why a treatment works, referring to the changes it causes in the body, a modern machine-learning system could only tell you that patients who are given this treatment tend, on average, to get better. (③) In these cases, supporting human reasoning with more structured AI-based tools may be helpful. (④) Researchers have been exploring the use of Bayesian Networks—an AI technology that can be used to map out the causal relationships between events, and to represent degrees of uncertainty around different areas—for decision support, such as to enable more accurate risk assessment. (⑤) These may be particularly useful for assessing the threat of novel or rare threats, where little historical data is available, such as the risk of terrorist attacks and new ecological disasters.

*notoriously: 악명 높게도

12

다음 글의 내용을 한 문장으로 요약하고자 한다. 빈칸 (A), (B)에 들어갈 말로 가장 적절한 것은?

> There is no question that losing weight is hard. According to one calculation, you must walk 35 miles or jog for seven hours to lose just one pound. One big problem with exercise is that we don't track it very scrupulously. A study in America found that people overestimated the number of calories they burned in a workout by a factor of four. They also then consumed, on average, about twice as many calories as they had just burned off. As Daniel Lieberman noted in *The Story of the Human Body*, a worker on a factory floor will in a year expend about 175,000 more calories than a desk worker—equivalent to more than sixty marathons. That's pretty impressive, but here's a reasonable question: how many factory workers look as if they run a marathon every six days? To be cruelly blunt, not many. That's because most of them, like most of the rest of us, replace all those burnt calories, and then some, when they are not working.
>
> *scrupulously: 용의주도하게

↓

> Losing weight is hard because people usually think they burned a ___(A)___ number of calories than they actually did and ___(B)___ exercise by eating a lot of food.

	(A)		(B)
①	larger	······	undo
②	larger	······	intensify
③	higher	······	supplement
④	smaller	······	continue
⑤	smaller	······	delay

13~14 다음 글을 읽고, 물음에 답하시오.

Surprisingly, consciousness might not be as crucial to creativity as we like to think. There are several different types of creativity—some of them conscious, some of them unconscious. Creativity can happen when you (a) <u>deliberately</u> try to create something or it can happen in your sleep. In any case, Arne Dietrich, a neuroscientist, believes that the creative brain might work much like software. Neuroscientists suspect that creativity is essentially about (b) <u>discovery</u> rather than anything mystical —driven by a mechanical process in the brain that generates possible solutions and then eliminates them systematically. He believes our tendency to dismiss computational creativity as (c) <u>inferior</u> to our own comes from an ingrained dualism in human culture. 'We are overvaluing ourselves and underestimating them,' he says.

As a neuroscientist, Dietrich says he tackles the brain as a machine—and does not see machine creativity as different. Considered in this way, the idea that the human brain has a unique claim to creative talents seems a (d) <u>proper</u> perspective. Will others accept that idea? The trick is to stop trying to compare computer artists to human ones. If we can (e) <u>embrace</u> computer creativity for what it is and stop trying to make it look human, not only will computers teach us new things about our own creative talents, but they might become creative in ways that we cannot begin to imagine.

제목 추론

13 윗글의 제목으로 가장 적절한 것은?

① Machines That Create Redefine Creativity
② The New Way Machines Learn and Think
③ How Brain Works During Unconsciousness
④ Potential Limits of Artificial Intelligence
⑤ High Technology Weakens Creativity

어휘 추론

14 밑줄 친 (a)~(e) 중에서 문맥상 낱말의 쓰임이 적절하지 <u>않은</u> 것은?

① (a)
② (b)
③ (c)
④ (d)
⑤ (e)

2021 3월 41~42번

13 정답률 47%　**14** 정답률 38%

정답 p. 43

단어 TEST ● 주어진 단어의 뜻을 쓰고, 예문을 올바르게 해석하세요.

1	**bystander** 방관자	a passive bystander	수동적 (방관자)
2	**status quo**	disrupt the status quo	( )를 무너뜨리다
3	**astonishing**	his astonishing powers of observation	그의 ( ) 관찰력
4	**predetermined**	a predetermined system	( ) 시스템
5	**spontaneity**	traces of spontaneity	( )의 흔적들
6	**elaboration**	prefer simplicity to elaboration	( )보다 단순함을 선호하다
7	**accustomed to**	accustomed to digital formats	디지털 포맷에 ( )
8	**sweep away**	sweep away the rules	그 규칙들을 ( )
9	**malicious**	a malicious website	( ) 웹 사이트
10	**prone to**	be prone to confusion	혼란에 ( )
11	**map out**	map out the causal relationships between events	사건들 간의 인과관계를 ( )
12	**blunt**	to be cruelly blunt	심히 ( )으로 말해서

구문 TEST ● 주어진 단어를 우리말에 맞게 배열하세요.

13 Some products change lives, (while others do not).
others / not / do / while

어떤 제품들은 삶을 바꾸고, 반면 다른 것들은 그렇지 않다.

14 ( ) often visits my house.
the neighborhood / roams / that / the cat

동네를 배회하는 그 고양이는 종종 우리 집에 온다.

15 Julie has explored the city ( ).
has / any of us / more extensively / than

Julie는 우리 중 누가 그랬던 것보다도 더 광범위하게 그 도시를 돌아다녔다.

16 The boss ( ) two days a week.
them / work / let / from home

사장은 그들더러 일주일에 이틀 재택 근무하도록 허락했다.

17 Not only ( ), but they will become creative themselves.
new things / computers / will / us / teach

컴퓨터는 우리에게 새로운 것을 가르쳐줄 뿐 아니라, 스스로 창의적이 될 것이다.

18 At no point ( ).
we / have / such a challenging obstacle / encountered

그 어느 시점에도 우리는 이렇게 어려운 장애물을 마주한 적이 없다.

기출 하프 모의고사

07

● 문제에 나오는 단어들을 확인하세요.

☐ sensible	a. 합리적인		☐ compound	n. 화합물 v. (문제를) 악화시키다
☐ validity	n. 타당성		☐ petroleum	n. 석유
☐ by design	일부러, 고의로		☐ nourishment	n. 영양(분)
☐ validate	v. 증명하다		☐ prevail	v. 우세하다, 만연하다
☐ acquaintance	n. 지인, 아는 사람		☐ deplete	v. 고갈시키다, 다 써버리다
☐ switch to	~로 바꾸다, 전환하다		☐ contaminant	n. 오염 물질
☐ abandon	v. 포기하다, 버리다		☐ unknowingly	ad. 자기도 모르게
☐ challenging	a. 어려운, 도전적인		☐ discriminatory	a. 차별적인
☐ base A on B	A의 근거를 B에 두다		☐ transplant	n. (장기) 이식
☐ flawed	a. 결함이 있는		☐ pitfall	n. 위험, 함정
☐ plot	n. (특정 용도의 작은) 토지, (이야기의) 구성, 줄거리		☐ rationalize	v. 합리화하다
☐ facility	n. 시설		☐ inequity	n. 불공평
☐ phenomenon	n. 현상		☐ pull oneself up by one's bootstraps	혼자 힘으로 해내다
☐ instinctive	a. 본능적인		☐ legitimate	a. 정당한, 합법적인
☐ appreciate	v. 감상하다, 진가를 알다, 고마워하다		☐ consensus	n. 합의, 의견 일치
☐ sign up for	~에 신청하다, 가입하다		☐ inevitably	ad. 반드시, 필연적으로
☐ accompany	v. 동행하다, 동반하다		☐ impose	v. 부과하다, 가하다
☐ countertendency	n. 반대 경향		☐ align with	~에 맞춰가다
☐ substitute	n. 대체(물) v. 대체하다		☐ familiarity	n. 친숙함
☐ forgetful	a. 잘 잊어버리는		☐ acknowledge	v. 아는 표시를 하다, 인정하다
☐ knowledgeable	a. 박식한		☐ embody	v. 구현하다
☐ ignorant	a. 무지한		☐ pat	v. 가볍게 두드리다
☐ shortsighted	a. 근시안적인		☐ deprived of	~이 박탈된, ~을 빼앗긴
☐ foresee	v. 예견하다, 미리 보다		☐ reluctant	a. 꺼리는, 마지못해 하는
☐ foundation	n. 토대, 기반		☐ digest	v. 소화하다

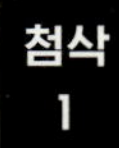

❶ 가주어 it

But **it's better** to disappoint a few people over small things, **than** to abandon your dreams for an empty inbox.

❷ 비교급+than

그러나 빈 수신함을 위해 여러분의 꿈을 포기하는 것보다, 사소한 것으로 몇 사람을 실망시키는 게 더 낫다.

첨삭 1

가주어 it

개　념 ▶ to부정사구, that절 등 긴 주어가 나올 때 주어를 대신하는 의미 없는 주어이다.

독해전략 ▶ it은 '그것'으로 해석되지 않으며, 문장의 핵심 소재는 동사 뒤를 읽어야 알 수 있다.

어법전략 ▶ 가주어 it은 원칙적으로 다른 대명사(that, this 등)로 대체되지 않는다.

다음 중 어법상 옳은 것을 고르세요.

a. It is common for people | experience | to experience | stress at some point in their lives.

b. | It | That | remains a mystery why she left all of a sudden, without saying goodbye to anyone.

c. It was clear | that | what | the team needed better communication to succeed.

첨삭 2

비교급+than

개　념 ▶ <비교급+than>은 '더 ~한/하게'의 의미를 나타낸다.

독해전략 ▶ than 뒤보다는 앞이 '더 ~한' 대상이므로 더 비중을 두고 읽어야 한다.

어법전략 ▶ than 앞뒤로 비교되는 두 대상은 병렬구조를 이룬다. than 앞의 비교대상을 중복해서 언급하는 것을 피하고자 지시대명사 that/those를 이용한다는 것도 기억해 둔다.

다음 중 어법상 옳은 것을 고르세요.

a. It's often easier to communicate via email than | makes | to make | a phone call.

b. Composing poetry involves more creativity than | writing | writes | technical reports.

c. His command of multiple languages is more advanced than | that | those | of most linguists.

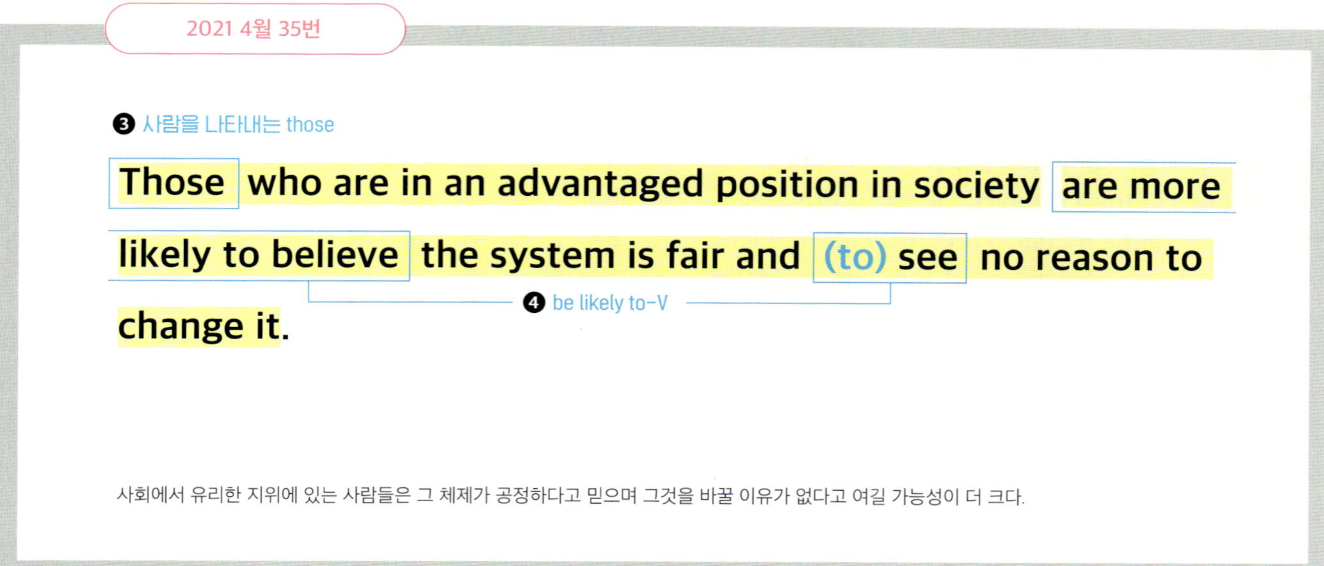

2021 4월 35번

❸ 사람을 나타내는 those

Those who are in an advantaged position in society **are more likely to believe** the system is fair and **(to) see** no reason to **change it.**

❹ be likely to-V

사회에서 유리한 지위에 있는 사람들은 그 체제가 공정하다고 믿으며 그것을 바꿀 이유가 없다고 여길 가능성이 더 크다.

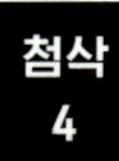

첨삭 3

사람을 나타내는 those

개 념 ▶ 지시대명사 those는 who로 시작하는 관계절과 함께 '~한 사람들'이라는 의미를 나타낼 수 있다.

독해전략 ▶ those가 어떤 사람들인지 파악하려면 who 뒤를 잘 읽어야 한다.

어법전략 ▶ those 뒤에 who are/were가 생략되고 형용사구나 분사구 등만 남기도 하므로, 수 일치에 주의한다.

다음 중 어법상 옳은 것을 고르세요.

a. Those | who | which | donate to charity believe in giving back to their community.

b. Those who embrace change | is | are | better equipped to succeed in today's fast-paced world.

c. Those | live | living | in big cities tend to be under pressure or stressed out.

첨삭 4

be likely to-V

개 념 ▶ 경향이나 가능성을 나타내는 표현으로, '~할 가능성이 크다, ~할 것 같다'라는 의미이다.

독해전략 ▶ likely 앞에 more나 less가 붙어 '더' 또한 '덜'한 경향을 나타내기도 한다.

어법전략 ▶ to 뒤에 동사원형이 온다는 점, be동사는 앞에 나온 주어에 수 일치된다는 점을 기억해 둔다.

다음 중 어법상 옳은 것을 고르세요.

a. If you plant these seeds in spring, they are likely to | bloom | blooming | by early summer.

b. Travelers who skip the weather report | is | are | likely to encounter unexpected conditions.

c. People who do not wear sunscreen when outdoors | are | being | likely to get sunburned.

정답 a. who b. are c. living / a. bloom b. are c. are

01 다음 글에 드러난 Mark의 심경으로 가장 적절한 것은?

Mark was participating in freestyle swimming competitions in this Olympics. He had a firm belief that he could get a medal in the 200m. Swimming was dominated by Americans at the time, so Mark was dreaming of becoming a national hero for his country, Britain. That day, Mark was competing in his very last race—the final round of the 200m. He had done his training and was ready. One minute and fifty seconds later, it was all over. He had tried hard and, at his best, was ranked number four. He fell short of a bronze medal by 0.49 of a second. And that was the end of Mark's swimming career. He was heartbroken. He had nothing left.

① worried → hopeful
② grateful → fearful
③ pleased → jealous
④ indifferent → upset
⑤ confident → disappointed

02 다음 글의 요지로 가장 적절한 것은?

When it comes to the Internet, it just pays to be a little paranoid (but not a lot). Given the level of anonymity with all that resides on the Internet, it's sensible to question the validity of any data that you may receive. Typically it's to our natural instinct when we meet someone coming down a sidewalk to place yourself in some manner of protective position, especially when they introduce themselves as having known you, much to your surprise. By design, we set up challenges in which the individual must validate how they know us by presenting scenarios, names or acquaintances, or evidence by which to validate (that is, photographs). Once we have received that information and it has gone through a cognitive validation, we accept that person as more trustworthy. All this happens in a matter of minutes but is a natural defense mechanism that we perform in the real world. However, in the virtual world, we have a tendency to be less defensive, as there appears to be no physical threat to our well-being.

*paranoid: 편집성의 **anonymity: 익명

① 가상 세계 특유의 익명성 때문에 표현의 자유가 남용되기도 한다.
② 인터넷 정보의 신뢰도를 검증하는 기술은 점진적으로 향상되고 있다.
③ 가상 세계에서는 현실 세계와 달리 자유로운 정보 공유가 가능하다.
④ 안전한 인터넷 환경 구축을 위해 보안 프로그램을 설치하는 것이 좋다.
⑤ 방어 기제가 덜 작동하는 가상 세계에서는 신중한 정보 검증이 중요하다.

2023 3월 19번　　정답률 88%

2023 6월 22번　　정답률 85%

함축 의미

03 밑줄 친 an empty inbox가 다음 글에서 의미하는 바로 가장 적절한 것은?

The single most important change you can make in your working habits is to switch to creative work first, reactive work second. This means blocking off a large chunk of time every day for creative work on your own priorities, with the phone and e-mail off. I used to be a frustrated writer. Making this switch turned me into a productive writer. Yet there wasn't a single day when I sat down to write an article, blog post, or book chapter without a string of people waiting for me to get back to them. It wasn't easy, and it still isn't, particularly when I get phone messages beginning "I sent you an e-mail *two hours* ago...!" By definition, this approach goes against the grain of others' expectations and the pressures they put on you. It takes willpower to switch off the world, even for an hour. It feels uncomfortable, and sometimes people get upset. But it's better to disappoint a few people over small things, than to abandon your dreams for <u>an empty inbox</u>. Otherwise, you're sacrificing your potential for the illusion of professionalism.

① following an innovative course of action
② attempting to satisfy other people's demands
③ completing challenging work without mistakes
④ removing social ties to maintain a mental balance
⑤ securing enough opportunities for social networking

주제 추론

04 다음 글의 주제로 가장 적절한 것은?

Environmental learning occurs when farmers base decisions on observations of "payoff" information. They may observe their own or neighbors' farms, but it is the empirical results they are using as a guide, not the neighbors themselves. They are looking at farming activities as experiments and assessing such factors as relative advantage, compatibility with existing resources, difficulty of use, and "trialability"—how well can it be experimented with. But that criterion of "trialability" turns out to be a real problem; it's true that farmers are always experimenting, but working farms are very flawed laboratories. Farmers cannot set up the controlled conditions of professional test plots in research facilities. Farmers also often confront complex and difficult-to-observe phenomena that would be hard to manage even if they could run controlled experiments. Moreover farmers can rarely acquire payoff information on more than a few of the production methods they might use, which makes the criterion of "relative advantage" hard to measure.

*empirical: 경험적인 **compatibility: 양립성
***criterion: 기준

① limitations of using empirical observations in farming
② challenges in modernizing traditional farming equipment
③ necessity of prioritizing trialability in agricultural innovation
④ importance of making instinctive decisions in agriculture
⑤ ways to control unpredictable agricultural phenomena

---

05 Brushwood National Park Tour Program에 관한 다음 안내문의 내용과 일치하지 <u>않는</u> 것은?

Brushwood National Park Tour Program

Walking in nature is a great way to stay fit and healthy. Enjoy free park walks with our volunteer guides, while appreciating the beautiful sights and sounds of the forest.

Details
- Open on weekdays from March to November
- Easy walk along the path for one hour (3 km)
- Groups of 15 to 20 per guide

Registration
- Scan the QR code to sign up for the tour.

Note
- A bottle of water will be provided to each participant.
- Children under 12 must be accompanied by an adult.
- Tours may be canceled due to weather conditions.

※ If you have any questions, please email us at brushwoodtour@parks.org.

---

① 자원봉사 안내자가 동행한다.
② 주말에 진행된다.
③ QR 코드를 스캔하여 신청한다.
④ 각 참가자에게 물이 한 병씩 제공될 것이다.
⑤ 날씨에 따라 취소될 수 있다.

---

06 다음 글의 밑줄 친 부분 중, 문맥상 낱말의 쓰임이 적절하지 <u>않은</u> 것은?

Just as there's a tendency to glorify technological progress, there's a countertendency to expect the worst of every new tool or machine. In Plato's *Phaedrus*, Socrates bemoaned the ① <u>development</u> of writing. He feared that, as people came to rely on the written word as a ② <u>substitute</u> for the knowledge they used to carry inside their heads, they would, in the words of one of the dialogue's characters, "cease to exercise their memory and become forgetful." And because they would be able to "③ <u>receive</u> a quantity of information without proper instruction," they would "be thought very knowledgeable when they are for the most part quite ignorant." They would be "filled with the conceit of wisdom instead of real wisdom." Socrates wasn't ④ <u>right</u>—the new technology did often have the effects he feared—but he was shortsighted. He couldn't ⑤ <u>foresee</u> the many ways that writing and reading would serve to spread information, spark fresh ideas, and expand human knowledge (if not wisdom).

*bemoan: 한탄하다   **conceit: 자만심

07   다음 빈칸에 들어갈 말로 가장 적절한 것은?

Ecological health depends on keeping the surface of the earth rich in humus and minerals so that it can provide a foundation for healthy plant and animal life. The situation is disrupted if the soil loses these raw materials or if ________________ ________________________________. When man goes beneath the surface of the earth and drags out minerals or other compounds that did not evolve as part of this system, then problems follow. The mining of lead and cadmium are examples of this. Petroleum is also a substance that has been dug out of the bowels of the earth and introduced into the surface ecology by man. Though it is formed from plant matter, the highly reduced carbon compounds that result are often toxic to living protoplasm. In some cases this is true of even very tiny amounts, as in the case of "polychlorinated biphenyls," a petroleum product which can cause cancer.

*humus: 부식토, 부엽토   **protoplasm: 원형질

① the number of plants on it increases too rapidly
② it stops providing enough nourishment for humans
③ climate change transforms its chemical components
④ alien species prevail and deplete resources around it
⑤ great quantities of contaminants are introduced into it

08   다음 빈칸에 들어갈 말로 가장 적절한 것은?

The designer in the Age of Algorithms poses a threat to American jurisprudence because the algorithm is only as good as ________________ ________________________________. The person designing the algorithm may be an excellent software engineer, but without the knowledge of all the factors that need to go into an algorithmic process, the engineer could unknowingly produce an algorithm whose decisions are at best incomplete and at worst discriminatory and unfair. Compounding the problem, an algorithm design firm might be under contract to design algorithms for a wide range of uses, from determining which patients awaiting transplants are chosen to receive organs, to which criminals facing sentencing should be given probation or the maximum sentence. That firm is not going to be staffed with subject matter experts who know what questions each algorithm needs to address, what databases the algorithm should use to collect its data, and what pitfalls the algorithm needs to avoid in churning out decisions.

*jurisprudence: 법체계   **probation: 집행 유예
***churn out: 잇달아 내다

① the amount of data that the public can access
② its capacity to teach itself to reach the best decisions
③ its potential to create a lasting profit for the algorithm users
④ the functionality of the hardware the designing company operates
⑤ the designer's understanding of the intended use of the algorithm

2022 10월 32번   정답률 20%

2021 7월 34번   정답률 33%

09 다음 글에서 전체 흐름과 관계 <u>없는</u> 문장은?

Research has shown that individuals—especially those who have benefited from a particular system—are prone to support and rationalize the status quo, even if there are clear problems. ① These people justify systemic inequity with familiar phrases like "If you just work hard enough you can pull yourself up by your bootstraps." ② A branch of psychology called *system justification theory* describes how people tend to see social, economic, and political systems as good, fair, and legitimate if they have succeeded as a result of those systems. ③ According to Erin Godfrey, a professor of applied psychology at New York University, "The people who are at the top want to believe in meritocracy because it means that they deserve their successes." ④ Indeed, it is not surprising that there exists a general consensus across social class about the definition and the results of meritocracy. ⑤ Those who are in an advantaged position in society are more likely to believe the system is fair and see no reason to change it.

*status quo: 현재 상태   **meritocracy: 능력주의

10 주어진 글 다음에 이어질 글의 순서로 가장 적절한 것은?

> Both ancient farmers and foragers suffered seasonal food shortages. During these periods children and adults alike would go to bed hungry some days and everyone would lose fat and muscle.

(A) Typically, in complex ecosystems when weather one year proves unsuitable for one set of plant species, it almost inevitably suits others. But in farming societies when harvests fail as a result of, for example, a sustained drought, then catastrophe emerges.

(B) This is firstly because foragers tended to live well within the natural limits imposed by their environments, and secondly because where farmers typically relied on one or two staple crops, foragers in even the harshest environments relied on dozens of different food sources and so were usually able to adjust their diets to align with an ecosystem's own dynamic responses to changing conditions.

(C) But over longer periods of time farming societies were far more likely to suffer severe, existentially threatening famines than foragers. Foraging may be much less productive and generate far lower energy yields than farming but it is also much less risky.

*forager: 수렵 채집인   **catastrophe: 참사
***staple: 주요한

① (A) – (C) – (B)   ② (B) – (A) – (C)
③ (B) – (C) – (A)   ④ (C) – (A) – (B)
⑤ (C) – (B) – (A)

11 글의 흐름으로 보아, 주어진 문장이 들어가기에 가장 적절한 곳은?

In the case of specialists such as art critics, a deeper familiarity with materials and techniques is often useful in reaching an informed judgement about a work.

Acknowledging the making of artworks does not require a detailed, technical knowledge of, say, how painters mix different kinds of paint, or how an image editing tool works. (①) All that is required is a general sense of a significant difference between working with paints and working with an imaging application. (②) This sense might involve a basic familiarity with paints and paintbrushes as well as a basic familiarity with how we use computers, perhaps including how we use consumer imaging apps. (③) This is because every kind of artistic material or tool comes with its own challenges and affordances for artistic creation. (④) Critics are often interested in the ways artists exploit different kinds of materials and tools for particular artistic effect. (⑤) They are also interested in the success of an artist's attempt—embodied in the artwork itself—to push the limits of what can be achieved with certain materials and tools.

*affordance: 행위유발성 **exploit: 활용하다

12 다음 글의 내용을 한 문장으로 요약하고자 한다. 빈칸 (A), (B)에 들어갈 말로 가장 적절한 것은?

There is a key difference between how humans and other intelligent animals learn. In a very telling experiment done by evolutionary psychologist Mike Tomasello at the Max Planck Institute in Germany, a puzzle box containing a treat is given to a human toddler and a chimpanzee. Neither is able to get the treat out. He then demonstrates a multi-step process of pulling and pushing pegs that eventually releases the treat. Among the motions, he includes an obviously nonsensical step—patting his head three times before the last step. Both the toddler and the chimp are able to copy his actions and get the treat, but only the toddler includes the head-patting step. The chimp, seeing this is not relevant to getting the treat, omits it from the routine. The human, however, unquestioningly copies all the steps. The toddler trusts the human teaching her to have a reason for each step in this situation, and so she overcopies. In fact, the less clear the goal of the procedure, the more carefully and precisely the human child will imitate even irrelevant steps.

*peg: 나무못 **omit: 생략하다

↓

According to the experiment above, when given multiple steps to get a treat, toddlers ___(A)___ every step of the procedure unlike chimpanzees, because toddlers do not doubt the ___(B)___ of each step.

	(A)		(B)
①	complete	……	relevance
②	complete	……	complexity
③	evaluate	……	flexibility
④	rearrange	……	variability
⑤	rearrange	……	usefulness

13~14 다음 글을 읽고, 물음에 답하시오.

In *What a Plant Knows*, the biologist Daniel Chamovitz describes sophisticated information-processing capacities that plants use to control their movements in response to stimulation. Plants not only "follow the sun" by bending their stems, they also align their leaves in such a way as to (a) maximize exposure to light and thereby promote growth. Some plants actually anticipate sunrise from "memory," and even when deprived of solar signals retain this information for several days. In *Brilliant Green*, Stefano Mancuso and Alessandra Viola argue that plants possess not only the senses of sight, touch, smell, and hearing, but more than a dozen other (b) sensory capacities that humans lack. For example, the roots of plants sense the mineral and water content of the soil and alter their direction of growth accordingly.

Some are (c) reluctant to label plant movements as behaviors, since they lack nerves and muscles. But just as they are able to breathe without lungs and digest nutrients without a stomach, plants have the ability to move (behave). We should not dismiss the (d) absence of behavioral capacities in an organism simply because it lacks the physiological mechanism that is responsible for the behavior in animals. Plants clearly sense the environment, learn, store information, and use that information to guide movements; they behave. One might say that there is certain "intelligence" to their behavior. This is true as long as intelligence is defined in terms of the ability to solve problems through behavioral (e) interactions with the environment, rather than with respect to mental capacity.

2022 3월 41~42번

제목 추론

13 윗글의 제목으로 가장 적절한 것은?

① Plant Growth Is Up to Soil Content
② Plants Do Behave and Have Intelligence
③ Plants Know the Secret of Solar Signals
④ What Plants and Animals Need for Survival
⑤ Benefits and Challenges of Living in Nature

어휘 추론

14 밑줄 친 (a)~(e) 중에서 문맥상 낱말의 쓰임이 적절하지 <u>않은</u> 것은?

① (a)
② (b)
③ (c)
④ (d)
⑤ (e)

13 정답률 78%   **14** 정답률 51%

정답 p. 50

단어 TEST ● 주어진 단어의 뜻을 쓰고, 예문을 올바르게 해석하세요.

1	**sensible**	합리적인	a sensible question	(합리적인) 의문
2	**validate**		validate how they know us	그들이 우리를 어떻게 아는지 ( )
3	**abandon**		abandon your dreams	당신의 꿈을 ( )
4	**knowledgeable**		be thought very knowledgeable	매우 ( )고 여겨지다
5	**foresee**		foresee the many ways	그 많은 방법을 ( )
6	**deplete**		deplete resources	자원을 ( )
7	**discriminatory**		discriminatory and unfair	( )이고 불공정한
8	**impose**		impose limits	제한을 ( )
9	**acknowledge**		acknowledge the making of artworks	예술 작품의 제작에 대해 ( )
10	**pat**		pat his own head	자기 머리를 ( )
11	**deprived of**		deprived of solar signals	태양 신호가 ( )
12	**reluctant**		reluctant to step forward	나서기를 ( )

구문 TEST ● 주어진 단어를 활용하여 우리말에 맞게 빈칸을 완성하세요.

13 It's okay (to disappoint a few people) over small things.
disappoint / a few

사소한 일로 몇 명의 사람들을 실망시키는 것은 괜찮다.

14 ( ) at some point in their lives.
it / common / for / experience / stress

사람들이 삶의 어느 순간 스트레스를 겪는 것은 흔하다.

15 It's often easier to communicate via email ( ).
make a phone call

전화하는 것보다 이메일로 소통하는 것이 흔히 더 쉽다.

16 ( ) tend to believe the system is fair.
those / be / in an advantaged position

유리한 지위에 있는 사람들은 체제가 공정하다고 믿는 경향이 있다.

17 ( ) tend to be under pressure.
those / live / big cities

대도시에 사는 사람들은 압박을 받곤 한다.

18 People who do not wear sunscreen ( ).
likely / get sunburned

선크림을 바르지 않는 사람들은 햇볕 화상을 입을 가능성이 있다.

기출 하프 모의고사

● 문제에 나오는 단어들을 확인하세요.

☐	eligible	a. 자격이 있는
☐	adversely	ad. 불리하게
☐	distribute	v. 배포하다, 분배하다
☐	concise	a. 간결한
☐	specific	a. 특정한, 구체적인
☐	transform A into B	A를 B로 바꾸다
☐	gather	v. 모으다, 모이다
☐	erroneous	a. 잘못된
☐	compel	v. 꼭 ~하게 하다, 강제하다
☐	extraordinary	a. 비범한
☐	speak ill of	~을 헐뜯다, 나쁘게 말하다
☐	mend	v. 고치다, 수리하다
☐	blacksmith	n. 대장장이
☐	fabrication	n. 제작, 날조
☐	province	n. (특정 지식, 관심) 영역
☐	comprehension	n. 이해
☐	subdivision	n. 세분, 분화
☐	conductor	n. 지휘자
☐	nominate	v. 지명하다
☐	downside	n. 부정적인 면
☐	qualification	n. 자격사항
☐	differentiate	v. 구별하다
☐	summarily	ad. 즉석으로
☐	credibility	n. 신뢰성
☐	regulatory	a. 규제의

☐	address	v. 처리하다, 다루다
☐	obstruction	n. 방해
☐	feature	n. 특징
☐	strip A of B	A에게서 B를 제거하다, 박탈하다
☐	subjectivity	n. 주관성
☐	independent of	~로부터 독립된, ~와 상관없이
☐	envision	v. 상상하다, (머릿속에) 그리다
☐	disengage	v. 분리하다, 해방시키다
☐	parenting	n. 양육
☐	enlightenment	n. 깨달음
☐	compensate	v. 보수를 주다, 보상하다
☐	settle	v. 해결하다, 합의하다
☐	optimally	ad. 최적으로
☐	surround	v. 둘러싸다
☐	decline	n. 쇠락, 감소
☐	genetic	a. 유전적인
☐	fall prey to	~의 먹이가 되다
☐	prolonged	a. (기간이) 오래 계속되는, 장기적인
☐	pour	v. 쏟아지다
☐	soar	v. 급증하다, 치솟다
☐	escalate	v. 증가하다
☐	alienate	v. 소외시키다
☐	lose sight of	~을 모르다, 놓치다
☐	constantly	ad. 끊임없이
☐	drawback	n. 불리한 점, 문제점

2021 7월 35번

❶ not A but B

The parenting experience is **not** one of parent *versus* child **but of parent *with* child.** The road to wholeness sits in our children's lap, and **all we need do is** take a seat.

❷ 원형부정사 주격보어

양육 경험은 부모 '대' 아이의 경험이 아니라, 부모가 아이와 '함께하는' 경험이다. 완전함으로 가는 길은 우리 아이들 무릎에 달렸으며, 우리가 해야 할 일은 자리에 앉아 있는 것뿐이다.

첨삭 1

not A but B

개　념 ▶ 상관접속사의 일종으로, 'A가 아니라 B인'이라는 뜻이다.

독해전략 ▶ 주제와 대비되는 A를 이용해 주제인 B를 강조하는 표현이므로, B의 내용에 주목한다.

어법전략 ▶ A와 B는 병렬구조를 이루며, <not A but B>가 주어 자리에 오면 B에 수 일치한다.

다음 중 어법상 옳은 것을 고르세요.

a. He does not want to criticize but helps / to help improve the situation.

b. Not one but three people is / are needed to lift this heavy object.

c. Not avoiding but facing your fears is / are the best way to overcome them.

첨삭 2

원형부정사 주격보어

개　념 ▶ be동사 앞의 주어가 <all/what/the only thing+주어 ~ do> 형태일 때, 주격보어로 원형부정사가 올 수 있다.

독해전략 ▶ 문장은 전체적으로 '~한 것은 …뿐이다'의 의미를 나타낸다. 즉 원형부정사 부분을 잘 읽어야 한다.

어법전략 ▶ 원형부정사 대신 to부정사를 써도 문법적으로 맞다는 것을 기억해 둔다.

다음 중 어법상 옳은 것을 고르세요.

a. All we need to do is meet / meets at the designated location at the agreed time.

b. The only thing I need to do is pay / paid the invoice, and my financial obligations will be settled.

c. What we must do is assess / to assess all the data thoroughly before making a decision.

정답 **a.** to help **b.** are **c.** is / **a.** meet **b.** pay **c.** assess, to assess

2021 7월 40번

The supply of high-skilled workers did grow, but new technologies were skill-biased and so `caused` **the demand for high-skilled workers** `to soar` **. The latter effect was** `so` **great** `that` **it overcame the former.**

❸ cause A to-V

❹ so ~ that …

고도로 숙련된 노동자의 공급은 실제로 증가했지만, 새로운 기술은 숙련 편향적이어서 고도로 숙련된 노동자에 대한 수요를 급증시켰다. 후자의 효과는 너무 커서 전자를 압도했다.

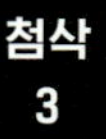

cause A to-V

개　념 ▶ 'A가 ~하게 만들다'라는 의미의 5형식 구문이다. 목적격보어 자리에 to부정사가 온다는 것이 포인트이다.

독해전략 ▶ 주어와 함께 읽으면서 '(주어)로 인해 A가 ~하게 되다'라는 인과관계를 파악한다.

어법전략 ▶ allow, force, enable, encourage, expect, persuade 등도 to부정사를 목적격보어로 취한다.

다음 중 어법상 옳은 것을 고르세요.

a. The sudden drop in temperature overnight caused the pipes `freezing` `to freeze` solid.

b. The loud noises coming from outside caused the dog `to bark` `bark` throughout the night.

c. His remarkable speech persuaded the committee `approved` `to approve` the proposed budget.

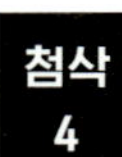

so ~ that …

개　념 ▶ '너무 ~해서 …하다'라는 의미의 결과 부사절 구문이다.

독해전략 ▶ that 앞이 원인, that 뒤가 결과를 나타내므로 인과관계를 잘 파악하며 읽는다.

어법전략 ▶ 접속사 that 뒤에는 완전한 절이 나오며, 이 that은 which나 what으로 대체할 수 없다.

다음 중 어법상 옳은 것을 고르세요.

a. The concert was `too` `so` loud that it could be heard from miles away.

b. The machine operates so quietly `that` `which` it doesn't disturb anyone in the office.

c. The view from the rooftop was so stunning `what` `that` it left me speechless.

정답 a. to freeze b. to bark c. to approve / a. so b. that c. that

---

01 다음 글의 목적으로 가장 적절한 것은?

Dear Staff,

My name is Laura Miller, the Human Resources Manager. As part of our efforts to reduce traffic on newly built area roadways, we are starting to offer flextime working hours to eligible employees. Under the plan, staffers could begin work 60 to 90 minutes before or after ordinary business hours, adjusting their scheduled departure time accordingly. All requests for flextime must be submitted to departmental supervisors and will be approved if they do not conflict with the staffing needs of the company. In addition, flextime schedules will be reviewed every four months to assure that they do not adversely affect company goals.

Best regards,
Laura Miller

① 유연 근무제 실시 계획을 안내하려고
② 직장 내 갈등 조정 기구 신설을 홍보하려고
③ 유연 근무제의 만족도 조사 참여를 독려하려고
④ 부서별 유연 근무 신청 승인 결과를 통보하려고
⑤ 교통량 감소를 위한 대중교통 이용을 장려하려고

02 다음 글에서 필자가 주장하는 바로 가장 적절한 것은?

Values alone do not create and build culture. Living your values only some of the time does not contribute to the creation and maintenance of culture. Changing values into behaviors is only half the battle. Certainly, this is a step in the right direction, but those behaviors must then be shared and distributed widely throughout the organization, along with a clear and concise description of what is expected. It is not enough to simply talk about it. It is critical to have a visual representation of the specific behaviors that leaders and all people managers can use to coach their people. Just like a sports team has a playbook with specific plays designed to help them perform well and win, your company should have a playbook with the key shifts needed to transform your culture into action and turn your values into winning behaviors.

① 조직 문화 혁신을 위해서 모든 구성원이 공유할 핵심 가치를 정립해야 한다.
② 조직 구성원의 행동을 변화시키려면 지도자는 명확한 가치관을 가져야 한다.
③ 조직 내 문화가 공유되기 위해서 구성원의 자발적 행동이 뒷받침되어야 한다.
④ 조직의 핵심 가치 실현을 위해 구성원 간의 지속적인 의사소통이 필수적이다.
⑤ 조직의 문화 형성에는 가치를 반영한 행동의 공유를 위한 명시적 지침이 필요하다.

2024 7월 18번   정답률 90%

2024학년도 수능 20번   정답률 75%

03 밑줄 친 *faulty storytelling*이 다음 글에서 의미하는 바로 가장 적절한 것은?

In recent years I've come to see that, amazingly, the key to almost all of our problems is *faulty storytelling*, because it's storytelling that *drives* the way we gather and spend our energy. I believe that stories—not the ones people tell us but the ones we tell ourselves—determine nothing less than our personal and professional destinies. And the most important story you will ever tell about yourself is the story you tell *to* yourself. So, you'd better examine your story, *especially* this one that's supposedly the most familiar of all. "The most erroneous stories are those we think we know best—and therefore never scrutinize or question," said paleontologist Stephen Jay Gould. Participate in your story rather than observing it from afar; make sure it's a story that compels you. Tell yourself the right story—the rightness of which only *you* can really determine. If you're finally living the story you want, then it needn't—it shouldn't and won't—be an ordinary one. It can and will be extraordinary. After all, you're not just the author of your story but also its main character, the hero. Heroes are never ordinary.

*scrutinize: 면밀히 조사하다 **paleontologist: 고생물학자

① failing to live a self-determined life
② obsessing over the regrets of the past
③ not thinking we are the same as others
④ attributing someone else's faults to ourselves
⑤ speaking ill of others by creating a false story

04 다음 글의 제목으로 가장 적절한 것은?

Mending and restoring objects often require even more creativity than original production. The preindustrial blacksmith made things to order for people in his immediate community; customizing the product, modifying or transforming it according to the user, was routine. Customers would bring things back if something went wrong; repair was thus an extension of fabrication. With industrialization and eventually with mass production, making things became the province of machine tenders with limited knowledge. But repair continued to require a larger grasp of design and materials, an understanding of the whole and a comprehension of the designer's intentions. "Manufacturers all work by machinery or by vast subdivision of labour and not, so to speak, by hand," an 1896 *Manual of Mending and Repairing* explained. "But all repairing *must* be done by hand. We can make every detail of a watch or of a gun by machinery, but the machine cannot mend it when broken, much less a clock or a pistol!"

① Still Left to the Modern Blacksmith: The Art of Repair
② A Historical Survey of How Repairing Skills Evolved
③ How to Be a Creative Repairperson: Tips and Ideas
④ A Process of Repair: Create, Modify, Transform!
⑤ Can Industrialization Mend Our Broken Past?

05 Antonia Brico에 관한 다음 글의 내용과 일치하지 <u>않는</u> 것은?

Antonia Brico was born in the Netherlands in 1902 and immigrated to the United States at the age of six. After attending a park concert when she was young, she was so inspired that she made up her mind to study music and become a conductor. In 1927, she entered the Berlin State Academy of Music and became the first American to graduate from its master class in conducting. In 1930, Brico made her debut as a professional conductor, for which she received positive reviews. She made an extensive European tour, and during the tour she was invited by Jean Sibelius to conduct the Helsinki Symphony Orchestra. Brico settled in Denver, where she continued to work as a conductor of the Denver Businessmen's Orchestra, later renamed the Brico Symphony Orchestra. In 1974, her most famous student, folk singer Judy Collins, made a documentary film about her, which was nominated for an Academy Award.

① 네덜란드에서 태어나 6살에 미국으로 이주했다.
② 공원 콘서트에 참석한 후 지휘자가 되기로 결심했다.
③ 전문 지휘자로서의 데뷔에서 부정적인 평가를 받았다.
④ Denver에 정착해서 지휘자로 계속 일했다.
⑤ 그녀에 관한 영화가 아카데미상 후보에 올랐다.

06 다음 글의 밑줄 친 부분 중, 문맥상 낱말의 쓰임이 적절하지 <u>않은</u> 것은?

Although the wonders of modern technology have provided people with opportunities beyond the wildest dreams of our ancestors, the good, as usual, is weakened by a downside. One of those downsides is that anyone who so chooses can pick up the virtual megaphone that is the Internet and put in their two cents on any of an infinite number of topics, regardless of their ① <u>qualifications</u>. After all, on the Internet, there are no regulations ② <u>preventing</u> a kindergarten teacher from offering medical advice or a physician from suggesting ways to safely make structural changes to your home. As a result, misinformation gets disseminated as information, and it is not always easy to ③ <u>differentiate</u> the two. This can be particularly frustrating for scientists, who spend their lives learning how to understand the intricacies of the world around them, only to have their work summarily ④ <u>challenged</u> by people whose experience with the topic can be measured in minutes. This frustration is then ⑤ <u>diminished</u> by the fact that, to the general public, both the scientist and the challenger are awarded equal credibility.

*put in one's two cents: 의견을 말하다
**disseminate: 퍼뜨리다   ***intricacy: 복잡성

2022 4월 26번   정답률 94%

2022 9월 30번   정답률 42%

07 다음 빈칸에 들어갈 말로 가장 적절한 것은?

Much of what we call political risk is in fact
________________. This applies to all types of
political risks, from civil strife to expropriations to
regulatory changes. Political risk, unlike credit or
market or operational risk, can be unsystematic
and therefore more difficult to address in classic
statistical terms. What is the probability that
terrorists will attack the United States again?
Unlike earthquakes or hurricanes, political actors
constantly adapt to overcome the barriers created
by risk managers. When corporations structure
foreign investments to mitigate risks of
expropriations, through international guarantees or
legal contracts, host governments seek out new
forms of obstruction, such as creeping
expropriation or regulatory discrimination, that are
very hard and legally costly to prove. Observation
of a risk changes the risk itself. There are ways to
mitigate high-impact, low-probability events. But
analysis of these risks can be as much art as
science.

*expropriation: 몰수   **mitigate: 줄이다

① injustice
② uncertainty
③ circularity
④ contradiction
⑤ miscommunication

08 다음 빈칸에 들어갈 말로 가장 적절한 것은?

Whatever their differences, scientists and artists
begin with the same question: *can you and I see
the same thing the same way? If so, how?* The
scientific thinker looks for features of the thing
that can be stripped of subjectivity—ideally, those
aspects that can be quantified and whose values
will thus never change from one observer to the
next. In this way, he arrives at a reality independent
of all observers. The artist, on the other hand,
relies on the strength of her artistry to effect a
marriage between her own subjectivity and that of
her readers. To a scientific thinker, this must sound
like magical thinking: *you're saying you will imagine
something so hard it'll pop into someone else's
head exactly the way you envision it?* The artist has
sought the opposite of the scientist's observer-
independent reality. She creates a reality
dependent upon observers, indeed a reality in
which ________________________________
in order for it to exist at all.

① human beings must participate
② objectivity should be maintained
③ science and art need to harmonize
④ readers remain distanced from the arts
⑤ she is disengaged from her own subjectivity

09 다음 글에서 전체 흐름과 관계 <u>없는</u> 문장은?

While we believe we hold the power to raise our children, the reality is that our children hold the power to raise *us* into the parents they need us to become. ① For this reason, the parenting experience isn't one of parent *versus* child but of parent *with* child. ② The road to wholeness sits in our children's lap, and all we need do is take a seat. ③ As our children show us our way back to our own essence, they become our greatest awakeners. ④ This means that how much we pay attention to awakening our children's minds can make a difference in their lives. ⑤ If we fail to hold their hand and follow their lead as they guide us through the gateway of increased consciousness, we lose the chance to walk toward our own enlightenment.

10 주어진 글 다음에 이어질 글의 순서로 가장 적절한 것은?

> The most commonly known form of results-based pricing is a practice called *contingency pricing*, used by lawyers.

(A) Therefore, only an outcome in the client's favor is compensated. From the client's point of view, the pricing makes sense in part because most clients in these cases are unfamiliar with and possibly intimidated by law firms. Their biggest fears are high fees for a case that may take years to settle.

(B) By using contingency pricing, clients are ensured that they pay no fees until they receive a settlement. In these and other instances of contingency pricing, the economic value of the service is hard to determine before the service, and providers develop a price that allows them to share the risks and rewards of delivering value to the buyer.

(C) Contingency pricing is the major way that personal injury and certain consumer cases are billed. In this approach, lawyers do not receive fees or payment until the case is settled, when they are paid a percentage of the money that the client receives.

*intimidate: 위협하다

① (A) – (C) – (B) 　② (B) – (A) – (C)
③ (B) – (C) – (A) 　④ (C) – (A) – (B)
⑤ (C) – (B) – (A)

11 글의 흐름으로 보아, 주어진 문장이 들어가기에 가장 적절한 곳은?

As a result, they are fit and grow better, but they aren't particularly long-lived.

When trees grow together, nutrients and water can be optimally divided among them all so that each tree can grow into the best tree it can be. If you "help" individual trees by getting rid of their supposed competition, the remaining trees are bereft. They send messages out to their neighbors unsuccessfully, because nothing remains but stumps. Every tree now grows on its own, giving rise to great differences in productivity. (①) Some individuals photosynthesize like mad until sugar positively bubbles along their trunk. (②) This is because a tree can be only as strong as the forest that surrounds it. (③) And there are now a lot of losers in the forest. (④) Weaker members, who would once have been supported by the stronger ones, suddenly fall behind. (⑤) Whether the reason for their decline is their location and lack of nutrients, a passing sickness, or genetic makeup, they now fall prey to insects and fungi.

*bereft: 잃은 **stump: 그루터기
***photosynthesize: 광합성하다

12 다음 글의 내용을 한 문장으로 요약하고자 한다. 빈칸 (A), (B)에 들어갈 말로 가장 적절한 것은?

A basic principle in economics is that when the supply of something goes up, its price should go down. The puzzle was that in the twentieth century, there were prolonged periods where the reverse appeared to happen in the world of work. In some countries, there was huge growth in the number of high-skilled people pouring out of colleges and universities, yet their wages appeared to rise rather than fall compared to those without this education. How could this be? The supply of high-skilled workers did grow, pushing their wages downward, but new technologies were skill-biased and so caused the demand for high-skilled workers to soar. The latter effect was so great that it overcame the former, so even though there were more educated people looking for work, the demand for them was so strong that the amount they were paid still went up.

↓

In the twentieth century, there were times where the wages of high-skilled workers ___(A)___ when the supply of them increased, and it was because new technologies ___(B)___ them.

	(A)		(B)
①	escalated	……	favored
②	stabilized	……	replaced
③	increased	……	devalued
④	declined	……	alienated
⑤	diminished	……	standardized

13~14 다음 글을 읽고, 물음에 답하시오.

Because personality is the innermost layer of your "personhood," it's easy (and very common) to lose sight of your personality. In fact, most people are (a) <u>unaware</u> of their personalities because from early childhood, they have spent most of their time *adopting out-of-sync identities* that completely mask their natural personalities. More often than not, the environments of our youth (for example, the way our parents raise us, the way society interacts with us, and the way our culture shapes us) (b) <u>mislead</u> us as adults into thinking we are one kind of person—when we are really another!

As children, we are surrounded by families and societies and cultures that are constantly making impressions on us, giving us (c) <u>feedback</u> about how we should be in the world, and teaching us "the right" ways to behave, the "right" thoughts and feelings to have, and the "right" groups to join. Although we come into the world being one way (our personalities), we often receive messages over time, from these (d) <u>outside</u> influences, that there are drawbacks to being our true selves and rewards for adopting identities that are out-of-sync with our true selves. So instead of developing behaviors, thoughts, and relationships that support our true selves, we develop ones that will (e) <u>disappoint</u> the people in our lives.

*out-of-sync: 맞지 않는

13 윗글의 제목으로 가장 적절한 것은?

① Let Your Social Skills Speak for You
② The Key to Building Character and Personality
③ Silence Your Impulses and Achieve Inner Peace
④ Why Do We Move Away from Our True Selves?
⑤ Can We Base Self-Worth on Social Achievements?

14 밑줄 친 (a)~(e) 중에서 문맥상 낱말의 쓰임이 적절하지 <u>않은</u> 것은?

① (a)
② (b)
③ (c)
④ (d)
⑤ (e)

2020 10월 41~42번

13 정답률 40%   14 정답률 50%

정답 p. 57

단어 TEST ● 주어진 단어의 뜻을 쓰고, 예문을 올바르게 해석하세요.

1	**eligible**	자격이 있는	eligible employees	(자격이 있는) 직원들
2	**erroneous**		erroneous stories	( ) 이야기
3	**speak ill of**		speak ill of others	남들을 ( )
4	**fabrication**		an extension of fabrication	( )의 연장
5	**downside**		one of those downsides	그 ( )들 중 하나
6	**summarily**		summarily challenged	( ) 반박당하는
7	**independent of**		independent of all observers	모든 관찰자들로부터 ( )
8	**envision**		envision something	무언가를 ( )
9	**optimally**		optimally divided	( ) 분배된
10	**fall prey to**		fall prey to insects	곤충의 ( )
11	**prolonged**		prolonged periods	( ) 기간
12	**lose sight of**		lose sight of your personality	당신의 성격을 ( )

구문 TEST ● 주어진 단어를 활용하여 우리말에 맞게 빈칸을 완성하세요.

13 **He does not want to criticize but (** to help (to) improve the situation **).**
help / improve / the situation

그는 비판하고 싶은 게 아니라, 상황이 나아지도록 돕기를 원하는 것이다.

14 **(** **) is the best way to overcome them.**
avoid / face / your fears

여러분의 두려움을 피하는 것이 아니라 직면하는 것이 최선의 극복 방법이다.

15 **What we must do is (** **).**
assess / all the data / before / make a decision

우리가 꼭 해야 할 일은 결정을 내리기 전에 모든 데이터를 평가하는 것이다.

16 **New technologies (** **).**
cause / the demand / high-skilled workers / soar

새로운 기술은 고도로 숙련된 노동자에 대한 수요가 급증하게 했다.

17 **The loud noises coming from outside (** **).**
cause / bark all night

밖에서부터 들어오는 큰 소리가 그 개로 하여금 밤내내 짖게 했다.

18 **The machine (** **) it doesn't disturb anyone in the office.**
operate / quietly

그 기계는 너무도 조용히 작동해서 사무실 안 그 누구도 방해하지 않는다.

기출 하프 모의고사

● 문제에 나오는 단어들을 확인하세요.

□	**numerous**	a. 수많은	□	**pinpoint**	v. 정확히 특정하다, 지적하다
□	**overflow with**	~로 가득하다, ~이 넘쳐나다	□	**unfold**	v. 전개되다, 펼쳐지다
□	**wander**	v. 배회하다, 돌아다니다	□	**involvement**	n. 몰입, 참여
□	**deserted**	a. 황량한, 버려진	□	**particularity**	n. 특수성
□	**incredible**	a. 놀라운, 믿을 수 없는	□	**be resolved into**	귀착되다, (서서히) ~이 되다
□	**execution**	n. 실행, 집행	□	**substance**	n. 실체, 물질, 본질, 핵심
□	**flip side**	이면, 뒷면	□	**subordinate to**	~에 종속되는, 부차적인
□	**sheer**	a. 순전한, 순수한	□	**deduce**	v. 추론하다, 연역하다
□	**ingredient**	n. 요소, 재료	□	**preferential**	a. 특별한, 특혜받은
□	**identify**	v. (신원을) 특정하다, 식별하다, 확인하다	□	**composition**	n. 구성
□	**simplify**	v. 단순화하다	□	**regeneration**	n. (생물) 재생
□	**counterintuitive**	a. 직관에 어긋나는	□	**ripen**	v. 숙성하다, 익다
□	**harmful**	a. 해로운	□	**interfere with**	~을 방해하다
□	**take measures**	조치를 취하다	□	**decay**	n. 부패
□	**demonstrate**	v. 입증하다, 보여주다	□	**misprint**	n. 오타
□	**synchronize**	v. 동조하다	□	**have an impact on**	~에 영향을 미치다
□	**consistently**	ad. 계속해서, 꾸준히	□	**displacement**	n. 위치 오류, 교체
□	**distinction**	n. 차이(점), 구별	□	**reproductive**	a. 생식의, 재생의
□	**marvel**	n. 놀라운 것, 경이	□	**accidental**	a. 우연한, 사고의
□	**self-reflective**	a. 자아 성찰적인	□	**substantial**	a. 상당한
□	**abstract**	a. 추상적인 n. (논문) 초록, 요약	□	**implement**	v. 실행하다
□	**primate**	n. 영장류	□	**be the case**	(사실이) 그러하다
□	**double-edged sword**	양날의 검(긍정, 부정 양면을 둘 다 지닌 상황)	□	**niche**	n. 틈새
□	**literature**	n. 문학, 문헌	□	**restrict**	v. 제한하다
□	**imaginatively**	ad. 상상력을 발휘하여, 창의적으로	□	**realm**	n. 영역, 분야

2022학년도 수능 19번

❶ 주격 관계대명사 생략

It was Evelyn's first time to explore the Badlands of Alberta, (which is) famous across Canada for its numerous dinosaur fossils. As a young amateur bone-hunter, she was overflowing with anticipation.

❷ 전치사 as

캐나다 전역에서 수많은 공룡 화석으로 유명한 앨버타주의 Badlands를 탐험하는 것이 Evelyn에게는 처음이었다. 젊은 아마추어 뼈 발굴자로서, 그녀는 기대감으로 가득 차 있었다.

첨삭 1 · 주격 관계대명사 생략

개　　념 ▶ 주격 관계대명사는 be동사와 함께 생략된다. 자유롭게 단독 생략되는 목적격 관계대명사와 비교해 둔다.

독해전략 ▶ 생략을 눈치채지 못하더라도, 뒤에 나오는 말이 앞의 명사를 수식 또는 보충 설명한다는 점을 파악하면 된다.

어법전략 ▶ 생략된 be동사 뒤에는 be동사의 보어 역할을 할 수 있는 형용사구, 분사구, 전치사구 등이 온다.

다음 중 어법상 옳은 것을 고르세요.

a. His major is forensic science, `instrumental` `instrumentally` in solving complex criminal cases.

b. We read *The Catcher in the Rye*, `known` `knowing` for its themes of teenage alienation.

c. The professor `is` `who is` lecturing today is an expert in medieval literature.

첨삭 2 · 전치사 as

개　　념 ▶ as가 전치사로 쓰이면 '~로서'라는 의미로 자격을 나타낸다.

독해전략 ▶ 전치사 as 앞뒤의 명사는 서로 동격이다. 즉 <A as B> 형태에서 'A = B'이다.

어법전략 ▶ 뒤에 <주어+동사>가 연결되는 접속사 as(~할 때, ~하면서, ~하므로)와 그 쓰임을 구별해야 한다.

다음 중 밑줄 친 부분의 품사로 옳은 것을 고르세요.

a. <u>As</u> a young aspiring scholar, he dedicated countless hours to studying ancient texts. `전치사` `접속사`

b. <u>As</u> a boy who grew up in a small town, he always dreamed of traveling to cities. `전치사` `접속사`

c. <u>As</u> the boy grew up, he became increasingly fascinated with science. `전치사` `접속사`

정답 a. instrumental b. known c. who is / a. 전치사 b. 전치사 c. 접속사

2024학년도 수능 39번

❸ 전치사+관계대명사

Most mutations have harmful consequences for the organism in which they occur. But sometimes a mutation may occur that increases its reproductive fitness.

❹ 선행사와 관계절의 분리

대부분의 돌연변이는 그것이 발생한 유기체에 해로운 결과를 가져온다. 하지만, 때때로 유기체의 적합성을 높이는 어떤 돌연변이가 발생할 수 있다.

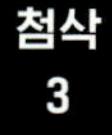

전치사+관계대명사

개   념 ▶ 본래 관계절 맨 끝에 위치하는 전치사를 관계대명사 앞으로 보낸 것이다.

독해전략 ▶ 전치사 앞에서 문장을 끊고, 선행사를 관계대명사 자리에 넣어 해석하면 의미를 파악하기 쉽다.

어법전략 ▶ 뒷구조에 유념해 둔다. <전치사+관계대명사>는 관계부사와 같아서 뒤에 완전한 문장이 온다.

다음 중 어법상 옳은 것을 고르세요.

a. The process which by which voters select their candidates is fundamental to democracy.

b. Conflict is the lens which through which we understand differences.

c. The period which during which the dinosaurs lived on Earth spanned over 160 million years.

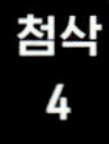

선행사와 관계절의 분리

개   념 ▶ 관계절은 보통 선행사 바로 뒤에 나오지만, 중간에 다른 말이 끼어들어 선행사와 분리되기도 한다.

독해전략 ▶ 주변 문맥을 잘 살피며 선행사를 정확하게 파악해야 한다.

어법전략 ▶ 관계대명사 뒤에서 동사 수 일치를 묻거나, 올바른 관계사를 선택하는 문제가 출제될 수 있다.

다음 중 어법상 옳은 것을 고르세요.

a. A change in the weather may occur that affect affects our travel plans.

b. Various developments in transportation have taken place what that redefine mobility.

c. A decision in politics will soon be made that determines determine the future of the nation.

01 다음 글에 나타난 Evelyn의 심경 변화로 가장 적절한 것은?

It was Evelyn's first time to explore the Badlands of Alberta, famous across Canada for its numerous dinosaur fossils. As a young amateur bone-hunter, she was overflowing with anticipation. She had not travelled this far for the bones of common dinosaur species. Her life-long dream to find rare fossils of dinosaurs was about to come true. She began eagerly searching for them. After many hours of wandering throughout the deserted lands, however, she was unsuccessful. Now, the sun was beginning to set, and her goal was still far beyond her reach. Looking at the slowly darkening ground before her, she sighed to herself, "I can't believe I came all this way for nothing. What a waste of time!"

① confused → scared
② discouraged → confident
③ relaxed → annoyed
④ indifferent → depressed
⑤ hopeful → disappointed

02 다음 글에서 필자가 주장하는 바로 가장 적절한 것은?

Bringing incredible creative projects to life demands much hard work down in the trenches of day-to-day idea execution. Genius truly is "1 percent inspiration and 99 percent perspiration." But we cannot forget the flip side of that 99 percent—it's impossible to solve every problem by sheer force of will. We must also make time for play, relaxation, and exploration, the essential ingredients of the creative insights that help us evolve existing ideas and set new projects in motion. Often this means creating a routine for breaking from your routine, working on exploratory side projects just for the hell of it, or finding new ways to hotwire your brain's perspective on a problem. To stay creatively fit, we must keep our minds engaged and on the move—because the greatest enemy of creativity is nothing more than standing still.

① 창의성을 유지할 다양한 경험과 활동을 지속해야 한다.
② 내적 비판과 성찰을 통해 숨은 잠재력을 일깨워야 한다.
③ 일상에서의 관찰을 통해 새로운 아이디어를 얻어야 한다.
④ 혁신적 아이디어를 내려면 기존 사고의 틀을 버려야 한다.
⑤ 추상적인 생각을 뛰어넘어 구체적인 적용을 모색해야 한다.

2022학년도 수능 19번   정답률 93%

2022 10월 20번   정답률 62%

03 밑줄 친 *everyone* is *no one*이 다음 글에서 의미하는 바로 가장 적절한 것은?

Many writers make the common mistake of being too vague when picturing a reader. When it comes to identifying a target audience, *everyone* is *no one*. You may worry about excluding other people if you write specifically for one individual. Relax— that doesn't necessarily happen. A well-defined audience simplifies decisions about explanations and word choice. Your style may become more distinctive, in a way that attracts people beyond the target reader. For example, Andy Weir wrote *The Martian* for science fiction readers who want their stories firmly grounded in scientific fact, and perhaps rocket scientists who enjoy science fiction. I belong to neither audience, yet I enjoyed the book. Weir was so successful at pleasing his target audience that they shared it widely and enthusiastically. Because Weir didn't try to cater to everyone, he wrote something that delighted his core audience. Eventually, his work traveled far beyond that sphere. It may be counterintuitive, but if you want to broaden your impact, tighten your focus on the reader.

① It is desirable to consider as broad a class of readers as possible.
② All readers want to buy best sellers regardless of their tastes.
③ A story can cause various reactions depending on its readers.
④ Trying to satisfy all readers leads to nobody's satisfaction.
⑤ To specifically target readers is harmful to fiction writers.

주제 추론

04 다음 글의 주제로 가장 적절한 것은?

Whenever possible, we should take measures to *re-socialize* the information we think about. The continual patter we carry on in our heads is in fact a kind of internalized conversation. Likewise, many of the written forms we encounter at school and at work—from exams and evaluations, to profiles and case studies, to essays and proposals—are really social exchanges (questions, stories, arguments) put on paper and addressed to some imagined listener or interlocutor. There are significant advantages to turning such interactions at a remove back into actual social encounters. Research demonstrates that the brain processes the "same" information differently, and often more effectively, when other human beings are involved—whether we're imitating them, debating them, exchanging stories with them, synchronizing and cooperating with them, teaching or being taught by them. We are inherently social creatures, and our thinking benefits from bringing other people into our train of thought.

*patter: 재잘거림　**interlocutor: 대화자
***at a remove: 조금 거리를 둔

① importance of processing information via social interactions
② ways of improving social skills through physical activities
③ necessity of regular evaluations of cognitive functions
④ influence of personality traits on social interactions
⑤ socialization as a form of internalized social control

2019 4월 21번　　정답률 43%

2023 3월 23번　　정답률 46%

05 다음 도표의 내용과 일치하지 <u>않는</u> 것은?

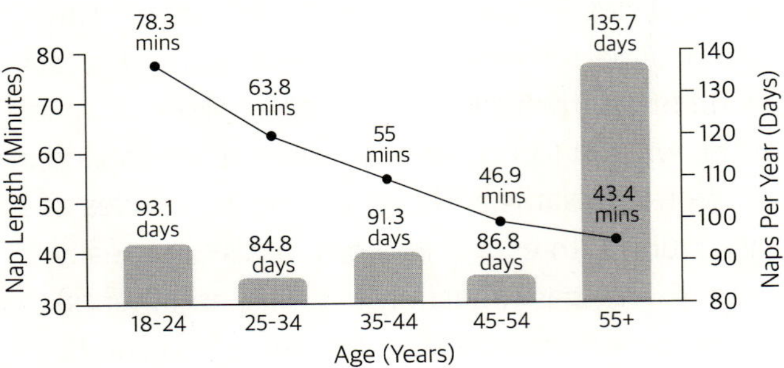

The above graph shows the nap length and the number of nap days per year by age group. ① As people get older, the nap length consistently decreases, but that is not the case with the number of nap days per year. ② The 18 to 24 age group, which has the longest nap length, naps over 30 minutes longer than the 55 and older age group, which has the shortest nap length. ③ As for the number of nap days per year, the 55 and older age group has the most days, 135.7 days, whereas the 25 to 34 age group has the fewest days, 84.8 days. ④ The 35 to 44 age group is ranked third in the nap length, and second in the number of nap days per year. ⑤ The nap length and the number of nap days per year of the 45 to 54 age group are lower than those of the 35 to 44 age group.

06 다음 글의 밑줄 친 부분 중, 어법상 <u>틀린</u> 것은?

Metacognition simply means "thinking about thinking," and it is one of the main distinctions between the human brain and that of other species. Our ability to stand high on a ladder above our normal thinking processes and ① <u>evaluate</u> why we are thinking as we are thinking is an evolutionary marvel. We have this ability ② <u>because</u> the most recently developed part of the human brain—the prefrontal cortex—enables self-reflective, abstract thought. We can think about ourselves as if we are not part of ③ <u>ourselves</u>. Research on primate behavior indicates that even our closest cousins, the chimpanzees, ④ <u>lacking</u> this ability (although they possess some self-reflective abilities, like being able to identify themselves in a mirror instead of thinking the reflection is another chimp). The ability is a double-edged sword, because while it allows us to evaluate why we are thinking ⑤ <u>what</u> we are thinking, it also puts us in touch with difficult existential questions that can easily become obsessions.

07 다음 빈칸에 들어갈 말로 가장 적절한 것은?

Literature can be helpful in the language learning process because of the ________________________ it fosters in readers. Core language teaching materials must concentrate on how a language operates both as a rule-based system and as a sociosemantic system. Very often, the process of learning is essentially analytic, piecemeal, and, at the level of the personality, fairly superficial. Engaging imaginatively with literature enables learners to shift the focus of their attention beyond the more mechanical aspects of the foreign language system. When a novel, play or short story is explored over a period of time, the result is that the reader begins to 'inhabit' the text. He or she is drawn into the book. Pinpointing what individual words or phrases may mean becomes less important than pursuing the development of the story. The reader is eager to find out what happens as events unfold; he or she feels close to certain characters and shares their emotional responses. The language becomes 'transparent'—the fiction draws the whole person into its own world.

*sociosemantic: 사회의미론적인
**transparent: 투명한

① linguistic insight
② artistic imagination
③ literary sensibility
④ alternative perspective
⑤ personal involvement

08 다음 빈칸에 들어갈 말로 가장 적절한 것은?

In Hegel's philosophy, even though there is interaction and interrelation between the universal and the individual, ________________________.
For Hegel, individuals are not distinguished in terms of Reason. In *Philosophy of Right* Hegel stresses particularity and universality as follows: "A man, who acts perversely, exhibits particularity. The rational is the highway on which everyone travels, and no one is specially marked." Here, Hegel maintains that individuals can be differentiated from each other in terms of their acts but they are not differentiated with respect to reason. There are specific thoughts, but they are finally resolved into the universal. One might say that Hegel seems to focus on the individual like Aristotle but in reality, he subtly treats the universal as fundamental whereas Aristotle considers the individual as primary substance and universal as secondary substance; in so doing Aristotle emphasizes the universal to be subordinate to the individual in contrast to Hegel.

*perversely: 별나게

① an individual stands alone apart from the universe
② the universal still has more priority than the individual
③ universal truth cannot be the key to individual problems
④ individuals can't deduce universal principles from reality itself
⑤ every individual should have his or her own particular universe

09 다음 글에서 전체 흐름과 관계 <u>없는</u> 문장은?

Because plants tend to recover from disasters more quickly than animals, they are essential to the revitalization of damaged environments. Why do plants have this preferential ability to recover from disaster? It is largely because, unlike animals, they can generate new organs and tissues throughout their life cycle. ① This ability is due to the activity of plant meristems—regions of undifferentiated tissue in roots and shoots that can, in response to specific cues, differentiate into new tissues and organs. ② If meristems are not damaged during disasters, plants can recover and ultimately transform the destroyed or barren environment. ③ You can see this phenomenon on a smaller scale when a tree struck by lightning forms new branches that grow from the old scar. ④ In the form of forests and grasslands, plants regulate the cycling of water and adjust the chemical composition of the atmosphere. ⑤ In addition to regeneration or resprouting of plants, disturbed areas can also recover through reseeding.

*revitalization: 소생

10 주어진 글 다음에 이어질 글의 순서로 가장 적절한 것은?

> The fruit ripening process brings about the softening of cell walls, sweetening and the production of chemicals that give colour and flavour. The process is induced by the production of a plant hormone called ethylene.

(A) If ripening could be slowed down by interfering with ethylene production or with the processes that respond to ethylene, fruit could be left on the plant until it was ripe and full of flavour but would still be in good condition when it arrived at the supermarket shelf.

(B) In some countries they are then sprayed with ethylene before sale to the consumer to induce ripening. However, fruit picked before it is ripe has less flavour than fruit picked ripe from the plant. Biotechnologists therefore saw an opportunity in delaying the ripening and softening process in fruit.

(C) The problem for growers and retailers is that ripening is followed sometimes quite rapidly by deterioration and decay and the product becomes worthless. Tomatoes and other fruits are, therefore, usually picked and transported when they are unripe.

*deterioration: (품질의) 저하

① (A) – (C) – (B) ② (B) – (A) – (C)
③ (B) – (C) – (A) ④ (C) – (A) – (B)
⑤ (C) – (B) – (A)

11 글의 흐름으로 보아, 주어진 문장이 들어가기에 가장 적절한 곳은?

> At the next step in the argument, however, the analogy breaks down.

Misprints in a book or in any written message usually have a negative impact on the content, sometimes (literally) fatally. (①) The displacement of a comma, for instance, may be a matter of life and death. (②) Similarly most mutations have harmful consequences for the organism in which they occur, meaning that they reduce its reproductive fitness. (③) Occasionally, however, a mutation may occur that increases the fitness of the organism, just as an accidental failure to reproduce the text of the first edition might provide more accurate or updated information. (④) A favorable mutation is going to be more heavily represented in the next generation, since the organism in which it occurred will have more offspring and mutations are transmitted to the offspring. (⑤) By contrast, there is no mechanism by which a book that accidentally corrects the mistakes of the first edition will tend to sell better.

*analogy: 유사   **mutation: 돌연변이

---

12 다음 글의 내용을 한 문장으로 요약하고자 한다. 빈칸 (A), (B)에 들어갈 말로 가장 적절한 것은?

A striving to demonstrate individual personality through designs should not be surprising. Most designers are educated to work as individuals, and design literature contains countless references to 'the designer'. Personal flair is without doubt an absolute necessity in some product categories, particularly relatively small objects, with a low degree of technological complexity, such as furniture, lighting, small appliances, and housewares. In larger-scale projects, however, even where a strong personality exercises powerful influence, the fact that substantial numbers of designers are employed in implementing a concept can easily be overlooked. The emphasis on individuality is therefore problematic—rather than actually designing, many successful designer 'personalities' function more as creative managers. A distinction needs to be made between designers working truly alone and those working in a group. In the latter case, management organization and processes can be equally as relevant as designers' creativity.

*strive: 애쓰다   **flair: 재능

↓

Depending on the ___(A)___ of a project, the capacity of designers to ___(B)___ team-based working environments can be just as important as their personal qualities.

	(A)		(B)
①	size	……	coordinate
②	cost	……	systematize
③	size	……	identify
④	cost	……	innovate
⑤	goal	……	investigate

13~14 다음 글을 읽고, 물음에 답하시오.

In many ways, the proliferation of news sources has been a wonderful thing. The public now has multiple ways to check facts and learn about (a) differing points of view. In theory, this access should improve our ability to have meaningful discussions with one another and our ability to form informed opinions. But this isn't always the case.

One of the most significant developments is that media has become like a Las Vegas buffet—we have too many choices. When you consider all of the information options—including niche media and personalized social media networks where developers utilize algorithms to serve up ideal content—there just isn't enough time to (b) explore them all. In this space it is easy to become trapped in an *echo chamber*, where your own opinions are reinforced by others without introducing new or conflicting content into the mix, which restricts public discourse and can lead to (c) extremes.

This is most evident in the realm of politics. Traditionally, mass media has been a place to tune in and hear nonpartisan reporting of facts about a situation or candidate, giving everyone (d) equal access to the vital information necessary to form opinions and make decisions. Cable news networks and partisan online sources can (e) enhance the audience's ability to access accurate, full-picture information. In some cases, audience members have made the conscious decision to only engage with content that is in line with their ideals.

*proliferation: 확산 **nonpartisan: 공정한

제목 추론

13 윗글의 제목으로 가장 적절한 것은?

① Efforts to Develop Ideal Content for Online Media
② Cable News Networks: Places for Public Discourse
③ Techniques of Utilizing Media Content for Political Data
④ Analysis of Quality Competition Among Media Platforms
⑤ Flood of Media Information: Barriers to Balanced Perspectives

어휘 추론

14 밑줄 친 (a)~(e) 중에서 문맥상 낱말의 쓰임이 적절하지 않은 것은?

① (a)
② (b)
③ (c)
④ (d)
⑤ (e)

2021 10월 41~42번

13 정답률 45%　14 정답률 40%

정답 p. 64

단어 TEST ● 　주어진 단어의 뜻을 쓰고, 예문을 올바르게 해석하세요.

1	**deserted**	황량한, 버려진	the deserted land	그 (황량한) 땅
2	**flip side**		the flip side of that 99 percent	그 99퍼센트의 ( )
3	**counterintuitive**		sound counterintuitive	( ) 것처럼 들리다
4	**synchronize**		synchronize with other human beings	다른 사람들에 ( )
5	**double-edged sword**		a double-edged sword	( )
6	**imaginatively**		engage imaginatively with literature	( ) 문학에 몰입하다
7	**unfold**		as events unfold	사건들이 ( )에 따라
8	**subordinate to**		subordinate to the individual	개별적인 것에 ( )
9	**regeneration**		regeneration of plants	식물의 ( )
10	**have an impact on**		have a negative impact on the content	내용에 부정적인 ( )
11	**reproductive**		the reproductive fitness	( ) 적합성
12	**restrict**		restrict public discourse	대중의 담론(공론화)을 ( )

구문 TEST ● 　주어진 단어를 활용하여 우리말에 맞게 빈칸을 완성하세요.

13　**She was exploring the area** (which[that] is) famous for its dinosaur fossils).
famous for / dinosaur fossils
그녀는 그곳의 공룡 화석으로 유명한 지역을 탐험 중이었다.

14　( ) **is an expert in medieval literature.**
the professor / lecture
오늘 강의하고 있는(강의할 예정인) 교수님은 중세 문학 전문가이다.

15　( ), **he dreamed of moving to cities.**
as / grow up / a small town
작은 마을에서 자란 소년으로서, 그는 도시로 이사 가기를 꿈꿨다.

16　**Conflict is the lens** ( ).
through / understand / differences
갈등은 우리가 차이를 이해하는 렌즈(통로)이다.

17　**A mutation may occur** ( ).
increase / the fitness of the organism
유기체의 적합성을 높이는 어떤 돌연변이가 발생할 수도 있다.

18　**A change in the weather may occur** ( ).
affect / our travel plans
우리 여행 계획에 영향을 미치는 어떤 날씨 변화가 일어날 수도 있다.

기출 하프 모의고사

10

DAY 10

● 문제에 나오는 단어들을 확인하세요.

a great deal	많은 것[양], 많이	concerned with	~와 관련된
verbally	ad. 말로, 언어로	exaggerate	v. 과장하다
overwhelm	v. 압도하다	interrupt	v. 방해하다, 중단시키다
tackle	v. 다루다	conventional	a. 전통적인
multifaceted	a. 다면적인	misleading	a. 오해의 소지가 있는
attribute A to B	A를 B의 탓으로 돌리다	smooth the way to	~로 가는 길을 닦다, 순탄하게 만들다
understate	v. 과소평가하다, 축소해서 말하다	divorce A from B	A와 B를 단절시키다
significant	a. 상당한, 많은, 중요한	project	v. (소리 등을 멀리까지) 내다, 던지다
in question	논의 중인, 문제의, 해당	sparingly	ad. 드물게
accommodation	n. 숙박 시설	authoritative	a. 권위적인
venture into	~을 탐험하다, (위험을 무릅쓰고) 들어가다	enforcement	n. (규제 등의) 집행, 시행
enhance	v. 향상시키다, 개선하다	contract	v. 계약하다, 수축하다 n. 계약
cornerstone	n. 초석, 디딤돌	devalue	v. 가치를 떨어뜨리다, 평가 절하하다
billion	n. 10억	reputation	n. 평판, 명성
neglect	v. 무시하다, 소홀히 하다	bond	n. (법적) 계약, 속박, 결속, 유대
endeavour	n. 노력	respiration	n. 호흡
devote oneself to	~에 전념하다	equator	n. 적도
noted for	~로 유명한	density	n. 밀도
anthem	n. 찬가, 축가, 성가	temperate	a. (기후) 온대의, 온화한
sacred	a. 성스러운	chances are (good) that	~할 가능성이 크다
applicable	a. 적용할 수 있는	prior	a. 이전의
enthusiastically	ad. 열광적으로	extinction	n. 멸종
vital	a. 매우 중요한	helpless	a. 무력한
aesthetic	a. 미적인	articulate	v. 분명히 말하다
disengagement	n. 이탈	signify	v. 의미하다

❶ 가정법 현재의 that절

However, I would always advise **that you (should) use** your **loudest voice incredibly sparingly and avoid shouting as much as possible**.

❷ 병렬구조

그러나 항상 나는 가장 큰 목소리는 놀랍도록 드물게 쓰고 소리치는 것은 최대한 피해야 한다고 조언하고자 한다.

첨삭 1 — 가정법 현재의 that절

개　념 ▶ '주장, 요구, 명령, 제안' 동사의 목적어인 that절에서 동사 자리에 should를 생략하고 동사원형을 쓸 수 있다.

독해전략 ▶ '~해야 한다고 주장/요구/명령/제안하다'라는 의미 특성상 중요한 내용이므로 주목해야 한다.

어법전략 ▶ that절이 '~해야 한다'라고 해석되는 한, that절의 주어의 인칭과 수에 관계없이 동사원형을 쓴다.

다음 중 어법상 옳은 것을 고르세요.

a. The counselor advised that the couple ┃ were ┃ be ┃ respectful to each other.

b. I suggest that he ┃ speaks ┃ speak ┃ with a financial advisor before making any major investments.

c. She requested that they ┃ did not disclose ┃ not disclose ┃ the confidential information.

첨삭 2 — 병렬구조

개　념 ▶ 등위접속사(and, but, or 등) 또는 비교구문의 as/than 앞뒤로 문법적으로 대등한 요소를 연결하는 것이다.

독해전략 ▶ 문법적으로는 대등해도, <A but/so B>, <B ~ than A>와 같이 어느 하나(B)가 의미상 더 중요할 수 있다.

어법전략 ▶ 기계적으로 같은 형태를 맞추기보다, 문맥 단서를 잘 활용해야 한다.

다음 중 어법상 옳은 것을 고르세요.

a. He took a more serious interest in running and thus ┃ devoting ┃ devoted ┃ himself to it.

b. She needs to decide whether to walk to the park or ┃ drive ┃ drives ┃ to the beach today.

c. She was injured, visibly in pain with a bruised shoulder, but ┃ continued ┃ continuing ┃ to play.

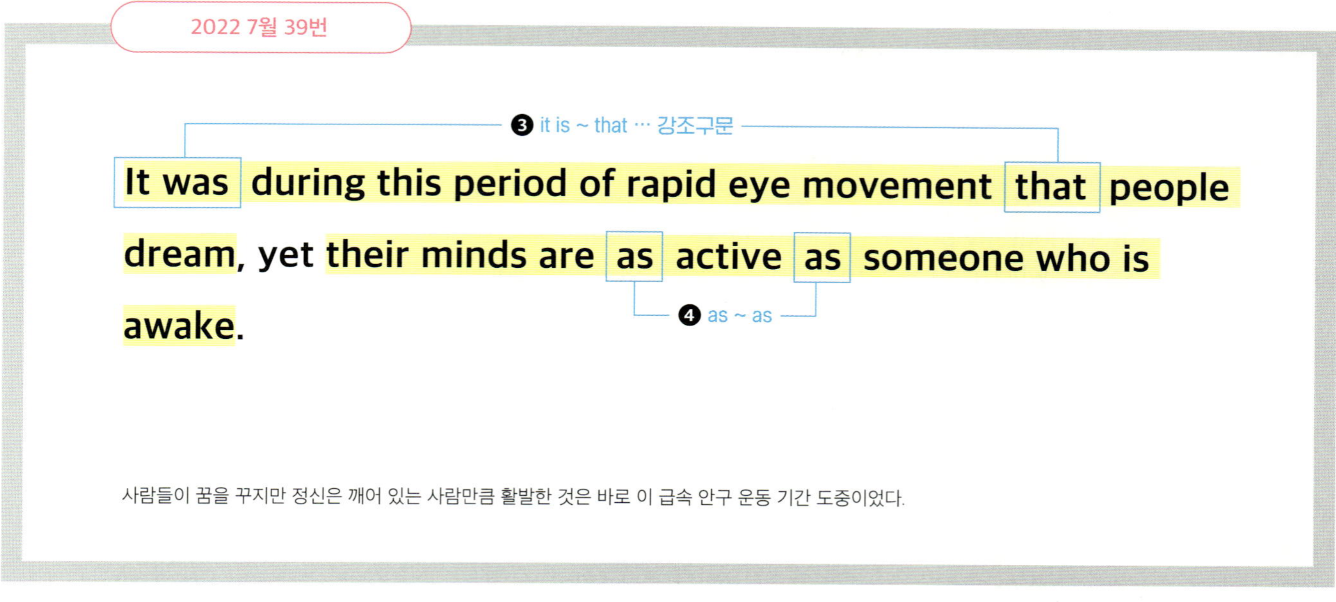

첨삭 3

it is ~ that … 강조구문

개　념 ▶ it is[was]와 that 사이에 명사구나 부사구를 넣어 강조하는 구문이다(…한 것은 바로 ~이다).

독해전략 ▶ that절이 강조되는 말을 꾸미는 것처럼 해석한다. 주로 글의 요지와 직결된다.

어법전략 ▶ it is[was]와 that 사이가 명사구면 that 뒤가 불완전하고, 부사구면 that 뒤가 완전하다. 강조 대상에 따라 who/which/when/where 등을 활용할 수도 있다.

다음 중 어법상 옳은 것을 고르세요.

a. It was during the darkest hours of the night | that | which | he found inspiration for his novel.

b. It is her resilience in the face of adversity | where | that | serves as an inspiration to us all.

c. It was at the peak of her career | that | what | she decided to pursue a different path.

첨삭 4

as ~ as

개　념 ▶ <as+원급+as>는 '~만큼 …한/하게'라는 의미로, 동등한 두 대상을 비교하는 표현이다.

독해전략 ▶ 도표 문제에서 twice 등 배수사와 함께 <배수사+as+원급+as(몇 배 더 ~한)>으로 응용될 때 주의한다.

어법전략 ▶ as 앞뒤의 두 비교 대상은 문법적으로 대등한 요소이다(= 병렬구조).

다음 중 어법상 옳은 것을 고르세요.

a. The car's fuel efficiency is as good as | that | those | of a hybrid vehicle.

b. The antique pieces of furniture in the museum are as valuable as | that | those | in private collections.

c. The athletic shoes provide twice as much support as standard sneakers | are | do |.

정답 a. that b. that c. that / a. that b. those c. do

목적 파악

01 다음 글의 목적으로 가장 적절한 것은?

Dear Readers,

As you've seen throughout my books, I've learned a great deal from people who have sent me their stories and advice. Let's keep it going. If you would like to send me an email about your experiences with disasters and what you've learned about escaping them, please send it to nodisaster@smail.com. I want you to note that, by sending me your story, you are giving me permission to use it in the books that I write. But I promise not to use your name unless you give me explicit permission. Thank you.

Very truly yours,
Robert Brown

① 신간 도서 출판 기념회에 초대하려고
② 저작물 사용에 대한 허락을 구하려고
③ 개인 정보의 무단 사용에 대해 항의하려고
④ 재난에 적절히 대처하는 요령을 안내하려고
⑤ 재난과 관련한 경험담을 보내 줄 것을 요청하려고

요지 파악

02 다음 글의 요지로 가장 적절한 것은?

Despite numerous studies on the influence of mediated agendas on politics, most studies examine text only—as if media only deliver words. These studies looked at how reporters, analysts, and commentators *verbally* describe and criticize the candidates. But they often neglect another important source of influence: visuals. As some communication scholars said, "Stories are often complex combinations of visual and verbal content—all too often the visual information is so powerful that it overwhelms the verbal." The challenge of tackling visuals to examine their influence is multifaceted. The difficulties of gathering and coding visual data and of attributing impact to specific parts of images have no doubt caused veritable scholars to shy away. But the potential impact of visuals on people's perceptions is simply too important to ignore. Furthermore, the importance of understanding both visuals and text in tandem cannot be understated.

*veritable: 진정한   **in tandem: 동시에

① 시각 자료는 정치 관련 보도 자료 연구의 중요한 대상이다.
② 전문가들의 의견도 철저하게 검증하고 보도할 필요가 있다.
③ 다양한 관심사를 반영하는 뉴스 프로그램 편성이 요구된다.
④ 지나치게 방대한 시각 자료는 보도 내용 이해에 방해가 된다.
⑤ 언론인은 보도에서 자신의 정치적 편향을 드러내서는 안 된다.

2022 10월 18번   정답률 87%

2021 3월 22번   정답률 44%

03 밑줄 친 from their *verandas*가 다음 글에서 의미하는 바로 가장 적절한 것은?

Around the turn of the twentieth century, anthropologists trained in the natural sciences began to reimagine what a science of humanity should look like and how social scientists ought to go about studying cultural groups. Some of those anthropologists insisted that one should at least spend significant time actually observing and talking to the people studied. Early ethnographers such as Franz Boas and Alfred Cort Haddon typically traveled to the remote locations where the people in question lived and spent a few weeks to a few months there. They sought out a local Western host who was familiar with the people and the area (such as a colonial official, missionary, or businessman) and found accommodations through them. Although they did at times venture into the community without a guide, they generally did not spend significant time with the local people. Thus, their observations were primarily conducted from their *verandas*.

*anthropologist: 인류학자   **ethnographer: 민족지학자

① seeking to build long-lasting relationships with the natives
② participating in collaborative research with natural scientists
③ engaging in little direct contact with the people being studied
④ cooperating actively with Western hosts in the local community
⑤ struggling to take a wider view of the native culture examined

04 다음 글의 주제로 가장 적절한 것은?

More recently there have been attempts to argue that unpaid work *is* work because 'it is an activity that combines labour with raw materials to produce goods and services with enhanced economic value'. Economists such as Duncan Ironmonger have attempted to impute a dollar value on volunteering to enable its 'economic' value to be counted. Yet despite this, unpaid work and volunteering still remain outside the defined economic framework of our capitalist system because capitalism has competition and financial reward as its cornerstones and volunteering does not. Having said that, it has been estimated that volunteering contributes about $42 billion a year to the Australian economy. Although attempts to quantify and qualify the financial importance of volunteering in supporting our economic structures and enhancing our social capital continue to be made, it is slow going. And while volunteering remains outside the GDP, its true value and importance is neglected. Governments continue to pay lip service to the importance of volunteering but ultimately deny it official recognition.

*impute: 귀속시키다

① efforts to utilise volunteering as a business strategy
② mistaken view of identifying volunteering with labour
③ obstacles to our understanding of the capitalist system
④ governmental endeavours to involve volunteers in public service
⑤ lack of appreciation for the economic significance of volunteering

05 Emil Zátopek에 관한 다음 글의 내용과 일치하지 <u>않는</u> 것은?

Emil Zátopek, a former Czech athlete, is considered one of the greatest long-distance runners ever. He was also famous for his distinctive running style. While working in a shoe factory, he participated in a 1,500-meter race and won second place. After that event, he took a more serious interest in running and devoted himself to it. At the 1952 Olympic Games in Helsinki, he won three gold medals in the 5,000-meter and 10,000-meter races and in the marathon, breaking Olympic records in each. He was married to Dana Zátopková, who was an Olympic gold medalist, too. Zátopek was also noted for his friendly personality. In 1966, Zátopek invited Ron Clarke, a great Australian runner who had never won an Olympic gold medal, to an athletic meeting in Prague. After the meeting, he gave Clarke one of his gold medals as a gift.

① 독특한 달리기 스타일로 유명했다.
② 신발 공장에서 일한 적이 있다.
③ 1952년 Helsinki 올림픽에서 올림픽 기록을 깨지 못했다.
④ 올림픽 금메달리스트인 Dana Zátopková와 결혼했다.
⑤ 자신의 금메달 중 하나를 Ron Clarke에게 주었다.

06 다음 글의 밑줄 친 부분 중, 어법상 <u>틀린</u> 것은?

According to its dictionary definition, an anthem is both a song of loyalty, often to a country, and a piece of 'sacred music', definitions that are both applicable in sporting contexts. This genre is dominated, although not exclusively, by football and has produced a number of examples ① <u>where</u> popular songs become synonymous with the club and are enthusiastically adopted by the fans. More than this they are often spontaneous expressions of loyalty and identity and, according to Desmond Morris, have 'reached the level of something ② <u>approached</u> a local art form'. A strong element of the appeal of such sports songs ③ <u>is</u> that they feature 'memorable and easily sung choruses in which fans can participate'. This is a vital part of the team's performance ④ <u>as</u> it makes the fans' presence more tangible. This form of popular culture can be said ⑤ <u>to display</u> pleasure and emotional excess in contrast to the dominant culture which tends to maintain 'respectable aesthetic distance and control'.

*synonymous: 밀접한 연관을 갖는
**tangible: 확실한

07 다음 빈칸에 들어갈 말로 가장 적절한 것은?

Humour involves not just practical disengagement but cognitive disengagement. As long as something is funny, we are for the moment not concerned with whether it is real or fictional, true or false. This is why we give considerable leeway to people telling funny stories. If they are getting extra laughs by exaggerating the silliness of a situation or even by making up a few details, we are happy to grant them comic licence, a kind of poetic licence. Indeed, someone listening to a funny story who tries to correct the teller—'No, he didn't spill the spaghetti on the keyboard and the monitor, just on the keyboard'—will probably be told by the other listeners to stop interrupting. The creator of humour is putting ideas into people's heads for the pleasure those ideas will bring, not to provide _______________ information.

*cognitive: 인식의 **leeway: 여지

① detailed
② accurate
③ useful
④ additional
⑤ alternative

08 다음 빈칸에 들어갈 말로 가장 적절한 것은?

We understand that the segregation of our consciousness into present, past, and future is both a fiction and an oddly self-referential framework; your present was part of your mother's future, and your children's past will be in part your present. Nothing is generally wrong with structuring our consciousness of time in this conventional manner, and it often works well enough. In the case of climate change, however, the sharp division of time into past, present, and future has been desperately misleading and has, most importantly, hidden from view the extent of the responsibility of those of us alive now. The narrowing of our consciousness of time smooths the way to divorcing ourselves from responsibility for developments in the past and the future with which our lives are in fact deeply intertwined. In the climate case, it is not that _______________________________________. It is that the realities are obscured from view by the partitioning of time, and so questions of responsibility toward the past and future do not arise naturally.

*segregation: 분리 **intertwine: 뒤얽히게 하다
***obscure: 흐릿하게 하다

① all our efforts prove to be effective and are thus encouraged
② sufficient scientific evidence has been provided to us
③ future concerns are more urgent than present needs
④ our ancestors maintained a different frame of time
⑤ we face the facts but then deny our responsibility

09 다음 글에서 전체 흐름과 관계 <u>없는</u> 문장은?

Actors, singers, politicians and countless others recognise the power of the human voice as a means of communication beyond the simple decoding of the words that are used. Learning to control your voice and use it for different purposes is, therefore, one of the most important skills to develop as an early career teacher. ① The more confidently you give instructions, the higher the chance of a positive class response. ② There are times when being able to project your voice loudly will be very useful when working in school, and knowing that you can cut through a noisy classroom, dinner hall or playground is a great skill to have. ③ In order to address serious noise issues in school, students, parents and teachers should search for a solution together. ④ However, I would always advise that you use your loudest voice incredibly sparingly and avoid shouting as much as possible. ⑤ A quiet, authoritative and measured tone has so much more impact than slightly panicked shouting.

10 주어진 글 다음에 이어질 글의 순서로 가장 적절한 것은?

> The potential for market enforcement is greater when contracting parties have developed reputational capital that can be devalued when contracts are violated.

(A) Similarly, a landowner can undermaintain fences, ditches, and irrigation systems. Accurate assessments of farmer and landowner behavior will be made over time, and those farmers and landowners who attempt to gain at each other's expense will find that others may refuse to deal with them in the future.

(B) Over time landowners indirectly monitor farmers by observing the reported output, the general quality of the soil, and any unusual or extreme behavior. Farmer and landowner reputations act as a bond. In any growing season a farmer can reduce effort, overuse soil, or underreport the crop.

(C) Farmers and landowners develop reputations for honesty, fairness, producing high yields, and consistently demonstrating that they are good at what they do. In small, close-knit farming communities, reputations are well known.

*ditch: 개천　**irrigation: 물을 댐

① (A) – (C) – (B)　　② (B) – (A) – (C)
③ (B) – (C) – (A)　　④ (C) – (A) – (B)
⑤ (C) – (B) – (A)

11 글의 흐름으로 보아, 주어진 문장이 들어가기에 가장 적절한 곳은?

> This is why it is difficult to wake up from or scream out during a nightmare.

Most dreaming occurs during REM sleep. (①) REM stands for Rapid Eye Movement, a stage of sleep discovered by Professor Nathaniel Kleitman at the University of Chicago in 1958. (②) Along with a medical student, Eugene Aserinsky, he noted that when people are sleeping, they exhibit rapid eye movement, as if they were "looking" at something. (③) Ongoing research by Kleitman and Aserinsky concluded that it was during this period of rapid eye movement that people dream, yet their minds are as active as someone who is awake. (④) Interestingly enough, studies have found that along with rapid eye movement, our heart rates increase and our respiration is also elevated—yet our bodies do not move and are basically paralyzed due to a nerve center in the brain that keeps our bodies motionless besides some occasional twitches and jerks. (⑤) To sum it up, during the REM dream state, your mind is busy but your body is at rest.

*twitch: 씰룩거림

12 다음 글의 내용을 한 문장으로 요약하고자 한다. 빈칸 (A), (B)에 들어갈 말로 가장 적절한 것은?

Why would languages and religions increase rapidly around the equator, and why is their frequency also related to ethnocentrism? The answer to these questions lies in the fact that pathogen density is much higher in the tropics than it is in temperate and cold climates. When you live in Sweden, chances are good that any group within five hundred miles has been exposed to the same few pathogens. In contrast, when you live in the Congo, the group on the other side of the valley may well have been exposed to a pathogen with which you've had no prior contact. For this reason, humans in the tropics learned that when they interacted with other groups they tended to get sick, so they would have stopped doing it. In a pre-scientific world, it was logical to blame their neighbors for their illness, and therefore to dislike them. Dislike and fear kept neighbors apart, and once you don't interact with others anymore, your languages and religions naturally divide as well.

*ethnocentrism: 자민족 중심주의
**pathogen: 병원균

↓

High pathogen density can contribute to the ____(A)____ of languages and religions by ____(B)____ people's interactions with their neighboring groups, as was shown in the regions around the equator.

	(A)		(B)
①	diversification	……	discouraging
②	extinction	……	delaying
③	extinction	……	expanding
④	unification	……	discouraging
⑤	diversification	……	expanding

13~14 다음 글을 읽고, 물음에 답하시오.

Although we humans are equipped with reflexive responses for survival, at birth we are (a) <u>helpless</u>. We spend about a year unable to walk, about two more before we can articulate full thoughts, and many more years unable to provide for ourselves. We are totally dependent on those around us for our survival. Now compare this to many other mammals. Dolphins, for instance, are born swimming; giraffes learn to stand within hours; a baby zebra can run within forty-five minutes of birth. Across the animal kingdom, our cousins are strikingly (b) <u>independent</u> soon after they're born.
On the face of it, that seems like a great advantage for other species—but in fact it signifies a limitation. Baby animals develop quickly because their brains are wiring up according to a largely preprogrammed routine. But that (c) <u>preparedness</u> trades off with flexibility. Imagine if some unfortunate rhinoceros found itself on the Arctic tundra, or on top of a mountain in the Himalayas, or in the middle of a metropolis. It would have no capacity to adapt (which is why we don't find rhinos in those areas). This strategy of arriving with a pre-arranged brain works inside a particular niche in the ecosystem—but put an animal outside of that niche, and its chances of thriving are (d) <u>low</u>.
In contrast, humans are able to thrive in many different environments, from the frozen tundra to the high mountains to crowded urban centers. This is possible because the human brain is born remarkably incomplete. Instead of arriving with everything wired up—let's call it "hardwired"—a human brain (e) <u>forbids</u> itself to be shaped by the details of life experience. This leads to long periods of helplessness as the young brain slowly molds to its environment. It's "livewired."

*niche: 적합한 장소

13 윗글의 제목으로 가장 적절한 것은?

① Rewire Your Brain to Enhance Your Courage!
② Born Unfinished: A Gift of Adaptability to Humans
③ Evolutionary Rivalry Between Humans and Animals
④ How Does Human-Centered Thinking Bring Tragedy?
⑤ Human Brains Develop Through Interaction with Other Species

14 밑줄 친 (a)~(e) 중에서 문맥상 낱말의 쓰임이 적절하지 <u>않은</u> 것은?

① (a)
② (b)
③ (c)
④ (d)
⑤ (e)

13 정답률 56%   **14** 정답률 43%

정답 p. 71

단어 TEST ●　주어진 단어의 뜻을 쓰고, 예문을 올바르게 해석하세요.

1	**a great deal** 많이	learn a great deal from others	남들로부터 (많이) 배우다
2	**accommodation**	find accommodations	(　　　　)들을 찾다
3	**devote oneself to**	devote oneself to running	달리기에 (　　　)
4	**noted for**	noted for his friendly personality	그의 다정한 성격으로 (　　　)
5	**disengagement**	practical disengagement	실제적 (　　)
6	**interrupt**	stop interrupting	(　　　)를 그만두다
7	**sparingly**	use your loudest voice sparingly	당신의 가장 큰 목소리를 (　　　) 쓰다
8	**devalue**	reputational capital that can be devalued	(　　　) 수 있는 평판 자본
9	**equator**	around the equator	(　　) 주변에서
10	**extinction**	mass extinction	대량 (　　)
11	**articulate**	articulate full thoughts	완전한 생각을 (　　　)
12	**signify**	signify a limitation	한계를 (　　　)

구문 TEST ●　주어진 단어를 활용하여 우리말에 맞게 빈칸을 완성하세요.

13　**I would always advise that you** ((should) avoid shouting as much as possible).
avoid / shout / much / possible

나는 항상 소리치는 것을 최대한 피하라고 조언하고자 한다.

14　**The counselor advised that the couple** (　　　　　　　　　　　).
respectful / to each other

상담사는 그 부부가 서로 존중해야 한다고 충고했다.

15　**He took a more serious interest in running and** (　　　　　　　).
devote oneself to

그는 달리기에 좀 더 진지한 관심을 갖고 그것에 전념했다.

16　**It was** (　　　　　　　　　　　　) **people dream.**
this period of rapid eye movement

사람들이 꿈을 꾸는 것은 바로 이 급속 안구 운동 동안이었다.

17　(　　　　　　　　　　) **that serves as an inspiration to us all.**
her positive personality

우리 모두에게 영감이 되는 것은 바로 그녀의 긍정적인 성격이다.

18　**The car's fuel efficiency is** (　　　　　　　　　).
good / of / a hybrid vehicle

이 차의 연비는 하이브리드 차량의 그것만큼 좋다.

기출 하프 모의고사

● 문제에 나오는 단어들을 확인하세요.

session	n. (특정한 활동을 위한) 시간		pursuit	n. 활동, 일, 추구
suspense	n. 긴장감, 서스펜스		cutting-edge	a. 최첨단의
impending	a. 임박한, 곧 닥칠		novel	a. 참신한, 새로운
neutral	a. 감정이 드러나지 않는, 중립적인		secondary	a. 부차적인
coffin	n. 관		attachment	n. 애착
precede	v. ~보다 앞서다, 선행하다		affection	n. 애정
suited	a. 적합한, 알맞은		afford	v. (격식) 제공하다, 주다
convergence	n. 수렴		heighten	v. 고조시키다, 고양시키다
proclaim	v. 분명히 말하다, 선언하다		inexperienced	a. 경험이 많지 않은, 미숙한
discern	v. 분별하다		coordination	n. 조정, 조직
deficient	a. 불충분한, 결함이 있는		bipedalism	n. (직립) 두 발 보행
statement	n. 진술		enormous	a. 엄청난, 거대한
notwithstanding	prep. 그럼에도 불구하고 (명사 뒤에 쓰기도 함)		digit	n. 손가락, (0부터 9까지의) 숫자
mutually exclusive	상호 배타적인(둘 중 하나가 참이면 나머지가 거짓인)		manipulation	n. 조작
virtuoso	n. (특히 음악의) 거장		leverage	n. 지렛대 v. 이용하다
distinguished	a. 유명한, 성공한		prerequisite	n. 전제 조건
remarkable	a. 놀라운, 주목할 만한		account for	(비율·비중을) 차지하다 ~을 설명하다
glowing praise	열렬한 찬사		frustrate	v. 좌절시키다, 방해하다
liberalize	v. 자유롭게 하다, 해방시키다		identification	n. (신원) 확인, 증명
continuity	n. 연속성		permanence	n. 영속성
absorb	v. 흡수하다		bound	n. 경계, 한계 v. 경계를 이루다
distort	v. 왜곡하다		quarrel	n. 다툼, 싸움
accommodate	v. ~에 맞추다, ~을 수용하다		conformity	n. 순응
come into existence	생겨나다, 발생하다		lose one's cool	냉정함을 잃다
discipline	n. 학과, (학문) 분야		passivity	n. 수동성

2021 6월 19번

❶ 비교급 강조부사

She actually started thinking that it was much more convenient than expected. She felt as if the counselor were in the room with her.

❷ as if 가정법

그녀는 실제로 그것이 예상했던 것보다 훨씬 더 편리하다고 생각하기 시작했다. 그녀는 마치 상담사가 자신과 함께 방 안에 있는 듯한 기분을 느꼈다.

첨삭 1 — 비교급 강조부사

개   념 ▶ much, far, even, still, a lot 등은 주로 비교급 앞에서 비교급을 수식한다.

독해전략 ▶ 원래 단어의 의미 대신 '훨씬'이라는 강조의 의미로 해석한다.

어법전략 ▶ 원급 또는 최상급을 수식하는 (the) very와 쓰임을 구별해 둔다.

다음 중 어법상 옳은 것을 고르세요.

a. Our garden has grown very much larger since we started using the new fertilizer.

b. He's been working hard and is very a lot more skilled at coding than he was last year.

c. The mystery novel was even very more fascinating than the summary suggested.

첨삭 2 — as if 가정법

개   념 ▶ <as if+주어+과거/과거완료 동사 ~>는 '(실제 ~하지 않지만) 마치 ~한/했던 것처럼'의 의미이다.

독해전략 ▶ 이해를 돕기 위한 예시나 부연 진술에 많이 활용되므로, 핵심 파악이 어려울 때 주목한다.

어법전략 ▶ as if절에 과거시제를 쓰면 주절과 같은 시점을, 과거완료 시제를 쓰면 주절보다 이전 시점을 나타낸다.

다음 중 어법상 옳은 것을 고르세요.

a. We should treat every day as if it is were our last.

b. She was holding the old book as if it were is a precious treasure.

c. The house looks as if it were had been hit by a storm last summer.

2022 9월 39번

The transition from magnetic stripe to embedded chip slightly slowed down transactions, sometimes frustrating customers in a hurry. Make a service too burdensome, and the potential customer will go elsewhere.

❸ 결과의 분사구문

❹ 명령문+and

마그네틱 띠에서 내장형 칩으로의 전환은 거래를 약간 느려지게 해서, 바쁜 고객을 간혹 좌절시켰다. 서비스를 너무 부담스럽게 만들어보라, 그러면 잠재적 고객은 다른 곳으로 갈 것이다.

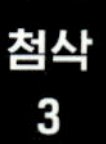

결과의 분사구문

개　　념 ▶ 주로 주절 뒤에 콤마와 함께 쓰여 '(그리고/그래서) ~하다'의 의미를 나타내는 표현이다.

독해전략 ▶ 분사구문을 주절보다 먼저 해석하지 않아도 된다. 콤마 앞에서부터 뒤로 의미를 순차적으로 파악한다.

어법전략 ▶ 의미상 주어(보통 문장의 주어)를 기준으로 능동(V-ing)과 수동(p.p.)을 잘 판단해야 한다. 본동사와도 혼동하지 않도록 한다.

다음 중 어법상 옳은 것을 고르세요.

a. The heavy rains flooded the main roads, forcing / forced people to seek alternative routes.

b. The concert was cancelled all of a sudden, disappointed / disappointing thousands of fans.

c. The decision to cut down the trees sparked public outrage, led / leading to several protests.

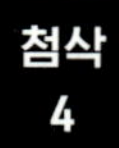

명령문+and

개　　념 ▶ <명령문+and>는 '~하라, 그러면 …'의 의미이다. <명령문+or(~하라, 그러지 않으면 …)>과 구별해 둔다.

독해전략 ▶ 명령문 형태이지만 실질적으로 '~하면 …하게 된다'의 조건문임을 염두에 둔다.

어법전략 ▶ 명령문의 동사원형을 준동사(to부정사, 동명사, 분사)와 구별하는 문제에 주의한다.

다음 중 어법상 옳은 것을 고르세요.

a. Bring / Bringing your camera, and we can capture stunning shots of the sunset.

b. To come / Come early, and we can grab a good seat at the front.

c. Save your work frequently, and / or you might lose your progress.

정답 a. forcing b. disappointing c. leading / a. Bring b. Come c. or

심경 파악

01 다음 글에 드러난 Natalie의 심경 변화로 가장 적절한 것은?

As Natalie was logging in to her first online counseling session, she wondered, "How can I open my heart to the counselor through a computer screen?" Since the counseling center was a long drive away, she knew that this would save her a lot of time. Natalie just wasn't sure if it would be as helpful as meeting her counselor in person. Once the session began, however, her concerns went away. She actually started thinking that it was much more convenient than expected. She felt as if the counselor were in the room with her. As the session closed, she told him with a smile, "I'll definitely see you online again!"

① doubtful → satisfied
② regretful → confused
③ confident → ashamed
④ bored → excited
⑤ thrilled → disappointed

요지 파악

02 다음 글의 요지로 가장 적절한 것은?

A visual scene can set up our emotional response. Suspense is driven by a sense of calm with the anticipation of impending terror. Indeed, anticipation or expectations play a key role in driving our emotions. The Russian silent filmmaker Lev Kuleshov considered such contextual influences. He interspersed shots of an actor exhibiting a neutral expression with shots of a child's coffin or a plate of soup. This same "neutral" expression was interpreted differently depending on what image preceded it. Thus, the same expression appeared to show sorrow or hunger, depending on the context. Psychological studies of the *Kuleshov* effect have confirmed the impact of the social context on emotion. For example, if a person smiles at you and then the smile turns into a neutral expression, that person will appear somewhat grumpy or disappointed. Conversely, if a person first looks angry and then the expression turns into a neutral expression, the person looks somewhat pleasant or positive.

*intersperse: (~ 사이에) 배치하다
**grumpy: 기분이 언짢은

① 영상과 음향의 대비가 긴장감을 조성한다.
② 사회적 상황에 따라 감정의 표현 방식이 다르다.
③ 시대의 상황을 반영한 영화는 관객의 공감을 얻는다.
④ 중립적인 태도 유지가 갈등을 해결하는 데 도움이 된다.
⑤ 선행 장면에 따라서 동일한 시각 정보가 다르게 해석된다.

2021 6월 19번   정답률 89%

2021 10월 22번   정답률 81%

03 밑줄 친 send us off into different far corners of the library가 다음 글에서 의미하는 바로 가장 적절한 것은?

You may feel there is something scary about an algorithm deciding what you might like. Could it mean that, if computers conclude you won't like something, you will never get the chance to see it? Personally, I really enjoy being directed toward new music that I might not have found by myself. I can quickly get stuck in a rut where I put on the same songs over and over. That's why I've always enjoyed the radio. But the algorithms that are now pushing and pulling me through the music library are perfectly suited to finding gems that I'll like. My worry originally about such algorithms was that they might drive everyone into certain parts of the library, leaving others lacking listeners. Would they cause a convergence of tastes? But thanks to the nonlinear and chaotic mathematics usually behind them, this doesn't happen. A small divergence in my likes compared to yours can <u>send us off into different far corners of the library</u>.

*rut: 관습, 틀 **gem: 보석 ***divergence: 갈라짐

① lead us to music selected to suit our respective tastes
② enable us to build connections with other listeners
③ encourage us to request frequent updates for algorithms
④ motivate us to search for talented but unknown musicians
⑤ make us ignore our preferences for particular music genres

04 다음 글의 제목으로 가장 적절한 것은?

Moral philosophy textbooks often proclaim that we can discern if a claim is ethical by attending to the use of the words "is" and "ought." On this suggestion, the claim "You ought to keep your promises," because it uses "ought," is ethical. "An atom is small," because it uses "is," is nonethical. Yet, despite being commonly invoked, this is-ought test is seriously deficient. Some is-statements have ethical content and some ought-statements do not. For example, consider the claims "Murder is wrong" and "Friendship is good." These claims obviously have ethical content. Whatever the is-ought test is tracking, these claims clearly fall on the ought side of that divide. Yet they both use "is." Similarly, consider the claim "The train ought to arrive in an hour." This statement is clearly nonethical, the use of "ought" notwithstanding. There is an important distinction between ethical and nonethical claims. But we can't simply rely on "is" and "ought" to make it. Instead we need to attend to the substance of the claim.

*invoke: 예로서 인용하다

① Mutually Exclusive Relationship Between "Is" and "Ought"
② Sounds Unethical to You? Check Your Moral Standard First
③ What Determines Ethicality of a Claim, Word Choice or Content?
④ How We Can Get to Harmony of Linguistic Forms and Functions
⑤ To Use "Is" or "Ought," That Is the Key to Ethical Statements!

05 Charles Rosen에 관한 다음 글의 내용과 일치하지 않는 것은?

Charles Rosen, a virtuoso pianist and distinguished writer, was born in New York in 1927. Rosen displayed a remarkable talent for the piano from his early childhood. In 1951, the year he earned his doctoral degree in French literature at Princeton University, Rosen made both his New York piano debut and his first recordings. To glowing praise, he appeared in numerous recitals and orchestral concerts around the world. Rosen's performances impressed some of the 20th century's most well-known composers, who invited him to play their music. Rosen was also the author of many widely admired books about music. His most famous book, *The Classical Style*, was first published in 1971 and won the U.S. National Book Award the next year. This work, which was reprinted in an expanded edition in 1997, remains a landmark in the field. While writing extensively, Rosen continued to perform as a pianist for the rest of his life until he died in 2012.

① 어려서부터 피아노에 재능을 보였다.
② 프랑스 문학으로 박사 학위를 받았다.
③ 유명 작곡가들로부터 그들의 작품 연주를 요청받았다.
④ *The Classical Style*이 처음으로 출판되고 다음 해에 상을 받았다.
⑤ 피아니스트 활동을 중단하고 글쓰기에 매진하였다.

06 다음 글의 밑줄 친 부분 중, 문맥상 낱말의 쓰임이 적절하지 않은 것은?

Technology has historically distinguished the way music is produced. In a live jazz concert a bass player can provide the audience with a ten-minute jam session but is ① <u>unable</u> to do so if making a record. Time and space limits on early discs made this liberalized performance style impossible. Often, pieces would be separated into a number of discs leading to a ② <u>lack</u> of continuity. In addition to length, musicians had to take into account how the machinery recorded and absorbed their sound. Especially in the early days of recording, human voices as well as instruments were often distorted once recorded. To prevent such distortion, it was up to the musician to ③ <u>alter</u> the sound to accommodate the recording technology that was just coming into existence. Jazz musicians and orchestras almost molded their works around recording parameters. Many musicians were ④ <u>resistant</u> to the limitations and benefits of technology and created their records accordingly. The recording limitations began to filter into stage performance. Musicians were restricted to three-minute songs in the recording studio and they soon ⑤ <u>kept</u> their songs to that length on stage too.

*jam session: 즉흥 연주 **mold: (틀에 맞추어) 만들다
***parameter: 한도, 기준

07 다음 빈칸에 들어갈 말로 가장 적절한 것은?

The growth of academic disciplines and sub-disciplines, such as art history or palaeontology, and of particular figures such as the art critic, helped produce principles and practices for selecting and organizing what was worthy of keeping, though it remained a struggle. Moreover, as museums and universities drew further apart toward the end of the nineteenth century, and as the idea of objects as a highly valued route to knowing the world went into decline, collecting began to lose its status as a worthy intellectual pursuit, especially in the sciences. The really interesting and important aspects of science were increasingly those invisible to the naked eye, and the classification of things collected no longer promised to produce cutting-edge knowledge. The term "butterfly collecting" could come to be used with the adjective "mere" to indicate a pursuit of ________________ academic status.

*palaeontology: 고생물학 **adjective: 형용사

① competitive
② novel
③ secondary
④ reliable
⑤ unconditional

08 다음 빈칸에 들어갈 말로 가장 적절한 것은?

Fans feel for feeling's own sake. They make meanings beyond what seems to be on offer. They build identities and experiences, and make artistic creations of their own to share with others. A person can be an individual fan, feeling an "idealized connection with a star, strong feelings of memory and nostalgia," and engaging in activities like "collecting to develop a sense of self." But, more often, individual experiences are embedded in social contexts where other people with shared attachments socialize around the object of their affections. Much of the pleasure of fandom ________________________________. In their diaries, Bostonians of the 1800s described being part of the crowds at concerts as part of the pleasure of attendance. A compelling argument can be made that what fans love is less the object of their fandom than the attachments to (and differentiations from) one another that those affections afford.

*embed: 끼워 넣다 **compelling: 강력한

① is enhanced by collaborations between global stars
② results from frequent personal contact with a star
③ deepens as fans age together with their idols
④ comes from being connected to other fans
⑤ is heightened by stars' media appearances

09 다음 글에서 전체 흐름과 관계 <u>없는</u> 문장은?

When approaching practical music making for the first time in the classroom, it is a good idea to avoid using instruments altogether. ① This will allow an inexperienced teacher to focus on the development of fundamental musical behaviour through listening, performing and composing; and allow the children to focus on the more controllable sound sources i.e. voices and body percussion (clapping, clicking, stamping etc). ② Music starts with these both developmentally and historically: the most expressive and immediate musical instrument is the human voice. ③ The sound quality of an instrument is a direct result of the quality of the materials, design, and making. ④ Body movements are not only an instinctive response to music but also instigate music making. ⑤ Activities which develop many of the coordination skills, aural sensitivity, responses to visual cues and symbols, and the musical understanding necessary to play an instrument can all be established without instruments.

*instigate: 부추기다   **coordination: 조정

10 주어진 글 다음에 이어질 글의 순서로 가장 적절한 것은?

Bipedalism, upright walking, started a chain of enormous evolutionary adjustments. It liberated hominin arms for carrying weapons and for taking food to group sites instead of consuming it on the spot. But bipedalism was necessary to trigger hand dexterity and tool use.

(A) This creates the ability to use each digit independently in the complex manipulations required for tool use. But without bipedalism it would be impossible to use the trunk for leverage in accelerating the hand during toolmaking and tool use.

(B) Hashimoto and co-workers concluded that adaptations underlying tool use evolved independently of those required for human bipedalism because in both humans and monkeys, each finger is represented separately in the primary sensorimotor cortex, just as the fingers are physically separated in the hand.

(C) Bipedalism also freed the mouth and teeth to develop a more complex call system as the prerequisite of language. These developments required larger brains whose energy cost eventually reached three times the level for chimpanzees, accounting for up to one-sixth of the total basal metabolic rate.

*hominin: 호미닌(인간의 조상으로 분류되는 종족)
**dexterity: (손)재주   ***sensorimotor cortex: 감각 운동 피질

① (A) – (C) – (B)　　② (B) – (A) – (C)
③ (B) – (C) – (A)　　④ (C) – (A) – (B)
⑤ (C) – (B) – (A)

2022 3월 35번　　정답률 51%　　　　2022 10월 37번　　정답률 31%

11 글의 흐름으로 보아, 주어진 문장이 들어가기에 가장 적절한 곳은?

On top of the hurdles introduced in accessing his or her money, if a suspected fraud is detected, the account holder has to deal with the phone call asking if he or she made the suspicious transactions.

Each new wave of technology is intended to enhance user convenience, as well as improve security, but sometimes these do not necessarily go hand-in-hand. For example, the transition from magnetic stripe to embedded chip slightly slowed down transactions, sometimes frustrating customers in a hurry. (①) Make a service too burdensome, and the potential customer will go elsewhere. (②) This obstacle applies at several levels. (③) Passwords, double-key identification, and biometrics such as fingerprint-, iris-, and voice recognition are all ways of keeping the account details hidden from potential fraudsters, of keeping your data dark. (④) But they all inevitably add a burden to the use of the account. (⑤) This is all useful at some level—indeed, it can be reassuring knowing that your bank is keeping alert to protect you—but it becomes tiresome if too many such calls are received.

*fraud: 사기

12 다음 글의 내용을 한 문장으로 요약하고자 한다. 빈칸 (A), (B)에 들어갈 말로 가장 적절한 것은?

The idea that *planting* trees could have a social or political significance appears to have been invented by the English, though it has since spread widely. According to Keith Thomas's history *Man and the Natural World*, seventeenth- and eighteenth-century aristocrats began planting hardwood trees, usually in lines, to declare the extent of their property and the permanence of their claim to it. "What can be more pleasant," the editor of a magazine for gentlemen asked his readers, "than to have the bounds and limits of your own property preserved and continued from age to age by the testimony of such living and growing witnesses?" Planting trees had the additional advantage of being regarded as a patriotic act, for the Crown had declared a severe shortage of the hardwood on which the Royal Navy depended.

*aristocrat: 귀족 **patriotic: 애국적인

↓

For English aristocrats, planting trees served as statements to mark the ___(A)___ ownership of their land, and it was also considered to be a(n) ___(B)___ of their loyalty to the nation.

(A)		(B)
① unstable	······	confirmation
② unstable	······	exaggeration
③ lasting	······	exhibition
④ lasting	······	manipulation
⑤ official	······	justification

13~14 다음 글을 읽고, 물음에 답하시오.

Once an event is noticed, an onlooker must decide if it is truly an emergency. Emergencies are not always clearly (a) <u>labeled</u> as such; "smoke" pouring into a waiting room may be caused by fire, or it may merely indicate a leak in a steam pipe. Screams in the street may signal an attack or a family quarrel. A man lying in a doorway may be having a coronary—or he may simply be sleeping off a drunk. A person trying to interpret a situation often looks at those around him to see how he should react. If everyone else is calm and indifferent, he will tend to remain so; if everyone else is reacting strongly, he is likely to become alert. This tendency is not merely blind conformity; ordinarily we derive much valuable information about new situations from how others around us behave. It's a (b) <u>rare</u> traveler who, in picking a roadside restaurant, chooses to stop at one where no other cars appear in the parking lot. But occasionally the reactions of others provide (c) <u>accurate</u> information. The studied nonchalance of patients in a dentist's waiting room is a poor indication of their inner anxiety. It is considered embarrassing to "lose your cool" in public. In a potentially acute situation, then, everyone present will appear more (d) <u>unconcerned</u> than he is in fact. A crowd can thus force (e) <u>inaction</u> on its members by implying, through its passivity, that an event is not an emergency. Any individual in such a crowd fears that he may appear a fool if he behaves as though it were.

*coronary: 관상 동맥증   **nonchalance: 무관심, 냉담

제목 추론

13 윗글의 제목으로 가장 적절한 것은?

① Do We Judge Independently? The Effect of Crowds
② Winning Strategy: How Not to Be Fooled by Others
③ Do Emergencies Affect the Way of Our Thinking?
④ Stepping Towards Harmony with Your Neighbors
⑤ Ways of Helping Others in Emergent Situations

어휘 추론

14 밑줄 친 (a)~(e) 중에서 문맥상 낱말의 쓰임이 적절하지 <u>않은</u> 것은?

① (a)
② (b)
③ (c)
④ (d)
⑤ (e)

2022 6월 41~42번

13 정답률 47%   **14** 정답률 39%

정답 p. 78

단어 TEST ●　주어진 단어의 뜻을 쓰고, 예문을 올바르게 해석하세요.

	단어	뜻	예문	해석
1	**impending**	임박한, 곧 닥칠	impending terror	(임박한) 공포
2	**precede**		preceding images	( ) 이미지들
3	**convergence**		a convergence of tastes	취향의 ( )
4	**mutually exclusive**		a mutually exclusive relationship	( ) 관계
5	**glowing praise**		to glowing praise	( ) 속에
6	**continuity**		a lack of continuity	( )의 결여
7	**secondary**		a secondary status	( ) 지위
8	**attachment**		shared attachments	공유된 ( )
9	**prerequisite**		the prerequisite of language	언어의 ( )
10	**frustrate**		frustrate customers	고객들을 ( )
11	**permanence**		the permanence of their claim	그들의 권리의 ( )
12	**conformity**		blind conformity	맹목적인 ( )

구문 TEST ●　주어진 단어를 활용하여 우리말에 맞게 빈칸을 완성하세요.

13　**It was (** much more convenient than expected **).**
much / convenient / than expected
그것은 예상했던 것보다 훨씬 더 편리했다.

14　**She felt (** **) with her.**
as if / the counselor / in the room
그녀는 마치 상담사가 자신과 함께 그 방 안에 있는 듯한 기분을 느꼈다.

15　**The house looks (** **) last summer.**
as if / be hit / a storm
그 집은 마치 그것이 지난 여름 폭풍우라도 맞았던 것처럼 보인다.

16　**Such a transition slowed down transactions, (** **).**
frustrate / customers in a hurry
이런 전환은 거래를 느려지게 해서, 바쁜 고객을 좌절시켰다.

17　**The rain flooded the main roads, (** **).**
force / seek / alternative routes
비가 대로를 침수시켜서, 사람들이 대체 경로를 찾을 수밖에 없게 만들었다.

18　**Make a service burdensome, (** **).**
the potential customer / go elsewhere
서비스를 부담스럽게 만들라, 그러면 잠재적 고객은 다른 곳으로 갈 것이다.

기출 하프 모의고사

12

● 문제에 나오는 단어들을 확인하세요.

□	regretful	a. 후회하는
□	hindrance	n. 방해
□	specialization	n. 전문화, 특화
□	generality	n. 일반성
□	specificity	n. 특수성
□	vagueness	n. 모호함
□	shallowness	n. 얕음
□	novelty	n. 새로움, 참신함
□	vulnerable	a. (~에) 취약한, 상처받기 쉬운
□	undermine	v. (기반을) 약화시키다
□	subsequent	a. 후속의, 이후의
□	blameworthy	a. 비난받을 만한
□	overstate	v. 과장해서 말하다
□	prestigious	a. 명성 있는
□	incompatibility	n. 상반(된 점), 양립 불가함
□	unsuited	a. 부적합한
□	allocate	v. 할당하다
□	inhabit	v. 살다, 거주하다
□	bear	v. (도움, 증언을) 주다, (아이를) 낳다
□	recollection	n. 기억, 회상
□	interpret A as B	A를 B로 이해하다
□	swiftly	ad. 빠르게
□	restlessly	ad. 쉴새없이
□	unconvinced	a. 확신하지 못하는
□	prehistoric	a. 선사 시대의

□	airborne	a. 공중에 있는, 하늘에 뜬
□	illusion	n. 환상, 착각
□	adhere to	~을 고수하다
□	intuition	n. 직관
□	irresistible	a. 거부[저항]할 수 없는
□	a myriad of	무수히 많은
□	stationary	a. 고정된, 정적인
□	inefficiency	n. 비효율(성)
□	economical	a. 경제적인, 절약하는
□	reference	n. 기준, 준거, 참고
□	paradigm	n. 전형적인 예
□	estimate	v. 추정하다
□	elementary	a. 기초적인
□	coherent	a. 일관된
□	disclose	v. 공개하다, 폭로하다, 드러내다
□	secrecy	n. 비밀(주의), 비밀 유지
□	impassable	a. 통과할 수 없는, 극복할 수 없는
□	dissolve	v. 해체하다
□	regulation	n. 규제
□	permissive	a. 허용적인
□	domination	n. 지배
□	causal relation	인과 관계
□	prosperity	n. 번영
□	superstition	n. 미신
□	illegitimate	a. 부당한

❶ 부사절 축약

Journalists, though (they are) blameworthy for this tendency, are encouraged by the scientists whose studies they cite.

❷ 소유격 관계대명사 whose

(그들이) 이런 경향에 관해 비난받을 만하기는 해도, 저널리스트들은 그들이 인용하는 연구를 한 과학자들에 의해 부추김을 당한다.

첨삭 1 부사절 축약

개　　념 ▶ 시간, 조건, 양보의 부사절에서 <대명사 주어 + be동사>는 함께 생략할 수 있다.

독해전략 ▶ 보통 주절에 대한 부연 설명이므로, 접속사 중심으로 의미를 간단하게 파악한다.

어법전략 ▶ 생략된 be동사의 보어 자리에서 '형용사 vs. 부사', '현재분사 vs. 과거분사'를 잘 판단해야 한다.

다음 중 어법상 옳은 것을 고르세요.

a. Though ｜ tiring ｜ tired ｜ from hours of intense work, she continued to push through her tasks.

b. While ｜ grateful ｜ gratefully ｜, she couldn't help but feel overwhelmed by the sudden attention.

c. Once ｜ receiving ｜ received ｜ by our office, your application will be processed within a week.

첨삭 2 소유격 관계대명사 whose

개　　념 ▶ 앞뒤로 절을 연결하는 동시에 선행사의 소유격을 나타낸다.

독해전략 ▶ whose 앞에서 문장을 끊고, 선행사에 '~의'를 붙여 whose를 해석한다.

어법전략 ▶ 뒷구조가 중요하다. 소유격 관계대명사 뒤는 관사 없는 명사로 시작하는 완전한 구조여야 한다.

다음 중 어법상 옳은 것을 고르세요.

a. Those ｜ who ｜ whose ｜ work reflects a commitment to innovation are often awarded grants.

b. She admires authors ｜ whose ｜ whom ｜ novels explore the complexities of identity and culture.

c. The botanist studies a plant ｜ which ｜ whose ｜ roots have the ability to clean polluted soil.

정답 a. tired b. grateful c. received / a. whose b. whose c. whose

2021 6월 29번

❸ 조동사+have p.p.　　　　❹ 목적의 to부정사

The stones **may even have been used** **to predict** eclipses.

그 돌들은 심지어 (해·달의) 식(蝕)을 예측하는 데 사용되었을지도 모른다.

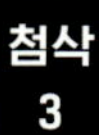

조동사+have p.p.

개　　념 ▶ 조동사 현재형/과거형에 have p.p.를 붙여 과거에 대한 추측이나 후회를 나타낼 수 있다.

독해전략 ▶ <should have p.p.(~했어야 했다)>, <must have p.p.(~했음에 틀림없다)> 등은 숙어처럼 기억해 둔다.

어법전략 ▶ 의미에 따라 조동사를 구별하거나, 동사 뒤에서 '동사원형 vs. have p.p.'를 구별하는 형태로 자주 나온다.

다음 중 어법상 옳은 것을 고르세요.

a. She │ may miss │ **may have missed** │ the first train, which is why she's running late.

b. They │ should check │ **should have checked** │ the weather before they left for the hike.

c. We │ **must have lost** │ should have lost │ the document during the move last weekend.

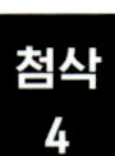

목적의 to부정사

개　　념 ▶ 주절의 목적이나 이유를 밝히는 표현으로, to부정사가 부사구 역할을 하는 대표적인 사례이다.

독해전략 ▶ '~하려면, ~하기 위해' 등으로 해석한다. so as to-V, in order to-V로 써도 같은 의미이다.

어법전략 ▶ 문장 앞, 뒤, 중간에 자유롭게 위치하여 동사와 혼동될 수 있으니 주의해야 한다.

다음 중 어법상 옳은 것을 고르세요.

a. │ See │ **To see** │ the stars more clearly, they drove out of the city and into the countryside.

b. The city, │ increases │ **to increase** │ green spaces for residents, plans to build a new park.

c. We organize monthly meetings in various local venues │ foster │ **to foster** │ community engagement.

정답 **a.** may have missed　**b.** should have checked　**c.** must have lost　/　**a.** To see　**b.** to increase　**c.** to foster

01 다음 글에 드러난 Jamie의 심경 변화로 가장 적절한 것은?

Putting all of her energy into her last steps of the running race, Jamie crossed the finish line. To her disappointment, she had failed to beat her personal best time, again. Jamie had pushed herself for months to finally break her record, but it was all for nothing. Recognizing how she felt about her failure, Ken, her teammate, approached her and said, "Jamie, even though you didn't set a personal best time today, your performances have improved dramatically. Your running skills have progressed so much! You'll definitely break your personal best time in the next race!" After hearing his comments, she felt confident about herself. Jamie, now motivated to keep pushing for her goal, replied with a smile. "You're right! Next race, I'll beat my best time for sure!"

① indifferent → regretful
② pleased → bored
③ frustrated → encouraged
④ nervous → fearful
⑤ calm → excited

02 다음 글에서 필자가 주장하는 바로 가장 적절한 것은?

Certain hindrances to multifaceted creative activity may lie in premature specialization, i.e., having to choose the direction of education or to focus on developing one ability too early in life. However, development of creative ability in one domain may enhance effectiveness in other domains that require similar skills, and flexible switching between generality and specificity is helpful to productivity in many domains. Excessive specificity may result in information from outside the domain being underestimated and unavailable, which leads to fixedness of thinking, whereas excessive generality causes chaos, vagueness, and shallowness. Both tendencies pose a threat to the transfer of knowledge and skills between domains. What should therefore be optimal for the development of cross-domain creativity is support for young people in taking up creative challenges in a specific domain and coupling it with encouragement to apply knowledge and skills in, as well as from, other domains, disciplines, and tasks.

① 창의성을 개발하기 위해서는 도전과 실패를 두려워하지 말아야 한다.
② 전문 지식과 기술을 전수하려면 집중적인 투자가 선행되어야 한다.
③ 창의적인 인재를 육성하기 위해 다양한 교육과정을 준비해야 한다.
④ 특정 영역에서 개발된 창의성이 영역 간 활용되도록 장려해야 한다.
⑤ 조기 교육을 통해 특정 분야의 전문가를 지속적으로 양성해야 한다.

2023학년도 수능 19번   정답률 91%

2023 6월 20번   정답률 83%

03 밑줄 친 news 'happens'가 다음 글에서 의미하는 바로 가장 적절한 것은?

Journalists love to report studies that are at the "initial findings" stages—research that claims to be the first time anyone has discovered a thing—because there is newsworthiness in their novelty. But "first ever" discoveries are extremely vulnerable to becoming undermined by subsequent research. When that happens, the news media often don't go back and inform their audiences about the change—assuming they even hear about it. Kelly Crowe, a CBC News reporter writes, quoting one epidemiologist, "There is increasing concern that in modern research, false findings may be the majority or even the vast majority of published research claims." She goes on to suggest that journalists, though blameworthy for this tendency, are aided and abetted by the scientists whose studies they cite. She writes that the "conclusions" sections in scientific abstracts can sometimes be overstated in an attempt to draw attention from prestigious academic journals and media who uncritically take their bait. Even so, Crowe ends her piece by stressing that there is still an incompatibility between the purposes and processes of news and science: Science 'evolves,' but news 'happens.'

*epidemiologist: 전염병학자
**aid and abet: 방조하다

① News follows the process of research more than the outcome.
② News focuses not on how research changes but on the novelty of it.
③ News attracts attention by criticizing false scientific discoveries.
④ Reporters give instant feedback to their viewers, unlike scientists.
⑤ Reporters create and strengthen trust in the importance of science.

04 다음 글의 주제로 가장 적절한 것은?

Difficulties arise when we do not think of people and machines as collaborative systems, but assign whatever tasks can be automated to the machines and leave the rest to people. This ends up requiring people to behave in machine-like fashion, in ways that differ from human capabilities. We expect people to monitor machines, which means keeping alert for long periods, something we are bad at. We require people to do repeated operations with the extreme precision and accuracy required by machines, again something we are not good at. When we divide up the machine and human components of a task in this way, we fail to take advantage of human strengths and capabilities but instead rely upon areas where we are genetically, biologically unsuited. Yet, when people fail, they are blamed.

① difficulties of overcoming human weaknesses to avoid failure
② benefits of allowing machines and humans to work together
③ issues of allocating unfit tasks to humans in automated systems
④ reasons why humans continue to pursue machine automation
⑤ influences of human actions on a machine's performance

05 다음 표의 내용과 일치하지 <u>않는</u> 것은?

Resident Patent Applications per Million Population for the Top 6 Origins, in 2009 and in 2019

2009			2019		
Rank	Origin	Resident patent applications per million population	Rank	Origin	Resident patent applications per million population
1	Republic of Korea	2,582	1	Republic of Korea	3,319
2	Japan	2,306	2	Japan	1,943
3	Switzerland	975	3	Switzerland	1,122
4	Germany	891	4	China	890
5	U.S.	733	5	Germany	884
6	Finland	609	6	U.S.	869

Note: The top 6 origins were included if they had a population greater than 5 million and if they had more than 100 resident patent applications.

The above tables show the resident patent applications per million population for the top 6 origins in 2009 and in 2019. ① The Republic of Korea, Japan, and Switzerland, the top three origins in 2009, maintained their rankings in 2019. ② Germany, which sat fourth on the 2009 list with 891 resident patent applications per million population, fell to fifth place on the 2019 list with 884 resident patent applications per million population. ③ The U.S. fell from fifth place on the 2009 list to sixth place on the 2019 list, showing a decrease in the number of resident patent applications per million population. ④ Among the top 6 origins which made the list in 2009, Finland was the only origin which did not make it again in 2019. ⑤ On the other hand, China, which did not make the list of the top 6 origins in 2009, sat fourth on the 2019 list with 890 resident patent applications per million population.

06 다음 글의 밑줄 친 부분 중, 어법상 틀린 것은?

Most historians of science point to the need for a reliable calendar to regulate agricultural activity as the motivation for learning about what we now call astronomy, the study of stars and planets. Early astronomy provided information about when to plant crops and gave humans ① <u>their</u> first formal method of recording the passage of time. Stonehenge, the 4,000-year-old ring of stones in southern Britain, ② <u>is</u> perhaps the best-known monument to the discovery of regularity and predictability in the world we inhabit. The great markers of Stonehenge point to the spots on the horizon ③ <u>where</u> the sun rises at the solstices and equinoxes—the dates we still use to mark the beginnings of the seasons. The stones may even have ④ <u>been used</u> to predict eclipses. The existence of Stonehenge, built by people without writing, bears silent testimony both to the regularity of nature and to the ability of the human mind to see behind immediate appearances and ⑤ <u>discovers</u> deeper meanings in events.

*monument: 기념비 **eclipse: (해·달의) 식(蝕)
***testimony: 증언

2022 6월 25번   정답률 90%

2021 6월 29번   정답률 44%

07 다음 빈칸에 들어갈 말로 가장 적절한 것은?

Science shows that _______________________ like gear teeth in a bicycle chain. Rich and novel experiences, like the recollections of the summers of our youth, have lots of new information associated with them. During those hot days, we learned how to swim or traveled to new places or mastered riding a bike without training wheels. The days went by slowly with those adventures. Yet, our adult lives have less novelty and newness, and are full of repeated tasks such as commuting or sending email or doing paperwork. The associated information filed for those chores is smaller, and there is less new footage for the recall part of the brain to draw upon. Our brain interprets these days filled with boring events as shorter, so summers swiftly speed by. Despite our desire for better clocks, our measuring stick of time isn't fixed. We don't measure time with seconds, like our clocks, but by our experiences. For us, time can slow down or time can fly.

*footage: 장면

① the memory functions of our brain wear out with age
② the richness of experiences relies on intellectual capacity
③ the information storage system in our mind runs restlessly
④ the temporal context of an event pulls our emotions awake
⑤ the size of a memory and our perception of time are coupled

08 다음 빈칸에 들어갈 말로 가장 적절한 것은?

If you are unconvinced that _______________________, consider the example of the "flying horse." Depictions of galloping horses from prehistoric times up until the mid-1800s typically showed horses' legs splayed while galloping, that is, the front legs reaching far ahead as the hind legs stretched far behind. People just "knew" that's how horses galloped, and that is how they "saw" them galloping. Cavemen *saw* them this way, Aristotle *saw* them this way, and so did Victorian gentry. But all of that ended when, in 1878, Eadweard Muybridge published a set of twelve pictures he had taken of a galloping horse in the space of less than half a second using twelve cameras hooked to wire triggers. Muybridge's photos showed clearly that a horse goes completely airborne in the third step of the gallop with its legs *collected* beneath it, not splayed. It is called the moment of suspension. Now even kids draw horses galloping this way.

*gallop: 질주(하다) **splay: 벌리다
***gentry: 상류층

① our beliefs influence how we interpret facts
② what we see is an illusion of our past memories
③ even photographs can lead to a wrong visual perception
④ there is no standard by which we can judge good or bad
⑤ we adhere to our intuition in spite of irresistible evidence

09 다음 글에서 전체 흐름과 관계 <u>없는</u> 문장은?

Some forms of energy are more versatile in their usefulness than others. For example, we can use electricity for a myriad of applications, whereas the heat from burning coal is currently used mostly for stationary applications like generating power. ① When we turn the heat from burning coal into electricity, a substantial amount of energy is lost due to the inefficiency of the process. ② But we are willing to accept that loss because coal is relatively cheap, and it would be difficult and inconvenient to use burning coal directly to power lights, computers, and refrigerators. ③ Finding an economical way to use coal to produce carbon fibers will help revitalize rural communities suffering from the decline in coal production. ④ In effect, we put a differing value on different forms of energy, with electricity at the top of the value ladder, liquid and gaseous fuels in the middle, and coal or firewood at the bottom. ⑤ Solar and wind technologies have an advantage in that they produce high-value electricity directly.

*versatile: 다용도의

10 주어진 글 다음에 이어질 글의 순서로 가장 적절한 것은?

Spatial reference points are larger than themselves. This isn't really a paradox: landmarks are themselves, but they also define neighborhoods around themselves.

(A) In a paradigm that has been repeated on many campuses, researchers first collect a list of campus landmarks from students. Then they ask another group of students to estimate the distances between pairs of locations, some to landmarks, some to ordinary buildings on campus.

(B) This asymmetry of distance estimates violates the most elementary principles of Euclidean distance, that the distance from A to B must be the same as the distance from B to A. Judgments of distance, then, are not necessarily coherent.

(C) The remarkable finding is that distances from an ordinary location to a landmark are judged shorter than distances from a landmark to an ordinary location. So, people would judge the distance from Pierre's house to the Eiffel Tower to be shorter than the distance from the Eiffel Tower to Pierre's house. Like black holes, landmarks seem to pull ordinary locations toward themselves, but ordinary places do not.

*asymmetry: 비대칭

① (A) – (C) – (B) ② (B) – (A) – (C)
③ (B) – (C) – (A) ④ (C) – (A) – (B)
⑤ (C) – (B) – (A)

2022 7월 35번　정답률 55%　　2021 6월 36번　정답률 23%

11 글의 흐름으로 보아, 주어진 문장이 들어가기에 가장 적절한 곳은?

> Without any special legal protection for trade secrets, however, the secretive inventor risks that an employee or contractor will disclose the proprietary information.

Trade secret law aims to promote innovation, although it accomplishes this objective in a very different manner than patent protection. (①) Notwithstanding the advantages of obtaining a patent, many innovators prefer to protect their innovation through secrecy. (②) They may believe that the cost and delay of seeking a patent are too great or that secrecy better protects their investment and increases their profit. (③) They might also believe that the invention can best be utilized over a longer period of time than a patent would allow. (④) Once the idea is released, it will be "free as the air" under the background norms of a free market economy. (⑤) Such a predicament would lead any inventor seeking to rely upon secrecy to spend an inordinate amount of resources building high and impassable fences around their research facilities and greatly limiting the number of people with access to the proprietary information.

*patent: 특허 **predicament: 곤경

12 다음 글의 내용을 한 문장으로 요약하고자 한다. 빈칸 (A), (B)에 들어갈 말로 가장 적절한 것은?

> The rise of large, industrial cities has had social consequences that are often known as urbanism. The city dissolves the informal controls of the village or small town. Most urban residents are unknown to one another, and most social interactions in cities occur between people who know each other only in specific roles, such as parking attendant, store clerk, or customer. Individuals became more free to live as they wished, and in ways that break away from social norms. In response, and because the high density of city living requires the pliant coordination of many thousands of people, urban societies have developed a wide range of methods to control urban behavior. These include regulations that control private land use, building construction and maintenance (to minimize fire risk), and the production of pollution and noise.
>
> *pliant: 유순한

↓

> The social conditions in large, industrial cities made urban societies ___(A)___ the informal controls of the village or small town, introducing ___(B)___ measures to effectively induce coordinated urban behaviors.

	(A)		(B)
①	limit	⋯⋯	permissive
②	maintain	⋯⋯	restrictive
③	evaluate	⋯⋯	indirect
④	remove	⋯⋯	restrictive
⑤	reinforce	⋯⋯	permissive

13~14 다음 글을 읽고, 물음에 답하시오.

The domination of nature is a familiar trope in environmental ethics and environmental political theory. Its history is tied more broadly to the rise of modern science, philosophy, and politics. The effort to understand the causal relations that govern the physical world so as to intervene in these relations in ways that could, as Francis Bacon put it, "ameliorate the human condition," marked the beginning of modernity in the West. For a long time, the "domination of nature" referred to this effort to understand and (a) control the nonhuman environment, and it was seen as a clearly good thing. This effort made (b) possible new technologies and rising economic prosperity, promised an end to many forms of human suffering, and demonstrated the triumph of reason over ignorance and superstition. Its costs began to be (c) invisible with industrialization in the nineteenth century, which generated obvious environmental damage and caused among many people a sense of alienation from the land and the more-than-human communities composing it. One sees a growing (d) unease about these costs in novels of the era such as Mary Shelley's *Frankenstein* (1818), in poems like Wordsworth's "Michael" (1800) and later Whitman's *Leaves of Grass* (1855), and in the early nature writing of Thoreau's *Walden* (1854). Yet systematic, critical analysis of the domination of nature as a problem came into its own only with the environmental studies movement in the 1970s. Since then, the trope has come to have a broadly (e) negative meaning, with the domination of nature being viewed as harmful and illegitimate, as well as dangerous to human interests.

*trope: 수사적 표현   **ameliorate: 개선하다

제목 추론

13 윗글의 제목으로 가장 적절한 것은?

① Changing Perspectives on the Domination of Nature
② Science Starts from a Desire for Knowledge
③ Ethics Is Central to Every Discipline
④ Nature in Literature Is Not Real
⑤ Is Going Green Really Green?

어휘 추론

14 밑줄 친 (a)~(e) 중에서 문맥상 낱말의 쓰임이 적절하지 <u>않은</u> 것은?

① (a)
② (b)
③ (c)
④ (d)
⑤ (e)

2023 10월 41~42번

13 정답률 84%   14 정답률 54%

정답 p. 85

단어 TEST ● 주어진 단어의 뜻을 쓰고, 예문을 올바르게 해석하세요.

1	**regretful**	후회하는	feel regretful	(후회하는) 기분이 들다
2	**novelty**		the novelty of news	뉴스의 ( )
3	**undermine**		undermine the discovery	발견의 기반을 ( )
4	**allocate**		allocate unfit tasks to humans	인간에게 부적합한 과제를 ( )
5	**restlessly**		run restlessly	( ) 돌아가다
6	**unconvinced**		be unconvinced	( )
7	**adhere to**		adhere to our intuition	우리의 직관을 ( )
8	**irresistible**		irresistible evidence	( ) 증거
9	**coherent**		coherent judgments	( ) 판단
10	**dissolve**		dissolve the informal controls	비공식적인 통제를 ( )
11	**prosperity**		economic prosperity	경제적 ( )
12	**illegitimate**		harmful and illegitimate	해롭고 ( )

구문 TEST ● 주어진 단어를 활용하여 우리말에 맞게 빈칸을 완성하세요.

13 (Though (she was) tired), she continued to push through her tasks.
though / tired
피곤했지만, 그녀는 일을 계속했다.

14 ( ), your application will be processed within a week.
once / receive
저희 사무실에 의해 접수되면, 귀하의 신청서는 일주일 이내에 처리됩니다.

15 She admires authors ( ).
novels / explore / identity / culture
그녀는 그들의 소설이 정체성과 문화를 탐구하는 작가들을 존경한다.

16 The stones ( ).
may / use / predict / eclipses
그 돌들은 (해·달의) 식을 예측하기 위해 사용되었을지도 모른다.

17 We ( ) during the move last weekend.
may / lose / the document
우리는 지난 주말 이사하다가 그 문서를 잃어버렸는지도 모른다.

18 ( ), they drove into the countryside.
see / clearly
그 별들을 더 분명하게 보기 위해, 그들은 시골로 차를 몰았다.

기출 하프 모의고사

13

● 문제에 나오는 단어들을 확인하세요.

☐	unclaimed	a. 주인이 나서지 않은	☐ fuel	v. 부추기다
☐	safekeeping	n. 보관	☐ suburban	a. 교외의, 근교의
☐	genuinely	ad. 진심으로, 진짜로	☐ downfall	n. 몰락
☐	one-off	a. 일회성의	☐ privatization	n. 사유화, 민영화
☐	delightful	a. 즐거운, 기쁜	☐ autobiographical	a. 자전적인
☐	favorable	a. 호의적인	☐ regularity	n. 규칙성
☐	ownership	n. 소유(권)	☐ bent on	~에 열중하는
☐	metaphor	n. 비유, 은유	☐ argumentation	n. 논쟁, 논증
☐	in reference to	~에 관해	☐ be comprised of	~로 구성되다
☐	make up	~을 구성하다	☐ involuntary	a. 자기도 모르게 하는
☐	give away	증여하다, 거저 주다	☐ embarrassment	n. 당혹, 난처
☐	split up	쪼개다, 나누다	☐ loss of face	체면 손상
☐	plumber	n. 배관공	☐ awkward	a. 어색한
☐	party	n. 관계자, (이해) 당사자	☐ bring on	~을 야기하다, 초래하다
☐	claim	v. (권리를) 주장하다	☐ lay off	~을 해고하다
☐	by definition	당연히	☐ ease	v. 완화하다 n. 쉬움, 편안함
☐	shelf life	유통 기한	☐ under-documented	a. 문서로 덜 기록된
☐	readiness	n. 준비(된 상태)	☐ flesh	n. 살
☐	spectacle	n. 구경거리, 장관	☐ bare	a. 맨, 벌거벗은
☐	orphanage	n. 보육원, 고아원	☐ insufficient	a. 불충분한
☐	attending	a. (의사로서) 병원에 소속된	☐ enrich	v. 풍부하게 하다
☐	legislature	n. 의회, 입법 기관	☐ clarification	n. 해명, 설명
☐	replacement	n. 보충, 대체	☐ controversy	n. 논란(의 여지)
☐	extraction	n. 추출	☐ misquote	v. 잘못 인용하다
☐	equivalent	a. 상응하는, 등가의	☐ media coverage	언론 보도

❶ 명령문　　　　　　　❷ 가정법 과거

Think about what it **would feel like** **if** you **were** personally **acknowledged by the brand manager**, for example.

예컨대 여러분이 브랜드 관리자로부터 개인적으로 인정받는다면 기분이 어떨지 생각해보라.

첨삭 1

명령문

개　념 ▶ 고정된 주어 You를 생략하고, 동사원형으로 문장을 시작해 '~하라'는 의미를 나타낸다.

독해전략 ▶ 주로 글의 주제를 제시하지만, think/imagine/suppose/consider 등으로 시작해 예를 들 때도 많다.

어법전략 ▶ 동사원형을 to부정사나 동명사와 비교하는 패턴으로 자주 출제된다.

다음 중 어법상 옳은 것을 고르세요.

a. **Avoid** **Avoiding** walking alone at night in areas without adequate lighting.

b. **To wash** **Wash** the vegetables thoroughly before chopping them into pieces.

c. **Capture** **To capture** the audience's attention, start your presentation with a personal story.

첨삭 2

가정법 과거

개　념 ▶ <if+주어+과거 동사/were ~, 주어+조동사 과거형+동사원형 ~>의 형태로, '현재' 사실이 아닌 것을 가정한다.

독해전략 ▶ '(실제 ~하지 않지만) 만일 ~한다면' 어떨지에 대한 가정이 주제를 어떻게 뒷받침하는지 파악해 본다.

어법전략 ▶ '과거'의 반대를 말하는 가정법 과거완료(if+주어+had p.p. ~, 주어+조동사 과거형+have p.p)와 구별한다.

다음 중 어법상 옳은 것을 고르세요.

a. If I **am** **were** a millionaire, I would donate a significant portion to charity.

b. If we lived closer, we **would see** **will see** each other more often.

c. If she **spoke** **had spoken** Spanish, she could communicate with the locals during her trip to Spain.

정답 a. Avoid b. Wash c. To capture / a. were b. would see c. spoke

2023 9월 40번

❸ 혼합가정법

If producers of historical fiction had strongly held the strict academic standards, many historical subjects would remain unexplored for lack of appropriate evidence.

❹ remain+형용사

역사 소설 제작자들이 엄격한 학술적 기준을 강력히 고수했었다면, 많은 역사적 주제는 적절한 증거 부족으로 탐구되지 못한 채로 남아 있을 것이다.

 첨삭 3

혼합가정법

개　　념 ▶ 과거의 행위가 달랐다면 현재의 결과 또한 달랐을 것이라는 후회나 안도를 주로 나타낸다.

독해전략 ▶ 가정법 과거와 마찬가지로, 주제를 뒷받침하는 진술로 많이 활용된다.

어법전략 ▶ 종속절은 가정법 과거완료(if+주어+had p.p.), 주절은 가정법 과거(주어+조동사 과거형+동사원형)의 형태이다.

다음 중 어법상 옳은 것을 고르세요.

a. If I | accepted | **had accepted** | that job offer abroad last year, I wouldn't be stuck in this career now.

b. If we had addressed the climate crisis earlier, we | won't | **wouldn't** | face such severe weather now.

c. If you had said sorry back then, our relationship might | be | **have been** | in a better place today.

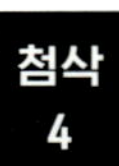 첨삭 4

remain+형용사

개　　념 ▶ '계속 ~한 상태이다'라는 의미의 2형식 구문이다. keep이나 stay도 같은 구조로 쓰인다.

독해전략 ▶ 동사보다는 보어가 의미 파악에 더 중요함을 기억한다.

어법전략 ▶ 여기서 형용사는 주격보어이므로, 형용사 대신 부사를 쓰면 안 된다.

다음 중 어법상 옳은 것을 고르세요.

a. Throughout the investigation, the witness remains | **silent** | silently |, offering no further information.

b. To keep | **safe** | safely | during the trip, the campers followed all recommended precautions.

c. The walls need to stay | covering | **covered** | during the rainy season to ensure the paint lasts longer.

정답 **a.** had accepted **b.** wouldn't **c.** be / **a.** silent **b.** safe **c.** covered

목적 파악

01 다음 글의 목적으로 가장 적절한 것은?

We hope this notice finds you in good health and high spirits. We are writing to inform you that a package was delivered to the Rosehill Apartment Complex on October 9th, specifically addressed to your home. However, despite multiple attempts to deliver the package to you, it has remained unclaimed at our front desk for an extended period. As the management office, it is our responsibility to ensure the safekeeping of all delivered items and help deliver them quickly to the right residents. Therefore, we kindly request that you visit the management office during our office hours to claim your package. We genuinely appreciate your cooperation in this matter.

① 관리 사무실 공사 일정을 알리려고
② 배달된 물품을 찾아갈 것을 요청하려고
③ 잘못 찾아간 물품의 반납을 부탁하려고
④ 배달 물품의 도난 방지 조치를 설명하려고
⑤ 관리 사무실 운영 시간 변경을 공지하려고

요지 파악

02 다음 글의 요지로 가장 적절한 것은?

Being able to prioritize your responses allows you to connect more deeply with individual customers, be it a one-off interaction around a particularly delightful or upsetting experience, or the development of a longer-term relationship with a significantly influential individual within your customer base. If you've ever posted a favorable comment—or any comment, for that matter—about a brand, product or service, think about what it would feel like if you were personally acknowledged by the brand manager, for example, as a result. In general, people post because they have something to say—and because they want to be recognized for having said it. In particular, when people post positive comments they are expressions of appreciation for the experience that led to the post. While a compliment to the person standing next to you is typically answered with a response like "Thank You," the sad fact is that most brand compliments go unanswered. These are lost opportunities to understand what drove the compliments and create a solid fan based on them.

*compliment: 칭찬

① 고객과의 관계 증진을 위해 고객의 브랜드 칭찬에 응답하는 것은 중요하다.
② 고객의 피드백을 면밀히 분석함으로써 브랜드의 성공 가능성을 높일 수 있다.
③ 신속한 고객 응대를 통해서 고객의 긍정적인 반응을 이끌어 낼 수 있다.
④ 브랜드 매니저에게는 고객의 부정적인 의견을 수용하는 태도가 요구된다.
⑤ 고객의 의견을 경청하는 것은 브랜드의 새로운 이미지 창출에 도움이 된다.

함축 의미

03 밑줄 친 a stick in the bundle이 다음 글에서 의미하는 바로 가장 적절한 것은?

Lawyers sometimes describe ownership as a *bundle of sticks*. This metaphor was introduced about a century ago, and it has dramatically transformed the teaching and practice of law. The metaphor is useful because it helps us see ownership as a grouping of interpersonal rights that can be separated and put back together. When you say *It's mine* in reference to a resource, often that means you own a lot of the sticks that make up the full bundle: the sell stick, the rent stick, the right to mortgage, license, give away, even destroy the thing. Often, though, we split the sticks up, as for a piece of land: there may be a landowner, a bank with a mortgage, a tenant with a lease, a plumber with a license to enter the land, an oil company with mineral rights. Each of these parties owns <u>a stick in the bundle</u>.

*mortgage: 저당잡히다   **tenant: 임차인

① a legal obligation to develop the resource
② a priority to legally claim the real estate
③ a right to use one aspect of the property
④ a building to be shared equally by tenants
⑤ a piece of land nobody can claim as their own

04 다음 글의 제목으로 가장 적절한 것은?

Before the web, newspaper archives were largely the musty domain of professional researchers and journalism students. Journalism was, by definition, current. The general accessibility of archives has greatly extended the shelf life of journalism, with older stories now regularly cited to provide context for more current ones. With regard to how meaning is made of complex issues encountered in the news, this departure can be understood as a readiness by online news consumers to engage with the underlying issues and contexts of the news that was not apparent in, or even possible for, print consumers. One of the emergent qualities of online news, determined in part by the depth of readily accessible online archives, seems to be the possibility of understanding news stories as the manifest outcomes of larger economic, social and cultural issues rather than short-lived and unconnected media spectacles.

*archive: 기록 보관소   **musty: 곰팡내 나는
***manifest: 분명한

① Web-based Journalism: Lasting Longer and Contextually Wider
② With the Latest Content, Online News Beats Daily Newspapers!
③ How Online Media Journalists Reveal Hidden Stories Behind News
④ Let's Begin a Journey to the Past with Printed Newspapers!
⑤ Present and Future of Journalism in the Web World

05 Dorothy Lavinia Brown에 관한 다음 글의 내용과 일치하지 <u>않는</u> 것은?

Dorothy Lavinia Brown was the first black female in the American South to become a surgeon. As an infant she was placed in an orphanage. After high school, she won a scholarship to Bennett College, and after graduating there in 1941, she entered Meharry Medical College in Nashville, Tennessee, graduating in 1948. Her medical internship was served at New York's Harlem Hospital but there she encountered gender resistance and was denied residency as a surgeon. She then returned to Meharry and completed her surgical residency in 1954. She later became chief of surgery and educational director of the Riverside-Meharry Clinic in Nashville, as well as an attending surgeon at George W. Hubbard Hospital and a professor of surgery at the Meharry Medical College. In 1966 she became the first African American woman elected to the Tennessee state legislature.

① 미국 남부에서 외과 의사가 된 최초의 흑인 여성이었다.
② 유아일 때 보육원에 맡겨졌다.
③ 고등학교 졸업 후 장학금을 받고 Bennett College에 들어갔다.
④ 뉴욕의 Harlem 병원에서 외과 레지던트 과정을 마쳤다.
⑤ 1966년에 Tennessee 주의회 의원으로 선출되었다.

06 다음 글의 밑줄 친 부분 중, 문맥상 낱말의 쓰임이 적절하지 <u>않은</u> 것은?

In economic systems what takes place in one sector has impacts on another; demand for a good or service in one sector is derived from another. For instance, a consumer buying a good in a store will likely trigger the replacement of this product, which will generate ① <u>demands</u> for activities such as manufacturing, resource extraction and, of course, transport. What is different about transport is that it cannot exist alone and a movement cannot be ② <u>stored</u>. An unsold product can remain on the shelf of a store until bought (often with discount incentives), but an unsold seat on a flight or unused cargo capacity in the same flight remains unsold and cannot be brought back as additional capacity ③ <u>later</u>. In this case an opportunity has been ④ <u>seized</u>, since the amount of transport being offered has exceeded the demand for it. The derived demand of transportation is often very difficult to reconcile with an equivalent supply, and actually transport companies would prefer to have some additional capacity to accommodate ⑤ <u>unforeseen</u> demand (often at much higher prices).

*reconcile: 조화시키다

07 다음 빈칸에 들어갈 말로 가장 적절한 것은?

In the post-World War II years after 1945, unparalleled economic growth fueled a building boom and a massive migration from the central cities to the new suburban areas. The suburbs were far more dependent on the automobile, signaling the shift from primary dependence on public transportation to private cars. Soon this led to the construction of better highways and freeways and the decline and even loss of public transportation. With all of these changes came a ________________ of leisure. As more people owned their own homes, with more space inside and lovely yards outside, their recreation and leisure time was increasingly centered around the home or, at most, the neighborhood. One major activity of this home-based leisure was watching television. No longer did one have to ride the trolly to the theater to watch a movie; similar entertainment was available for free and more conveniently from television.

*unparalleled: 유례없는

① downfall
② uniformity
③ restoration
④ privatization
⑤ customization

08 다음 빈칸에 들어갈 말로 가장 적절한 것은?

In trying to explain how different disciplines attempt to understand autobiographical memory the literary critic Daniel Albright said, "Psychology is a garden, literature is a wilderness." He meant, I believe, that psychology seeks to make patterns, find regularity, and ultimately impose order on human experience and behavior. Writers, by contrast, dive into the unruly, untamed depths of human experiences. What he said about understanding memory can be extended to our questions about young children's minds. If we psychologists are too bent on identifying the orderly pattern, the regularities of children's minds, we may miss an essential and pervasive characteristic of our topic: the child's more unruly and imaginative ways of talking and thinking. It is not only the developed writer or literary scholar who seems drawn toward a somewhat wild and idiosyncratic way of thinking; young children are as well. The psychologist interested in young children may have to _______________________________ in order to get a good picture of how children think.

*unruly: 제멋대로 구는　**pervasive: 널리 퍼져 있는
***idiosyncratic: 색다른

① venture a little more often into the wilderness
② help them recall their most precious memories
③ better understand the challenges of parental duty
④ disregard the key characteristics of children's fiction
⑤ standardize the paths of their psychological development

09 다음 글에서 전체 흐름과 관계 <u>없는</u> 문장은?

Argument is "reason giving", trying to convince others of your side of the issue. One makes claims and backs them up. The arguer tries to get others to "recognize the rightness" of his or her beliefs or actions. ① Interpersonal argumentation, then, has a place in our everyday conflicts and negotiations. ② One of the positive features of interpersonal arguments is that they are comprised of exchanges between two people who feel powerful enough to set forth reasons for their beliefs. ③ That's why one person reveals a sense of superiority and the other ends up realizing his or her inferiority. ④ If two people are arguing, it is because they are balanced enough in power (or in their desire to reestablish a power balance) to proceed. ⑤ Lack of argument, in fact, may show that one of the parties feels so powerless that he or she avoids engaging directly with the other.

10 주어진 글 다음에 이어질 글의 순서로 가장 적절한 것은?

Darwin saw blushing as uniquely human, representing an involuntary physical reaction caused by embarrassment and self-consciousness in a social environment.

(A) Maybe our brief loss of face benefits the long-term cohesion of the group. Interestingly, if someone blushes after making a social mistake, they are viewed in a more favourable light than those who don't blush.

(B) If we feel awkward, embarrassed or ashamed when we are alone, we don't blush; it seems to be caused by our concern about what others are thinking of us. Studies have confirmed that simply being told you are blushing brings it on. We feel as though others can see through our skin and into our mind.

(C) However, while we sometimes want to disappear when we involuntarily go bright red, psychologists argue that blushing actually serves a positive social purpose. When we blush, it's a signal to others that we recognize that a social norm has been broken; it is an apology for a faux pas.

*faux pas: 실수

① (A) – (C) – (B)　　② (B) – (A) – (C)
③ (B) – (C) – (A)　　④ (C) – (A) – (B)
⑤ (C) – (B) – (A)

11 글의 흐름으로 보아, 주어진 문장이 들어가기에 가장 적절한 곳은?

> Retraining current employees for new positions within the company will also greatly reduce their fear of being laid off.

Introduction of robots into factories, while employment of human workers is being reduced, creates worry and fear. (①) It is the responsibility of management to prevent or, at least, to ease these fears. (②) For example, robots could be introduced only in new plants rather than replacing humans in existing assembly lines. (③) Workers should be included in the planning for new factories or the introduction of robots into existing plants, so they can participate in the process. (④) It may be that robots are needed to reduce manufacturing costs so that the company remains competitive, but planning for such cost reductions should be done jointly by labor and management. (⑤) Since robots are particularly good at highly repetitive simple motions, the replaced human workers should be moved to positions where judgment and decisions beyond the abilities of robots are required.

12 다음 글의 내용을 한 문장으로 요약하고자 한다. 빈칸 (A), (B)에 들어갈 말로 가장 적절한 것은?

> Research for historical fiction may focus on under-documented ordinary people, events, or sites. Fiction helps portray everyday situations, feelings, and atmosphere that recreate the historical context. Historical fiction adds "flesh to the bare bones that historians are able to uncover and by doing so provides an account that while not necessarily true provides a clearer indication of past events, circumstances and cultures." Fiction adds color, sound, drama to the past, as much as it invents parts of the past. And Robert Rosenstone argues that invention is not the weakness of films, it is their strength. Fiction can allow users to see parts of the past that have never—for lack of archives—been represented. In fact, Gilden Seavey explains that if producers of historical fiction had strongly held the strict academic standards, many historical subjects would remain unexplored for lack of appropriate evidence. Historical fiction should, therefore, not be seen as the opposite of professional history, but rather as a challenging representation of the past from which both public historians and popular audiences may learn.

↓

> While historical fiction reconstructs the past using ___(A)___ evidence, it provides an inviting description, which may ___(B)___ people's understanding of historical events.

	(A)		(B)
①	insignificant	……	delay
②	insufficient	……	enrich
③	concrete	……	enhance
④	outdated	……	improve
⑤	limited	……	disturb

2022학년도 수능 38번   정답률 25%

2023 9월 40번   정답률 36%

13~14 다음 글을 읽고, 물음에 답하시오.

One way to avoid contributing to overhyping a story would be to say nothing. However, that is not a realistic option for scientists who feel a strong sense of responsibility to inform the public and policymakers and/or to offer suggestions. Speaking with members of the media has (a) <u>advantages</u> in getting a message out and perhaps receiving favorable recognition, but it runs the risk of misinterpretations, the need for repeated clarifications, and entanglement in never-ending controversy. Hence, the decision of whether to speak with the media tends to be highly individualized. Decades ago, it was (b) <u>unusual</u> for Earth scientists to have results that were of interest to the media, and consequently few media contacts were expected or encouraged. In the 1970s, the few scientists who spoke frequently with the media were often (c) <u>criticized</u> by their fellow scientists for having done so. The situation now is quite different, as many scientists feel a responsibility to speak out because of the importance of global warming and related issues, and many reporters share these feelings. In addition, many scientists are finding that they (d) <u>enjoy</u> the media attention and the public recognition that comes with it. At the same time, other scientists continue to resist speaking with reporters, thereby preserving more time for their science and (e) <u>running</u> the risk of being misquoted and the other unpleasantries associated with media coverage.

*overhype: 과대광고하다 **entanglement: 얽힘

13 윗글의 제목으로 가장 적절한 것은?

① The Troubling Relationship Between Scientists and the Media
② A Scientist's Choice: To Be Exposed to the Media or Not?
③ Scientists! Be Cautious When Talking to the Media
④ The Dilemma over Scientific Truth and Media Attention
⑤ Who Are Responsible for Climate Issues, Scientists or the Media?

14 밑줄 친 (a)~(e) 중에서 문맥상 낱말의 쓰임이 적절하지 <u>않은</u> 것은?

① (a)
② (b)
③ (c)
④ (d)
⑤ (e)

2024학년도 수능 41~42번

13 정답률 44% **14** 정답률 42%

정답 p. 92

단어 TEST ● 주어진 단어의 뜻을 쓰고, 예문을 올바르게 해석하세요.

1	**unclaimed**	주인이 나서지 않은	remain unclaimed	(주인이 나서지 않은) 채로 남아 있다
2	**in reference to**		in reference to a resource	어떤 자원에 ( )
3	**make up**		make up the full bundle	전체 다발을 ( )
4	**plumber**		a plumber with a license to enter the land	토지 진입 면허를 가진 ( )
5	**claim**		legally claim the real estate	법적으로 그 부동산에 대한 권리를 ( )
6	**extraction**		resource extraction	자원 ( )
7	**bent on**		bent on identifying the orderly pattern	질서 있는 패턴을 밝히는 데 ( )
8	**be comprised of**		be comprised of exchanges	언쟁으로 ( )
9	**involuntary**		an involuntary physical reaction	( ) 신체적 반응
10	**lay off**		the fear of being laid off	( ) 것에 대한 두려움
11	**under-documented**		under-documented ordinary people	( ) 보통 사람들
12	**controversy**		never-ending controversy	끝없는 ( )

구문 TEST ● 주어진 단어를 활용하여 우리말에 맞게 빈칸을 완성하세요.

13 (Avoid walking alone at night) **in areas without adequate lighting.**
avoid / alone
적절한 조명이 없는 지역에서 밤에 혼자 걸어다니는 것을 피하라.

14 ( ), **I would donate a significant portion to charity.**
a millionaire
내가 백만장자라면, 나는 (재산의) 상당 부분을 자선 단체에 기부할 텐데.

15 **What would it feel like (**) **by the manager?**
acknowledge
당신이 매니저에게 인정받는다면 어떤 기분일까?

16 **If (**), **we wouldn't face this weather now.**
address / the climate crisis / earlier
우리가 예전에 기후 위기를 해결했었다면, 지금 이런 날씨를 맞닥뜨리지 않을 텐데.

17 **If you had said sorry back then, (**) **today.**
our relationship / may / better
네가 그때 사과했었더라면, 오늘 우리 관계가 더 좋을 텐데.

18 **Many historical subjects (**).
remain / overlook / for / lack / evidence
많은 역사적 주제는 증거 부족 때문에 간과된 채로 남아 있다.

기출 하프 모의고사

● 문제에 나오는 단어들을 확인하세요.

desperately	ad. 필사적으로, 간절히
injury	n. 부상
dysfunction	n. 기능 장애, 역기능
superficial	a. 표면적인, 피상적인
restore	v. 회복하다, 복구하다
glimpse	n. 얼핏 봄
vessel	n. 혈관
cast	v. (그림자, 빛 등을) 드리우다
momentarily	ad. 잠시
stabilization	n. 고정, 안정(화)
tune out	~을 무시하다, 듣지 않다
approximate	a. 근사치의, 대략의 v. (~에) 가까워지다
blurry	a. 흐릿한
shaky	a. 떨리는, 불안정한
profound	a. 깊은, 심오한
dispute	n. 논쟁
randomness	n. 무작위성
facilitate	v. 용이하게 하다, 촉진하다
allow for	~을 가능하게 하다, 참작하다
comprehensive	a. 종합적인, 포괄적인
outstanding	a. 뛰어난
snap judgment	성급한 판단
override	v. 무시하다, ~보다 더 중요하다
deliberative	a. 신중한, 깊이 생각하는
built-in	a. 내재한, 내장된
offend	v. 불쾌하게 하다
obligation	n. 의무
have no choice but to-V	~할 수밖에 없다
centralize	v. 중앙 집중화하다
score	n. 악보, (음악) 작품
corporation	n. 기업, 회사
negotiable	a. (어음, 증권 등이) 양도 가능한, 협상의 여지가 있는
occupy	v. (공간 등을) 차지하다, 점유하다
authentic	a. 진정한
consent	n. 동의, 합의 v. 동의하다
prioritize	v. 우선시하다
idealistic	a. 이상주의적인
popularize	v. 대중화하다, 보급하다
emission	n. 배출(물)
disincentive	n. 저해 요소
taxation	n. 과세 (제도)
residual	a. 잔여의, 남은
discharge	n. 배출, 방출 v. 내보내다, 석방하다
property	n. 특성, 재산
toxicity	n. 유독성
appreciably	ad. 눈에 띄게, 상당히
variability	n. 변동성, 가변성
prescribe	v. 규정하다, 지시하다, 처방하다
in accordance with	~에 따라, 맞게
coincide	v. 일치하다, 비슷하다, 동시에 일어나다

2024 5월 21번

❶ 명사절 접속사 if

Now you might wonder if you could cause an image to fade just by staring at something unmoving.

❷ by V-ing

이제 여러분은 움직이지 않는 것을 단지 쳐다봄으로써 어떤 이미지가 사라지게 할 수 있는지 궁금할지도 모르겠다.

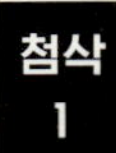

명사절 접속사 if

개　념 ▶ 접속사 if가 명사절을 이끄는 경우 whether와 마찬가지로 '~인지 아닌지'라는 의미를 나타낸다.

독해전략 ▶ if가 wonder(궁금해하다), see(알아보다), check(점검하다) 뒤에 나오면 '~인지 아닌지'를 대입해본다.

어법전략 ▶ if가 이끄는 명사절은 원칙적으로 동사의 목적어 자리에만 쓰인다는 점을 기억해 둔다. 같은 의미의 whether는 주어, 보어, 전치사의 목적어까지 고루 쓰인다.

다음 중 어법상 옳은 것을 고르세요.

a. I wonder if　that he finished the report on time, considering how busy he was with other projects.

b. He will see if　whether he can join us for dinner after his meeting, which is supposed to end by six.

c. Whether　If the policy changes will affect us remains to be clarified by the legal team.

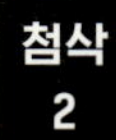

by V-ing

개　념 ▶ 전치사 by 뒤에 동명사가 나와 수단(~함으로써)의 의미를 나타낼 수 있다.

독해전략 ▶ <in V-ing(~할 때, ~함에 있어)>, <(up)on V-ing(~하자마자)> 등과 의미를 구별해 둔다.

어법전략 ▶ by 뒤의 동명사는 부사의 수식을 받으며, to부정사로 대체될 수 없음에 주의해야 한다.

다음 중 어법상 옳은 것을 고르세요.

a. She stayed well-informed about current events by reading　read the news every morning.

b. You can avoid mistakes by attentive　attentively checking your work before submitting it.

c. She succeeded by staying focused on her goals and steadily improving　to improve her skills.

2024 3월 32번

❸ the+비교급 ~, the+비교급 …

The *more* altruistic someone is, the more they insist that they have done no more than all of us would be expected to do, lest we avoid our basic moral obligation to humanity.

❹ lest S (should) V

누군가 '더' 이타적일수록, 그들은 우리가 인류에 대한 기본적인 도덕적 의무를 피하지 않도록 모두가 기대받았을 정도로만 행동한 것이라고 더 주장한다.

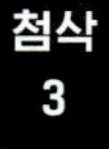 첨삭 3

the+비교급 ~, the+비교급 …

개 념 ▶ '~할수록 더 …하다'라는 의미를 나타낸다. 비교급을 강조하는 구문이기도 하다.

독해전략 ▶ 글의 핵심을 담을 때가 많다. 특히 대의파악(주장, 요지, 제목, 주제 등) 유형에서 주의 깊게 봐야 한다.

어법전략 ▶ 비교급 자리에서 '형용사 vs. 부사'를 구별하려면 <the+비교급> 바로 뒤의 문장구조를 살펴 봐야 한다.

다음 중 어법상 옳은 것을 고르세요.

a. The | more patient | more patiently | you wait, the greater the reward will be.

b. The more you practice, the | more proficient | more proficiently | you become at playing the piano.

c. The | quieter | more quietly | the library, the more suitable it is for studying.

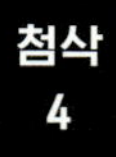 첨삭 4

lest S (should) V

개 념 ▶ '~하지 않기 위해'라는 의미로 주절의 목적이나 이유를 보충 설명하는 부사절이다.

독해전략 ▶ <so that S (can) V(~할 수 있도록, ~하기 위해)>의 반대 표현으로 함께 기억해 둔다.

어법전략 ▶ 3인칭 단수 주어 뒤로 should가 생략된 뒤 바로 동사원형이 나올 때 이를 어색하게 여기지 않도록 한다.

다음 중 어법상 옳은 것을 고르세요.

a. She locks all the doors and windows each night lest an intruder | enter | enters | the house.

b. She rehearsed her presentation several times lest she | forget | forgot | a single word.

c. He had his online map turned on during his hikes lest he | lose | to lose | his way in the dense forest.

정답 a. more patiently b. more proficient c. quieter / a. enter b. forget c. lose

심경 파악

01 다음 글에 드러난 Timothy의 심경 변화로 가장 적절한 것은?

Timothy sat at his desk, desperately turning the pages of his science book. His science project was due in a few days and he had no idea where to start. Finally, he closed his book, hit the table, and shouted, "This is impossible!" His sister, Amelia, drawn by the noise, came into his room. "Hey, little brother, can I help?" Timothy explained his situation and Amelia immediately had a solution. She knew that Timothy enjoyed learning about environmental issues and suggested he do a project about climate change. Timothy thought about the idea and agreed that his sister was right. "Oh, Amelia, your idea is fantastic! Thank you. You are the best sister ever!"

① frustrated → grateful
② disappointed → envious
③ hopeful → thrilled
④ encouraged → ashamed
⑤ fearful → indifferent

주장 파악

02 다음 글에서 필자가 주장하는 바로 가장 적절한 것은?

When you are middle-aged, the risk of connective tissue injuries peaks as decreased load tolerance combines with continued high activity levels. The path of least resistance is to stop doing the things that hurt—avoid uncomfortable movements and find easier forms of exercise. However, that's the exact opposite of what you should do. There is a path forward. But it doesn't involve following the typical pain management advice of rest, ice, and medicine, which multiple reviews have shown is not effective for treating age-related joint pain and dysfunction. These methods do nothing more than treat superficial symptoms. The only practical solution is to strengthen your body with muscle training. Whether you've been training for a few years or a few decades, or haven't ever stepped foot in the weight room, it's not too late to restore your body, build real strength, and achieve your physical potential.

① 관절의 노화를 늦추기 위해 적절한 체중을 유지해야 한다.
② 근육을 강화하기 위해 다양한 강도의 운동을 병행해야 한다.
③ 중년층은 근 손실 예방을 위해 식단을 철저히 관리해야 한다.
④ 노화와 관련된 관절 질환에는 치료보다 예방이 우선되어야 한다.
⑤ 중년에는 통증이 따르더라도 근력 운동으로 신체를 강화해야 한다.

2024 6월 19번   정답률 95%

2024 5월 20번   정답률 85%

함축 의미

03

밑줄 친 Approximate perfection is better than perfect perfection이 다음 글에서 의미하는 바로 가장 적절한 것은?

Turn the lights out and point the beam of a small flashlight up into one of your eyes. Shake the beam around while moving your gaze up and down. You should catch glimpses of what look like delicate branches. These branches are shadows of the blood vessels that lie on top of your retina. The vessels constantly cast shadows as light streams into the eye, but because these shadows never move, the brain ceases responding to them. Moving the flashlight beam around shifts the shadows just enough to make them momentarily visible. Now you might wonder if you could cause an image to fade just by staring at something unmoving. But that is not possible because the visual system constantly jiggles the eye muscles, which prevents the perfect stabilization of images of the world. These muscle movements are unbelievably small, but their effect is huge. Without them, we would go blind by tuning out what we see shortly after fixating our gaze! It's an interesting notion: Approximate perfection is better than perfect perfection.

*retina: 망막 **jiggle: 가볍게 흔들다

① What makes your vision blurry actually protects your eyes.
② The more quickly an object moves, the more sensitively eyes react.
③ Eyes exposed to intense light are subject to distortion of images.
④ Constant adjustment of focusing makes your eye muscles tired.
⑤ Shaky eye-muscle movements let us see what the brain might ignore.

주제 추론

04

다음 글의 주제로 가장 적절한 것은?

Natural disasters and aging are two problems that societies have been dealing with for all of human history. Governments must respond to both, but their dynamics are entirely different and this has profound consequences for the nature of the response. Simply by plotting the aging slope, policy makers go a long way toward understanding the problem: People get older at a constant and reliable rate. There can be disagreements over how to solve the aging problem (this is political complexity), but the nature of the problem is never in dispute. Plotting the number of people killed in natural disasters does very little to advance understanding of this problem other than emphasizing the randomness of natural disasters. Preparing a policy response is, therefore, much easier in some areas than in others. When inputs are reliable and easy to predict, it greatly facilitates information processing and allows for anticipatory problem-solving. When problems are causally complex and multivariate, determining the appropriate response is a reactionary endeavor.

① risks of hasty decision-making during natural disasters
② reasons for governmental concern about aging populations
③ significance of studying the comprehensive history of policy making
④ different approaches of governments depending on the nature of the problem
⑤ advantages of anticipatory problem-solving in dealing with social problems

2024 5월 21번   정답률 31%

2024 7월 23번   정답률 42%

05 Will Rogers에 관한 다음 글의 내용과 일치하지 않는 것은?

Will Rogers (1879–1935) was a famous American public figure. He was born as the eighth child. When he was young, he was clever and mature but he dropped out of school after the 10th grade. He was very interested in cowboys and horses, and he even learned how to do rope tricks. He left the U.S. in 1902 and worked as a cowboy and roping artist in South Africa and Australia. After returning to the U.S., he appeared in more than 50 movies and was often heard on the radio as an entertainer. He was also an outstanding newspaper columnist with his wit and humor, writing more than 4,000 columns. He unfortunately died at the height of his career in 1935. Rogers was so popular that after his death his statue was installed in the U.S. Capitol. He will be remembered as a great American of many talents.

① 여덟 번째 아이로 태어났다.
② 카우보이와 말에 매우 관심이 있었다.
③ 미국에 돌아온 후 50편이 넘는 영화에 출연했다.
④ 뛰어난 신문 칼럼니스트였다.
⑤ 생전에 그의 동상이 U.S. Capitol에 설치되었다.

06 다음 글의 밑줄 친 부분 중, 문맥상 낱말의 쓰임이 적절하지 않은 것은?

We all like to think of ourselves as rational actors, careful and considered in our thinking, capable of sound and reliable judgments. We might believe that we generally consider different points of view and make ① informed decisions. We are, in fact, "predictably irrational," as psychologist Dan Ariely titled his book on the topic. All of us engage in automatic, reflexive thinking, typically taking the ② easier path and conserving mental effort. Although we each may have the subjective impression that we are careful thinkers, we often make snap judgments or no real judgments at all. In addition, numerous biases inhibit or override reflective, deliberative thought; intuitive theories can also interfere with ③ acceptance of accurate scientific explanations. Understanding more about how our minds work and how biases may operate can make us each ④ less subject to fallacious reasoning, more rational, and more aware of the problems in others' thinking. Learning to understand the built-in ⑤ rationality of our mental processes can also help us improve our ability to inform others more effectively.

*intuitive: 직관적인   **fallacious: 오류가 있는

07 다음 빈칸에 들어갈 말로 가장 적절한 것은?

The commonsense understanding of the moral status of altruistic acts conforms to how most of us think about our responsibilities toward others. We tend to get offended when someone else or society determines for us how much of what we have should be given away; we are adults and should have the right to make such decisions for ourselves. Yet, when interviewed, altruists known for making the largest sacrifices—and bringing about the greatest benefits to their recipients—assert just the opposite. They insist that they _______________ _______________. Organ donors, and everyday citizens who risk their own lives to save others in mortal danger are remarkably consistent in their explicit denials that they have done anything deserving of high praise as well as in their assurance that anyone in their shoes should have done exactly the same thing. To be sure, it seems that the *more* altruistic someone is, the more they are likely to insist that they have done no more than all of us would be expected to do, lest we shirk our basic moral obligation to humanity.

*altruistic: 이타적인 **lest: ~하지 않도록
***shirk: (책임을) 회피하다

① had absolutely no choice but to act as they did
② should have been rewarded financially
③ regretted making such decisions
④ deserved others' appreciation in return
⑤ found the moral obligations inapplicable in risky situations

08 다음 빈칸에 들어갈 말로 가장 적절한 것은?

Centralized, formal rules can _______________ _______________. The rules of baseball don't just regulate the behavior of the players; they determine the behavior that constitutes playing the game. Rules do not prevent people from playing baseball; they create the very practice that allows people to play baseball. A score of music imposes rules, but it also creates a pattern of conduct that enables people to produce music. Legal rules that enable the formation of corporations, that enable the use of wills and trusts, that create negotiable instruments, and that establish the practice of contracting all make practices that create new opportunities for individuals. And we have legal rules that establish roles individuals play within the legal system, such as judges, trustees, partners, and guardians. True, the legal rules that establish these roles constrain the behavior of individuals who occupy them, but rules also create the roles themselves. Without them an individual would not have the opportunity to occupy the role.

*constrain: 속박하다

① categorize one's patterns of conduct in legal and productive ways
② lead people to reevaluate their roles and practices in a society
③ encourage new ways of thinking which promote creative ideas
④ reinforce one's behavior within legal and established contexts
⑤ facilitate productive activity by establishing roles and practices

09 다음 글에서 전체 흐름과 관계 <u>없는</u> 문장은?

In a context in which the cultural obligation to produce the self as a distinctive, authentic individual is difficult to fulfill, the burdensome work of individualizing the self is turned over increasingly to algorithms. ① The "personalization" that is promised on every front—in the domains of search, shopping, health, news, advertising, learning, music, and entertainment—depends on ever more refined algorithmic constructions of individuality. ② As it becomes more difficult to produce our digital selves as unique individuals, we are increasingly being produced as unique individuals from the outside. ③ When AI algorithms learn more about our identities, it becomes essential to safeguard this information and ensure that individuals have control and consent over the data collected about them. ④ Individuality is redefined from a cultural practice and reflexive project to an algorithmic process. ⑤ Our unique selfhood is no longer something for which we are wholly responsible; it is algorithmically guaranteed.

10 주어진 글 다음에 이어질 글의 순서로 가장 적절한 것은?

Today, historic ideas about integrating nature and urban/suburban space find expression in various interpretations of sustainable urban planning.

(A) But Landscape Urbanists find that these designs do not prioritize the natural environment and often involve diverting streams and disrupting natural wetlands. Still others, such as those advocating for "just sustainabilities" or "complete streets," find that both approaches are overly idealistic and neither pays enough attention to the realities of social dynamics and systemic inequality.

(B) However, critics claim that Landscape Urbanists prioritize aesthetic and ecological concerns over human needs. In contrast, New Urbanism is an approach that was popularized in the 1980s and promotes walkable streets, compact design, and mixed-use developments.

(C) However, the role of social justice in these approaches remains highly controversial. For example, Landscape Urbanism is a relatively recent planning approach that advocates for native habitat designs that include diverse species and landscapes that require very low resource use.

*divert: 우회시키다, 방향을 바꾸게 하다
**compact: 고밀도, 촘촘한

① (A) – (C) – (B)　　② (B) – (A) – (C)
③ (B) – (C) – (A)　　④ (C) – (A) – (B)
⑤ (C) – (B) – (A)

11 글의 흐름으로 보아, 주어진 문장이 들어가기에 가장 적절한 곳은?

Continuous emissions measurement can be costly, particularly where there are many separate sources of emissions, and for many pollution problems this may be a major disincentive to direct taxation of emissions.

Environmental taxes based directly on measured emissions can, in principle, be very precisely targeted to the policy's environmental objectives. (①) If a firm pollutes more, it pays additional tax directly in proportion to the rise in emissions. (②) The polluter thus has an incentive to reduce emissions in any manner that is less costly per unit of abatement than the tax on each unit of residual emissions. (③) The great attraction of basing the tax directly on measured emissions is that the actions the polluter can take to reduce tax liability are actions that also reduce emissions. (④) Nevertheless, the technologies available for monitoring the concentrations and flows of particular substances in waste discharges have been developing rapidly. (⑤) In the future, it may be possible to think of taxing measured emissions in a wider range of applications.

*abatement: 감소 **liability: 부담액

12 다음 글의 내용을 한 문장으로 요약하고자 한다. 빈칸 (A), (B)에 들어갈 말로 가장 적절한 것은?

People often assume that synthetic food ingredients are more harmful than natural ones, but this is not always the case. Typically, synthetic ingredients can be made in a precisely controlled fashion and have well-defined compositions and properties, allowing careful evaluation of their potential toxicity. On the other hand, natural ingredients often vary appreciably in their composition and properties depending on their origin, the time of year they were harvested, the climate they experienced throughout their lifetime, the soil quality, and how they were isolated and stored. These variations can make testing their safety extremely difficult—one is never sure about the potential toxicity of minor components that may vary from time to time. In some cases, a natural food component has been consumed for hundreds or thousands of years without causing any obvious health problems and can, therefore, be assumed to be safe. However, one must still be very careful.

*synthetic: 합성의

↓

The ____(A)____ of the production process for synthetic food ingredients and the variability of natural food ingredients may ____(B)____ people's commonly held assumption that the natural ingredients are more secure.

	(A)		(B)
①	controllability	……	challenge
②	predictability	……	support
③	manageability	……	intensify
④	affordability	……	reverse
⑤	accessibility	……	question

13~14 다음 글을 읽고, 물음에 답하시오.

If we understand critical thinking as: 'the identification and evaluation of evidence to guide decision-making', then ethical thinking is about identifying ethical issues and evaluating these issues from different perspectives to guide how to respond. This form of ethics is distinct from higher levels of conceptual ethics or theory. The nature of an ethical issue or problem from this perspective is that there is no clear right or wrong response. It is therefore (a) essential that students learn to think through ethical issues rather than follow a prescribed set of ethical codes or rules. There is a need to (b) encourage recognition that, although being ethical is defined as acting 'in accordance with the principles of conduct that are considered correct', these principles vary both between and within individuals. What a person (c) values relates to their social, religious, or civic beliefs influenced by their formal and informal learning experiences. Individual perspectives may also be context (d) dependent, meaning that under different circumstances, at a different time, when they are feeling a different way, the same individual may make different choices. Therefore, in order to analyse ethical issues and think ethically it is necessary to understand the personal factors that influence your own 'code of behaviour' and how these may (e) coincide, alongside recognizing and accepting that the factors that drive other people's codes and decision making may be different.

제목 추론

13 윗글의 제목으로 가장 적절한 것은?

① Critical Reasoning: A Road to Ethical Decision-making
② Far-reaching Impacts of Ethics on Behavioural Codes
③ Ethical Thinking: A Walk Through Individual Minds
④ Exploring Ethical Theory in the Eyes of the Others
⑤ Do Ethical Choices Always Take Priority?

어휘 추론

14 밑줄 친 (a)~(e) 중에서 문맥상 낱말의 쓰임이 적절하지 <u>않은</u> 것은?

① (a)
② (b)
③ (c)
④ (d)
⑤ (e)

2024 6월 41~42번

13 정답률 62%　　**14** 정답률 35%

정답 p. 99

단어 TEST ● 주어진 단어의 뜻을 쓰고, 예문을 올바르게 해석하세요.

1	**desperately** 필사적으로, 간절히	desperately turn the pages	(필사적으로) 페이지를 넘기다
2	**dysfunction**	pain and dysfunction	통증과 ( )
3	**stabilization**	the perfect stabilization of images	이미지의 완벽한 ( )
4	**shaky**	shaky movements	( ) 움직임
5	**outstanding**	an outstanding newspaper columnist	( ) 신문 칼럼니스트
6	**snap judgment**	make snap judgments	( )을 하다
7	**offend**	get offended	( )
8	**authentic**	a distinctive, authentic individual	독특하고 ( ) 개인
9	**prioritize**	prioritize the natural environment	자연환경을 ( )
10	**disincentive**	a major disincentive	주요한 ( )
11	**residual**	residual emissions	( ) 배출물
12	**in accordance with**	in accordance with the rules	규칙에 ( )

구문 TEST ● 주어진 단어를 활용하여 우리말에 맞게 빈칸을 완성하세요.

13 **You might wonder** (if[whether] you could cause an image to fade) **just by staring at it.**
could / cause / an image / fade

여러분은 그것을 단지 쳐다봄으로써 어떤 이미지를 사라지게 할 수 있는지 궁금할지도 모르겠다.

14 **He will** (   ) **after his meeting.**
see / can / join / for dinner

그는 그가 미팅 후에 저녁 식사를 위해 우리와 합류할 수 있는지 알아볼 것이다.

15 **Avoid mistakes** (   ).
attentively / check / work

당신의 일을 주의 깊게 점검함으로써 실수를 피하라.

16 (   ), **the greater the reward will be.**
patiently / wait

당신이 더 참을성 있게 기다릴수록, 보상은 더 클 것이다.

17 (   ), **the more suitable it is for studying.**
quiet / the library

도서관이 더 조용할수록, 공부에 더 적합하다.

18 **She rehearsed her presentation several times** (   ).
lest / forget / a single word

그녀는 한 단어도 잊어버리지 않도록 발표를 여러 차례 연습했다.

MEMO

매 3 영

기출 | 하프

모의고사

정답 및 해설

교육 R&D에 앞서가는
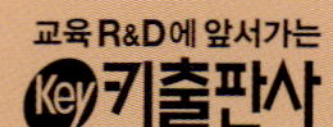
Key 키출판사

매
3
영

모의
고사

기출 | 하프

정답 및 해설

01 정답 ② 94% 2025학년도 수능 19번

해석 금요일은 밸런타인데이였고, Peter는 아내 Amy가 자신의 깜짝 선물을 좋아할 거라고 확신하고 있었다. Peter는 온라인에서 Amy와 함께 시간을 보낼 새로운 방법이 되어줄 이벤트를 오랫동안 검색했었다. 그는 마침내 Amy에게 딱 맞는 것을 찾았다. 그녀는 전에 한 번도 가보지 않은 곳에 가는 게 좋다고 그에게 자주 말했고, 그는 Amy가 시내에 있는 새로 생긴 5성 레스토랑에 가면 좋아할 거라고 전적으로 확신했다. 그는 레스토랑에 전화를 걸어 금요일에 예약해 달라고 요청하며 미소를 지었다. 안타깝게도, 그의 미소는 레스토랑 예약이 다 찼다는 말을 들었을 때 순식간에 사라졌다. "너무 아쉽네요." 그는 조용히 말했다. "전 제가 알맞은 곳을 찾았다고 생각했는데."

지문 간단히 보기

> 밸런타인데이 이벤트로 아내 Amy를 위해 5성 레스토랑을 찾아둔 Peter: 아내가 분명 좋아할 거라고 '확신'

↓

> 예약이 다 찼다는 말에 미소가 사라진 채 '아쉬움'을 표현한 Peter

해설 아내를 위해 5성 레스토랑에 방문할 이벤트를 계획하며 아내가 좋아할 거라고 확신하던 Peter가 레스토랑 예약이 이미 다 찼다는 이야기에 미소가 사라진 얼굴로 아쉬움을 표했다는 내용이다. 따라서 Peter의 심경 변화로 ② '확신하는 → 실망한'이 적절하다.

오답풀이

보기 해석	선택률
① 느긋한 → 무관심한	0%
③ 혼란스러운 → 만족한	1%
④ 질투하는 → 낙담한	2%
⑤ 당황한 → 즐거운	0%

구문 [6행] She often told him [**that** she liked to go to places she had never visited before], ~
▶ <tell A B(A에게 B를 말하다)>의 4형식 구조이다. B에 해당하는 [ ]는 접속사 that이 이끄는 명사절(~것)이다.
▶ 밑줄 부분은 선행사 places를 꾸미는 수식어로, 목적격 관계대명사가 생략되고 <주어+동사>만 남은 불완전한 구조이다.

02 정답 ③ 87% 2024 9월 22번

해석 개가 선택과 계획을 할 수 있는 지각력이 있는 존재라고 여길 타당한 이유가 있다 해도, 그래서 우리가 '개가 다른 식으로 행동할까 생각했을 수도 있었을' 거라고 가정할지 몰라도, 우리는 개가 아이를 공격한다고 해서 그 개가 사악하고 부도덕하다고 생각하지는 않을 것이다. 도덕적 책임은 엔트로피나 온도처럼 어떤 보편적인 개념, 즉 똑같이 적용되고 우주 어디서나 비슷하게 측정될 수 있는 그런 것이 아니다. 그것은 인간이 사용하기 위해 특별히 만들어진 개념으로, 언어와 별반 다르지 않다. 지각력과 의지가 마음 및 주체성의 측면인 반면, 도덕성은 사회적 행동에 영향을 미칠 목적으로, 즉 바람직한 것을 함양하고 해로운 것을 막기 위해서 만들어진 문화적 도구이다. 이는 태어날 때 주어진 것이 아니고, 학습된 것이다. 우리는 다른 사람과 협력하려는 성향을 지니고 태어날 수 있고 실제로 그럴 가능성도 높지만, 오로지 인간 사회 안에서만 우리는 이것을 '도덕적인' 행동이라고 이해하게 된다.

지문 간단히 보기

> 개가 아이를 공격한다고 '부도덕'하게 여겨지지는 않음

↓

> 도덕적 책임은 어디서나 보편 타당하게 적용되는 개념이 아니라, 인간이 '만들어서' 사용하는 개념이기 때문
> = 도덕성은 '문화적인' 도구
> = 타고난 것이 아니라, 후천적으로 '학습되는' 개념

↓

> 도덕적 판단은 오로지 인간 사회에서만 이루어짐

해설 도덕성은 인간이 '만들어서' 사용하는 문화적 도구나 다름없기 때문에, 어떤 행위의 도덕성에 관한 판단은 인간 사회에서만 이뤄질 수 있다는 내용이다. 마지막 문장에서 협력 성향을 예로 들어 결론을 잘 제시한다. 따라서 요지로 ③ '도덕성은 학습되는 문화적 도구로서 인간 사회에만 나타난다.'가 가장 적절하다.

오답풀이

보기 해설	선택률
① 도덕성에 관해 언급하고는 있지만, 이를 '선택에 따른 책임'으로 규정하고 있지는 않다.	1%
② '도덕'이라는 키워드가 아예 빠져 있다.	2%
④ '협력 성향'이 마지막 문장에서 언급되었지만, 이것이 동물과 인간의 공통점과 연관되지는 않았다.	2%
⑤ '문화적 도구, 도덕성' 등 핵심 표현이 포함되었지만, 이것이 '의사 결정'과 연관된다는 내용을 글에서 다루지 않았기에 오답이다.	7%

구문 [1행] ~ so that we might suppose 'it **could have conceived** of acting otherwise' ~
▶ <could have p.p.(~할 수 있었을 텐데)>의 의미를 잘 기억해 둔다. <조동사+have p.p.>는 과거에 대한 추측 또는 가정법 과거완료(과거 사실이 아닌 내용을 가정)의 의미를 나타낸다.

03 정답 ② 25%

해석 (번아웃의) 폭(모두가 약간 지쳤다고 느낀다)과 깊이(일부가 너무 지쳐서 일을 더 이상 하지 못한다)에 대한 필요의 균형을 맞추려면, 우리는 번아웃을 '상태'가 아니라 '범위'로 간주해야 한다. 번아웃에 대한 대부분의 대중적 논의에서, 우리는 '번아웃 된' 노동자에 대해서 마치 그 상태가 (명확하게 나뉘는) 흑백 상태인 것처럼 이야기한다. 그러나, 흑백 논리식 관점은 번아웃 경험의 다양성을 설명할 수 없다. 번아웃 상태와 그렇지 않은 상태 사이에 마치 전구에서 그렇듯(켜지거나 꺼져 있음) 분명한 경계가 있는 거라면, 우리는 본인이 번아웃 되었다고 말하지만 여전히 그런대로 본인 일을 유능하게 해내는 사람들을 분류할 좋은 방법이 없다. 번아웃을 범위로 간주하면 이러한 문제를 해결할 수 있다. 번아웃을 주장하지만 그로 인해 쇠약해지지 않는 사람은 그것을 일부 또는 덜 심각한 형태로 겪고 있을 뿐이다. 그들은 번아웃'인 상태가' 아니면서 번아웃을 경험하고 있다. 번아웃은 최후 발언을 (아직) 하지 않았다.

지문 간단히 보기

'번아웃': 상태 X 범위 O

↓

대중적 논의에서의 번아웃 분류 = 흑백 논리식(맞다, 아니다)
→ '부분적으로, 덜 심각하게' 번아웃을 겪는 이들을 포괄 X

↓

'번아웃은 최후 발언을 하지 않았다' = **'번아웃'이라는 표현으로 특정 정도의 소진 상태를 단정지을 수 없다**

해설 번아웃은 '맞다, 아니다'의 이분법적 상태 개념으로 볼 수 없고, 다양한 강도와 양상으로 나타나는 '범위' 개념으로 봐야 한다는 내용이다. 마지막 문장 또한 '번아웃'이라는 말로 '소진감의 양상, 정도, 한계를 특정할 수 없다'는 의미이므로, ② '소진 정도가 더 클 여지가 아직 있다.'가 정답이다.

오답풀이

보기 해석	선택률
① 번아웃에 대한 대중적 논의는 아직 끝나지 않았다.	25%
③ 양자택일식 기준은 번아웃 증상에 적용될 수 있다.	21%
④ 소진은 그 심각성에 근거해 여러 방법으로 극복된다.	13%
⑤ 소진의 정도는 개인의 인식에 의해 형성된다.	16%

구문 [13행] ~ **those** who claim burnout but are not debilitated by it **are** simply dealing with a partial or less-severe form of it.
▶ 주어가 복수대명사인 those(~한 사람들)이므로, be동사도 복수형인 are로 쓰였다. who가 이끄는 관계절이 주어를 꾸민다.

04 정답 ④ 76%

해석 개방형 사무실 설계가 유행하게 된 타당한 이유가 있지만, 개방형 사무실은 '모든' 시대에 채택될 설계는 아닐 수도 있다. 그보다는, 올바른 설계란 변화의 문화를 구축하는 것인 듯하다. 지나치게 굳은 관례와 관습은 아무리 잘 숙고되었거나 선의라고 하더라도 혁신을 위협한다. 시간 흐름에 따라 사무실 설계를 분석할 때 아주 중요한 핵심은 답이 계속 바뀐다는 것이다. 일직선으로 발전하는 것처럼 보이기도 하겠지만, 이는 근거 없는 믿음이다. 지난 80년의 사무실 공간을 조사해 보면 반복되는 주기를 확인할 수 있다. 1940년대의 사무실과 현대의 사무실 공간을 비교해보면, 칸막이벽과 작은 개인 방이 보다 표준적이던 1980년대를 거쳐서, 본질적으로 같은 스타일로 다시 돌아왔음을 알 수 있다. 기술과 색상은 다를 수도 있지만, 1940년대와 2000년대의 설계는 비슷한데, 중앙에서 내려오는 기둥까지 그렇다.

지문 간단히 보기

(예시) (현대에 유행하는) 개방형 사무실: '모든' 시대에 채택될 방식은 아닐 수도 있음

↓

사무실 설계에 관한 '답은 계속 바뀜'
= 발전 방향이 일직선이라는 생각은 '근거 없는 믿음'

↓

1940년대 사무실과 현대(2000년대) 사무실: '본질상 같은' 스타일
- 칸막이, 개인 방이 표준이던 시기(1980년대)도 있지만, 결국 같은 스타일로 돌아옴
- (예시) 중앙에서 내려오는 기둥

해설 시간 흐름에 따라 사무실 공간 설계 양식을 분석해보면 '답은 계속 바뀐다'는 것을 알 수 있다는 내용이다. 마지막 두 문장에서 '바뀐다'의 의미가 구체화되는데, 변화가 직선으로 이뤄지기보다는 같은 스타일이 주기적으로 반복된다는 것이다. 따라서 글의 제목으로 ④ '사무실 설계: 유행은 돌고 돈다'가 가장 적절하다.

오답풀이

보기 해석	선택률
① 개방형 사무실 설계는 왜 비용 효율적일까	6%
② 사무실 공간에 복고 스타일을 통합하는 방법	8%
③ 분리형 사무실: 왜 칸막이는 생산성을 제한하는가	3%
⑤ 현대 사무실 공간 관리를 위한 조언	4%

구문 [5행] Overly rigid habits and conventions, **no matter how well-considered or well-intentioned (they are)**, threaten innovation.
▶ 밑줄 친 주어-동사 사이에 삽입된 <no matter how+형/부+주어+동사>는 '아무리 ~하더라도'라는 뜻의 부사절이다. <대명사 주어+be동사>인 they(= the habits and conventions) are는 생략되었다.

05 정답 ④ 86%　　2024 3월 26번

해석　Ilya Prigogine은 모스크바의 한 유대인 가정에서 태어났다. 1921년에 그와 그의 가족은 러시아를 떠나서 결국 벨기에에 정착했다. 그의 부모님은 그가 변호사가 되기를 권했고, 그는 처음에 Free University of Brussels에서 법학을 공부했다. 바로 그때 그는 심리학과 행동 연구에 관심을 갖게 되었다. 결과적으로 이러한 주제에 관해 읽으면서 화학에 대한 그의 관심이 생겨났는데, 화학 작용은 정신과 신체에 영향을 미치기 때문이었다. 그는 결국 법대를 중퇴했다. 이후 Prigogine은 Free University of Brussels에서 화학과 물리학을 동시에 공부했다. 1939년에 그는 두 분야 모두에서 석사 학위에 상응하는 것을 취득했고, 1941년에는 Free University of Brussels에서 화학 박사 학위를 취득했으며, 여기서 1947년에 교수직을 수락했다. 복잡계 과학의 창시자 중 한 명으로 여겨지는 Ilya Prigogine은 1977년에 노벨 화학상을 수상했다.

지문 간단히 보기

> Ilya Prigogine의 생애
> ① 모스크바 출생 → 1921년 벨기에에 정착
> ② 변호사가 되라는 부모의 권유 → 법대 진학했으나 중퇴
> ③ Free University of Brussels에서 화학, 물리학 동시 공부
> ④ 1941년에 박사 학위 → 1947년에 교수직 수락
> ⑤ 1977년에 노벨 화학상 수상

해설　'~ he accepted the position of professor in 1947.'에 따르면 Ilya Prigogine이 교수직을 수락한 것은 1947년이다. 1941년은 그가 화학 박사 학위를 취득한 해이다. 따라서 ④ '1941년에 Free University of Brussels의 교수직을 수락했다.'가 일치하지 않는다.

오답풀이

보기 해설	선택률
① In 1921, he and his family left Russia, ~	1%
② His parents encouraged him to become a lawyer, ~	1%
③ ~ studied chemistry and physics at the same time at the Free University of Brussels.	9%
⑤ ~ was awarded the Nobel Prize in Chemistry in 1977.	0%

구문　[5행] **It was** then **that** he became interested in psychology and behavioral research.
▶ <it is[was] ~ that …(…한 것은 바로 ~이다[였다])> 강조 구문으로, 부사인 then이 강조되고 있다.

06 정답 ⑤ 27%　　2024 5월 30번

해석　기억은 경험과 연결된 감정에 의해 형성된다. 이러한 이유로 부정확성은 일어났던 일의 전체적인 상황을 종종 숨긴다. 예를 들어, 한 회사가 중대한 프로젝트를 도와줄 어느 자문 위원을 고용하기로 결정했을 수 있다. 이 프로젝트 동안 그 자문 위원은 관련 임원 몇몇과 충돌하는 몇 가지 성격 특성들을 드러냈다. 프로젝트 과정 동안 그들은 그들의 비전이 실현되는 것을 보고자 그 성격 갈등을 제쳐둘 수 있었다. 결국 프로젝트는 성공하여, 회사가 발전하고 이득을 볼 수 있게 해주었다. 뒷날 그 회사는 이전의 성공을 기억하며 같은 자문 위원을 또 다른 큰 프로젝트에 고용하는 데 관심을 표했다. 저번에 그의 성격으로 고생했던 임원들은 그의 성격을 극복하는 것의 어려움과 (그와) 연관된 감정들을 아마 가장 생생히 기억할 것이다. 이 경우, 그들이 불편한 감정으로 물든 이전 경험에 집중함에 따라, 프로젝트의 성공에 대한 기억은 희미해진다. 그 결과로, 그들은 회사가 그 자문 위원을 재고용하도록 (→ 배제하도록) 설득하여, 프로젝트 완성을 더 어려워지게 한다.

지문 간단히 보기

> 기억은 경험과 연결된 감정에 영향을 받음

> (예시) 프로젝트를 성공시켰지만 성격 이슈가 있었던 자문 위원
> → 그와 충돌했던 임원들은 그의 성격 때문에 불편해함
> → 이 감정이 성공에 대한 기억까지 흐려지게 함
> ▶ **그를 다시 고용하지 '말자고' 설득하게 됨**

해설　④가 포함된 문장에서 성격 갈등을 빚었던 자문 위원과의 '불편한' 경험에 집중하게 되면 그가 도와 프로젝트를 성공시켰던 기억도 희미해진다고 한다. 그 결과 해당 자문 위원을 다른 프로젝트에 포함하는 대신 '배제'하기를 권하게 된다는 내용이 자연스러우므로, ⑤에는 rehire 대신 exclude를 써야 옳다.

오답풀이

보기 해설	선택률
① hide(숨기다)	5%
② conflicts(갈등)	12%
③ interest(관심, 흥미)	17%
④ discomfort(불편)	38%

구문　[22행] As a result, they convince the company to rehire(→ exclude) the consultant, **making project completion more difficult**.
▶ 콤마 뒤는 결과를 나타내는 분사구문으로, '그리고 ~하다'라는 의미이다. 이는 '~ and make ~'로 바꿀 수 있다.

07 정답 ① 32%

해석 도시의 질은 선택적 활동에 매우 중요해서, 머무는 활동의 정도가 흔히 도시의 공간뿐 아니라 도시의 질을 측정하는 잣대로 사용될 수 있다. 도시에 보행자가 많은 것이 반드시 우수한 도시 질의 지표는 아닌데, 많은 사람들이 걸어서 돌아다닌다는 것은 흔히 교통 선택권이 부족하거나 도시 내 다양한 기능 (시설)끼리 거리가 멀다는 지표일 수 있다. 역으로, 많은 사람이 걸어다니지 않는 도시가 흔히 우수한 도시 질을 시사한다는 주장도 가능하다. 로마 같은 도시에서는 걸어다니기보다는 광장에 서 있거나 앉아 있는 사람이 많다는 것이 눈에 띈다. 그리고 이것은 (그렇게 할) 필요성 때문이 아니라, 그 도시의 질이 아주 매력적이기 때문이다. 머물게 하는 유혹이 많은 도시 공간에서 계속 움직이기는 어렵다. 반대로, 많은 사람이 걸어서 지나가지만 거의 멈추거나 머무르지 않는 여러 새로운 구역과 단지들이 있다.

지문 간단히 보기

'머무는' 활동의 정도 = 도시의 질을 측정하는 기준
- 걷는 사람이 많다 = 교통 선택권이 부족하거나 시설 간 거리가 멀다
  = 도시 질↓
- 걷는 사람이 많지 않다 = 도시 질↑

↓

(예시) 로마 같은 도시: 걷는 사람 < 서거나 앉은 사람
= 도시 공간에 '머물' 유인이 많음 ▶ **도시 질이 '좋음'**

해설 걸어 다니는 사람보다 머무는 사람이 많은 도시의 질이 좋다는 설명 뒤로, 로마의 예시가 언급된다. 로마에서 사람들은 걷기보다는 광장에 서거나 앉아 '머무르는' 모습이 눈에 많이 띄는데, 빈칸 바로 뒤에 따르면 이는 그 공간이 사람들을 머물도록 유혹할 정도로 매력적이기 때문이다. 따라서 빈칸에는 ① '그 도시의 질이 아주 매력적이기'가 들어가야 한다.

오답풀이

보기 해석	선택률
② 공공장소가 이미 점유되었기	24%
③ 대중교통을 이용할 수 없기	15%
④ 주요 관광지가 걸어서 갈 거리 내에 있기	20%
⑤ 도시의 행정 건물이 밀집되어 있기	9%

구문 [17행] In contrast **are many new quarters and complexes** [that many people walk through but rarely stop or stay in].
▶ <동사+주어> 어순의 도치 구문이다. [ ]의 수식을 받는 주어가 너무 길어서, 짧은 동사 are를 주어보다 먼저 쓴 것이다.

08 정답 ⑤ 20%

해석 '어미나무(모수)'라는 용어는 임업에서 유래한다. 부모 나무가 자기 자손을 기르는 데 너무도 중요한 역할을 해서 인간 부모에 비할 만하다는 점은 수 세기 동안 분명했다. 어미나무는 자기 뿌리를 이용해서 주변의 어떤 묘목이 자기 자손인지를 알아볼 수 있다. 그러고 나서 그 나무는 정교한 연결을 통해서 당 용액으로 묘목을 부양하는데, (이는) 인간 어머니가 아이를 수유하는 것과 비슷한 과정이다. 부모에 의해 제공되는 그늘은 또 다른 돌봄의 형태인데, 이것(그늘)은 부모의 수관 아래에서 살고 있는 묘목들의 성장을 억제하기 때문이다. 그늘 없이 완전한 햇빛에 노출된 상태라면, 어린 나무들은 너무 급속히 자라 나무 몸통의 너비를 너무 빨리 확장시킨 나머지 겨우 한두 세기 뒤면 소진되어 버릴 것이다. 그러나 만약 어린나무들이 수십 년 혹은 심지어 수 세기 동안 그늘 속에 굳건하게 서 있다면, 그것들은 장수할 수 있다. 그늘은 더 적은 햇빛, 그리하여 상당히 더 적은 당(에 대한 노출)을 의미한다. 수 세대의 산림 감독관들이 관찰했듯이, 어미나무가 부드럽게 강제하는 느린 삶의 속도는 우연이 아니다. 지금까지도 사람들은 독일어로 'erzieherischer Schatten', 즉 '유익한 그늘'이라고 알려진 것에 대해 이야기한다.

지문 간단히 보기

'어미나무': 자손을 알아보고 돌볼 수 있음 = 인간 부모

(예시) 그늘 제공 → **(지나친)** 성장을 억제
- 그늘X → 나무가 지나치게 성장 → 일찍 소진
- 그늘O → 느리지만 적당한 성장 → 오래 생존

↓

따라서, 어미나무의 그늘 ▶ **자손 나무의 삶의 속도를 늦추어 오래 존속할 수 있도록 도와주는 의도적 장치**

해설 글에 따르면 어미나무는 그늘을 통해 자손 나무가 너무 빨리 많이 자라지 않도록 막아 궁극적으로 더 오래 살아남을 수 있도록 도와준다고 한다. 즉 그늘은 성장을 '적절히 늦춰주려는' 돌봄 행위라는 의미에 맞게, 빈칸에는 ⑤ '어미나무가 부드럽게 강제하는 느린 삶의 속도는 우연이 아니다'를 넣어야 한다.

오답풀이 보기 해석

		선택률
①	사람들은 큰 나무 그늘 아래서 기분 좋게 더위를 식힐 수 있다	18%
②	나무들은 수원(水源)을 향해 뿌리를 가까스로 뻗는다	15%
③	주변 묘목을 앞질러 성장하려는 시도는 성공할 확률이 높다	21%
④	어미나무는 그늘을 제공해 자손의 성장을 가속화한다	26%

구문 [11행] **Without** the shade ~, the young trees **would shoot up and expand** the width of their trunks <u>so</u> quickly (<u>that</u>) they**'d be exhausted** ~
▶ 주절에 가정법 과거 동사(조동사 과거형+동사원형)가 쓰인 것으로 볼 때, 문장 맨 처음의 Without은 'If it were not for(~이 실제 있지만 만일 없다면)'의 의미이다.
▶ 밑줄 친 부분은 <so ~ that …(너무 ~해서 …하다)> 구문이다. 결과의 부사절 접속사 that은 생략되었다.

09 정답 ④ 82%   2024 6월 35번

해석 조류의 노래 학습은 두 단계로 이뤄지는데, 먼저 노래를 암기해야 하고 다음으로 노래를 연습해야 한다. 일부 종에서는 이 두 사건이 겹쳐서 일어나지만, 다른 종에서는 연습 이전 몇 달에 걸쳐 암기가 이뤄질 수 있고, (이는) 장기 기억 저장의 인상적인 예를 제공한다. 어린 새가 외운 노래를 재현해보려 하는 초기의 시도는 대체로 성공적이지 못하다. 이러한 초기 노래에는 고르지 않은 음정과 불규칙한 박자, 그리고 순서가 맞지 않거나 제대로 재현되지 않은 음이 있을 수도 있다. 하지만 몇 주 또는 몇 달에 걸쳐 녹음된 노래의 음향 그래프를 보면, 이 연습 기간 중 새는 미세 조정의 노력을 기울여서 비로소 암기된 본보기를 정확히 모방하게 된다는 것이 드러난다. (새소리 연구를 통해 나타나는 한 가지 중요한 개념은 노래 학습이 선호와 한계에 의해 형성된다는 것이다.) 이 과정에서는 자신이 노래하는 것을 들어야 해서, 만약 새들이 암기 이후더라도 연습 기간 이전에 청각을 잃으면 외운 노래를 재현할 수 없다.

지문 간단히 보기

새의 노래 학습 단계: 암기+연습

↓

① 처음에는 암기한 노래를 잘 재현하기 쉽지 않음
② 음정, 박자, 음의 순서 등에서 놓치는 부분들이 생김

↓

③ 하지만, 연습 기간을 거치면서 노래가 제대로 재현됨
⑤ 이 과정(**연습**) 동안 새들은 자기 노래를 들어야 함
 → 연습 전에 청각을 잃으면 암기해도 재현 X

해설 새가 암기와 연습을 통해 노래를 학습하는 과정을 설명하는 글인데, ④는 노래 학습이 선호나 한계에 영향을 받는다는 내용이어서, '과정'과 연관이 없다. 따라서 무관한 문장은 ④이다.

오답풀이

보기 해설	선택률
① 앞에서 암기를 언급한 후 '암기 직후'의 상황을 적절히 부연하는 문장이다.	2%
② 암기 직후(초기)에 재현하는 노래가 어떤 식으로 성공적이지 않은지 부연하는 문장이다.	4%
③ 역접어 However와 함께 암기에서 연습으로 흐름을 전환하는 문장이다.	7%
⑤ 주어인 This process가 ③의 'during this practice period ~'를 가리킨다.	2%

구문 [11행] ~ the bird fine-tunes his efforts **until** he produces an accurate copy of the memorized template.
▶ <A until B(B할 때까지 A하다)>는 'A하고 나서 (비로소) B하다'의 의미로 볼 수 있다.

10 정답 ③ 47%   2024 5월 36번

해석 시간의 본질을 이해하려는 철학자들은 시간 여행의 가능성을 고려할지 모른다. 그러나 시간 여행의 실제 사례는 없다.
(B) 이와 같은 상황에서 철학자들은 흔히 사고 실험, 즉 사람들의 판단에 기초가 되는 생각 및 전제를 이끌어내는 가상의 시나리오를 구성한다. 간혹 이런 시나리오들은 책과 영화, 텔레비전에서 얻어진다. 다른 경우에는 철학자들이 그냥 본인만의 시나리오를 지어낸다.
(C) (둘 중) 어느 쪽이든, 요점은 그러한 개념들을 시험해 보는 것이다. 가령 시간 여행의 경우 흔한 사고 실험은 만약 여러분이 시간을 거슬러 가서 본인이 결코 태어나지 않는 방식으로 개입할 수 있는 입장임을 깨달으면 무슨 일이 생길지 상상해보는 것이다.
(A) 여러분이 이렇게 하지 못하게 막으려면 무슨 일이 생겨야 할 듯 한데, 만약 여러분이 성공한다면 여러분은 존재하지 않을 것이고 그리하여 시간을 거슬러 갈 수도 없었을 것이기 때문이다. 이런 식의 사례들을 통해 생각한 결과, 일부 철학자들은 시간 여행이라는 개념 자체가 말이 되지 않는다고 주장한다.

지문 간단히 보기

시간 여행: 실제 사례가 없는 개념

↓

(B) '이런 상황'에서 '사고 실험'이 이뤄짐 → 시나리오 구성
 (다른 소스 참고 or 그냥 지어냄)

(C) '어느 방법이든' 시험이 목적 → (예시) 과거로 돌아가 '안 태어나는' 방식으로 상황에 개입할 수 있다고 상상

↓

(A) '이런 개입'이 성공하면 시간을 거슬러 갈 주체가 사라지고, 시간 여행도 불가능 → 시간 여행은 '말이 안 됨'

해설 주어진 글에서 시간 여행의 실제 사례가 없다고 하는데, (B)는 '이런 상황'에서 사고 실험 기법이 이용된다고 말하며, 가상 시나리오를 구축하는 두 가지 방법을 제시한다. (C)는 '둘 중 어느 방식이든' 개념을 시험하는 것이 중요하다고 말하며 과거로 돌아가 보는 사고 실험의 예시를 들고, (A)는 예시를 마무리하며 시간 여행이 성립하기 어렵다는 결론을 내린다. 따라서 ③ '(B)-(C)-(A)'가 적절하다.

오답풀이 보기 해설

	선택률
① (A) 첫 문장의 doing this는 주어진 글의 time travel이 아닌, (C)의 'interfere ~ never born'이다.	5%
② '시나리오를 지어낸다'는 (B) 말미의 내용을 (A)의 doing this에 대입하면 어색하다.	19%
④, (C)의 Either way가 자연스러우려면 앞에서 '두 가지'를	15%
⑤ 말해야 하므로 (B)-(C)는 고정이다.	13%

구문 [C-2행] ~ **what would happen if you went back** in time and **found** yourself in a position ~
▶ 현재 사실이 아닌 상황을 상상하는 가정법 과거 문장이다. 주절에 <would+동사원형>, if절에 과거시제 동사가 쓰였다.

11 정답 ② 22%

해석 지금 우리에게 익숙한 거의 모든 구상화는 원근법으로 그린 것이다. 그것들은 그림의 초점에서 멀어짐에 따라 작아지는 축소된 인물들과 사물들을 나타낸다. 원근법으로 그린 그림은 공간 속 어느 특정 위치에서 그 장면을 보는 사람에게 세상이 어떻게 '보이는지'를 나타낸다. 이것은 초기 구상화와는 대조적이었는데, 이 그림은 화가가 자신이 그리고 있는 사물 및 공간이 어떻게 '보이는지' 표현하는 것만큼이나 그들이 그것들에 관해 '알고 있는' 바를 나타내는 데 초점이 맞춰져 있었다. 이런 그림들은 그 자체로 아름답기는 하나, 만일 우리가 그것을 본다고 할 때 (실제로) 볼 수도 있는 장면들을 나타내지는 않는다. 또한 이것들은 묘사된 공간의 배치에 대해서도 덜 알려준다. 시점과 공간 배치 정보가 함께 어우러진다는 사실은 '본다는 것'에 관해 중요한 것을 드러낸다. 우리는 자기중심적인 틀을 통해 세상을 볼 뿐 아니라, 우리 자신과 사물들 간 서로 상대적인 거리와 크기에 관한 정보 추출이 가능한 방식으로도 사물을 본다는 것이다.

지문 간단히 보기

> 오늘날 구상화: 원근법 → 대상이 '어떻게 보이는지'가 초점

↓

> 반면, 초기 구상화: 화가가 대상에 대해 '아는 바'가 중요
> = '어떻게 보일지'를 나타내지 않음 = 공간 배치 정보도 덜 제공

해설 ② 앞은 특정 위치에서 대상이 '보이는 바'를 묘사하는 원근법 회화에 관한 내용인데, ② 뒤에서는 갑자기 '이 그림들'이 장면을 보이는 대로 나타내지 않는다고 하므로 흐름이 끊긴다. 이때 주어진 문장을 보면 원근법 회화와 대조되는 '초기 구상화'를 언급하는데, 이것이 ② 뒤의 These pictures로 이어져야 흐름이 자연스럽다. 따라서 주어진 문장은 ②에 들어가야 한다.

오답풀이

보기 해설	선택률
① 앞뒤로 in perspective라는 표현이 반복되며 원근법 그림에 관해 설명하고 있다.	8%
③ 앞문장의 주어 These pictures와 뒷문장의 주어 They가 모두 '초기 구상화'를 지칭한다.	26%
④, ⑤ ④ 앞까지 초기 구상화에 관한 설명이 마무리되고, ④ 뒤부터는 '보는 행위'에 대한 일반적 결론이다. 따라서 '초기 구상화'를 다루는 주어진 문장을 ④, ⑤에 넣으면 어색하다.	28% 17%

구문 [1행] ~ earlier figurative art, **which** had been **as focused on representing** [what the artist *knew* about the objects and the space he or she was painting] **as** on (representing) [how they *looked*].
▶ 계속적 용법의 which가 earlier figurative art를 보충 설명한다.
▶ <as ~ as(~만큼 …한)> 구문을 잘 파악해야 한다. focused에 연결되는 <on+동명사>가 병렬구조를 이룬다. 두 번째 as 뒤에서 중복되는 동명사 representing은 생략되었다.
▶ [ ]은 representing의 목적어 역할을 하는 명사절이다.

12 정답 ② 32%

해석 일단 비상사태의 소요가 진정되고 나면, 주로 강화된 경제 성장이나 지방 경제의 회복, 혹은 경제 활동의 다각화에서 기아(굶주림) 취약성의 감소를 모색하는 경향이 있다. 더 큰 경제적 성공의 잠재적 기여는 만일 그것이 취약 계층을 포괄한다면 부인될 수 없다. 그와 동시에, 상당수 인구가 불확실한 원천에서부터 생계를 마련하는 국가들은 아무리 빨리 성장한다 해도 직접적인 공적 개입을 포함하는 특화된 재정 지원 혜택의 보호 기제 없이는 기아 예방을 기대할 수 없다는 점을 인식하는 것이 중요하다. 보츠와나의 경제, 케냐의 농업 부문, 혹은 짐바브웨의 식량 생산에 있어 급속한 성장은 반복되는 기아 위험을 방지하는 데 성공한 것 중 기껏해야 작은 일부만을 설명할 뿐이다. 이들 국가의 진정한 성과는 위기 상황에서 국민들에게 직접적인 공적 지원을 제공했던 데 있다.

→ 비록 경제 성장이 국가의 기아 위험을 줄이는 데 어느 정도 (A)효과적일 수 있지만, 피해 입은 사람들을 돕기 위한 직접적 접근이 이 과정에서 (B)중요한 역할을 한다.

지문 간단히 보기

> 경제 성장을 통해 기아 취약성을 줄이려는 경향

↓

> 하지만, '직접적 공적 개입'이 함께 이뤄져야 기아 예방 O

↓

> (예시) 보츠와나, 케냐, 짐바브웨: 성장도 큰 역할을 했지만, 위기에 처한 국민에게 '직접적 공적 지원을 해서' 성공

해설 흔히 경제 성장을 촉진해 기아 예방을 모색하려는 경향이 있지만, 위기 상황일 때 '직접적인 공적 지원'을 해주려는 노력이 함께 있어야 한다는 내용이다. 따라서 요약문의 빈칸에는 ② '효과적일 - 중요한'이 들어가야 한다.

오답풀이

보기 해설	선택률
① 생산적일 - 복잡한	30%
③ 우세할 - 포괄적인	14%
④ 제한적일 - 적절한	17%
④ 바람직할 - 비용 효율이 높은	7%

구문 [8행] At the same time, <u>it</u> is important <u>to recognize</u> **that,** ~, **countries** [**where** a large part of the population **derive** their livelihood **from** uncertain sources] **cannot hope** to prevent famines ~
▶ 가주어(it)-진주어(to recognize ~) 구문이며, 접속사 that이 이끄는 명사절이 to recognize의 목적어 역할을 한다.
▶ that절의 주어 countries와 동사 cannot hope 사이에 주어를 꾸미는 관계부사절 [ ]이 왔다.
▶ [ ]에서 <derive A from B(A를 B에서부터 끌어내다, 얻다)> 구문도 확인해 둔다.

13~14 정답 ① 55% / ③ 42%　　2024 9월 41~42번

 사람들이 문자 기반 사회의 글로 된 시와 문자에 의존하지 않는 사회의 말로 전해지는 시(에 쓰인 언어)가 공동체에서 사용되는 일상 언어와 꽤 다르다고 느낀다면 그들은 옳다. 청자(감상자)는 단어의 낯선 사용, 어순의 재배열, 유운, 두운, 운율, 각운, 사고의 압축 등을 받아들일 뿐만 아니라, 시에서 이런 요소들을 발견하기를 실제로 기대하며, 시가 '시적으로' 들리지 않으면 실망한다. 그러나 시를 완전히 다른 범주의 언어로 간주하는 사람들은 시인의 진정한 업적에 귀 기울이지 않는다. 그보다는(완전히 다른 언어를 쓰기보다는), 시인은 일상 발화에서 사용되는 바로 그 언어 원료를 교묘히 조작한다. 그의 솜씨(재주)란 이미 언어에 있는 자원에서 새로운 가능성을 찾아내는 것이다. 바닷가에 사는 사람들이 파도 소리에 너무 익숙해져서 더 이상 그 소리를 듣지 못하는 것과 꼭 마찬가지로, 우리 대부분은 고막을 때리는 하루 수백만 단어의 홍수에 민감해진다(→ 무관심해진다). 시의 한 가지 기능은 세상을 신선한 인식으로 묘사하여, 즉 그것을 낯설게 만들어서 우리가 다시 한 번 언어에 귀 기울이게 하는 것이다. 그러나 성공한 시인은 결코 아무 청자도 못 따라올 만큼 멀리까지 낯선 언어의 세계로 벗어나는 법이 없다. 그는 여전히 (효과적인) 전달자, 즉 능숙한 언어 사용자로 남아 있다.

지문 간단히 보기

> 시적 언어는 일상 언어와 다르다는 일반적 생각

↓

> 하지만 실제로, 시인이 쓰는 원료는 일상 언어와 동일
> → 다만, 이 원료를 '교묘히 조작'해 '새로운 가능성' 모색

↓

> 파도 소리에 익숙해져 소리를 못 듣는 바닷가 사람처럼, 언어 홍수에 노출되어 단어들에 둔감해진 일상의 우리

↓

> 이러한 우리를 '신선한 인식'으로 일깨워 다시금 언어에 귀 기울이게 하는 것이 곧, '시'

구문 [26행] But the successful poet **never** departs **so** far into the strange world of language **that** none of his listeners can follow him.
▶ <so ~ that …> 구문에 never가 붙어서 '결코 너무 ~해서 …하는 법이 없다'라는 의미를 나타낸다.

---

13 **해설** 시는 일상 언어와 완전히 다른 언어를 사용하기보다는, 일상 언어를 재주껏 가공하여 '신선한 인식'을 더하고 사람들의 이목을 끈다는 내용이다. 따라서 제목으로 가장 적절한 것은 ① '새롭게 하다: 시가 일상의 언어를 새로이 하는 방법'이다.

오답풀이

보기 해석	선택률
② 왜 시인들은 더 이상 자연에서 영감을 구하지 않을까?	6%
③ 자연의 소리가 시적 표현에 끼치는 영향	16%
④ 일상 발화에서 시적 표현을 인용하는 방법	17%
⑤ 재발견된 아름다움: 구전 시의 귀환	5%

14 **해설** 앞에서 파도 소리에 너무 익숙해져 더 이상 그 소리를 사실상 '듣지 못하는' 사람들을 언급한다. 이 비유를 일상 언어의 '홍수'에 맞닥뜨린 사람들에 적용해보면, 단어들에 '민감'해지기보다는 '무관심, 둔감'해진다는 결론이 자연스럽다. 따라서 ③ (c)의 sensitive를 deaf로 바꾸어야 한다.

오답풀이

보기 해석	선택률
① strange(낯선)	5%
② different(다른)	15%
④ fresh(신선한)	21%
⑤ follow(따르다, 이해하다)	16%

STEP PLUS+ 수능 기출 마무리 복습

단어 TEST
02 당황한, 난처한　**03** 소진, 탈진　**04** 유행하다, 통용되다　**05** ~와 충돌하다　**06** 매력적인, 솔깃한　**07** 자손　**08** 가속화하다　**09** 재현하다, 복제하다　**10** ~에 기초가 되다　**11** 작아지다, 축소시키다　**12** 반복되는

구문 TEST
14 Reaching for the top shelf　**15** will be awarded a scholarship　**16** The fact that she apologized　**17** Every student who passes the final exam[passing the final exam] is invited　**18** The magazines piled on the table tell

01   정답 ①   93%   2023 4월 19번

해석 "5,000달러가 입금되었다고요? 감사합니다. 바로 확인해 보겠습니다." Jerry Shaw는 얼굴에 미소를 띤 채 전화를 끊었다. 콧노래를 부르며 그는 약간의 현금을 인출하기 위해 은행으로 향했다. 그는 현금 인출기에 멈춰서 카드를 넣고 비밀번호를 눌렀다. "카드가 유효하지 않습니다. 창구 직원에게 문의하세요."라는 메시지가 화면에 떴다. '뭐라고? 내 보너스는 방금 입금되었다고!' 은행에 들어가서 Jerry는 창구 직원에게 무슨 일이 일어났는지 말했다. 그녀는 화면을 살펴보더니 얼굴을 찌푸렸다. "Shaw 씨, 고객님의 계좌는 해지되었습니다. 고객님이 계좌를 해지하셨을 때 모든 예금이 인출되었습니다."라고 그녀가 말했다. "그게 무슨 뜻이죠? 난 절대 그런 적이 없어요! 이건 신분 도용이 틀림없어요!" Jerry는 목소리를 거의 억누르지 못하고 소리쳤다.

지문 간단히 보기

보너스 5,000달러를 받은 Jerry → 미소 & 콧노래 ▶ **기쁨**

↓

현금 인출을 시도했는데 카드가 유효하지 않다고 뜸

↓

Jerry가 계좌 해지 및 전액 출금 사실을 듣고, 목소리를 억누르지 못함 ▶ **당황**

해설 보너스를 입금받았다는 소식에 즐거워했던 Jerry가 모든 현금이 인출된 사실을 알고 당황했다는 내용이므로, 심경 변화로 ① '기쁜 → 당황한'이 적절하다.

오답풀이

보기 해석	선택률
② 불안한 → 부러운	1%
③ 연민 어린 → 지친	1%
④ 고마운 → 무관심한	1%
⑤ 혼란스러운 → 열정적인	1%

구문 [8행] **Entering the bank**, Jerry told the teller **what had happened.**
▶ 콤마 앞은 분사구문(~하면서)이다.
▶ told의 직접목적어로 what이 이끄는 명사절(~것)이 왔다.

02   정답 ⑤   43%   2023 7월 22번

해석 성공적이고 공평하려면, 생태계 관리는 빈곤 감소와 연결되어야 한다. 도시 기반 시설 프로젝트는 보존, 생계, 그리고 자원의 공평한 분배 사이의 균형(상충 관계)을 다루어야 한다. 역사적으로 보호 구역을 만드는 보존 모델이 지역사회로서는 접근할 수 없는 것으로 인식될 때 긴장이 있었다. 흔히, 이러한 모델은 가난하고 소외된 거주자와 그 지역에서 나는 자원 사용자들의 희생으로 실행된다. 생태계 서비스를 보호할 필요성과, 지역사회의 필요를 해결할 목적으로 자원을 사용하려는 욕구 사이에 균형이 없기 때문에, 사회적, 경제적, 및 환경적 개발 프로그램은 지속 가능한 발전에 있어 장애물이었다. 지역사회는 스스로 선택 가능한 것을 파악하여 협상하고 예상치 못한 변화에 대처할 수 있는 유연성을 높일 수 있어야 한다.

지문 간단히 보기

생태계 관리는 빈곤 감소와 연관되어야 함

↓

(생태계) 보호 구역 모델은 빈곤층을 희생시켰고, 생태계 보호 목적과 지역사회의 필요가 조화를 이루지 못하는 상태로 실행되어 옴

↓

지역사회가 자기 필요에 따라 협상할 수 있게 해야 함
▶ **빈곤층, 지역사회의 요구가 반영되게 할 필요 있음**

해설 생태계 관리는 빈곤 감소와 연관되어야 하므로, 지역사회와 빈곤층의 필요를 희생시키며 생태계를 관리하던 지금까지의 관행을 바로잡아야 한다는 내용이다. 따라서 요지로 ⑤ '생태계 관리 시 빈곤층을 포함한 지역사회의 요구를 고려할 필요가 있다.'가 가장 적절하다.

오답풀이

보기 해설	선택률
① '도시 개발'은 언급되지 않았다.	8%
② '기반 시설 확충, 재정 지원'에 관해서는 언급되지 않았다.	4%
③ 지역 '간의' 협력은 언급되지 않았다. 빈곤층의 필요를 고려하라는 것이 핵심이다.	11%
④ 자원의 '순환'에 관해서는 언급되지 않았다. '지속가능한 발전'만 보고 고르지 않도록 한다.	34%

구문 [1행] **In order to be** successful and equitable, ecosystem management must be linked to poverty reduction.
▶ in order to-V는 so as to-V와 마찬가지로 목적(~하려면, ~하기 위해서)을 나타낸다. 혹은 이를 to-V(To be ~)로만 써도 같은 의미를 나타낼 수 있다.

03 정답 ② 29%   2023 9월 21번

해석 프로젝트에서 금도금이란 예상되는 결과를 불필요하게 향상하는 것, 즉 비용이 많이 들면서 필수적이지는 않고 목표와 관련해서는 부가 가치가 낮은 특성을 더하는 것을 뜻한다. 다시 말해, (작업자) 본인의 재능을 입증한다는 것 외에는 실질적인 명분 없이 더 많이 준다는 뜻이다. 금도금은 특히 프로젝트 팀원들에게 흥미로운데, 이는 전문적 요소가 뚜렷한 프로젝트, 즉 검증된 경력과 폭넓은 전문적 자율성을 갖춘 전문가들이 참여하는 프로젝트에서 흔하기 때문이다. 이런 환경에서 전문가들은 흔히 프로젝트가 자신의 다양한 기술을 테스트하고 강화할 기회라고 본다. 따라서 전적으로 선의에서 금도금에 참여하려는 유혹, 즉 전문가들은 만족시키지만 고객의 요청에는 가치를 더하지 않으면서 동시에 프로젝트의 귀중한 자원을 없애는, 더 많거나 더 질 높은 성과를 달성하려는 강한 유혹이 있다. 속담에서 말하듯이, '최고는 좋음의 적이다'.

지문 간단히 보기

> 금도금의 정의: 부가 가치가 크지 않은 '불필요한' 특징을 작업자가 자기 재능을 보여줄 목적으로 덧붙이는 것
> = 명분 없이 더 많이 주는 것

↓

> 전문적 요소가 강한 프로젝트에서 일어나기 쉬움

↓

> (비유) '최고는 좋음의 적이다' ▶ **'명분이나 필요도 없이 고품질만 추구하는'** 상황을 비판

해설 글에 따르면 금도금이란 재능이나 기술을 입증하려는 것 외에는 명분도 없이 작업의 퀄리티와 양을 계속 높여가는 과정이다. 밑줄 부분은 이를 비판하는 비유이므로, ② '오로지 자기 자신(의 실력)을 입증하기 위해서 작업의 질을 높이는 것은 바람직하지 않다.'가 그 의미로 적절하다.

오답풀이

보기 해석	선택률
① 일에서 완벽을 추구하면 팀원 간 갈등이 야기된다.	9%
③ 필요 이상의 자격을 갖춘 전문가를 프로젝트에 끌어들이면 나쁜 결과로 이어진다.	28%
④ 변화하는 고객 요구에 대응하는 것은 불필요하다.	17%
⑤ 프로젝트를 위해 다양한 기술을 습득한다고 해서 성공이 보장되지는 않는다.	16%

구문 [1행] Gold plating in the project means **needlessly enhancing the expected results**, namely, **adding characteristics ~**
▶ <mean V-ing(~하는 것을 뜻하다)>의 동명사구 2개가 namely를 사이에 두고 구조상 동격을 이룬다.

04 정답 ① 47%   2023 4월 23번

해석 대규모의 장기적인 변화에 직면하는 것은 버거워 보일 수 있다. 세계적 전염병이나 경제적 불평등 같은 문제는 너무 복잡해서 어떤 개입이든 변화를 가져올지도 모른다고 믿기 어려울 수 있다. 무슨 일이 있을지에 대한 두려움을 극복하는 것은 추상적인 것과의 연결에 달려 있다. 예컨대 기후 변화와 같은 문제를 우리의 이웃, 직업, 그리고 관계와 연결하는 것은 개념적인 생각을 구체적인 감정으로 바꾼다. 우리가 사랑하는 해변이 어떻게 사라지고, 더 잦은 홍수가 어떻게 우리 집을 파괴할 수도 있는지, 혹은 커지는 산불 위험을 피하려면 우리가 어떻게 이동해야 할 수도 있을 것인지 생각하는 것은 분노, 슬픔 혹은 죄책감 같은 감정을 불러일으킨다. 우리가 행동하도록 자극하는 감정 말이다. 최근 한 연구는 사람들이 잠재적인 기후 변화로 개인적으로 영향을 받는다고 느낄 때 탄소 감소 노력을 지지하고 사전적 정책을 요구할 가능성이 더 크다는 점을 발견했다. 잠재적 미래와의 감정적인 연결을 형성하는 것은 우리가 부정과 절망에서 행동으로 이동하도록 도와준다.

지문 간단히 보기

> 대규모의 장기적 변화에 대한 두려움을 극복하려면, 추상적인 것과의 연결이 필요

↓

> (예시) 기후 변화와 개인적인 것(이웃, 직업 등)을 연결
> → 감정적 반응(분노, 슬픔, 죄책감)
> → 행동 자극(탄소 감소 지지, 정책 요구 등)

↓

> (결론) 잠정적 미래와 감정적인 연결을 형성하면 우리가 실제 행동에 나서는 데 도움이 됨

해설 너무 복잡하고 크게, 즉 '멀게' 느껴지는 문제를 우리의 직업, 인간관계 등 '개인적인' 요소와 연관지어 생각하면 문제 해결을 위해 행동하기 쉬워진다는 내용이다. 따라서 주제로 ① '동떨어진 문제를 개인적으로 만드는 것의 효과'가 가장 적절하다.

오답풀이

보기 해석	선택률
② 뉴스의 부정적인 어조가 문제 해결에 미치는 영향	16%
③ 대규모 문제 해결을 위한 전문가들의 기여	17%
④ 기후 변화를 최소화하는 데 있어 개인적인 개입의 한계	15%
⑤ 한정된 정보로 사건을 예측하려는 시도의 위험성	6%

구문 [5행] Working through fears of what could be **depends** on connecting with the abstract.
▶ 동명사구 주어는 단수 취급한다(depends).

05 정답 ② 92%　　　　　2024학년도 수능 26번

해석　가장 영향력 있는 미국의 물리학자 중 한 사람인 Charles H. Townes는 사우스캐롤라이나에서 태어났다. 어린 시절에 그는 하늘에 있는 별들을 관찰하면서 농장에서 성장했다. 그는 1939년에 California Institute of Technology에서 박사 학위를 받았고, 이후 뉴욕시에 있는 Bell Labs에 일자리를 얻었다. 제2차 세계 대전 후에 그는 Columbia 대학교의 물리학 부교수가 되었다. 1958년에 Townes와 그의 공동 연구자는 레이저의 개념을 제안했다. 레이저 기술은 산업과 연구에서 빠르게 수용되었다. 그는 1964년에 노벨 물리학상을 수상했다. 또한 그는 달 착륙 프로젝트인 Project Apollo에 관여했다. 인터넷과 모든 디지털 미디어가 레이저 없이는 상상할 수 없을 것이라는 점에서, 그의 공헌은 대단히 귀중하다.

지문 간단히 보기

> Charles H. Townes의 생애
> ① 어린 시절 별을 관찰하며 농장에서 자람
> ② 1939년 박사 학위 취득 → 이후 Bell Labs에서 근무
> ③ 1958년 동료와 함께 레이저 개념 제안
> ④ 1964년 노벨 물리학상 수상
> ⑤ 달 착륙 프로젝트인 Project Apollo에 관여

해설　'He earned his doctoral degree ~, and then he took a job at Bell Labs in New York City.'에 따르면, Charles H. Townes가 Bell Labs에서 근무한 것은 박사 학위를 취득하고 '나서'이다. and then이 선후 관계를 잡는 결정적 단서이다. 따라서 일치하지 않는 것은 ② '박사 학위를 받기 전에 Bell Labs에서 일했다.'이다.

오답풀이

보기 해설	선택률
①　In his childhood, he grew up on a farm, ~	1%
③　In 1958, ~ proposed the concept of the laser.	3%
④　He received the Nobel Prize in Physics in 1964.	0%
⑤　He was also involved in ~ the moon landing project.	1%

구문　[1행] Charles H. Townes, **one of the most influential American physicists,** was born in South Carolina.
▶ 2개의 콤마 사이에 주어의 지위를 보충 설명하는 동격 명사구로 <one of the+최상급+복수명사(가장 ~한 …들 중 하나)>가 삽입되었다.

06 정답 ② 28%　　　　　2023학년도 수능 29번

해석　유행은 사람들이 본인을 다시 (새롭게) 선보일 새로운 기회를 끊임없이 제시하며 변화의 때를 나타낸다. 유행이 궁극적으로 어떻게 개인에게 힘과 자유를 줄 수 있는지를 이해하려면, 먼저 변화의 기반이 되는 패션의 중요성을 논해야 한다. 왜 패션이 그토록 매력적인지에 관해 나의 정보 출처원들이 준 가장 흔한 설명은 그것이 일종의 연극적 의상을 구성한다는 것이다. 옷은 사람들이 본인을 세상에 보여주는 방식의 일부이고, 패션은 현재 사회 상황과 패션 자체의 역사와 관련지어 이들을 현재에 위치시킨다. 표현 형태로서, 패션은 다수의 모호함을 담고 있어 개인이 특정 의상과 연관된 의미를 재창조할 수 있게 한다. 패션은 자기표현의 가장 단순하고 값싼 방법 중 하나이다. 즉, 옷은 저렴하게 구매될 수 있는 한편, 부, 지적 능력, 휴식 또는 환경 의식(비록 이중 아무것도 해당되지 않는다 해도)의 개념을 전달하기 쉽게 만든다. 또한 패션은 다양한 방법으로 행동성을 강화하여, 행동의 여지를 열어줄 수 있다.

지문 간단히 보기

> 유행은 사람들이 본인을 다시 선보일 기회를 계속 제공

↓

> 변화의 기반이 되는 패션의 중요성(= 개인에게 힘과 자유 부여)
> - 패션은 자기표현의 수단
> - 특정 옷의 의미는 개인에 의해 계속 재창조됨
> - 패션은 행동의 여지를 열어주기도 함

해설　문맥상 ②가 포함된 문장은 옷을 사람들이 '자기 자신'을 표현하는 수단으로 이해할 수 있다는 의미다. 즉 동사 present의 주어와 목적어가 모두 people이다. 이렇듯 특정 행위의 주어와 목적어가 일치할 때 목적어 자리에는 재귀대명사를 써야 하므로, ②에는 them 대신 themselves를 써야 옳다.

오답풀이

보기 해설	선택률
①　is 뒤로 주격 보어 역할을 하는 명사절을 이끌기 위해 접속사 that을 바르게 썼다.	9%
③　the meanings가 특정 옷과 '연관지어진' 대상이므로 과거분사로 수식한다.	22%
④　동사구 <can be p.p.>를 꾸미는 부사이다.	15%
⑤　콤마 앞의 주절을 보충하는 분사구문(그리고 ~하다)이다. 분사구문의 의미상 주어 Fashion이 '열어주는' 주체이므로 현재분사를 썼다.	26%

구문　[6행] **The most common explanation** offered by my informants as to why fashion is so appealing **is** that it constitutes a kind of theatrical costumery.
▶ 주어가 단수명사이므로 동사도 단수형(is)으로 쓰였다.
▶ 밑줄 부분은 explanation을 꾸미는 과거분사구이다. as to는 '~에 관해서'라는 뜻이다. 뒤에 what, why, how 등 의문사가 이끄는 명사절이 주로 나온다.

07 정답 ③ 53%

해석 목표에 몰두하는 사고방식이 실수가 될 수도 있다고 우려할 만한 근거가 있다. 많은 연구에 따르면, 우리는 자기 통제를 한다는 게 얼마나 쉬운지에 관해 과신하는 경향이 있다. 바로 이 이유로, 우리 중 매우 많은 사람이 방문당 이용료를 내는 것이 더 저렴할 텐데도 낙관적이게도 비싼 체육관 회원권을 사고, 절대 끝내지 못할 온라인 강좌에 등록하며, 한 달 치 간식 예산을 줄일 목적으로 할인하는 대형 과자를 사 놓고는 결국 앉은 자리에서 한 번에 마지막 부스러기까지 다 먹는다. 우리는 '미래의 나'가 좋은 선택을 할 수 있을 거라 생각하지만, '현재의 나'는 너무도 자주 유혹에 굴복한다. 사람들에게는 본인의 실패를 무시하는 놀라운 능력이 있다. 거듭 실패하면서도, 우리 중 많은 사람은 과거의 실수로부터 배우기보다는, 다음에는 더 잘할 수 있다는 것에 관한 장밋빛 낙관주의를 용케 유지한다. 우리는 새로운 시작, 그리고 낙관적인 태도를 유지할 다른 이유들에 매달리는데, 이는 우리가 아침에 일어나는 데 도움이 될지는 모르지만, 최대한 현명한 방식으로 변화에 접근하지는 못하게 막을 수 있다.

지문 간단히 보기

사람들은 자기 통제가 얼마나 쉬울지를 과신하곤 함

↓

'미래의 나'에 대한 낙관적 기대("다음에는 잘할 거야")
vs. 유혹에 쉽게 굴복하는 '현재의 나'

↓

이런 괴리에도 불구, 낙관주의는 유지되는 경향이 있음
▶ 사람들이 자신의 실패를 '무시하기' 때문

해설 빈칸 뒤에서 사람들은 자기 통제에 거듭 실패하면서도 그 실수로부터 배우기보다는 앞으로 잘할 수 있다는 기대를 고수한다고 한다. 이는 결국 실수를 '무시하면서' 낙관을 유지한다는 의미이므로, 빈칸에는 ③ '무시하는'이 가장 적절하다.

오답풀이

보기 해석	선택률
① 비판하는	10%
② 상기시키는	20%
④ 감지하는	7%
⑤ 과대평가하는	10%

구문 [4행] This is why so many of us optimistically <u>buy</u> ~, <u>register</u> for online classes ~, and <u>purchase</u> family-size chips on discount to trim our monthly snack budget, **only to consume** every last crumb in a single sitting.
▶ 밑줄 친 동사들이 <A, B, and C> 형태로 병렬구조를 이룬다.
▶ <only to+동사원형>은 주로 부정적인 결과(결국 ~하다)를 나타내는 부사구이다.

08 정답 ④ 22%

해석 도시에서 운전하거나 걷거나 교통 카드를 (카드) 인식기에 찍는 모든 사람은 현관문을 나서는 순간부터 자기가 교통 전문가라고 여긴다. 그리고 그 사람이 도로를 바라보는 방식은 그 사람이 돌아다니는 방식과 매우 밀접하게 일치한다. 이 이유로 우리는 선의와 시민 의식을 가진 매우 많은 사람이 서로 언쟁하는 모습을 보게 된다. 학교 강당에서 열리는 주민 회의에서, 도서관과 교회의 뒷방에서, 전국의 지역 주민들이 모여 도시의 도로를 바꿀 교통 제안에 대해 흔히 논쟁적인 토론을 벌인다. 그리고 모든 정치와 마찬가지로, 모든 교통은 지역적이고 지극히 개인적이다. 수만 명의 이동 속도를 높일 수 있는 교통 프로젝트는 주차 공간 몇 개가 없어지는 것에 대한 반대, 또는 프로젝트가 효과가 없을 것이라는 단순한 두려움 때문에 중단될 수 있다. 그것은 데이터나 교통 공학 또는 계획의 문제가 아니다. 도로에 대한 대중 토론은 변화가 개인의 통근, 주차 능력, 무엇이 안전하고 또 안전하지 않은가에 대한 신념, 또는 지역 사업체의 순익에 어떤 영향을 미칠지에 대한 감정적인 추정에 보통 뿌리를 둔다.

지문 간단히 보기

사람들은 각자 자신이 지역 도로의 전문가라고 여김

↓

그래서 도로에 대한 대중 토론은 논쟁이 많이 수반됨

↓

교통은 지역적이고, 지극히 개인적인 이슈 ▶ **'각자의 이동 방식'에 따라 인식되는 문제**

↓

도로에 대한 대중 토론: 통근, 주차, 안전 등에 관한 사람들 나름의 감정적 추정치에 바탕을 둠

해설 도로 교통은 지역적이고도 '개인적인' 이슈로, 통근이나 주차 등 등의 이슈에 대해 사람들은 '나름의 감정적 추정'을 갖고 토론에 임하기 때문에 논쟁이 많다는 내용이다. 본문의 personal이 정답의 how she gets around와 가장 가깝다는 점에서, ④ '그 사람이 돌아다니는 방식과 매우 밀접하게 일치한다'가 빈칸에 적절하다.

오답풀이

보기 해석	선택률
① 자신의 도시 도로를 타인이 어떻게 보는지에 크게 의존한다	20%
② 새로운 각 대중교통 정책에 맞춰 업데이트된다	29%
③ 그 사람이 다니는 도로와 별개로 생겨난다	9%
⑤ 그 사람의 도시가 운영되는 방식과 긴밀하게 관련 있다	20%

구문 [5행] **That's why** we **find** so many well-intentioned and civic-minded citizens **arguing** past one another.
▶ that's why는 '그 이유로 ~하다'라는 뜻이다.
▶ 밑줄 부분은 <find+목적어+현재분사>의 5형식 구문이다. argue past는 '~와 (엇갈리며) 언쟁하다'라는 뜻이다.

09 정답 ④ 50%

해석 초기 근대 유럽에서 철학과 과학을 특징짓고 이전 전통과의 분리를 나타내는 것은 이론을 권위나 전통보다는 증거에 맞추려는 관심이다. Galileo Galilei, Francis Bacon, René Descartes 등등은 이전 사상가들의 선언에 호소하지 않고 하늘, 주변 자연 세계, 그리고 인간의 본성과 사회에 대한 설명을 정립했다. 종교의 원칙과 교회의 교리도 이들을 이끈 빛이 아니었다. 그보다는, 이들은 일부 사상가들이 '자연의 빛'이라고 불렀던 이성, 그리고 경험을 따랐다. (이성과 경험 사이의 우위에 관한 격렬한 논쟁이 계속되었지만, 모든 진지한 사상가들은 근대 과학과 철학의 발전 과정에서 결국 경험을 버렸다.) 이들이 연역의 논리에 따랐든, 혹은 경험적 자료 분석을 통해 나아갔든, 이들이 발전시킨 근대 과학의 방법은 이성에 따라, 그리고 이용 가능한 증거에 비춰 이론을 검증하는 데 있다.

지문 간단히 보기

근대 과학: 이론을 전통보다 증거에 맞추려 함

↓

①~③ (예시) Galilei, Bacon, Descartes 등의 학자들: 이전의 사상과 종교에 기대지 않고, 이성과 경험을 따름

↓

⑤ (결론) 근대 과학의 방법론: 이성과 증거에 입각한 이론 검증

해설 근대 과학에 이르러 이론을 전통이나 종교보다도 이성, 증거, 경험에 따라 검증하고자 했다는 내용이다. 하지만 ④는 과학자들이 이성과 경험 사이 우월성에 관한 논쟁의 결과로 '경험을 버렸다'는 내용이므로 흐름상 어울리지 않는다.

오답풀이

보기 해설		선택률
①	이전의 권위에 기대지 않은 학자들의 예를 들며 첫 문장을 뒷받침한다.	4%
②	①의 사상가들이 종교라는 기존의 권위와 전통에 따르지 않았다는 내용이므로 첫 문장과 같은 흐름이다.	19%
③	①의 사상가들이 권위보다 '이성과 경험'에 의지했다는 내용이므로 첫 문장과 같은 흐름이다.	19%
⑤	첫 문장의 재진술로, 근대 과학 방법론의 핵심이 이성과 근거임을 다시금 제시한다. they가 여전히 ①의 사상가들을 가리킨다.	7%

구문 [9행] **Nor were religious principles and ecclesiastic dogma** their guiding lights.

▶ 부정어구가 강조되기 위해 문장 맨 앞에 나오면 뒤따르는 주어와 동사는 의문문 어순으로 도치된다. 그리하여 <nor+be+주어(~도 않다)> 어순의 도치 구문이 완성되었다.

10 정답 ⑤ 27%

해석 식물은 영양분이 제한적일 때 미세 조정된 적응 반응을 보인다. 정원사는 노란 잎이 영양 부족과 비료의 필요성에 대한 신호임을 아마도 알아차릴 것이다.
(C) 그러나 식물에게 보충 미네랄을 공급해 줄 관리자가 없다면, 식물은 뿌리를 증식하거나 길게 늘이고 뿌리털을 발달시켜, 더 먼 토양에서 (영양분을) 구하러 다닐 수 있게 할 것이다. 또한 식물은 기억을 사용해서 영양 혹은 자원 가용성의 시간적 또는 공간적 변화의 역사에 대응할 수 있다.
(B) 이 분야의 연구는 식물이 공간 및 시간 모두의 측면에서 환경 속 자기 위치를 계속 인식한다는 것을 보여주었다. 과거에 다양한 영양 가용성을 경험한 식물은 잎 생산 대신 뿌리 길이 연장에 에너지를 소비하는 등, 위험을 감수하는 행동을 보이는 경향이 있다.
(A) 반대로, 영양분이 풍부했던 이력을 가진 식물은 위험을 회피하고 에너지를 절약한다. 모든 발달 단계에서 식물은 성장, 생존, 번식에 에너지를 사용할 수 있도록 환경 변화나 불균형에 대처하는 동시에, 귀중한 에너지의 손상과 비생산적인 사용을 제한한다.

지문 간단히 보기

식물의 영양분 부족 신호 → 정원사가 보고 파악

↓

(C) 하지만 관리자(정원사)가 없다면, 식물은 뿌리 연장 등의 방법을 동원하면서, 자신의 '기억'도 이용해 시공간적 변화에 대처

↓

(B) (자신의 위치를 시간·공간 측면에서 모두 인식해 대응하는 예시)
영양 상태 변동이 큰 환경에서 자랐던 식물 → 위험 감수
(A) 반면, 영양분이 풍부했던 식물 → 위험 회피

해설 주어진 글과 (C)는 (C) 처음의 But을 기준으로 식물이 영양분 부족에 관해 보내는 신호를 알아줄 관리자가 '있는 vs. 없는' 상황으로 대비된다. 한편 (C) 후반부와 (B) 초반부는 식물이 환경의 '시공간적 변화'를 인식하고 이에 대처한다는 공통된 내용을 다룬다. (A)는 (B)와 '반대되는' 사례를 다루므로 마지막에 온다. 따라서 ⑤ '(C)-(B)-(A)'가 적절하다.

오답풀이 보기 해설

		선택률
①	주어진 글과 (A)가 반대되는(In contrast) 내용이 아니므로 (A)부터 배치하면 어색하다.	5%
②,	'연구'만 보고 (B)를 주어진 글의 예시라고 오해하지 않도록 한다. 주어진 글과 (C)가 '관리자'라는 공통된 소재를	21%
③	언급한다는 점에서 첫 단락은 (C)일 수밖에 없다.	25%
④	(A)의 '영양분이 풍부한 환경을 경험한 식물'과 대비될 만한 대상이 (C)에 언급되지 않는다.	22%

구문 [A-2행] ~ **while limiting** damage and non-productive uses of their valuable energy.

▶ <접속사+현재분사(~하는 동시에, 한편)> 형태의 분사구문이다. 접속사를 남겨 분사구문의 의미를 분명히 했다.

11 정답 ⑤ 16%

해석 아날로그 기술에서 디지털 기술로의 전환은 음악 제작 방식에 크게 영향을 미쳤다. 무엇보다도, 소리의 디지털화, 즉 숫자로의 변환은 음악 제작자들이 이미 끝낸 작업을 되돌릴 수 있게 해 주었다. 다시 말해, 원본을 희생하지 않고도 소리를 비틀고 구부려서 새로운 뭔가로 만들 수 있었다. 이 '되돌리기' 기능은 실수를 훨씬 덜 중대하게 만들어, 창작 과정을 촉발하고 대체로 더 실험적인 사고방식을 촉진했다. 또한, 디지털로 변환된 소리는 물리적인 도구를 사용하기보다는 디지털 메시지를 프로그래밍하는 것만으로 조작될 수 있어서, 편집 과정을 크게 간소화했다. 가령, 한때 편집 과정에는 음성 녹음테이프를 물리적으로 자르고 합쳐 이으려면 면도기 칼날이 필요했지만, 이제는 컴퓨터에 기반한 순서기 프로그램의 커서와 마우스 클릭이 수반되어, 확실히 시간이 덜 소모됐다. 디지털로 변환된 소리 조작이란 2진법 정보를 다시 프로그래밍한다는 의미였으므로, 편집 작업은 1,000분의 1초의 정밀도로 수행될 수 있었다. 이런 초미세 수준의 접근은 (무음 지점에서 트랙을 결합하는 것 같은) 그 어떤 조작 흔적이든 즉시 숨기기 더 쉽게 만들어주었고, 잘 들리고 실험적인 방식으로 소리를 조작할 새로운 가능성을 내놓았다.

지문 간단히 보기

> 소리의 디지털화 → '되돌리기' 작업 가능 → 편집 작업 간소화

> 디지털화 이전: 물리적 작업(테이프를 자르고 붙임)
> vs. 오늘날: 마우스 클릭, 커서 조작 = 1,000분의 1초 단위의 정밀도

> '이러한 초미세 접근' → 실험적 시도에 대한 가능성 ↑

해설 과거에는 음악을 편집하려면 면도날로 테이프를 자르고 이어야 했지만 현재에는 클릭만 하면 된다는 것이 ⑤ 앞의 내용인데, ⑤ 뒤에서는 갑자기 대명사 This와 함께 '초미세 접근'을 언급하므로 흐름이 끊긴다. 이때 주어진 문장을 보면 '1,000분의 1초'라는 표현이 등장하여 '초미세 접근'이라는 표현과 자연스럽게 연결되므로, ⑤에 주어진 문장을 넣어야 한다.

오답풀이

보기 해설	선택률
① 앞뒤 문장이 in other words로 연결되는 동일한 내용이다.	3%
② 앞의 'twist and bend sounds ~'를 뒤에서 간단하게 This "undo" ability로 받았다.	7%
③ 창의적 과정이 촉진되었다는 앞 내용에 이어 과정 자체도 간단해졌다는 설명이 In addition으로 잘 연결된다.	24%
④ 앞에서 '편집 과정의 간소화'라는 일반적 내용을 말하고 뒤에서 예를 드는 흐름이다(For example).	51%

구문 [24행] This microlevel access at once **made it easier to conceal** any traces of manipulations ~
▶ <make+가목적어+형용사+to부정사> 형태의 5형식 가목적어 구문이다. it을 '그것'으로 해석하지 말고, to부정사를 목적어로 해석해야 한다.

12 정답 ① 48%

해석 햄스터를 쳇바퀴에 올려놓으면 달리기 시작할 것이다. 햄스터에게 먹을 것을 주면 훨씬 더 오래 달릴 것이다. 먹을 것을 그만 주면 햄스터는 달리기를 완전히 멈출 것이다. 그것으로 원래의 동기는 소멸되었다. 학교 시스템은 어린 아이들의 자연스러운 호기심과 발견의 기쁨을 칭찬, 성적, 그리고 다른 단기적인 성취 촉진책으로 대체하여 이런 심리적 특징을 이용해 왔다. 이야기에 따르면, 옛날에 자기 집 현관에서 노을 보기를 즐기던 한 노인이 있었다. 어느 날, 아이들 한 무리가 오더니 그의 집 앞에서 시끄럽게 놀기 시작했다. 그 남자는 아이들에게 비켜달라고 요청했지만, 그들은 그의 말을 무시했다. 다음날 아이들이 다시 왔다. 그 남자는 그들을 불러서, 각 아이들에게 5센트씩 주고, 가능한 한 최대로 시끄러운 소리를 내 달라고 요청했고, 이들은 그 말에 즐겁게 따랐다. 남자는 계속 규칙적으로 동전을 나누어 주다가, 어느 날 아이들에게 돈을 더 이상 주지 않겠다고 말했다. 아이들은 "그럼 우리는 할아버지를 위해 시끄러운 소리를 내지 않겠어요."라고 알리고는 가 버렸다.
→ (어떤) 행동에 대한 (B)보상을 일정 기간 지속해서 제공하다가 이후 그것(보상)을 주지 않으면 개인이 그 무언가를 하려는 의지를 (A)없애는 것이 가능하다.

지문 간단히 보기

> 쳇바퀴를 달리던 햄스터에게 보상을 주다가 끊으면, 햄스터가 달릴 동기를 잃고 멈춰버림

> 마찬가지로, 소음을 일으키는 아이들에게 그에 대한 보상을 주다가 끊으면, 아이들은 동기를 잃고 더 이상 시끄러운 소리를 내지 않음

해설 달리는 햄스터와 소음을 내는 아이들의 사례에서 공통된 결론은, 어떤 행동에 관해 일정 기간 보상이 주어지다가 보상이 없어지고 나면 그 행동을 지속할 자연스러운 동기가 사라지게 된다는 것이다. 따라서 요약문의 빈칸에는 ① '없애는 - 보상'이 들어가야 한다.

오답풀이

보기 해설	선택률
② 없애는 - 처벌	11%
③ 강화하는 - 설명	6%
④ 평가하는 - 처벌	7%
⑤ 강화하는 - 보상	28%

구문 [15행] The man ~ **asked them to make** as much noise as they possibly could—**to which** they happily obliged.
▶ <ask+목적어+to부정사(~에게 …해 달라고 요청하다)>의 5형식 구문이다.
▶ to which는 밑줄 친 부분을 보충 설명하는 <전치사+관계대명사>로, 뒤에 완전한 문장이 연결된다.

13~14 정답 ④ 43% / ③ 69%   2023 7월 41~42번

해석 일반화는 인지 경제성을 촉진하고, 그래서 우리는 중요하지 않은 세부 사항에는 집중하지 않는다. 러시아의 위대한 신경심리학자인 Alexander Luria는 Solomon Shereshevsky라는 한 환자를 연구했는데, 그는 우리가 일반적으로 듣는 것과 반대되는 기억력 장애를 가지고 있었다. 즉, Solomon은 기억을 잃는 증상인 기억상실증을 지닌 것이 아니었다. 그는 Luria가 기억과잉증이라고 부른 것을 갖고 있었다(그의 초능력이 뛰어난 기억력이었다고 말할 수 있을 것이다). 그의 과한 기억력은 그가 단 한 번 들은 연설의 마디마디, 또는 복잡한 수학 공식, 긴 숫자 배열, 그리고 그가 심지어 구사할 줄도 모르는 외국어로 된 시를 암송하는 것 같은 놀라운 재주를 선보이게 해주었다. 그런 환상적인 기억력을 갖는 건 좋을 거라고 생각하기도 전에, 여기에는 대가가 따랐다. Solomon은 모든 세부 사항을 별개의 것으로 기억했기 때문에 추상화를 할 수 없었다. 그는 사람들을 알아보는 데 특별한 어려움이 있었다. 신경인지적 관점에서, 여러분이 어떤 얼굴을 볼 때마다 지난번과는 적어도 약간 다르게 보일 가능성이 없다(→ 가능성이 있다). 여러분은 전과 다른 각도와 거리에서 그것을 보고 있으며, 어쩌면 다른 표정을 마주치고 있을지도 모른다. 여러분이 어떤 사람과 상호작용하는 동안, 그들의 얼굴에 일련의 표정이 지나간다. 여러분의 뇌가 일반화할 수 있기 때문에, 여러분은 이 모든 다른 얼굴 표정이 같은 사람에게 속한다고 여긴다. Solomon은 그렇게 할 수 없었다. 그가 Luria에게 설명했듯이, '모두에게는 얼굴이 너무 많아서' 그가 친구와 동료를 알아보기란 거의 불가능했다.

지문 간단히 보기

> 일반화로 인해, 우리는 중요하지 않은 세부 사항에 집중하지 않을 수 있음

⬇

> 반대 예시: Solomon이라는 환자
> - '초능력 같은, 과한' 기억력 보유
> - 단 한 번 들은 연설, 복잡한 숫자 공식, 외국어로 된 시 암기 가능

⬇

> 하지만, 과한 기억력의 '대가': 얼굴 인식 불가능
> = 매 순간 달라지는 디테일을 '일반화, 추상화'하지 못함
> ▶ **완벽한 기억력으로 인해 오히려 인식에 '결함' 발생**

구문 [1행] Generalization promotes cognitive economy, **so that** we don't focus on particulars that don't matter.
▶ 접속사 so that은 목적(~하기 위해) 또는 결과(그래서 ~하다)의 의미를 나타낸다. 문맥상 더 자연스러운 의미로 해석하면 된다.
▶ 밑줄 부분은 particulars를 꾸미는 관계절이다. 선행사가 복수명사이므로, 주격 관계대명사 that 뒤에 복수동사(don't matter)가 왔다.

13

해설 기억 과잉증 때문에 모든 세부사항을 완벽히 기억할 수 있었지만 적절한 일반화를 하지 못해 안면 인식에 어려움을 겪었던 Solomon의 사례를 소개하는 글이다. 따라서 제목으로 ④ '완벽한 기억력 때문에 생긴 인식 결함'이 가장 적절하다.

오답풀이

보기 해석	선택률
① 얼굴 인식 기술: 축복인가 아닌가?	15%
② 더 빨리 암기할수록, 더 빨리 잊어버린다	11%
③ 일반화는 지름길이자 함정일 수 있다!	26%
⑤ 나이 들수록 세부 사항을 기억하기 어려워지는 이유	6%

14

해설 'you're viewing it ~ a different expression'에서 우리는 타인의 얼굴을 매번 조금씩은 다른 각도와 표정으로 마주하게 된다고 한다. 즉 우리가 같은 얼굴을 보더라도 조금씩은 세부 사항이 달라질 가능성이 '있다'는 의미로, ③ (c)의 unlikely를 likely로 바꿔야 한다.

오답풀이

보기 해석	선택률
① opposite(반대)	3%
② cost(대가)	6%
④ generalize(일반화하다)	14%
⑤ recognizing(알아보기, 인식하기)	4%

STEP PLUS+ 수능 기출 마무리 복습

단어 TEST
02 유효한, 타당한 **03** 뚜렷한, 두드러진 **04** (감정을) 불러일으키다 **05** 모호함, 애매함 **06** 과대평가하다 **07** 지극히, 강렬하게 **08** 생기다, 발생하다 **09** 우위, 우월성 **10** 풍부함 **11** 희생하다 **12** 재주, 기량

구문 TEST
14 Once reaching[having reached] the summit **15** to find it difficult to play **16** What characterizes modern science is **17** What I find astonishing **18** take time rather than (to) rush

01　정답 ① 77%

2023 3월 18번

해석　Arkansas 주의 중심부에 위치한 Morganic Corporation은 훌륭한 유기농 작물을 경쟁력 있는 가격에 제공하면서 지난 10년을 보냈고, 국내 9위의 선도적인 유기농 회사로 성장했습니다. Morganic의 설립자이자 회장인 Richard Taylor와 친분이 있는 노련한 작가로서, 저는 Taylor에 대한 인물 소개 기사 작성을 귀 잡지에 제안합니다. 저는 유기농 산업에서 (이뤄진) Morganic의 성공을 취재할 때가 왔다고 믿습니다. 그 기사는 Taylor와 Morganic의 이용 가능한 사진들과 함께 통상적 단어 범주인 800~1,200단어로 작성될 것입니다. 이 기사를 고려해 주셔서 고맙습니다. 귀하로부터 곧 소식 듣기를 바랍니다.

지문 간단히 보기

Morganic Corporation: 선도적인 유기농 회사

↓

이 회사 창업주를 소개하는 인물 기사 작성 제안: 사진 포함 800~1,200단어 분량 예상

↓

마무리 인사: 검토 후 회신 요청

해설　선도적인 유기농 회사 창업주를 소개하는 기사를 작성해보겠다고 제안하는 글로, 'I propose ~' 문장에 글의 목적이 직접 제시된다. 따라서 정답으로 ① '잡지사에 기사 기고를 하겠다고 제안하려고'가 가장 적절하다.

오답풀이

보기 해설	선택률
② '지면을 늘려달라'는 요청은 제시되지 않았다. '기사'만 보고 고르지 않도록 한다.	10%
③ 유기농 회사 '제품'이 아닌, 'CEO'를 소개하고 싶다는 내용이다.	5%
④ 기사를 쓰기 전이므로 피드백도 오기 전이다.	4%
⑤ '창업'에 관해서는 언급되지 않았다.	1%

구문　[1행] Morganic Corporation, <u>located in the heart of Arkansas</u>, **spent the past decade providing** great organic crops at a competitive price, ~

▶ 밑줄 친 과거분사구는 주어와 동사 사이에 삽입되어 주어인 Morganic Corporation을 보충 설명한다.

▶ <spend+시간+동명사(~하는 데 …을 보내다)> 구문이다.

02　정답 ① 60%

2021 4월 20번

해석　종종 현대 부모들은 자녀를 어떤 이유로든 꾸짖는다면 더는 자녀가 자신을 좋아하지 않거나 심지어는 사랑해주지 않을 거라는 두려움으로 마비된다. 이들은 무엇보다 자녀와의 우정을 원하며, 이를 얻기 위해 존경을 기꺼이 희생한다. 좋지 않은 일이다. 자녀에게 친구는 많겠지만, 부모는 기껏해야 단 둘뿐이며, (그래서) 부모는 친구 이하가 아니라 이상이다. 친구들은 바로잡아줄 수 있는 권한이 매우 제한적이다. 따라서, 모든 부모는 필요한 교정 조치가 이뤄진 후에는, 자녀가 장기적 결과를 인식하거나 신경쓸 수 있는 능력이 제한되어 있어서 부모를 향해 느끼는 순간적인 분노나 심지어 증오까지도 견디는 법을 배워야 한다. 부모는 사회의 심판관이다. 그들은 다른 사람들이 의미 있고도 생산적으로 자녀와 상호 작용할 수 있도록 자녀에게 잘 처신하는 법을 가르친다.

지문 간단히 보기

현대 부모들은 자녀를 혼냈다가 미움을 살까 몹시 두려워함
→ 자녀와 친구처럼 지내려 함

↓

하지만, 부모는 자녀에게 '친구 이상'
= 분노나 증오를 사더라도, 행동을 바로잡아줘야 함
= '사회의 심판관'
= 올바른 상호작용과 처신 방법을 알려줘야 함

해설　부모는 아이에게 미움을 살까 봐 두려워하지 말고 아이가 올바르게 행동하고 상호 작용할 수 있도록 행동을 고쳐주어야 한다는 내용이다. 따라서 필자의 주장으로 ① '부모는 두려워 말고 자녀의 잘못된 행동을 바로잡아 주어야 한다.'가 가장 적절하다.

오답풀이

보기 해설	선택률
② 양육 태도의 '일관성'에 관해 언급되지 않는다.	2%
③ '다양한 경험 제공'에 관해 언급되지 않는다.	11%
④ 친구와 부모의 역할을 비교할 뿐, 부모가 자녀의 친구 관계에 개입한다는 내용은 다루지 않았다.	16%
⑤ 친구 '이상'의 역할, 즉 행동을 바로잡아주는 역할을 해야 한다는 것이 핵심이다.	7%

구문　[1행] ~ the fear [**that** they will no longer be liked or even loved by their children if **they** scold **them** for any reason].

▶ the fear 뒤로 동격의 that절이 '두려움'의 내용을 설명한다. 동격 접속사 that 뒤에는 완전한 절이 나온다.

▶ scold의 주어인 they는 parents를, 목적어인 them은 their children을 가리킨다. 즉 주어와 목적어가 서로 달라 재귀대명사를 쓰지 않았다.

03 정답 ② 31%

해석 협업의 전등 스위치를 탁 누르는 것은 지도자들이 직위상 고유하게 맡은 일인데, 왜냐하면 몇 가지 장애물이 자발적으로 혼자 일하는 사람들을 방해하기 때문이다. 우선, 상황을 잘 모르고 혼자 남겨진다는 두려움은 이들이 기업 소셜미디어에 계속 매달리게 할 수 있다. 개인들은 고립되거나 고립된 것처럼 보이는 상황을 원치 않는다. 또 다른 이유로는, 팀 동료들이 무엇을 하고 있는지 아는 것이 편안하고 안전하다는 느낌을 제공하는데, 사람들은 집단과 조화를 이룰 수 있도록 자기 행동을 조정할 수 있기 때문이다. 혼자 벗어나서 아마도 바로 처음부터 성공적이지 않을 새로운 뭔가를 시도하는 것은 위험천만하다. 하지만 사람들이 과잉 연결되는 것이 안도감을 줄지라도, 그들이 주기적으로 자리를 떠나 혼자 생각하여, 그다지 성숙하지는 않더라도 다양한 아이디어를 창안하는 것이 조직을 위해 더 좋다. 따라서, 사람들이 (전체에 유익한 여건을) 스스로 선택하지 않는 때에도, 처벌처럼 보이게 하지 않으면서 간헐적인 상호작용을 시행하여 전체에 유익한 여건을 조성하는 것이 지도자의 임무가 된다.

지문 간단히 보기

'협업의 스위치를 누르는 것': 리더만의 역할

↓

사람들은 혼자 있기 두렵다는 이유로, 혹은 동료가 뭘 하는지 알아야 안심된다는 이유로 '과잉 연결' 유지

↓

조직을 위해서는 '혼자' 생각해보는 것이 유익
→ 상호작용이 '간헐적으로' 이뤄질 여건을 조성해줘야 함
▶ **사람들이 종종 연결을 중단하고 혼자 일하게 해줘야 함**

해설 리더는 직원들이 집단과의 과도한 연결에서 벗어나 혼자 생각해볼 시간을 갖게 해줘야 한다는 내용으로 보아, 밑줄 친 부분은 협업을 때때로 '중단시킨다'는 의미일 것이다. 따라서 ② '사람들이 협업을 그만두고 개인 작업을 시작하게 하는 것'이 답으로 적절하다.

오답풀이

보기 해석	선택률
① 협력을 방해하는 물리적 장벽과 집단 규범을 깨는 것	17%
③ 사람들이 온라인 협업에 시간을 더 들이도록 격려하는 것	11%
④ 더 높은 생산성이 요구되는 환경을 조성하는 것	12%
⑤ 직원들이 집단 프로젝트에 주의 집중하도록 요구하는 것	27%

구문 [13행] But even though **it** feels reassuring **for** individuals **to be** hyperconnected, ~
▶ <it ~ for … to ~> 형태의 가주어-진주어 구문으로, <for+목적격>이 to부정사의 의미상 주어를 표시한다.

04 정답 ② 46%

해석 영국의 저명한 통계학자인 F. Yates에 관한 이야기가 있다. Cambridge의 St. John's College에서의 학창 시절에, Yates는 일종의 스포츠에 매우 관심이 많았다. (그 스포츠란) 밤에 대학 건물들의 지붕과 탑들을 올라타는 것이었다. 특히, St. John's College 예배당에는 성인들의 동상으로 장식된 거대한 신고딕 양식의 탑이 있는데, Yates에게는 이 성인들에게 흰 가운으로 적절히 옷을 입히면 분명히 더 품위 있어 보일 듯했다. 어느 밤 그는 기어올라서 그렇게 했고(가운을 옷처럼 입었고), 다음날 아침 그 결과는 대체로 많은 칭찬을 받았다. 하지만 대학 관계자들은 인정해 주지 않았으며, 그 성인 (동상)들이 새로 얻은 의복을 벗길 방법을 생각하기 시작했다. 이는 쉽지 않은 일이었는데, 그것들이 어느 일반 사다리든 도무지 닿을 수 없는 곳에 있었기 때문이다. 갈고리가 달린 밧줄을 사용해 위에서 흰 가운을 들어올리려는 시도는 성공하지 못했다. 아무 진전도 이뤄지지 않다가, 결국 Yates가 나서서 자원해 대낮에 올라가서 옷을 갖고 내려오기로 했다. 그는 이 일을 하여 모인 군중을 감탄하게 했다.

지문 간단히 보기

대학 시절 F. Yates의 특이한 취미: 건물 타고 오르기

↓

어느 밤 예배당 탑의 조각상까지 올라가서 가운을 입혀준 Yates
→ 대학 관계자들의 반대

↓

가운을 벗기려는 노력이 실패하자, Yates가 직접 올라감
▶ **'스스로 일으킨 문제를 해결'한 사례**

해설 건물을 올라타는 취미가 있었던 Yates가 대학 시절 탑 위에 있는 조각상에 가운을 입혀주었다가 대학 관계자들의 반발을 사자 다시 직접 올라가 가운을 회수해 왔다는 일화이다. 따라서 글의 제목으로는 ② '자기가 일으킨 문제를 해결한 학생'이 가장 적절하다.

오답풀이

보기 해석	선택률
① St. John's College의 동상들에 관한 으스스한 전설	23%
③ 사람마다 다른 미의 기준	6%
④ 범죄자를 찾아낸 어느 똑똑한 교수	6%
⑤ 어느 신비로운 건축가의 성공 이야기	11%

구문 [21행] **This he did** to the admiration of the crowd that assembled.
▶ <목적어+주어+동사> 어순의 도치 구문이다. 목적어 도치 구문은 부사구나 보어의 도치와는 달리 일반적으로 주어와 동사의 어순에 변화가 없다. 여기서 목적어 This는 앞 문장의 'to climb up ~ and bring them down'을 가리킨다.

05 정답 ④ 93% 2024학년도 수능 25번

해석 위 도표는 2017년, 2019년 및 2022년에 가끔 또는 자주 뉴스를 적극적으로 회피한 다섯 개 국가의 응답자 비율을 보여준다. 세 해 모두, 아일랜드는 도표의 국가들 가운데 가끔 또는 자주 뉴스를 적극적으로 회피한 응답자 비율이 가장 높게 나타났다. 독일의 경우, 가끔 또는 자주 뉴스를 적극적으로 회피한 응답자 비율이 세 해 모두 30%보다 낮았다. 덴마크의 경우, 2019년에 가끔 또는 자주 뉴스를 적극적으로 회피한 응답자 비율이 2017년보다 더 높았으나 2022년보다는 더 낮았다. 핀란드의 경우, 2019년에 가끔 또는 자주 뉴스를 적극적으로 회피한 응답자 비율이 2017년보다 더 낮았으며, 이는 일본에서도 마찬가지였다(→ 일본은 그 반대였다). 일본의 경우, 가끔 또는 자주 뉴스를 적극적으로 회피한 응답자 비율이 세 해 모두 15%를 넘지 않았다.

지문 간단히 보기

> 국가별 뉴스 회피 응답자 비율
> ① 아일랜드: 세 해 모두 최고치
> ② 독일: 세 해 모두 30% 미만
> ③ 덴마크: 2017년 < 2019년 < 2021년
> ④ 핀란드: 2017년 > 2019년
>   일본: 2017년 < 2019년 ▶ **핀란드와 '반대'**
> ⑤ 일본: 세 해 모두 15% 미만

해설 도표에 따르면 일본에서 뉴스를 가끔 혹은 자주 회피했다고 답한 비율은 2017년에 6%였으나 2019년에는 11%로 상승했다. 따라서 도표와 일치하지 않는 것은 이 비율이 핀란드와 마찬가지로 '떨어졌다'는 의미를 나타내는 ④이다.

오답풀이

보기 해설	선택률
① For each of the three years, Ireland showed the highest percentage ~	0%
② In Germany, ~ less than 30% in each of the three years.	1%
③ In Denmark, ~ higher than that in 2017 but lower than that in 2022.	2%
⑤ In Japan, ~ did not exceed 15% in each of the three years.	1%

구문 [10행] In Denmark, the percentage of the respondents who sometimes or often actively avoided news in 2019 was higher than **that** in 2017 but lower than **that** in 2022.
▶ that은 the percentage를 가리키는 지시대명사이다.

06 정답 ② 32% 2022 7월 30번

해석 가난한 나라에서는 생활 수준을 허용 가능한 수준으로 끌어올리려면 수년간의 빠른 성장이 필요할 수도 있다. 그러나 성장은 원하는 목표를 달성하기 위한 수단이지, 그 자체로 목적은 아니다. 부유한 세계에서는 적어도 관습적으로 측정되는 것으로서의 성장 개념 전체가 유지(→ 재구성)되어야 할 수도 있다. 서비스가 지배하는 경제에서는, 우리 개개인의 필요에 맞춘 재화와 서비스가 우리 사회의 진보를 결정하는 요인일 것이다. 이것(개인에 맞춘 재화와 서비스)은 게놈 맞춤형 약에서부터 개별화된 관리 또는 맞춤 정장까지 어느 것이든 될 수 있다. 이는 점점 더 많은 물건, 즉 무기의 확대 경쟁과는 다르다. 그보다는 이는 질적인 향상을 의미하는데, 이는 GDP가 제대로 측정하지 못하는 것이다. 약 50년 전 미국의 한 경제학자는 그가 '카우보이' 경제라고 칭했던, 생산과 자원 이용 및 오염에 집중된 경제와, 품질과 복합성이 '처리량'을 대신해 성공의 척도가 되었던 '우주인' 경제를 대조했다. 제조업에서 서비스업, 그리고 아날로그에서 디지털로의 이동은 카우보이에서 우주인으로의 전환이다. 하지만 우리는 여전히 올가미 밧줄의 크기를 측정하고 있다.

지문 간단히 보기

> 가난한 나라의 성장: (양적으로) 빠른 성장 = 카우보이 경제(양 중시)

↓

> 부유한 세계의 성장: '개인 맞춤형' 재화, 서비스의 성장
> = 우주인 경제(질 중시)
> ≠ 단순한 확대 경쟁, GDP 성장

↓

> (비유) 시대는 변했는데, '아직도 우리는 올가미 크기만 측정 중'
> ▶ **성장을 양적 개념으로 파악하는 기존의 관념을 '재구성'할 필요**

해설 글 중간의 Instead 앞뒤로, 오늘날 경제에서는 양적 확대보다는 질적 향상이 중요하다는 설명이 나온다. 그렇기에 적어도 개인 맞춤 재화와 서비스를 확대해 가는 부유한 나라에서라면 기존의 성장 개념을 '재구성해야' 한다는 의미로, ②에는 maintained 대신 reconstructed 등을 써야 옳다.

오답풀이

보기 해설	선택률
① end(목적)	6%
③ individual(개개인의)	22%
④ quality(질)	28%
⑤ move(이동)	13%

구문 [15행] ~ **contrasted** [**what he called the "cowboy" economy**], bent on production, exploitation of resources, and pollution, **with the "spaceman" economy**, in which ~
▶ <contrast A with B(A와 B를 대조하다)> 구문이다. 밑줄 친 부분이 A에 해당하는 [ ]를 보충 설명한다.

해석　현대 번역가들과 교사들이 스토아 철학을 비판하는 것 중 하나는 반복의 정도이다. 예를 들어, Marcus Aurelius는 그의 글이 다른 앞선 스토아 철학자들의 글과 비슷하다는 이유로 학자들에게 독창적이지 않다고 무시받았다. 이러한 비판은 핵심을 놓친다. Marcus 시대 이전에도 Seneca는 철학자들 사이에 차용과 중복이 많다는 것을 잘 알고 있었다. 진정한 철학자들이 원저자라는 것에 관심을 두지 않고 오직 효과가 있는 것에만 관심을 두었기 때문이다. 더 중요한 것은, 그들은 말로 한 것이 행동으로 한 것보다 덜 중요하다고 믿었다는 점이다. 이는 그때처럼 지금도 사실이다. 여러분은 원한다면 위대한 철학자들의 모든 말을 가져다가 취향에 맞게 사용해도 된다(그들은 죽었으니 개의치 않는다). 원하는 대로 맘껏 수정하고 개선하라. 이를 실제 세계의 실제 여건에 맞게 적용하라. 여러분이 직접 말하고 쓴 것을 정말 이해하고 있다는 것, 자신이 진정 독창적임을 증명하는 방법은 그것들을 실행에 옮기는 것이다.

지문 간단히 보기

> 스토아 철학에 관한 글은 그 내용이 자주 반복되었다는 이유로 독창성을 비판당함

> 하지만 스토아 철학자들은 누가 원래 저자였는가보다 '무엇이 효과적인지'에 관심을 뒀으며, 말보다도 행동을 중시함

> (결론) 오늘날의 우리 또한 누구의 말이든 가져다가 수정하고 개선하며 '실제 여건에 적용해보는**(실천)**' 것이 중요함

해설　스토아 학파 철학자들이 어떤 말의 출처를 따지기보다도 그 내용을 실천해보는 것을 중요하게 여겼듯이, 우리도 철학자의 말을 '실제 여건에 적용해보는' 것이 중요하다는 내용이다. 따라서 빈칸에는 ① '그것들을 실행에 옮기는'이 들어가야 한다.

오답풀이

보기 해석	선택률
② 본인이 쓴 글을 혼자 간직하는	28%
③ 말과 글로 전해진 전통을 결합하는	16%
④ 철학 이론들을 비교해보는	15%
⑤ 그것들을 차용하기를 피하는	7%

구문　[12행] And this is true now as it **was** then.
▶was는 was true를 뜻하는 대동사이다. 앞에 나온 is true를 과거시제로 대신한 것이다.

해석　고대 여행에서 태양의 역할을 이해하려고 할 때, 자료는 더 적어지고 알려진 여행은 더 적어진다. Herodotus는 기원전 600년경 고대 이집트 왕 Necho 2세가 의뢰했던 탐험 항해에 대해 기록한다. 전하는 바에 따르면, Necho 2세는 페니키아 원정대에게 아프리카 주위를 시계 방향으로 항해해서 홍해에서 출발해 나일강 하구로 돌아오도록 명령했다고 한다. 그들은 3년 동안 떠나있었다. Herodotus가 기록하기로, 페니키아인들은 영웅적인 탐험을 마치고 돌아오자마자, 그들이 남쪽으로 항해하다가 서쪽으로 방향을 바꾸고 나서 태양이 오른쪽에 있는 것을 발견했다고 보고했는데, 이는 그들이 늘 태양을 보았거나 태양이 있을 거라고 예상했던 것과는 정반대 방향이었다. 당대의 천문 과학은 적도를 지나 남반구로 항해한 후 태양이 어디에 있을지에 관해 그렇게 정확하고 기초적이지만 평범한 세부 사항을 꾸며 낼 만큼 결코 충분히 뛰어나지 않았다. 오늘날의 역사가 중 많은 이들이 그 여행은 틀림없이 이뤄졌다고 결론을 내리게 되는 것이 바로 이 때문이다.

지문 간단히 보기

> 핵심 소재: 페니키아 사람들의 항해 기록

> 남쪽으로 항해하다가 서쪽으로 방향을 바꾸자, 태양이 '오른쪽에 있었다' = 당시 사람들의 예상과 반대

> 당대 천문학 지식상, '꾸며내기 어려운' 내용
> ▶ **여행이 실제 이뤄진 일이라는 증거**

해설　페니키아 원정대의 항해 당시 천문 과학은 항해 도중 태양의 위치를 자세히 꾸며낼 만큼 정교하지 않았다는 설명으로 보아, '여행이 실제로 이뤄졌어야만' 태양의 위치를 구체적으로 밝힐 수 있었다는 결론이 적합하다. 따라서 ① '틀림없이 이뤄졌다'가 정답이다.

오답풀이

보기 해석	선택률
② 전혀 보고되지 않았다	25%
③ 시간을 들일 가치가 없었다	18%
④ 더 잘 계획되었어야만 했다	18%
⑤ 언제든 중단될 수 있었다	9%

구문　[19행] It is this **that** leads many of today's historians to conclude [that the journey **must have taken place**].
▶ 주절은 <it is ~ that …> 강조 구문으로, '…한 것은 바로 ~이다'의 의미이다. 앞 문장 내용을 가리키는 this가 강조되고 있다.
▶ [ ]는 to conclude의 목적어 역할을 하는 명사절이다. 과거에 대한 강한 추측을 나타내는 <must have p.p.(~했음에 틀림없다)>를 기억해 둔다.

09 정답 ③ 67%

해석 조직들이 과거 어느 때보다 재택근무 프로그램을 더 많이 제공하고 있지만, 이러한 프로그램의 수용과 활용은 여전히 많은 요인에 의해 제한된다. 이들 요인에는 대면 관리 관행에 대한 관리자의 의존, 조직 내 재택근무 교육 부족, 유연 근무 프로그램에 대한 오해와 불편, 그리고 재택근무가 조직의 총 결산에 미치는 효과에 대한 정보 부족 등이 있다. 이러한 한계에도 불구하고, 21세기 초에는 '언제 어디서나' 일할 수 있는 새로운 직장 문화가 부상하고 있다. (개인 및 업무 특성이 재택근무에 가장 적합한 직원들을 선발하기 위해 주의를 기울여야 한다.) 정보 기술의 지속적인 발전, 세계적 인력의 확대, 일과 가정 사이에서 균형을 이루려는 욕구의 증가는 재택근무가 지배적인 인력 개발(체제)이 되는 데 대한 현재의 장벽을 점진적으로 낮출 많은 요인 중 세 가지에 불과하다(이외에도 재택근무 장벽을 낮출 요인이 많다). 특히 더 낮은 시설 비용, 직원의 (시간적) 유연성 증가 및 생산성과 관련하여 조직의 비용 절감에 대한 영향으로 인해, 재택근무는 많은 조직에 점점 더 큰 관심사가 되고 있다.

지문 간단히 보기

재택근무에는 많은 제한 요인이 있음
→ ① (예시) 대면 관리에 대한 의존, 교육 부족, 유연 근무에 대한 오해 등등

↓

② 그래도 21세기 초, 재택근무는 부상 중
④ 재택근무에 대한 장벽을 낮출 요인이 많음

↓

⑤ (결론) 재택근무: 많은 조직의 관심사

해설 재택근무의 제한 요인을 설명한 후, '이런 요인들에도 불구하고' 재택근무가 확산되어 가는 추세임을 다룬 글이다. 하지만 ③은 재택근무에 적합한 직원 선발에 관해 언급하고 있으므로 글의 흐름에서 벗어난다.

오답풀이

보기 해설	선택률
① 앞의 a number of factors가 ①의 These factors로 자연스럽게 연결된다.	1%
② 여러 제한에도 '불구하고' 재택근무가 부상하고 있다는 내용으로, 글의 주제를 제시한다.	8%
④ ②에 대한 부연 설명으로, 재택근무의 장벽을 낮출 요인이 많은데 그중 세 가지만 예를 든다는 의미이다.	18%
⑤ 재택근무의 부상이라는 주제가 다시 반복된다.	3%

구문 [13행] ~ employees [**whose** personal and working characteristics are best suited for telecommuting].
▶소유격 관계대명사 whose가 employees를 수식하는 절을 이끈다. whose 뒤에는 관사 없는 명사로 시작하는 완전한 문장이 온다.

10 정답 ② 45%

해석 셰익스피어는 "이름 안에 무엇이 있죠(이름이라는 것이 무슨 소용인가요)? 우리가 장미라고 부르는 건 그 어떤 다른 이름으로 불러도 그만큼 달콤한 향이 날 거예요."라고 썼다.
(B) Stanford 대학교의 심리학 교수인 Lera Boroditsky에 따르면, 그게 꼭 그렇지는 않다. 독일어와 스페인어의 문법적 성 차이에 초점을 맞춘 Boroditsky의 연구가 시사하기로, 우리의 언어가 어떤 특정 명사에 부여하는 성은 우리가 무의식적으로 그 명사에 문법적 성의 특성을 부여하도록 영향을 미친다고 한다.
(A) '다리'라는 단어를 보자. 독일어로 '다리'(die brücke)는 여성 명사이지만, 스페인어로 '다리'(el puente)는 남성 명사이다. Boroditsky는 독일어 원어민이 다리를 묘사하라는 요청을 받으면 '아름다운', '우아한', '날씬한' 같은 단어를 사용한다는 사실을 알아냈다. 스페인어 원어민들이 같은 질문을 받았을 때, 이들은 '강한', '튼튼한', '우뚝 솟은' 같은 단어를 사용했다.
(C) 이것은 반대의 경우에도 마찬가지였다. '열쇠'라는 단어는 독일어에서는 남성형이고 스페인어에서는 여성형이다. 열쇠를 묘사하라는 요청을 받았을 때, 독일어 원어민은 '뾰족뾰족한', '무거운', '단단한', '금속의' 같은 단어를 사용했다. 스페인어 화자는 '정교한', '황금빛의', '사랑스러운' 같은 단어를 사용했다.

지문 간단히 보기

셰익스피어: "장미를 장미라 부르지 않아도 향은 같을 것"
▶ **이름과 사물의 본질이 서로 무관함**

↓

(B) 반박: Boroditsky의 연구(언어적 성과 사물 인식)

↓

(A) (예시) '다리': 독일어(여성) vs. 스페인어(남성)
(C) (대조) '열쇠': 독일어(남성) vs. 스페인어(여성)
▶ **명사의 언어적 성에 따라, 연상되는 형용사가 다름**

해설 주어진 글은 이름이 사물의 본질과 인식에 영향을 주지 못한다는 의미의 인용구를 제시하고, (B)는 '그게' 꼭 사실은 아닐 수 있다며 언어적 성별과 사물 인식의 영향 관계에 관한 연구를 언급한다. 이어서 (A)는 '다리', (C)는 '다리'와 반대되는 '열쇠'의 예시로 (B)를 뒷받침한다. 따라서 ② '(B)-(A)-(C)'가 정답이다.

오답풀이

보기 해설	선택률
① (B) 첫 문장의 주어 that이 주어진 글의 내용을 가리키므로 가장 먼저 올 단락은 (B)이다.	6%
③, (A)에서 예시가 하나 먼저 나와야 (C)에서 '이와 반대되는	16%
④ 경우(the other way around)'를 언급할 수 있다.	21%
⑤ (C)의 This에 주어진 글을 대입해보면 어색하다. 이 This는 (A)의 마지막 두 문장으로 봐야 한다.	11%

구문 [1행] **That** which we call a rose ~ would smell as sweet.
▶ which가 이끄는 관계절이 주어 That을 꾸민다. 이 That은 지시대명사로, 뒤에 수식어를 동반할 수 있다. That which를 한꺼번에 What으로 바꾸어 What we call a rose로 써도 같은 의미이다.

11 정답 ⑤ 22%

해석 식품 선택을 결정하는 사회적 역학이 점점 복잡해지면서 마케팅 담당자와 광고주의 업무가 점점 더 어려워지고 있다. 과거에, 대량 생산은 제품의 광범위한 유통뿐 아니라 제품의 접근성과 경제성을 허용했고, 발전의 신호로 이해되었다. 요즘에는 이것(대량 생산)이 개인의 선호를 반영해야 하는 점점 더 작은 부문 사이에서 소비자의 파편화(단편화)로 점차 대체되고 있다. 모든 사람은 (각자) 다르고 특별하다고 느끼고, 자신의 기호를 만족시키는 제품을 기대한다. 실제로는, 개인적 선호라고 생각되는 이런 것들은 문화적 감성, 사회 정체성, 정치적 감성, 식생활과 건강에 관한 관심을 중심으로 확고해지는, 최근에 생겨난 잠정적이고 항상 바뀌며 거의 부족적인 형성물과 결국 겹치게 된다. 개인의 이야기가 더 큰 이야기와 연결되어 새로운 정체성을 생성하는 것이다. 이 소비자 집단들은 국경을 넘어 전 세계적으로 널리 공유된 개념, 이미지, 관습의 저장소로 인해 더 강화된다.

지문 간단히 보기

식품 선택에 관여하는 사회적 역학 변화 → 식품 마케팅 변화

↓

과거: 대량 생산, 광범위 유통, 적정한 가격 vs. 오늘날: 소비자의 파편화, 개인마다 다른 선호 반영

↓

개인의 선호는 다 고유해 보이지만, '부족적' 선호와 중복 → '새로운 정체성'(= '소비자 집단') 형성

해설 ⑤ 앞은 개인의 선호가 다 별개인 것이 아니라 부족적 선호와 겹치게 된다는 내용인데, ⑤ 뒤에서는 갑자기 '이 소비자 집단'을 언급하므로 흐름이 끊긴다. 이때 주어진 문장을 보면 ⑤ 앞과 사실상 같은 내용으로, '개인의 선호가 더 큰 것과 연결되어 새로운 정체성을 형성한다'고 한다. 여기서 언급된 '새로운 정체성'이 ⑤ 뒤에서 '이 소비자 집단'으로 서술되는 것이므로, ⑤에 주어진 문장을 넣어야 한다.

오답풀이

보기 해설	선택률
① 식품 마케팅이 점점 바뀌고 있다는 일반론 뒤로 '옛날'을 대비하는 흐름이 자연스럽다.	4%
② '옛날'에서 다시 '현재'로 넘어오는 흐름이다. 뒷문장의 주어 it이 앞문장의 mass production을 적절히 지칭하고 있다.	9%
③ 앞에서 말했듯 '소비자가 파편화되는' 이유는 뒤에서 말하듯 '개인이 각자 남과 다르다고 느끼는' 것과 관련이 있다.	27%
④ In reality가 역접어 역할을 한다. '개인은 각기 다르다 → 실상은 선호가 서로 겹친다'는 흐름 전환이 자연스럽다.	36%

구문 [3행] ~ **makes** the job of marketers and advertisers increasingly **more difficult**.
▶ <make+목적어+비교급 형용사> 형태의 5형식 구조이다. '(주어)로 인해 (목적어)가 더 ~하게 되다'의 의미로 파악할 수 있다.

12 정답 ① 34%

해석 실험에 따르면, 동물은 인간과 마찬가지로 과장되고 비범한 자극을 선호하곤 하며, 선호는 빠르게 극단적인 수준까지 치달을 수 있다('정점 변경 효과'). 한 실험에서, 쥐는 음식 보상을 통해 정사각형을 다른 기하학 형태보다 선호하도록 조건화되었다. 다음 단계로 정사각형이 아닌 직사각형이 제시되었고, 정사각형보다 훨씬 더 큰 보상과 연관되었다. 예상했듯이 쥐는 직사각형을 확실히 선호하도록 학습했다. 덜 예측 가능했던 것은 실험의 세 번째 부분이었다. 쥐는 그들이 이미 알고 있고 큰 보상과 연관되었던 직사각형과, 비율상 정사각형과 훨씬 차이 나는 또 다른 직사각형 중에서 선택할 기회를 제공받았다. 흥미롭게도, 쥐는 새로운 변형에 대한 보상 기반의 조건화를 전혀 경험하지 않고서도 새로운 변형을 골랐다. 그러므로 가능한 설명은, 그들이 원래의 정사각형보다 더 큰 차이(즉 '비(非) 정사각형'의 과장)를 선택했다는 것이다.

→ 한 실험에서 처음에는 정사각형, 이후 정사각형이 아닌 직사각형에 대한 (A)선호를 확립하고 나자, 쥐는 심지어 아무 추가 보상 없이도 (B)극단적인 직사각형의 성질을 추구하는 것으로 보였다.

지문 간단히 보기

정점 변경 효과: 인간과 마찬가지로, 동물도 선호가 극단적 수준까지 발전 가능

↓

(예시) 쥐를 대상으로 한 도형 선호 실험
 - 1차: 정사각형을 다른 도형보다 선호하게 만듦
 - 2차: 정사각형 vs. 직사각형 → 직사각형을 선호하게 만듦
 - 3차: 기존 직사각형 vs. 과장된 직사각형
  → 보상 경험 없이도, 쥐들이 후자를 선택
  ▶ 더 '과장된' 자극을 자동적으로 선호

해설 동물의 선호 구조가 더 극단적이고 과장된 자극 쪽으로 발전할 수 있다는 것을 쥐 실험의 사례로 보여주는 글이다. 실험 결과를 제시하는 마지막 두 문장에 요지가 있다. 따라서 요약문의 빈칸에는 ① '선호 - 극단적인'이 들어가야 한다.

오답풀이

보기 해설	선택률
② 반대 - 친숙한	19%
③ 선호 - 모호한	21%
④ 반대 - 예상치 못한	22%
⑤ 애착 - 미묘한	5%

구문 [11행] **Less predictable** was the third part of the experiment.
▶ <보어+동사+주어> 어순의 도치 구문이다. 보어가 문장 맨 앞으로 나오면 주어와 동사의 어순이 서로 바뀐다.

13~14 정답 ③ 57% / ③ 44% 2022 9월 41~42번

해석 기후 변화 전문가들과 환경 인문주의자들 모두, 기후 위기가 근원적으로 상상력의 위기이며, 대중적 상상력의 많은 부분이 소설에 의해 형성된다는 데 동의한다. 인류학자이자 소설가인 Amitav Ghosh는 자신의 2016년도 책 <The Great Derangement>에서 상상과 환경 관리 사이의 이러한 관계를 다루면서, 인간이 기후 변화에 대응하지 못한 것은 적어도 부분적으로는 소설이 그것을 믿을 만하게 표현하지 못하기 때문이라고 주장한다. Ghosh가 설명하기로, 기후 변화는 대체로 현대 소설에 존재하지 않는데 그 이유는 기후 변화가 상기시키는 사이클론, 홍수, 그리고 다른 큰 재해들이 그야말로 일상생활에 관한 이야기에 속하기에는 너무 '있을 법하지 않아' 보여서라고 한다. 그러나 기후 변화는 일련의 놀라운 사건들로만 드러나지는 않는다. 사실, Rachel Carson에서 Rob Nixon에 이르는 환경론자들과 생태 비평가들이 지적했듯이, 환경 변화는 '감지되지 못할' 수 있다. 그것은 빠르게(→ 점진적으로) 진행되며, 단지 가끔 '폭발적이고 극적인' 사건들을 만들어 낼 뿐이기에 그렇다. 대부분의 기후 변화의 영향은 매일 관찰될 수는 없지만, 우리가 그 축적된 영향에 직면할 때 눈에 띄게 된다.
기후 변화는 중요한 표현상의 문제를 제기한다는 점에서 우리의 상상에서 벗어난다. 그것은 '인간의 시간' 동안에는 관찰될 수 없는데, 그 이유로 빙하와 산호초에 미치는 기후 변화의 영향을 추적하는 다큐멘터리 영화 제작자 Jeff Orlowski는 수개월 간격으로 같은 장소에서 찍은 '전후' 사진을 이용하여 점진적으로 일어난 변화를 강조한다.

지문 간단히 보기

> 기후 위기는 곧 '상상력의 위기'

↓

> 기후 변화 대처에 미흡했던 이유:
> : 소설 속에서 기후 변화가 '믿을 만하게' 묘사되지 못함
>   ('큰 재해' 형태로 많이 묘사됨)

↓

> 하지만, 기후 변화는 '영향이 누적되었을' 때 드러남
> = 평소에는 '감지되지 못함' ▶ **점진적 진행**

↓

> (결론) 기후 변화는 우리 상상에서 자꾸 벗어남
> ▶ **상상력이 기후 변화에 관해 제대로 말해주지 못함(= '침묵')**

구문 [11행] ~ the cyclones, floods, and other catastrophes [(that) it brings to mind] simply seem <u>too "improbable" to belong</u> in stories about everyday life.
▶ 선행사 the cyclones, floods, and other catastrophes를 꾸미는 형용사절 [ ]에서 목적격 관계대명사가 생략되었다. [ ]의 주어 it은 climate change를 가리킨다.
▶ 밑줄 부분은 <too ~ to …(…하기에는 너무 ~한, 너무 ~해서 …할 수 없다)> 구문이다.

13

해설 기후 변화는 소설 속에서 놀라운 사건으로만 주로 그려져 실제로 있을 법하게 느껴지지 않고, 이 때문에 대중에게 제대로 인식되지 못한다는 내용이다. 결국 기후 변화는 '상상력의 위기'라는 지적으로 보아, 제목으로 가장 적절한 것은 ③ '기후 변화 표현에 있어 상상력의 침묵'이다.

오답풀이

보기 해석	선택률
① 현재 기후 이슈에 대한 다양한 태도	15%
② 느리지만 중대하다: 생태학적 운동의 역사	14%
④ 뚜렷한 위협: 국소 지역에 퍼지는 기후 재난	11%
⑤ 환경보호주의와 생태학적 비평의 흥망성쇠	4%

14

해설 기후 변화는 '영향이 축적됐을 때' 눈에 보인다는 설명으로 보아 기후 변화가 '빠르게' 진행된다는 설명은 어색하다. '점진적 기후 변화'를 보여주고자 몇 달 간격을 두고 같은 장소를 찍어 비교한다는 마지막 문장의 예로 볼 때, ③ (c)에는 rapidly 대신 gradually가 적절하다.

오답풀이

보기 해석	선택률
① fails(~하지 못하다, 실패하다)	9%
② extraordinary(놀라운)	15%
④ visible(눈에 띄는, 보이는)	23%
⑤ highlight(강조하다)	10%

STEP PLUS+ 수능 기출 마무리 복습

단어 TEST
02 마비된 **03** 견디다, 참다 **04** 주기적으로 **05** 관계자, 당국 **06** 무시하다, 묵살하다 **07** 천문학의 **08** 오해 **09** 튼튼한, 강건한 **10** 부문, 분야 **11** 있을 법하지 않은, 사실 같지 않은 **12** 점진적으로, 점점

구문 TEST
14 being selected for the band **15** made her voice heard **16** (which was) an incredible feat **17** which delighted all the residents[delighting all the residents] **18** was truly spectacular

01 정답 ③ 85% 2022 3월 19번

해석 마침내 내 차례가 되었다. 난 절벽에서 뒤로 걸어가기로 되어 있었다. 절벽 아래를 내려다보기만 했는데 다리가 후들거리기 시작했다. 의식을 잃을 때를 대비해 내 몸에 안전 밧줄이 감겨 있다는 것은 알고 있었다. 머리로는 모든 상황을 이해했고, 머리로는 안전하다고 느꼈다. 그런데도 내 머리카락은 곤두섰고 온몸이 떨렸다. 절벽에서 그 첫발을 내딛는 것이 가장 힘든 순간이었지만, 다른 사람들이 해낸 것처럼, 나는 해냈다. 나는 도전에 성공한 것을 매우 기뻐하며 무사히 바닥에 도착했다. 마치 구름 위를 걷는 것 같은 기분이었다(몹시 기뻤다).

지문 간단히 보기

> 절벽에서 뒤로 걸어 (내려)가기로 한 상황
> → 머리카락이 곤두서고 온몸이 떨림 ▶ **무서움**

> 다른 사람들처럼 성공 → 공중을 걷는 기분 ▶ **기쁨**

해설 절벽 아래를 내려다보면서 두려움에 떨었던 필자가 무사히 성공한 후 '구름 위를 걷는 것 같은' 기쁨을 느꼈다는 내용이므로, ③ '무서운 → 기쁜'이 심경 변화로 가장 적절하다.

오답풀이

보기 해석	선택률
① 느긋한 → 긴장한	3%
② 화난 → 수치스러운	2%
④ 부러운 → 연민을 느끼는	5%
⑤ 실망한 → 희망을 품은	3%

구문 [8행] That first step off the cliff was the most difficult moment, but I made it—**as did others**.
▶ <as+대동사+주어> 어순의 도치 구문이 '~듯이, ~대로'의 의미를 나타낸다. did는 앞의 일반동사구 made it을 대신한다.

02 정답 ① 46% 2021 9월 22번

해석 역사적으로 전문직과 사회는 그들 관계의 조건을 규정할 목적으로 계획된 협상 과정에 참여해 왔다. 이 과정의 핵심에는 전문직의 자율성 추구와 대중의 책임 요구 사이의 긴장이 있다. 사회가 전문직에 권한과 특권을 부여한 것은 이들이 사회 복지에 기여하고 더 넓은 사회적 가치에 부합하는 방식으로 일을 수행하려는 의지와 능력을 전제로 한다. 오랫동안, 전문직의 전문 지식과 특권적 지위가 그들이 봉사하는 사람들을 희생시킨 채 그들 본인의 이익을 증진시키고자 쉽게 이용될 수 있는 권위와 권한을 준다고 인식되어 왔다. Edmund Burke가 두 세기 전에 말했듯이, "인간은 딱 자신의 욕구를 도덕적으로 구속하려는 성향에 비례해서 시민적 자유를 누릴 자격이 부여된다." 자율성은 일방통행로였던 적이 없었으며, 결코 절대적이고 비가역적으로 부여되지 않는다.

지문 간단히 보기

> 핵심 소재: 전문직의 '자율성 vs. 책임'

> 전문직의 권한과 특권
> = '사회적 가치에 따라' 일할 의지와 능력에서 기원
> = "욕구를 도덕적으로 구속하는 정도에 비례해서" 부여
> = 일방통행로 X, 절대적, 비가역적 X
> ▶ **사회적 책임의 중요성**

해설 전문직의 자율성과 특권은 사회가 요구하는 책임을 수행한다는 전제로 부여되는 것이라는 내용이다. 따라서 ① '전문직에 부여되는 자율성은 그에 상응하는 사회적 책임을 수반한다.'가 글의 요지로 적절하다.

오답풀이

보기 해설	선택률
② 'It has long been recognized ~' 문장의 내용과 일치하지만, 여기서 나아가 권위와 특권이 '책임'과 함께 온다고 말하는 것이 글의 핵심이다.	19%
③ '제도 정비'에 관해 언급되지 않았다.	5%
④ 전문직의 '자격 요건'에 관해 언급되지 않았다.	6%
⑤ 전문직의 '성과'를 '자율성, 특권'과 연관 지어 언급하지 않았다.	22%

구문 [10행] ~ authority and power that could readily **be used to advance** their own interests ~
▶ <be used to-V(~하기 위해 사용되다)> 구문이다. <be used to V-ing(~하는 데 익숙하다)>, <used to-V(~하곤 했다)> 등과 구별해 둔다.

03 정답 ② 49%

해석 '사자가 자신의 역사가를 둘 때까지, 사냥 이야기는 항상 사냥꾼을 미화하기 마련이다'라는 아프리카 속담이 있다. 이 속담은 권력과 통제, 그리고 법 제정에 관한 것이다. 환경 저널리스트들은 '사자의 역사가' 역할을 해야 한다. 그들은 법을 만드는 사람들에게 환경의 관점을 이해시켜야 한다. 그들은 인도 야생 자연의 목소리(대변자)가 되어야 한다. 현재 인간의 소비 속도는 완전히 지속 불가하다. 숲, 습지, 황무지, 해안 지대, 환경 민감 지역 (등등은) 모두 인류의 가속화되는 수요를 위해 마음대로 쓰일 수 있다고 여겨진다. 하지만 소비를 줄이는 것이든, 생활 방식을 바꾸는 것이든, 아니면 인구 증가를 줄이는 것이든, 인간의 행동에 그 어떤 변화라도 요구하는 것은 인권 침해로 간주된다. 그러나 어느 지점에 이르면 인권은 '잘못된 것'이 된다. 인간의 권리와 나머지 환경의 권리 사이에 차이가 없도록, 우리가 생각을 바꿔야 할 때이다.

지문 간단히 보기

> (비유) '사자의 역사가'가 되어야 하는 환경 저널리스트들
> = 입법자들에게 환경의 관점을 이해시키는 역할
> = 야생 자연을 대변하는 역할

↓

> 현재 인간 소비는 지속 불가한 수준이지만, 인권 침해 이슈 때문에 사람들에게 변화를 촉구하기도 쉽지 않음

> 하지만, '인권과 환경의 권리 간에 차이를 두지 않는' 사고방식 필요
> ▶ **'환경을 위해 행동을 바꾸도록' 촉구해야 함**

해설 환경 저널리스트들은 입법자들에게 '환경의 관점을 이해시켜야(put across)' 한다는 진술로 보아, 이들의 역할을 설명하는 비유의 의미로 가장 적절한 것은 ② '자연을 위해 지속 가능한 인간 행동으로 바뀌어갈 것을 촉구하는 것'이다.

오답풀이

보기 해석	선택률
① 한 종의 생물학적 진화의 역사를 밝혀내는 것	4%
③ 만연한 인권 침해에 맞서 싸우는 것	19%
④ 더 부당하게 서술된 사람들을 위해서 역사를 다시 쓰는 것	8%
⑤ 환경 입법자들의 권한을 제한하는 것	18%

구문 [13행] But **to ask for any change in human behaviour**—whether it be to cut down on consumption, alter lifestyles or decrease population growth—**is seen** ~
▶ 주어가 to부정사구이므로 단수 취급했다(is).
▶ 밑줄 부분은 <whether it be A, B or C(A, B, 혹은 C이든 간에)> 구문이다. 종종 whether가 생략되고 주어-동사가 도치되어 <be it ~>으로도 쓰인다.

04 정답 ⑤ 36%

해석 가장 혁신적인 팀들은 뜻밖의 환경 변화에 대응하여 스스로 재구성될 수 있는 팀들로, 이들은 무엇을 해야 할지를 알려주는 강력한 리더를 필요로 하지 않는다. 게다가, 이들은 자발적으로 형성되는 경향이 있어서, 생각이 비슷한 사람들이 서로를 발견할 때 집단이 생겨난다. 집단 전체의 즉흥적인 협업은 개인적 창의성의 순간을 집단 혁신으로 바꾼다. 이러한 자발적 조직 (집단의) 출현이 발생할 여지를 허용하는 것은 많은 관리자에게 어려운 일인데, 왜냐하면 그 결과는 관리팀의 일정으로 통제되지 않으며, 그렇기에 덜 예측 가능하기 때문이다. 대부분의 기업 관리자들은 큰 그림에서 시작하고 그다음에 세부 사항을 해결하기를 좋아한다. 그런 이유로 그토록 많은 최고의 즉흥적 혁신 사례가 공식적인 조직 밖에서 일어난다. 즉흥적 혁신을 할 때, 팀은 세부 사항에서 시작하고 차츰 큰 그림에 이르게 된다. 이는 더 위험하고 덜 효율적이지만, 성공적인 혁신이 일어나면 이는 흔히 매우 놀랍고 창의적이다.

지문 간단히 보기

> 가장 혁신적인 팀들: 리더 없이 자발적으로 형성(= 즉흥적 협업)

↓

> 리더들이 이런 혁신의 기회를 마련해주기는 쉽지 않음
> : 이들은 큰 그림부터 잡고 세부 사항으로 내려가는 경향

↓

> 그래서, 즉흥적 혁신은 공식적인 조직 밖에서 일어남
> = 세부 사항부터 큰 그림으로 ▶ **상향식**
> = 안정성이나 효율성은 덜해도, 매우 놀랍고 창의적임

해설 가장 혁신적인 팀은 강력한 리더 없이 스스로 형성되고, 이들이 이룩하는 '즉흥적 혁신'은 '세부 사항에서 시작해 큰 그림에 이르는' 특징을 지닌다는 내용이다. 따라서 ⑤ '즉흥적 혁신은 상향식으로 시작된다'는 제목이 가장 적절하다.

오답풀이

보기 해석	선택률
① 혁신의 시작: 리더의 큰 그림	21%
② 예측 불가한 변화: 혁신의 어려움	21%
③ 상충하는 아이디어가 최고의 혁신으로 이어진다	11%
④ 비상 상황에서 나타나는 즉흥적인 팀의 취약점	8%

구문 [1행] The most innovative teams are **those** that can restructure themselves in response to unexpected shifts in the environment; ~
▶ those는 복수명사 teams를 나타내는 지시대명사이다. 지시대명사 that/those는 수식어를 동반할 수 있다는 점에서 it/them과 다르다.
▶ 밑줄 친 부분이 바로 those를 수식하는 주격 관계대명사절이다.

05 정답 ⑤ 88%

해석 Josef Sudek은 체코 공화국에서 태어났다. 원래 책 제본 기술자였던 Sudek은 제1차 세계 대전 중에 심한 부상을 입어 그 결과 오른팔을 잃었다. 부상 이후 그는 여러 병원에서 3년을 보냈고, 무료함 때문에 사진을 찍기 시작했다. 1922년, 그는 Prague에 있는 State School of Graphic Arts에 등록하여 그곳에서 2년간 사진술을 공부했다. 그는 군인 장애 연금 덕에 수입 걱정 없이 예술 창작을 할 수 있었다. 그는 Prague의 많은 야경과 나무가 우거진 Bohemia의 풍경을 사진에 담았다. Sudek은 자신의 장애가 방해가 되도록 내버려 두지 않았고, 팔이 하나밖에 없음에도 불구하고 매우 무겁고 부피가 큰 장비를 사용했다. 흔히 'Prague의 시인'으로 알려진 Sudek은 결혼한 적이 없었으며 수줍음이 많고 내성적인 사람이었다. 그는 자신의 전시회 개막식에 나타난 적이 없었다. 그는 80세였던 1976년 9월 15일에 사망했다.

지문 간단히 보기

> Josef Sudek의 생애
> ① 1차 대전 때 오른팔을 잃음
> ② Prague의 State School of Graphic Arts에서 2년간 사진술 공부
> ③ 군인 장애 연금 → 수입 걱정 없이 창작
> ④ 왼팔만으로 매우 무겁고 부피가 큰 장비를 사용
> ⑤ 수줍고 내성적 → 전시회 개막식에 참석한 경험 X

해설 'He never appeared at his exhibition openings.'에 따르면 Josef Sudek은 자신의 전시회 개막식에 간 적이 없다고 하므로, 일치하지 않는 것은 ⑤ '자신의 전시회 개막식에 항상 참석했다.'이다.

오답풀이

보기 해설	선택률
① ~ resulting in the loss of his right arm.	2%
② ~ he studied photography for two years.	2%
③ His army disability pension ~ without worrying about an income.	3%
④ ~ he used very heavy and bulky equipment.	2%

구문 [2행] **(Having been)** Originally a bookbinder, Sudek was badly injured during World War I, **resulting** in the loss of his right arm.

▶ 주어 앞은 주절보다 과거인 시점에 있었던 일을 설명하는 완료분사구문이다. 부사절 'Although he had been originally a bookbinder ~'에서 접속사와 주어를 생략하고 had been을 having been으로 바꾼 후, 다시 having been을 생략하면 만들어지는 형태다.

▶ 'resulting ~'은 결과의 분사구문으로, 앞 내용에 이어서 순차적으로 해석한다(그리고/그 결과 ~하다).

06 정답 ② 21%

해석 서양의 과학 연구에 국한된 사람들은 오감으로 감지할 수 없고 반복해서 측정하거나 정량화할 수 없는 것은 무엇이든 사실상 무시해왔다. 연구는 원인과 결과에 의해 과학적으로 설명될 수 없으면 미신적이고 무효한 것으로 일축된다. 많은 사람이 과학의 힘, 더 구체적으로는 과학이 그들에게 주는 힘에 대한 이 문화적 패러다임에 거의 종교적인 열정으로 계속 반대한다(→ 집착한다). 비서양의 과학적 패러다임을 잘해야 열등하고 최악의 경우 부정확하다고 일축함으로써, 기존 서양 의학 연구 단체의 가장 완고한 구성원들은 대체 (의학) 요법과 연구가 자신들의 연구, 행복, 그리고 세계관에 가하는 위협에 대응하려 한다. 그럼에도 불구하고, 생물 의학 연구는 돌봄 치료 과정에 관해서 대체 의학 시술자들이 연관되어 있는 여러 현상을 설명할 수 없다. 침술이나 동종 요법 같은 치료법이 생물 의학적 모델로 설명될 수 없는 생리적 또는 임상적 반응을 초래하는 것이 관찰될 때, 많은 이들은 과학적인 모델을 수정하기보다는, 그 결과를 부정하려 애썼다.

지문 간단히 보기

> 서양 과학 연구에 국한된 사람들: 비정량적 데이터를 무시하고, 과학적으로 설명되지 않는 연구를 일축함

> (예시) 완고한 서양 의학 단체 구성원들
> → 대체 의학의 데이터나 연구를 반박하거나 부정함
> ▶ **거의 종교 수준으로 자신들의 패러다임에 '집착'함**

해설 글에 따르면 서양 과학 연구에 국한된 사람들은 과학적으로 설명되지 않는 데이터를 '무효하다, 열등하다, 부정확하다'고 무시한다고 한다. 따라서 ②에는 이들이 과학의 힘에 관한 패러다임에 '반대한다(object)'는 표현보다는 '집착한다(cling)'는 표현이 적합하다.

오답풀이

보기 해석	선택률
① ignored(무시해온)	6%
③ counter(위험이나 악영향에 대응하다)	21%
④ concern(~와 연관되다, ~의 관심사이다)	20%
⑤ deny(부정하다)	24%

구문 [1행] ~ **anything** [that <u>cannot be perceived</u> by the five senses and <u>(cannot be) repeatedly measured or quantified</u>].

▶ [ ]이 anything을 꾸민다. anything that을 한꺼번에 whatever(~한 것은 무엇이든)로 바꿀 수 있다.

▶ <cannot be p.p.(~될 수 없다)>의 조동사 수동태 구문에서 과거분사구가 and 앞뒤로 병렬구조를 이룬다.

07 정답 ⑤ 21% 2022 4월 34번

해석 동물들을 50살에 저절로 죽게 만드는 어떤 돌연변이가 나타난 다고 상상해 보라. 이것은 분명히 불리하지만 지극히 미미하게 그렇다. 이 돌연변이를 지닌 동물 중 99% 이상은 이것이 작용할 기회가 있기도 전에 죽을 것이므로, 결코 그 부작용을 경험하지 못할 것이다. 이는 그 돌연변이가 개체군에 남을 가능성이 꽤 있다는 의미인데, 그게 좋아서가 아니라, 그 정도 고령에는 '자연 선택의 힘'이 그것을 없앨 정도로 충분히 강하지 않기 때문이다. 반대로, 만약 한 돌연변이가 동물들을 2살에 죽게 해서, 다수가 아직 살아 새끼를 낳게 될 거라고 마땅히 기대할 때 이들의 목숨을 앗아간다면, 진화는 이것을 매우 신속히 없앨 것이다. 그 돌연변이를 가진 동물들은 곧 그것을 갖고 있지 않을 정도로 운 좋았던 개체들에게 경쟁에서 밀릴 것인데, 자연 선택은 번식 연령 이하의 기간에는 강력하기 때문이다. 그러므로 문제가 되는 돌연변이들은 동물들이 (이미) 번식했을 만큼 충분히 나이 든 후에야 겨우 동물들에게 영향을 미치는 한, 축적될 수 있다.

지문 간단히 보기

동물을 50살(**번식 이후**)에 사망케 하는 돌연변이
: 부작용을 겪기 전에 수명이 다함 → 개체군에 잔존할 확률 ↑

↓

반대로, 2살(**번식 이전**)에 발현하는 돌연변이
: 번식 가능성에 영향을 미침 → 개체군에 잔존할 확률 ↓

↓

즉, 돌연변이가 제거되지 않고 남으려면? ▶ **이미 번식이 끝나 자연 선택의 힘이 약할 때 효과가 나타나는 것이어야 함**

해설 자연 선택의 힘은 번식 연령 이전에 강하기 때문에, 번식 이전의 이른 나이에 발현되는 돌연변이는 제거될 확률이 높다고 한다. 빈칸은 이와 반대로 돌연변이가 '남는' 상황에 관한 설명이므로, '자연 선택이 충분히 강하지 않을' 때에 관한 설명이어야 한다. 따라서 ⑤ '동물들이 번식했을 만큼 충분히 나이 든 후에야 겨우 동물들에게 영향을 미치는'이 정답이다.

오답풀이

보기 해석	선택률
① 동물이 나이 들수록 자연 선택의 힘이 커지는	26%
② 그것의 축적이 주로 그 진화적 이득 때문인	19%
③ 진화가 동물의 번식 성공을 억누르며 작용하는	20%
④ 동물들이 자신의 능력 저하를 즉시 보충할 수 있는	13%

구문 [11행] Conversely, if a mutation **killed** the animals at two years, ~ evolution **would get rid of** it very promptly: ~
▶ 현재 사실이 아닌 내용을 가정하기 위해 <if+주어+과거시제 동사 ~, 주어+조동사 과거형+동사원형>의 가정법 과거 구문을 썼다.

08 정답 ② 27% 2022 6월 34번

해석 전개부는 매우 복잡하고 기발해질 수 있다. 요한 제바스티안 바흐의 푸가는 이 과정이 어디까지 갈 수 있는지를 보여줘서, 그 작곡가(바흐)가 통일성 있는 구조 안에서 여러 복잡한 전개부가 포함된 뛰어난 작품을 만들어 내는 데 멜로디 라인 하나, 가끔은 음 몇 개만 있으면 되었다. 루트비히 판 베토벤의 유명한 5번 교향곡은 클래식 작곡가가 음 몇 개와 간단하고 리듬감 있는 박자로 얼마나 많은 것을 이끌어낼 수 있는지에 관한 탁월한 예시를 제공한다. 모든 사람들이 어디선가 들어본 시작부의 다-다-다-덤은 일종의 반복 악구나 연결 끈처럼, 첫 악장뿐 아니라 나머지 3악장에 걸쳐 엄청나게 다양한 방식으로 나타난다. 우리가 그림 작품 하나를 창작하는 데 들어가는 복잡한 붓놀림을 항상 볼 수 있는 게 아닌 것처럼, 베토벤이 어떻게 계속 반복 악구를 새롭게 사용해낼 방법을 찾는지, 혹은 어떻게 제재를 거대하고 통일성 있는 진술로 전개하는지를 항상 알아채지는 못할 수도 있다. 그러나 그 웅장한 교향곡에서 우리가 얻는 즐거움의 많은 부분은 그 이면의 독창성, 즉 음악적 아이디어의 인상적인 전개에서 비롯된다.

지문 간단히 보기

매우 복잡하고 기발해질 수 있는 음악의 전개부

↓

(예시) 바흐의 푸가, 베토벤의 5번 교향곡
- 단순한 음, 멜로디, 리듬만으로 복잡한 전개부 구성
→ 반복 악구를 '계속 새롭게 사용'해서 가능

↓

음악 감상의 즐거움은 인상적인 전개부에서 비롯됨
▶ **반복 악구를 얼마나 다양하고 독창적으로 제시하는지가 중요**

해설 바흐의 푸가와 베토벤의 5번 교향곡을 예로 들어, 멜로디 라인 하나, 음 몇 개, 간단한 박자만 갖고도 '계속 새로운 사용'을 통해 놀라운 전개부를 만들 수 있다고 서술하는 글이다. 따라서 빈칸에는 ② '엄청나게 다양한 방식으로 나타난다'가 들어가야 한다.

오답풀이

보기 해석	선택률
① 작곡가의 음악적 아이디어를 모순되게 만든다	19%
③ 광범위한 음악적 지식을 창의적으로 제공한다	18%
④ 구조 안에서 꽤 조용하게 유지된다	18%
⑤ 사람들 본인의 즐거움과 깊이 관련된다	17%

구문 [16행] **Just as** we don't always see the intricate brushwork that goes into the creation of a painting, we may not always notice ~
▶ <just as A, B(A와 마찬가지로 B하다)> 구문이다.
▶ 밑줄 친 부분은 선행사 the intricate brushwork를 꾸미는 주격 관계대명사절이다. 선행사가 단수명사이므로 that절의 동사 또한 단수형(goes)으로 쓰였다.

09 정답 ③ 80%

해석 흥미롭게도, 전문가들은 복잡한 과제를 수행하거나 많은 과제를 결합할 때 초보자만큼 어려움을 겪지 않는다. 전문가는 한정된 영역 안에서 엄청난 연습을 하기 때문에, 자기 분야에서의 핵심 기술 요소는 고도로 숙련되고 더 자동화되어 있는 경향이 있다. 그러면 고도로 숙련된 이 각 기술은 비교적 적은 인지 자원을 필요로 하여, 전문가가 경험하는 총 인지 부하를 효과적으로 낮춘다. 따라서 전문가는 비교적 쉽게 복잡한 과제를 수행하고 많은 과제를 결합할 수 있다. (게다가, 초보자는 과제가 분할되고 분리되어 있을 때 그 과제 처리에 탁월하다.) 이는 그들(전문가들)이 반드시 초보자보다 인지적 자원이 더 많기 때문이 아니고, 그보다는 핵심 기술을 수행하면서 달성한 고도의 능숙함 때문에 이들은 자신들이 가진 것으로 더 많은 것을 해낼 수 있는 것이다. 반면에, 초보자는 각 기술 요소에서 (전문가와) 동일한 수준의 능숙함과 자동성을 달성하지 못했으며, 그렇기에 그들은 전문가가 비교적 쉽게 효율적으로 결합하는 기술들을 결합하느라 고생한다.

지문 간단히 보기

> 전문가는 초보자보다 복잡한 과제를 쉽게 처리하고 과제 결합에 능숙
> = 핵심 기술이 고도로 숙련되고 자동화돼 있음

> ① 기술 수행 시 인지 자원이 덜 듦
> ② 그래서 복잡한 과제 수행과 과제 결합이 쉬워짐
> ④ 인지 자원 자체가 더 많아서가 아니라, 능숙함 때문에 할 수 있는 게 더 많아진 것

> (대비) ⑤ 초보자: 아직 덜 능숙 → 전문가보다 고생함

해설 전문가가 초보자보다 쉽게 일을 처리하는 이유에 관한 글인데, ③은 초보자가 오히려 작업 수행에 더 탁월한 상황을 언급하므로 흐름에서 벗어난다.

오답풀이

보기 해설	선택률
① 전문가는 숙련되어 있어 인지 부하도 적게 든다는 보충 설명이다.	1%
② ①에서 말하듯 인지 부하가 적게 들기 '때문에' 복잡한 일 처리가 더 쉬워진다는 주제가 다시 언급된다. Thus를 기준으로 인과 흐름이 잘 형성된다.	5%
④ ②의 내용이 This로 연결된다. 일 처리가 쉬워지는 이유는 '고도의 능숙함' 때문임을 다시 강조하는 흐름이다.	8%
⑤ on the other hand 앞뒤로 '전문가 vs. 초보자'의 상황이 자연스럽게 대비된다.	3%

구문 [6행] **Each of these highly practiced skills** then **demands** relatively few cognitive resources, ~
▶ <each of+복수명사>가 주어이면 단수 취급한다(demands).

10 정답 ④ 50%

해석 언어 습득 과정에서, 아이들은 일련의 유한한 발화에만 노출된다. 하지만 그들은 무한한 문장들을 사용하고 이해하게 된다.
(C) 이것은 언어 사용의 창조적인 측면이라 일컬어져 왔다. 이 '창의성'은 시나 소설을 쓸 수 있는 능력이라기보다, 이전에 결코 말하거나 듣지 못한 새로운 문장을 무한히 만들어내고 이해할 수 있는 능력을 말한다. 아이들이 받는 구체적인 언어 입력은 아이마다 다르고, 어느 두 아이도 정확히 똑같은 발화를 접하지 않는다.
(A) 하지만 그들은 모두 거의 동일한 문법에 도달한다. 보호자들이 아이들에게 특정 문법 사항을 보여줄 목적으로 말을 걸지는 않는다는 점에서, 아이들이 받는 입력은 무작위적이다. 그렇지만 모든 아이들이 체계적인 언어 지식을 발달시킨다.
(B) 따라서, 아이들이 받는 (언어) 입력과 또한 개인적 상황의 극심한 한계와 변동에도 불구하고, 이들은 모두 풍부하고 균일한 언어 지식 체계를 발달시킨다. 습득된 지식은 다양한 방식으로 그 입력을 넘어선다.

지문 간단히 보기

> 유한한 발화를 접해도, 무한한 문장을 말하게 되는 아이들
> (C) 언어의 '창의성' 개념으로 설명 가능

> (C) 아이들마다 각기 접하는 입력이 다름
> (A) 하지만, 결국 같은 문법 수준에 도달

> (A) 입력은 무작위적이지만, 체계적인 언어 지식이 습득됨
> (B) 습득된 지식은 다양한 방식으로 입력을 '넘어선' 결과물

해설 주어진 글의 언어 습득 과정을 (C)에서 '창의성'이라는 개념으로 정리한다. 이어서 (A)는 아이들이 제한된 입력만 갖고도 동일한 문법을 습득한다고 말한다. (B)는 '그 모든 한계와 차이에도 불구하고' 입력을 넘어선 언어 지식이 발달된다는 최종 결론이므로 마지막에 온다. 따라서 ④ '(C)-(A)-(B)'가 자연스럽다.

오답풀이

보기 해설	선택률
① 주어진 글의 두 번째 문장과 (A) 첫 문장의 내용이 동일하므로, (A)의 Yet을 기준으로 대비될 수 없다.	6%
②, ③ 주어진 글과 (B) 첫 문장은 사실상 같은 내용이므로, 인과 관계를 나타내는 Thus로 연결되기 어렵다.	12% / 17%
⑤ (B)의 마지막 문장과 (A) 첫 문장의 내용이 동일하므로, (A)의 Yet을 기준으로 대비될 수 없다.	16%

구문 [C-1행] This **has been referred to as** the creative aspect of language use.
▶ 현재완료 수동태인 <have been p.p.(~되어 왔다)>가 쓰였다.
▶ 구동사 <refer to A as B(A를 B라고 일컫다)>를 수동태로 바꾸면 <A be referred to as B(A가 B라고 일컬어지다)>가 된다.

11 정답 ③ 41%

해석 바빌로니아의 천문학자들은 하늘의 천체 운동에 대한 자세한 기록을 만들어서, 그 결과표를 사용하여 불규칙성을 걸러내고, 그것들로 신의 은총을 가려냈다. 이것이 우리가 현재 과학적인 방법이라고 부르는 것, 즉 세상에 대한 정확한 관찰이 미래 예측에 사용될 수 있다는 것을 보여 주는 씨앗이었다. 이런 식의 우주의 이해에 있어 측정의 중요성은 수 세기 동안 원활하게 발전하지는 않았다. 사실, 중세 유럽 시대에는 손과 눈으로 측정하는 것이 간혹 다소 터무니없는 종류의 지식, 즉 추상적인 사고보다 열등한 지식을 만들어낸다고 여겨졌다. 그 의심은 당시의 스콜라 철학에서 고대 그리스인들의 영향, 특히 물질 세계는 끊임없는 변화와 불안정의 세계라고 역설했던 플라톤과 아리스토텔레스의 영향 때문이었다. 그들은 현실이 플라톤적인 형태이든 아리스토텔레스적인 원인이든, 비물질적인 자질을 참조하면 가장 잘 이해된다고 강조했다. 이러한 직관을 완전히 대체하려면 과학 혁명이라는 뜻밖의 새로운 발견이 필요했을 것이고, 밤하늘의 관찰은 다시금 결정적인 것으로 판명되었다.

지문 간단히 보기

바빌로니아의 천문학자들: 천체 운동을 '보고 기록'
→ 관찰이 미래 예측에 사용될 수 있음을 시사

↓

(하지만) 측정은 한동안 제대로 중시되지 못함
→ (예시) 중세 유럽: 관찰과 측정을 '열등하게' 여김

↓

'이런 의심': 그리스 학자들의 영향(비물질적 요소 중시)
→ 과학 혁명 이후에야 변화가 일어났을 것(관찰 중시)

해설 ③ 앞은 관측과 측정이 수 세기 동안 발전하지 못했다는 내용인데, 주어진 문장은 그런 시기의 예로 중세 유럽을 언급한다. 이어서 ③ 뒤에서는 The suspicion으로 주어진 문장의 내용을 지칭하며, '측정이 열등한 지식을 만들어낸다'는 중세 유럽의 '의심'이 어디서 비롯되었는지 설명한다. 따라서 주어진 문장은 ③에 들어가야 한다.

오답풀이 보기 해설　　　　　　　　　　　　　　　　선택률

① 앞문장에서 설명한 바빌로니아 천문학자들의 연구 방법을 뒷문장에서 This로 요약한다. 5%

② 앞문장의 accurate observations of the world가 뒷문장에서 measurement로 재진술되었다. 10%

④ 앞문장의 ancient Greeks가 뒷문장의 They이다. 즉 ④ 앞뒤가 모두 측정보다 비물질적 자질을 중시한 그리스인들의 연구법을 다룬다. 25%

⑤ 앞의 '직관', 즉 '비물질적 자질을 중시한 관점'을 깨고자 과학 혁명이 필요했다는 결론이 뒤에 잘 제시된다. 이 결론은 '관찰이 현대 과학적 연구 방법의 씨앗이 되었다'는 주제와 연결된다. 19%

구문 [22행] ~ with observations ~ proving decisive.
▶ <with+명사+분사(~한 채로)>는 주절에 연속되거나 주절과 동시에 일어나는 상황을 설명한다. 분사 앞의 명사가 분사의 의미상 주어이다.

12 정답 ① 37%

해석 컴퓨터는 정보를 획득하고 보존하고 추출하는 문제를 상당 부분 해결했다. 데이터는 사실상 무한한 양과 다루기 쉬운 형태로 저장될 수 있다. 컴퓨터는 책의 시대에는 얻을 수 없던 다양한 데이터를 이용할 수 있게 한다. 컴퓨터는 데이터를 효과적으로 짜임새 있게 담아내서, 그것을 이용 가능하게 만들 (특수한) 방식은 더 이상 필요하지 않고, 암기도 필요 없다. 맥락과 분리된 단일한 결정을 처리할 때, 컴퓨터는 10년 전만 해도 상상할 수 없었던 도구들을 제공한다. 하지만 이는 관점을 축소시키기도 한다. 정보에 매우 쉽게 접근할 수 있고 의사소통이 순간적이기 때문에, 그것의 중요성이나 심지어 중요한 것의 정의에 관한 관심이 감소한다. 이런 역학은 정책 입안자들이 쟁점을 예상하기보다는 발생하기를 기다리게 하고, 결정의 순간을 역사적 연속체의 일부라기보다는 일련의 고립되어 일어나는 일로 간주하게 한다. 이런 일이 일어나면, 정보 조작이 주요한 정책 도구로서의 숙고를 대체한다.
→ 컴퓨터는 탈맥락화된 방식으로 정보를 처리하는 데 틀림없이 (A)유능하지만, 정책 결정 과정에서 볼 수 있는 것처럼 더 광범위한 맥락과 관련된 (B)종합적 판단을 내리는 데 방해가 된다.

지문 간단히 보기

데이터 획득, 보존, 추출에 도움이 되는 컴퓨터
→ '맥락과 분리된' 단일한 결정 처리에 유용
▶ **탈맥락화된 정보 처리에 유능함**

하지만, '관점을 축소시키는' 한계도 있음
→ 의사소통의 '순간성'으로 인해 데이터의 중요성에 대한 관심↓
→ 의사결정의 각 순간을 '고립된' 일로 여기게 됨
▶ **종합적 판단에 방해**

해설 컴퓨터는 맥락에서 분리된 정보 처리에 분명 도움이 되지만, 한편으로 정보를 연속체 안에서 보지 못하게 하고 고립된 것으로 취급하게 한다는 점에서 한계가 있다는 내용이다. 따라서 요약문의 빈칸에는 ① '유능하지만 - 종합적'이 적절하다.

오답풀이

보기 해석　　　　　　　　　　　　　　　　　선택률

② 우세하지만 - 편향된 23%

③ 불완전하지만 - 정보에 근거한 17%

④ 인상적이지만 - 합법적 15%

⑤ 비효율적이지만 - 시기적절한 6%

구문 [5행] The computer **makes available** a range of data unattainable in the age of books. **It** packages **it** effectively; ~
▶ makes 뒤에 짧은 목적격보어 available이 긴 목적어인 'a range of data ~'보다 먼저 왔다.
▶ 첫 번째 It은 The computer를, 두 번째 it은 data를 받는다. 즉 동사 packages의 주어와 목적어가 서로 다르므로 목적어 자리에 재귀대명사 itself를 쓰지 않았다.

13~14 정답 ① 44% / ④ 51% 2023학년도 수능 41~42번

해석 매우 간단한 알고리즘일지라도 간단한 예측 문제에 관해서는 전문가의 판단을 능가할 수 있다는 증거가 있다. 예를 들어, 가석방으로 풀려난 죄수가 계속해서 또 다른 범죄를 저지를 것인지 예측하거나, 잠재적 (입사) 후보자가 장차 직장에서 일을 잘할 것인지를 예측할 때 알고리즘이 인간보다 더 정확하다는 것이 입증되었다. 여러 다양한 영역에 걸친 100건 이상의 연구에서, 모든 사례의 절반은 간단한 공식이 인간 전문가보다 중요한 예측을 더 잘한다는 것을 보여주며, (아주 적은 소수를 제외한) 나머지는 둘 사이의 무승부(비등함)를 보여준다. 여러 다양한 요인이 관련돼 있고 상황이 매우 불확실할 때, 간단한 공식은 가장 중요한 요소에 초점을 맞추고 일관성을 유지하여 (예측에) 성공할 수 있는 반면, 인간의 판단은 특히 두드러지지만 어쩌면 무관한 고려 사항에 너무 쉽게 영향받는다. '체크리스트'는 사람들이 편안하다고(→ 일이 너무 많다고) 느낄 때 중요한 조치나 고려 사항을 놓치지 않게 해서 다양한 영역에서 전문가의 결정의 질을 향상할 수 있다는 추가적인 증거가 유사한 생각을 뒷받침한다. 예를 들어, 중환자실에 있는 환자를 치료하려면 하루에 수백 가지의 작은 조치가 필요할 수 있으며, 작은 실수 하나로 목숨을 앗아갈 수 있다. 체크리스트를 사용해 어떠한 중요한 조치라도 놓치지 않는 것은 활성 감염의 예방부터 폐렴 감소에 이르기까지, 다양한 의학적 상황에서 현저히 효과가 있다는 것이 입증되었다.

지문 간단히 보기

> 간단한 알고리즘(= 공식)이 전문가보다 예측을 더 잘함

> 알고리즘: 중요한 요인에만 초점을 두고 일관적임
> vs. 사람: 관련 없는 요인에도 영향을 잘 받음

> 비슷한 추가 증거: 의료 상황에서의 체크리스트 활용
> → 중요한 고려사항을 놓치지 않게 도와줌
> → 전문가의 의사 결정의 질 향상

구문 [28행] **Using** checklists to ensure [that no crucial steps are missed] **has proved** to be remarkably effective in a range of medical contexts, <u>from preventing live infections to reducing pneumonia</u>.
▶ 동명사구 주어는 단수 취급한다(has). that절의 동사 are missed와 문장 전체의 동사 has proved를 잘 구별하도록 한다.
▶ 밑줄 부분은 <from A to B(A부터 B까지)> 구문으로, A와 B에 동명사구가 각각 나왔다.

13 **해설** 간단한 공식이나 알고리즘이 인간의 판단 능력을 도울 수 있다는 내용으로, 각종 연구 증거와 의학적 상황에서의 체크리스트 활용을 예시로 든다. 따라서 글의 제목으로 ① '의사 결정 시 간단한 공식의 힘'이 가장 적절하다.

오답풀이

보기 해석	선택률
② 항상 우선순위를 결정하라: 빅 데이터 관리 요령	9%
③ 알고리즘의 실수: 단순함에 관한 근거 없는 믿음	12%
④ 대비하라! 만일을 대비해 체크리스트를 만들라	22%
⑤ 인간의 판단은 어떻게 알고리즘을 이기는가	14%

14 **해설** 체크리스트가 유용한 경우에 관한 예시로 '작은 실수 하나로 환자의 목숨이 좌우되는' 중환자실이 언급되는데, 이는 사람들이 '편안함'보다는 '압박감'을 느낄 상황이다. 따라서 ④ (d)의 relaxed를 overloaded로 바꿔야 한다.

오답풀이

보기 해석	선택률
① accurate(정확한)	3%
② better(더 나은)	7%
③ irrelevant(무관한)	34%
⑤ effective(효과가 있는)	6%

STEP PLUS+ 수능 기출 마무리 복습

단어 TEST
02 책임(성) **03** ~을 줄이다 **04** 내성적인, 남과 잘 어울리지 않는 **05** (위협 등에) 대응하다, (주장 등에) 반대하다 **06** ~의 목숨을 앗아가다 **07** 신속히, 즉시 **08** 유한한, 한정된 **09** 터무니없는 **10** 끊임없는 **11** 얻을 수 없는 **12** 감염

구문 TEST
14 lies a cozy couch **15** The collaboration between art and science **16** you learned to drive[you should learn to drive, for you to learn to drive] **17** so that the room would be warmer **18** so that I would not oversleep

01   정답 ⑤ 86%   2020 7월 19번

해석 호텔 로비는 품격 있고 조명이 잘 되어 있었다. 연갈색 목조와 철조도 훌륭했다. 짧은 열차가 임원들을 태우고 이곳을 지나 달린다. 나는 짙은 회색의 정장을 잘 차려입고 어울리는 넥타이와 검정 구두를 착용했다. 나는 어떠한 군중도 매료시킬 준비가 되어 있다고 생각하니 기분이 매우 좋다. 하지만 나는 내 서류 가방과 노트북을 어디에 두었는지 잊는다. 나는 열차를 세우고, 유리창이 있는 짐칸에 내 가방이 있는지 확인해 봐야겠다고 말한다. 온갖 종류의 가방이 보이는데 내 것만 없다. 그것을 이 나라에 가져오긴 한 것인지 의심스럽다. 나는 멋진 남자라서 다른 사람들을 기다리게 하고 싶지 않다. 내가 열차를 보내고, 그것이 재빨리 움직여 거의 시야에서 사라져갈 때, 나는 내 값비싼 신발 한 짝이 없어졌다는 것을 깨닫는다! 가방을 찾는 동안 그 신발을 칸에 둔 게 틀림없고, 열차는 가 버렸다. 나는 내 얼굴이 빨개지는 것을 느낀다.

지문 간단히 보기

정장, 넥타이, 구두 차림의 '멋진 신사'인 '나': 기분이 좋음 ▶ **흡족함**

↓

서류 가방과 노트북을 어디에 뒀는지 잊음
→ 짐칸을 뒤졌으나 찾지 못함

↓

일단 기차를 보냈는데, 신발 한 짝이 없어진 것을 발견
→ 얼굴이 달아오름 ▶ **당황함**

해설 정장을 잘 차려입고 기분 좋게 열차로 이동 중이던 필자가 서류 가방과 노트북을 어디에 두었는지 잊어 짐칸에서 찾아보다가 일단 기차를 보냈는데 신발 한 짝이 없어져 있어 당황한다는 이야기다. 따라서 심경 변화로 ⑤ '흡족한 → 당황한'이 적절하다.

오답풀이

보기 해석	선택률
① 긴장한 → 안도한	4%
② 기쁜 → 지루한	2%
③ 호기심 많은 → 실망한	4%
④ 놀란 → 무관심한	2%

구문 [15행] I **must have left** it in the cabin while looking for the bag and the metro has left.
▶ <must have p.p.>는 '~했음에 틀림없다'라는 의미로, 과거에 대한 강한 추측을 나타낸다.

02   정답 ① 77%   2022 4월 20번

해석 우리는 과도한 분석을 통해 불확실성을 피하려고 노력한다. 그러나 우리는 미래가 어떻게 전개될지를 완벽히 통제할 수 없다. 여러분이 단지 '걱정(되는) 문제'에 완전히 답할 수만 있다면, 여러분은 만족할 것이고 마침내 반추를 중단할 수 있다고 느낄지도 모르지만, 이런 일이 실제로 여러분에게 일어난 적이 있는가? 여러분이 걱정을 그만두게 해주었던 정답이 있었던 적이 있는가? 이 소용돌이에서 벗어날 수 있는 유일한 방법이 있는데, 통제권을 얻으려고 노력하는 것이 아니라, 통제를 포기하는 것이다. 불확실성에 맞서는 대신, 그것을 수용하라. 여러분의 걱정(되는) 문제에 답하기 위해 노력하는 대신, 그것을 미해결 상태로 두는 것을 의도적으로 연습하라. 다른 사람들에게 물어보지 말고, 그것에 대해 생각하지 말라. 분석은 해결책이 '아니라', 실제로는 단지 똑같은 문제에 불과하다고 스스로에게 말하라.

지문 간단히 보기

과도한 분석으로 불확실성을 피하려는 경향

↓

(반박) 미래를 완벽히 통제하기는 불가능
→ 걱정이 중단되지 않고 '소용돌이'만 생겨날 뿐임

↓

통제권을 쥐기보다, 오히려 포기해야 함
= 불확실성에 맞서지 말고, 수용하기
= 문제를 해결되지 못한 상태로 놔두기
= 분석은 해결이 아니라 '문제'임을 상기하기

해설 과도할 정도의 분석을 통해 미래를 확실히 통제하려고 시도하기보다는, 불확실성을 있는 그대로 수용하라는 내용이다. 명령문 형태의 마지막 네 문장에 주장이 잘 제시된다. 따라서 ① '분석을 통해 미래의 불확실성을 통제하기보다 수용해야 한다.'가 주장으로 가장 적절하다.

오답풀이

보기 해설	선택률
② 문제에 관해 '타인에게 묻지 말라'는 문장을 '의존하지 말라'는 의미로 해석하지 않도록 한다.	12%
③ '객관적 판단'에 관해서 언급되지 않았다.	5%
④ 분석을 '피하라'가 핵심 내용이다.	2%
⑤ '계획을 세우라'는 내용은 언급되지 않았다.	1%

구문 [11행] Instead of trying to answer your worry question, deliberately **practice leaving it unanswered**.
▶ <practice V-ing(~하는 것을 연습하다)> 구조이다. 목적어인 동명사구는 <leave+목적어+과거분사(~을 …된 상태로 두다)>의 5형식 구조이다.

03 정답 ④ 51%　　2024학년도 수능 21번

해석　여러분이 주의 집중하는 방식은 여러분이 스트레스에 대처하는 방식에 중요한 역할을 한다. 주의가 분산되면 스트레스를 해소하는 능력이 손상되는데, 왜냐하면 여러분의 주의가 분산되더라도, 여러분은 경험 가운데 스트레스가 많은 부분에만 집착할 수 있기에 그것이 좁게 집중되기 때문이다. 여러분의 주의 초점 범위가 넓어지면, 여러분은 스트레스를 더 쉽게 해소할 수 있다. 여러분은 어떤 상황이든 그 상황의 더 많은 측면을 균형 있는 시각으로 볼 수 있으며, 피상적이고 불안을 유발하는 주의 수준에 여러분을 옭아매는 어느 한 부분에 갇히지 않을 수 있다. 초점이 좁으면 각 경험의 스트레스 수준이 높아지지만, 초점이 넓으면 여러분은 각 상황을 더 넓은 시각으로 더 잘 볼 수 있기 때문에 스트레스 수준이 낮아진다. 불안감을 유발하는 하나의 세부 사항은 더 큰 그림(전체 상황)보다 덜 중요하다. 그것은 스스로를 (음식이) 눌어붙지 않는 프라이팬으로 변모시키는 것과 같다. 여러분은 여전히 달걀을 부칠 수 있지만, 그 달걀은 팬에 눌어붙지 않을 것이다.

지문 간단히 보기

> 주의 집중 방식: 스트레스 대처 방식에 큰 역할

↓

> 주의 초점 범위가 좁아지면 → 스트레스 ↑
> 주의 초점 범위가 넓어지면 → 스트레스 ↓

↓

> (비유) 음식이 눌어붙지 않는 프라이팬
> = 불안을 유발하는 세부사항보다, 전체 그림을 보는 것
> ▶ **주의 초점 범위를 넓히는 것**

해설　글에서 반복되는 핵심 내용은, 스트레스가 되는 어느 한 부분에 집중하는 대신 '집중의 범위를 넓혀서' 큰 그림을 봐야 스트레스를 덜 받게 된다는 것이다. 따라서 밑줄 친 부분의 의미로 가장 적절한 것은 ④ '스트레스가 되는 측면을 넘어 경험을 더 넓게 바라보는 것'이다.

오답풀이

보기 해석	선택률
① 일상생활에서 스트레스가 되는 그 어떤 경험도 절대 맞닥뜨리지 않는 것	9%
② 시각을 넓혀 스트레스의 원인을 찾아내는 것	17%
③ 경험의 긍정적 측면에 주의를 좀처럼 국한시키지 않는 것	8%
⑤ 넓은 시각을 키우는 원천으로서 스트레스를 생각하는 것	16%

구문　[1행] **How you focus your attention** plays a critical role in **how you deal with stress**.
▶ how가 이끄는 2개의 명사절(~하는 방식)이 각각 문장의 주어와 전치사 in의 목적어 역할을 한다. 절 주어는 단수 취급한다(plays).

04 정답 ⑤ 44%　　2023 9월 23번

해석　민영 음악 라디오 방송의 주된 목적은 청취자를 광고주와 후원자 집단에게로 인도하는 것이다. 상업적 성공을 달성하려면, 그 청취자는 가능한 한 대규모여야 한다. (인구 통계학적 또는 심리 통계학적 개요, 구매력, 관심 수준, 만족도, 주목의 질, 또는 정서 상태 등) 다른 어떤 특성보다도, 집단으로 모인 청취자의 규모는 음악 라디오를 수익 목적에 맞게 만들려는 방송사들에게 가장 중요한 측정 기준이다. 결과적으로 방송사들은 인기 있는 음악, 또는 적어도 청취자가 라디오를 끄거나 채널을 바꾸게 하지 않을 거라고 여겨지는 음악을 틀어 청취자의 규모를 극대화하려고 애쓴다. 청취자 유지는 많은 음악 프로그램 제작자와 라디오 방송국 경영진에게 있어 (유일한 핵심 가치까지는 아니더라도) 핵심 가치 중 하나다. 그 결과 높은 수준의 위험 회피는 흔히 '성공한' 라디오 음악 프로그램 제작자를 구분 짓는다. 재생 목록은 제한적이고, 흔히 매우 적다.

지문 간단히 보기

> 민영 음악 라디오 방송: 상업적 성공이 목적

↓

> 이 목표를 달성하려면, 대규모 청취자 확보가 중요

↓

> 청취자 유지를 위해 인기 있는 음악 위주로 재생(위험 회피)
> → 재생 목록이 제한되고 적어지는 결과 초래

해설　민영 음악 라디오 방송이 대규모 청취자 확보에 주력하면서 인기 음악을 주로 내보내고, 위험을 회피하려고 하며, 이에 따라 재생 목록도 제한되는 결과가 나타난다는 내용이다. 따라서 주제로 ⑤ '음악 사업체들이 대규모 청중을 모으려고 시도한 결과'가 가장 적절하다.

오답풀이

보기 해석	선택률
① 국제적 청중의 관심을 끄는 음악 재생 목록의 특징	6%
② 광고주가 라디오 청취자의 음악적 선호에 미치는 영향	18%
③ 라디오 음악 프로그램에서 청취자 규모를 키우는 것의 어려움	17%
④ 라디오 사업에서 청취자의 다양한 요구를 충족할 필요성	16%

구문　[11행] ~ music that **can be relied upon not to cause** audiences **to switch off** their radio **or change** the station.
▶ <rely (up)on A not to-V(A가 ~하지 않을 거라고 믿다)>를 수동태로 바꾸면 <A be relied (up)on not to-V>가 된다.
▶ 밑줄 부분은 <cause+목적어+to부정사(~이 …하게 하다)> 구문이다. 목적격보어인 to부정사가 <A or B>로 병렬 연결되었다.

05 정답 ④ 96% 2023 6월 26번

해석 프랑스 영화감독인 Jean Renoir(1894~1979)는 프랑스 파리에서 태어났다. 그는 유명 화가 Pierre-Auguste Renoir의 아들이었다. 그와 나머지 Renoir 일가 사람들은 그의 아버지의 그림 중 다수의 모델이었다. 제1차 세계대전이 발발했을 때, Jean Renoir는 프랑스 군에서 복무하다가 다리에 부상을 입었다. 1937년에 그는 그의 비교적 잘 알려진 영화 중 하나인 <La Grande Illusion>을 만들었다. 그것은 엄청나게 흥행했지만, 독일에서는 상영이 허용되지 않았다. 제2차 세계대전 중, 1940년에 나치가 프랑스를 침공했을 때 그는 미국 할리우드로 가서 거기서 경력을 이어갔다. 그는 영화계에 남긴 평생의 업적으로 1975년 아카데미 공로상을 받은 것을 포함해, 경력 내내 수많은 훈장과 상을 받았다. 전반적으로, 영화 제작자이자 예술가로서 Jean Renoir의 영향력은 지속되고 있다.

지문 간단히 보기

> Jean Renoir의 생애
> ① 아버지가 유명 화가였음(Pierre-Auguste Renoir)
> ② 1차 대전 당시 프랑스 군 복무 → 다리 부상
> ③ 1937년 <La Grande Illusion> 제작 → 대흥행(독일 제외)
> ④ 2차 대전 중 미국 할리우드로 이동
> ⑤ 1975년 아카데미 공로상 수상

해설 'During World War II, when the Nazis invaded France in 1940, he went to Hollywood in the United States ~'에 따르면 2차 대전 당시 Jean Renoir는 미국 할리우드로 갔다고 하므로, 일치하지 않는 것은 ④ '제2차 세계대전 내내 프랑스에 머물렀다.'이다.

오답풀이

보기 해설	선택률
① ~ the son of the famous painter Pierre-Auguste Renoir.	0%
② At the outbreak of World War I, Jean Renoir was serving in the French army ~	1%
③ In 1937, he made *La Grande Illusion*, ~	0%
⑤ He was awarded ~ the Academy Honorary Award ~	0%

구문 [13행] He **was awarded numerous honors and awards** throughout his career ~
▶ 간접목적어를 주어로 삼은 4형식 문장의 수동태는 <be p.p.+직접목적어> 형태로 구성된다. <be p.p.> 뒤에 여전히 목적어가 나올 수 있다는 것이 포인트이다.

06 정답 ⑤ 47% 2021학년도 수능 30번

해석 편승 효과가 어떻게 발생하는지는 빛의 속도 측정의 역사로 입증된다. 이 속도는 상대성 이론의 기초이기 때문에, 과학에서 가장 자주 면밀하게 측정된 물리량 중 하나이다. 우리가 아는 한, 그 속도는 시간이 흐르는 동안 변함이 없었다. 하지만 1870년부터 1900년까지 모든 실험에서 너무 빠른 속도가 발견되었다. 이후, 1900년부터 1950년까지는 반대되는 현상이 일어났는데, 모든 실험에서 너무 느린 속도를 발견했다! 결과가 항상 실제 값의 어느 한쪽에 있는 이런 오류는 '편향'이라 불린다. 아마도 그것은 시간이 지나면서 실험자들이 자신들이 발견하리라 예상했던 것과 일치하도록 결과를 잠재의식적으로 조정했기 때문에 생겨났을 것이다. 결과가 그들이 예상한 것과 부합하면, 그들은 그것을 취했다. 결과가 부합하지 않으면, 그들은 그것을 버렸다. 그들은 고의로 부정직했던 것이 아니고, 그저 통념에 영향을 받았을 뿐이다. 그 패턴은 누군가 예상된 것 대신에 실제로 측정된 것을 보고할 용기가 부족했을(→ 있었을) 때에야 겨우 바뀌었다.

지문 간단히 보기

> 빛의 속도: 변하지 않은 값임에도, 측정값에 많은 '편향'이 있었음
> - 1870~1900: '너무 빠른' 측정값
> - 1900~1950: '너무 느린' 측정값

↓

> (이유) 실험자들이 자기 예상에 맞춰 측정값 조정
> - 결과가 예상과 부합하면 → 그 값을 취함
> - 결과가 예상과 다르면 → 그 값을 버림
> ▶ **누군가 실제 측정값을 보고할 용기를 '냈을' 때 이 패턴이 깨짐**

해설 실험자들은 빛의 속도 값에 대한 당대의 통념에 영향을 받아 무의식적으로 측정값을 조정했다는 설명에 이어, 마지막 문장은 이 패턴이 '변화한' 이유를 설명하고 있다. 즉 누군가 측정된 결과를 보고할 용기를 '지녔을' 때 이러한 패턴이 '바뀌었다'는 의미가 되도록, ⑤의 lacked를 had로 고쳐야 한다.

오답풀이

보기 해석	선택률
① quantities(양)	6%
② opposite(반대; 정반대인)	12%
③ match(부합하다, 맞다)	15%
④ influenced(영향을 받은)	12%

구문 [17행] They weren't being intentionally dishonest, just **influenced** by the conventional wisdom.
▶ 원래 문장은 <not A but B> 형태의 'They weren't being intentionally dishonest, but they were just influenced ~'이다. 여기서 접속사 but과 중복되는 주어 they를 지우고, were를 being으로 바꾼 뒤 생략하여 과거분사구 'just influenced ~'만 남은 분사구문으로 만들었다.

07 정답 ② 35%

해석 사람들은 항상 먹을 것이 필요했으며, 또 항상 그럴 것이다. 자기표현 가치에 대한 강조가 커지는 것이 물질적 욕구를 없애지는 않는다. 하지만 우세한 경제적 성향이 서서히 재편되고 있다. 지식 부문에서 일하는 사람들은 계속 높은 급료를 추구하지만, 그들은 아주 흥미로운 일을 하고 본인의 시간 계획을 따를 수 있는 데 그 이상의 중점을 둔다. 소비는 생존에 대한 필요와 소비되는 재화의 실용적 사용에 점차 덜 좌우된다. 사람들은 여전히 먹지만, 음식 가치의 구성 요소는 그것의 비물질적인 측면에 의해 더 많이 결정된다. 사람들은 할증금을 내서 흥미로운 경험을 제공하거나 독특한 생활 방식을 상징하는 이국적인 요리를 먹으려고 한다. 탈공업화 사회의 대중은 생산이 생태적 또는 윤리적 기준을 위반하는 상품의 구매를 거부하는 것과 같은 '정치적 소비주의'에 점점 더 많은 중점을 둔다. 소비는 점점 덜 생존의 문제이며, 점점 더 생활 방식, 그리고 선택의 문제이다(점점 생존 문제라기보다는 생활 방식 및 선택 문제이다).

지문 간단히 보기

과거에는 생존 때문에 먹었지만, 이제는 그렇지 않음
: 경제적 성향 재편

↓

일자리에서 흥미나 자기만의 시간을 급료보다 중시
= 현대 소비 생활에서도, 생존적 필요나 실용성의 비중 ↓
▶ **비물질적 측면(경험)을 더 중시**

(결론) 소비 = 점점 생존보다는 생활 방식과 선택의 문제

해설 빈칸 뒤에서 '경험'을 위해 비싼 돈을 주고 이국적인 음식을 먹는 소비 사례를 들며, 소비가 점점 생존 문제보다는 '무형의' 생활 방식 및 선택의 문제가 되어간다고 설명하고 있다. 따라서 빈칸에는 ② '비물질적인'이 적절하다.

오답풀이

보기 해석	선택률
① 양적인	12%
③ 영양의	16%
④ 불변의	11%
⑤ 경제적인	26%

구문 [17행] ~ such as boycotting goods **whose** production violates ecological or ethical standards.
▶ 소유격 관계대명사 whose는 관사 없는 명사로 시작하는 완전한 절을 이끌며, 선행사 goods의 소유격을 나타낸다.

08 정답 ① 46%

해설 얼굴 (표정)과 마찬가지로, 움직임은 간혹 우리를 속여서 어떤 것이 생각을 갖고 있다고 믿게 할 수 있다. 예를 들어, 살아 움직이는 것처럼 보이는 장난감은 아이들을 매료시킨다. 나 때 인기 있었던 장난감 중 하나는 'Slinky'라고 불리던, 촘촘하게 나선형으로 감긴 한 뭉치의 철사였다. 이것은 한쪽 끝을 늘리면서 다른 쪽 끝 위로 들어 올려서 경사면 아래로 걷는 것처럼 보일 수 있는데, 약간 곡예를 부리는 애벌레 같다. 크리스마스 날 Slinky의 매력은 누군가가 밟거나 스프링을 비틀어 그것을 영원히 망가뜨릴 때까지 그것이 계단을 내려오면서 보여준 생동감 있는 움직임이었다. 살아 있는 것처럼 보이는 장난감은 우리가 생각하는 무생물과 생물의 당연한 행동 방식을 거스른다는 점에서 진기한 물건이다. 오늘날 많은 장난감이 이 원리를 이용해 큰 효과를 내려고 하지만, 모든 아기가 문득 살아 있는 것처럼 보이는 물건을 좋아하지는 않는다는 점에 주의하라. 이러한 불안감은 아마도 "이게 살아 있는 거야 뭐야?"라는 질문에 대한 그들의 혼란을 나타낸다. 아기는 일단 무언가가 살아 있다고 판단하면, 그것의 움직임을 의도적인 것으로 보는 경향이 있다.

지문 간단히 보기

'살아 있어' 보이는 장난감 → (예시) Slinky
= 무생물과 생물의 행동 방식에 대한 생각을 거스름
= 아이들에게 신기하고 매력적인 대상

하지만 이런 장난감들은 '혼란, 불안'을 야기
: 움직임에 '의도**(생각)**가 있다'고 여겨지기 때문

해설 글의 결론에 따르면 아이들은 어떤 장난감의 움직임이 마치 '살아 있는' 것처럼 보이면 그것이 생물처럼 자기만의 '의도나 생각'도 갖고 있을 것이라고 추측한다고 한다. 따라서 빈칸에는 ① '우리를 속여서 어떤 것이 생각을 갖고 있다고 믿게 할'이다.

오답풀이

보기 해석	선택률
② 우리가 어떤 감정을 표출하고 처리하는 데 도움이 될	21%
③ 우리의 에너지와 보호 기제를 바꿀	10%
④ 말로는 드러낼 수 없는 감정을 남몰래 드러낼	10%
⑤ 확실한 성취감을 만들어 낼	10%

구문 [1행] ~ movement can **fool us into thinking** [that something has a mind].
▶ <fool A into B(A를 속여 B하게 하다)> 구문이다.
▶ [ ]은 동명사 thinking의 목적어 역할을 하는 명사절이다.

09 정답 ④ 74%

해석 정보 시스템은 도입 이래로 사업 수행 방식을 상당히 변화시켰다. 이는 특히 다수의 부문에 걸쳐 가치 사슬(기업 활동에서 부가 가치 창출에 직·간접적으로 연관된 모든 활동의 연계)을 통합하는 기업 간 협력의 사업 형태 및 유형에 특히 해당된다. 그 결과로 생기는 네트워크는 단일 기업의 (여러) 사업 부문을 포함할 뿐만 아니라, 서로 다른 기업의 여러 부문을 포함하기도 한다. 결과적으로, 기업은 지속 가능한 사업 성과를 보장하려면 내부 조직에 주의를 기울여야 할 뿐만 아니라, 주변 부문들의 전체 생태계를 고려할 필요도 있다. (많은 주요 기업들은 수익성이 있는 부문에 집중하고 수익성이 낮은 부문은 쳐내서 사업 모델을 근본적으로 변화시키고 있다.) 이 서로 다른 부문들이 성공적으로 협력할 수 있게 하려면, 공동 플랫폼의 존재가 매우 중요하다.

지문 간단히 보기

정보 시스템 도입 → 사업 수행 방식의 변화

①~② (예시) 다수 부문에 걸쳐 가치 사슬 통합
→ 기업 내 혹은 기업 간 여러 사업부의 통합 네트워크 출현

③ 내부 조직뿐 아니라 주변 부문의 전체적 생태계도 고려 필요
⑤ 성공적인 협력을 위한 공동 플랫폼이 필요

해설 정보 시스템 도입 이후로 여러 기업과 사업 부문이 활발하게 결합하고 있어, 협력을 장려할 수 있는 공동 플랫폼이 중요해졌다는 내용이다. 하지만 ④는 기업이 수익성에 따라 어떤 부문에 집중할지 정한다는 내용이므로 흐름상 어색하다.

오답풀이

보기 해설	선택률
① 첫 문장 내용이 주어인 This로 자연스럽게 이어진다.	1%
② ①의 cooperation between firms가 The resulting networks로 자연스럽게 연결된다.	4%
③ 부문 간, 기업 간 통합을 언급하는 ②를 근거로 주변 부문까지 포함된 '큰 그림'을 봐야 한다는 결론을 자연스럽게 제시하고 있다.	15%
⑤ 각기 다른 부문들 간 '협력'을 제고할 방안(공동 플랫폼)을 언급한다는 점에서 전체 흐름과 일치한다.	3%

구문 [13행] Many major companies are fundamentally changing their business models **by focusing** on profitable units and **cutting off** less profitable ones.
▶ by의 목적어인 동명사구가 <A and B> 형태로 병렬구조를 이룬다. 이는 '~하고 …함으로써'라는 수단의 의미를 나타낸다.

10 정답 ⑤ 28%

해석 한 회사가 조선업에 투자할지 말지를 판단하고 있다. 만약 충분히 대규모로 생산할 수 있다면, 이 회사는 그 모험(과도 같은 투자)이 수익성이 있을 것임을 알고 있다.
(C) 하지만 한 가지 핵심 투입 요소는 저가의 강철이고, 그것은 근처에서 생산되어야 한다. 그 회사의 결정은 결국 다음과 같다. 만약 근처에 강철 공장이 있다면 조선업에 투자하고, 그렇지 않으면 투자하지 않는다는 것이다. 이제, 그 지역에 있는 잠재적 강철 투자자들의 생각을 고려해 보라.
(B) 조선소가 유일한 잠재적 강철 소비자라고 가정하라. 강철 생산자들은 자신의 강철을 구매할 조선소가 있으면 돈을 벌 것이고, 그렇지 않으면 못 벌 거라고 생각한다. 이제 우리는 경제학자들이 '복수 균형'이라고 부르는 두 가지 가능한 결과를 갖게 된다.
(A) '좋은' 결과가 있는데, 이때는 두 가지 투자 형태가 모두 이루어지고, 조선소와 제강업자 모두 결국 이득을 얻고 만족하게 된다. 균형이 이루어지는 것이다. 그다음에 '나쁜' 결과가 있는데, 이때는 (둘 중) 어떤 투자 형태도 이루어지지 않는다. 이 두 번째 결과 또한 균형인데, 왜냐하면 투자하지 않겠다는 결정이 서로를 강화하기 때문이다.

지문 간단히 보기

주어진 상황: 조선업 투자 결정
(C) 주변에 강철 공장이 있어야 투자하기 좋음

(C) 반대로, 강철 투자자 입장도 생각해봐야 함
(B) 이들은 주변에 조선소가 있어야 투자

(B) 결국, 가능한 결과가 2개: '복수 균형'
(A) 복수 균형의 의미 상술(좋은 결과, 나쁜 결과)

해설 조선업 투자를 고려하는 상황을 언급한 주어진 글 뒤로, 이들은 주변에 강철 회사가 있어야 투자하기 좋다는 내용의 (C), 반대로 강철 투자자 입장을 언급한 뒤 2가지 가능한 결과가 생긴다고 언급하는 (B), 2가지 결과를 각각 설명하는 (A)가 차례로 연결되어야 한다. 따라서 ⑤ '(C)-(B)-(A)'가 적절하다.

오답풀이

보기 해설	선택률
① (A)는 '결과'에 관한 내용이므로 가장 마지막에 온다.	5%
②, (C)의 The company는 조선업 투자를 결정하는 주체로,	32%
③ 주어진 글의 A firm이다. 따라서 (C)가 가장 먼저 연결되어야 한다.	21%
④ 조선업 투자를 다루는 (C)와 대비되는 입장(강철 투자)에 대한 설명이 곧 (B)이므로, (B)는 (A)의 '결과'보다 앞에 와야 한다.	12%

구문 [1행] A firm is deciding **whether to invest** in shipbuilding.
▶ <whether+to부정사(~할지 안 할지)>가 동사 is deciding의 목적어 역할을 한다.

11 정답 ⑤ 33%

해석 패션 경향에 대한 영감의 필요성에 관한 초기 징후들은 아마도 1825년경에 미국을 방문하여 겉옷용으로 제작된 경량 울 혼방 옷감에 크게 영감을 받았던 많은 영국 제조업자들에 의해 나타난다. 기성복 부문은 영국보다 미국에서 훨씬 먼저 확립되었고 이와 함께 새로운 도전이 생겨났다. 이전에 의복은 나중에 패션 디자이너로 알려지거나 인정받은 기술자들에 의해 맞춤 제작되었다. 당시의 상류 사회 의상이었다고 지금은 받아들여진 이 수제 의류는 오직 그것에 돈을 지불할 수단(재력)을 가진 사람들을 위해서만 만들어졌다. 특권을 덜 가진 일반 대중들은 집에서 만들고 물려받은 옷을 입었다. 나중에 산업혁명이 끝나갈 무렵, 패션은 모든 계층에게 더욱 쉽게 이용 가능해지고 가격이 적당해졌다. 그 무렵 디자이너들은 주로 공장에서 일했고, 더 이상 개인이 아닌 대량 판매 시장을 위해서 디자인했다. 그러므로 디자이너와 고객 사이의 직접적인 소통 연결이 더 이상 존재하지 않았고, 디자이너들은 새로운 패션 소비자의 필요와 욕구를 예상하는 데 의존해야 했다.

지문 간단히 보기

기존의 의복: 기술자가 만들고 특권층이 소비
(vs. 대중: 집에서 만들고 물려받아 입음)

↓

산업혁명 이후: 패션의 대중화
- '이 무렵'의 디자이너들은 개인 대신 대량 판매 시장 겨냥
→ 고객과 디자이너 간의 직접 소통은 단절되고, 새로운 소비자
　(= 대량 판매 시장)의 수요 예측에 의존

해설 ⑤ 앞의 by the end of the industrial revolution이 주어진 문장의 By now로 연결되어, '산업혁명 이후' 디자이너들이 개인보다는 대중을 위한 의류를 만들게 되었다는 내용을 전개한다. ⑤ 뒤에서는 '그 결과' 디자이너와 고객의 직접적 연결이 끊어졌다고 한다. 따라서 주어진 문장은 ⑤에 들어간다.

오답풀이 보기 해설　　　　선택률

① Previously 앞뒤로 기성복 체제와 그 이전 상황이 자연스럽게 대비된다. — 3%

② 앞의 custom-made가 뒤에서 handmade로 적절히 재진술되어 '맞춤복'에 관해 계속 설명한다. — 12%

③ '특권층'과 대비되는 '비특권층'의 상황을 말하므로 흐름이 갑자기 전환되는 듯 하지만, 크게 보면 기성복 체제 '이전' 상황에 대한 추가 설명이므로 연결이 자연스럽다. — 32%

④ Later로 인해 글의 흐름이 '산업화 이후'로 자연스럽게 전환된다. '패션이 모든 계층에 더 이용 가능해졌다'는 설명은 '기성복 체제'를 암시한다. — 20%

구문 [9행] The ready-to-wear sector was established much earlier in America than in Britain and **with it came new challenges.**
▶ and 뒤는 <전치사구+동사+주어> 어순의 도치 구문이다. 원래 '~ new challenges came with it.'인 문장에서 전치사구를 강조하기 위해 앞에 쓰자 주어와 동사가 도치되었다.

12 정답 ③ 40%

해석 비교 문화적 관점에서 대중적 리더십과 지배력 사이의 방정식은 의심스럽다. '지배력'이란 말의 의미는 무엇인가? 강제를 뜻하는 것인가? 아니면 '가장 가치 있는 것'에 대한 통제인가? '정치' 체제는 둘 다 또는 하나와만 관련이 있거나, 아마도 둘 다 관련이 없을 수도 있다. 많은 부족에게 '통제'라는 관념은 성가실 것인데, 예시로 모든 공동체 구성원이 개인의 자율성을 좋아하고 통제나 강제가 명백하게 표현되면 무엇이든 몹시 싫어하는 아마존의 많은 원주민 부족 사이에서 그렇다. 서양의 고정관념일지 모르겠지만, '강제적인' 힘으로서의 정치 권력이라는 개념은 보편적이지 않다. 아마존의 지도자가 명령을 내리는 것은 매우 이례적이다. 많은 부족이 정치 권력을 강제적인 힘으로도, '가장 가치 있는 영역으로도' 여기지 않는다면, '정치적인 것'에서 (강제로서의) '지배'로, '그리고 그로부터' '여성에 대한 지배'로 비약하는 것은 불안정하다. Marilyn Strathern이 말한 것처럼, '정치적인 것'과 '정치적 개성'이라는 개념은 우리 자신의 문화적 강박 관념으로, 인류학적 구성 개념에 오랫동안 반영된 편견이다.
→ 우리가 정치 권력에 대해 지닌 개념을 통해 다른 문화에서의 정치 권력을 이해하는 것은 (A)잘못된 것인데, 정치적 힘에 대한 관념들이 여러 문화에 걸쳐 (B)똑같지 않기 때문이다.

지문 간단히 보기

'정치적 지배력 = 강제 or 통제'로 보는 시각
: '보편적이지' 않고, 서양의 고정관념일 수 있음

↓

(예시) 아마존의 부족들: 사람들이 자율성을 지지하고 통제를 싫어하므로, 지도자들이 명령을 잘 내리지 않음**(정치 권력 ≠ 강제)**

↓

'정치 권력 → 강제 → 여성에 대한 지배'로의 흐름은 '비약'일 수 있으며, 문화적 강박 관념이자 편견일 수 있음

해설 정치 권력을 '지배력, 강제력'으로 이해하는 시각은 보편적이지 않고 서양에 국한된 것일 수 있으므로, 이를 바탕으로 다른 문화권이나 부족의 정치 권력을 이해하기는 어렵다는 내용이다. 따라서 요약문의 빈칸에는 ③ '잘못된 - 똑같지'이 가장 적절하다.

오답풀이 보기 해석　　　　선택률

① 합리적인 - 유연하지 — 21%

② 적절한 - 아주 흔하지 — 18%

④ 불합리한 - 다양하지 — 11%

⑤ 효과적인 - 객관적이지 — 7%

구문 [17행] ~ **the leap** from 'the political' to 'domination' (as coercion), *and from there* to 'domination of women', **is** a shaky one.
▶ 주어는 the leap, 동사는 is이다. 밑줄 친 <from A to B>가 주어를 보충 설명한다.

13~14 정답 ④ 42% / ⑤ 46%

2020 3월 41~42번

해석 임상 심리학자들이 간혹 말하기로, 두 부류의 사람들이 치료를 찾는데, 긴장이 필요한 사람들과 이완이 필요한 사람들이다. 그러나 더 조직화되고, 자기를 잘 통제하고, 자기 미래를 책임지는 데 도움을 구하는 환자(가 한 명 있을 때)마다, 긴장을 풀고, 여유를 찾고, 어제 직원 회의에서 했던 바보 같은 말 또는 다음날 점심 데이트 뒤에 분명 있을 거라고 확신하는 거절을 덜 걱정하고 싶어 하는 사람들이 대기실을 꽉 채운다(긴장이 필요한 사람이 한 명 있다고 하면, 이완이 필요한 사람은 방 하나에 가득 찰 정도로 많다). 대부분의 사람들에게 있어, 잠재의식은 너무 많은 것을 나쁘게 보고 좋은 것은 충분치 않게 여긴다. 일리가 있다. 만약 당신이 물고기의 정신을 설계하고 있다면, 기회에도 위협만큼 강렬하게 반응하게 만들겠는가? 절대 아니다. 먹이를 알리는 단서를 놓친 대가는 적다. 바다에 다른 물고기가 있을 가능성이 있고, 한 번의 실수가 아사로 이어지지는 않을 것이다. 그러나 근처에 있는 포식자의 신호를 놓친 대가는 재앙일 수 있다. 게임 끝이고, 그 유전자로서는 혈통의 종말이다. 물론 진화에는 설계자가 없지만, 자연 선택에 의해 창조된 정신은 결국 마치 설계된 것처럼 (우리에게) 보이게 되는데, 그것이 대체로 생태학적으로 알맞은 장소에서 유연하게 적응하는 행동을 만들어 내기 때문이다. 동물의 어떠한 공통점들은 심지어 우리가 설계 원칙이라고 부를 수도 있는, 여러 종에 걸친 유사성을 만들어 낸다. 그러한 원칙 중 하나 나쁜 것이 좋은 것보다 더 약하다(→ 더 강하다)는 것이다. 위협과 불쾌함에 대한 반응은 기회와 유쾌함에 대한 반응보다 더 빠르고, 더 강하고, 억제하기가 더 어렵다.

지문 간단히 보기

우리의 잠재의식은 좋은 것보다 나쁜 것을 더 많이 보는 경향
→ (예시) 심리 치료 환자들(걱정, 긴장을 다스리러 오는 경우가 더 많음)

↓

좋은 신호보다 나쁜 신호를 놓쳤을 때 그 결과가 더 치명적

↓

자연 선택에 따라, 마치 설계된 듯한 공통된 원칙이 생김
= '기회, 유쾌함'보다 '위협, 불쾌'에 대해 더 빠르고 강하게 반응
▶ **나쁜 것이 좋은 것보다 더 '강함'**

구문 [3행] ~ a waiting room full of people {hoping to loosen up, lighten up, and worry less **about** the stupid things [they said at yesterday's staff meeting] or **about** the rejection [(that) they are sure will follow tomorrow's lunch date]}.

▶ { }는 people을 꾸미는 현재분사구이다. worry less에 연결되는 <about+명사>의 병렬구조를 확인해 둔다.

▶ 밑줄 친 they are sure은 추측(~라고 확신하다)의 의미를 더하는 삽입절로, 앞에 the rejection을 꾸미는 주격 관계대명사 that이 생략되었다. 본래 주격 관계대명사는 be동사와 함께 생략되는 것이 원칙이지만 여기서는 단독 생략되었다.

13

해설 사람들은 좋은 것보다 나쁜 것을 더 빠르고 강렬하게 지각하는 무의식적인 경향이 있음을 언급하고, 왜 이런 기제가 발달하게 되었는지 설명하는 글이다. 따라서 제목으로 ④ '우리는 위협에 더 예민하도록 프로그램된 것일까?'가 적절하다.

오답풀이

보기 해석	선택률
① 진화적 설계의 개념: 생물학적 넌센스	19%
② 즐거움을 추구하는 본능이 우리를 모험으로 내몬다	17%
③ 우리는 왜 터무니없어 보이는 약속에 매달릴까?	13%
⑤ 걱정: 계속 행동하지 않는 것에 대한 변명	10%

14

해설 위협이나 불쾌에 대한 반응이 기회나 쾌락에 대한 반응보다 더 빠르고 강렬하게 나타난다는 마지막 문장 내용으로 보아, ⑤에는 나쁜 것이 좋은 것보다 '강하다'는 진술이 적합하다. 따라서 ⑤ (e)의 weaker를 stronger로 고쳐야 옳다.

오답풀이

보기 해석	선택률
① hoping(~하고 싶어 하는, 바라는)	7%
② low(적은, 낮은)	18%
③ predator(포식자)	16%
④ designed(설계된)	14%

STEP PLUS+ 수능 기출 마무리 복습

단어 TEST

02 의도적으로　**03** 분산시키다, 흩뜨리다　**04** 유지, 보유　**05** 발발, 급증　**06** 아주 흥미로운, 자극이 되는　**07** 매료시키다　**08** 강화하다　**09** 기성복의　**10** ~에 알레르기가 있는, ~을 몹시 싫어하는　**11** 긴장을 풀다, 몸을 풀다　**12** 터무니없는, 불합리한

구문 TEST

14 brings something to read　**15** for[because] my car had broken down[broke down]　**16** where we celebrated our anniversary　**17** where his patience was tested to its limits　**18** The success was made possible

01 정답 ① 88%

2022 3월 18번

해석 Lorenzo Romano 씨께
귀하께서 다양한 천연 가죽으로 수출용 수제 장갑을 생산하고 있다고 로마의 Antonio Ricci 씨께 들었습니다. 귀하의 웹 사이트에서 귀하의 사업에 관해 읽어 보았습니다. 우리나라에서는 고급 가죽 장갑에 대한 수요가 꾸준하며, 제가 좋은 가격을 매길 수 있습니다. 귀하께서 추천하고 싶은 장갑에 대한 모든 세부 사항을 알려 주시기 바랍니다. 또한 귀하께서 생산하는 장갑의 견본을 몇 개 보내 주실 수 있으면 도움이 될 것 같습니다. 곧 답변 주시기를 바랍니다.
Jonathan Turner 드림

지문 간단히 보기

> 편지 수신자: 천연 가죽 수제 장갑 생산자

↓

> 필자네 나라에서도 고급 가죽 장갑 수요가 꾸준함

↓

> 수신자가 추천하고자 하는 장갑 세부 사항과 견본 요청

↓

> 마무리 인사

해설 'Please let me know ~'와 'It would also help if~'가 핵심 문장으로, 추천하고 싶은 장갑의 세부 사항과 견본을 요청하는 글이다. 따라서 ① '제품의 모든 세부 사항과 견본을 요청하려고'가 글의 목적으로 가장 적절하다.

오답풀이

보기 해설	선택률
② '가격 인상 요인'에 관해 언급되지 않았다.	2%
③ 제품 견본을 요청한다는 내용은 있지만, '전수 검사'에 관한 내용은 없다.	4%
④ 웹 사이트에 들어가봤다는 내용은 있지만, '정보 수정'을 요청하는 내용은 없다.	2%
⑤ '품질 개선'도, '회의'도 언급되지 않았다.	2%

구문 [8행] It would also help if you could **provide** me **with** some samples of the gloves you produce.
▶ <provide A with B(A에게 B를 제공하다)> 구문이다.
▶ 밑줄 부분은 선행사 the gloves를 꾸미는 형용사절로, 목적격 관계대명사는 생략된 채 <주어+동사>만 남았다.

02 정답 ① 49%

2022 6월 22번

해석 흔히 간과되지만 못지않게 중요한 이해관계자는 개인정보 역설이라는 개념에서 큰 역할을 하는 소비자이다. 모든 방식의 디지털 경험과 공동체에서 소비자의 참여 수준은 그야말로 폭발적으로 증가했으며, 이는 둔화될 기미가 거의 또는 전혀 보이지 않는다. 소비자들 사이에서는 이러한 회사들이 제공하는 풍부한 경험을 추진하는 데 자신들의 개인정보가 도움이 될 뿐 아니라, 이 정보를 공유하는 것이 이러한 경험에 대해 전체적이든 부분적이든 치르는 대가이기도 하다는 인식이 있다. 정보 수집 및 이용의 내용과 시기, 이유를 더 잘 이해하지 못한다면, 소비자는 흔히 취약함과 갈등을 느끼게 된다. '내 전화기에 있는 이 식당 검색 앱이 마음에 드는데, 그 앱이 내 현재 위치를 이용해도 되는지 물을 때 'ok'를 누르면 내 정보는 어떻게 되는 걸까?' 이들에게 선택권을 제공할 수 있는 도구로 무장한 소비자는 수동적 방관자에서 능동적 참여자로 바뀐다.

지문 간단히 보기

> '개인정보 제공 = 디지털 경험의 대가'라는 소비자 인식

↓

> (하지만) 정보 제공의 구체적 사항을 모르면 '취약함'을 느낌

↓

> 소비자는 (정보 제공) 선택권을 줄 수 있는 도구를 갖춰야 함
> **= 정보 제공에 관한 구체적 사항을 알아야 함**
> → 소비자가 '능동적 참여자'로 바뀔 수 있음

해설 기업에서 개인정보를 수집 또는 이용하는 내용과 시기, 이유 등을 잘 모르면 소비자들은 불안을 느낄 수 있으므로, 이들이 이런 내용을 '잘 알아야' 능동적 참여자가 될 수 있다는 내용이다. 따라서 글의 요지로 ① '개인정보 제공의 속성을 심층적으로 이해하면 주체적 소비자가 된다.'가 가장 적절하다.

오답풀이

보기 해설	선택률
② '앱 활용'을 권하는 글이 아니다.	10%
③ 현명한 소비자의 조건으로 '데이터 활용'이 언급되지 않았다.	13%
④ '디지털 서비스 이용의 대가'가 글의 쟁점이 아니다. 개인정보 제공의 세부 내용을 '모를 때' 위기감이 들 수 있기 때문에 '알게 하자'는 내용이 핵심이다. digital experiences, the price 등만 보고 끼워맞추면 안 된다.	21%
⑤ '개인정보 유출' 경로를 설명하는 글이 아니다.	7%

구문 [1행] Often overlooked, but just as important a stakeholder, **is the consumer** ~
▶ 본래 'The consumer ~ is often overlooked, but just as important a stakeholder.'인 문장에서, is의 보어를 강조하기 위해 앞으로 보낸 도치 구문이다. 결과적으로 <보어+동사+주어>의 어순이 되었다.

03 정답 ⑤ 38%

해석 사용자 습관은 그것들을 창출할 만큼 운 좋은 기업에게는 요긴하지만, 그것들의 존재는 '현재 상태'를 무너뜨리려는 새로운 혁신과 스타트업이 성공할 가능성을 본질적으로 낮춘다. 사실, 장기적인 사용자 습관을 성공적으로 바꾸는 것은 대단히 드문 일이다. 행동을 변화시키려면 사람들이 행동하도록 설득하는 방법에 대한 이해뿐만 아니라, 그들이 오랫동안, 이상적으로는 남은 인생 동안, 행동 방식을 반복하게 하는 것 또한 필요하다. 습관 형성 사업을 성공적으로 이룬 기업은 판도를 바꾸는, 널리 성공한 혁신과 자주 관련된다. 하지만 여느 분야와 마찬가지로, 습관 설계에는 어떤 제품들은 삶을 바꾸는 한편 다른 것들은 그렇지 않은 이유를 규정하고 설명하는 규칙이 있다. 한 예로 새로운 행동 방식은 짧은 반감기를 갖는데, 우리의 마음은 예전 사고방식과 행동 방식으로 되돌아가는 경향이 있기 때문이다. 여러 실험에서 보여주기로, 새로운 행동 방식에 익숙해졌던 실험 동물들이 시간이 지남에 따라 처음 배운 행동 방식으로 되돌아가는 경향이 있다고 한다. 회계 용어를 빌리자면, 행동 방식은 LIFO이다. 즉, '마지막으로 들어온 것이 제일 먼저 나간다.'

지문 간단히 보기

> 사용자 습관을 장기적으로 정착시키기는 어려움

↓

> 우리 마음은 예전의 사고/행동으로 돌아가려 하기 때문
> : 여러 실험 동물들의 예시로 입증

↓

> (결론) 행동 방식 = '마지막으로 들어온 것이 제일 먼저 나간다'
> ▶ **새로 배운 습관부터 잊어버린다**

해설 새로운 습관을 익혀도 시간이 지나면 새로운 것부터 다시 잊어버리고 원래 습관으로 돌아가기 쉽다는 설명으로 보아, 밑줄 친 부분은 ⑤ '가장 최근에 얻은 습관이 제일 빨리 사라진다.'이다.

오답풀이

보기 해석	선택률
① 처음에 목격된 행동이 가장 먼저 잊힌다.	8%
② 거의 어떤 행동이든 시간이 지나며 변한다.	13%
③ 오래된 습관이 깨진 후에 새로운 것이 형성된다.	15%
④ 마지막에 형성된 습관이 없애기 가장 어렵다.	18%

구문 [1행] While user habits are a boon to companies **fortunate enough to generate them**, their existence inherently **makes success less likely** ~
▶ <형/부+enough to-V(~할 만큼 충분히 …한)> 구문이 companies를 수식한다. 대명사 them은 user habits를 가리킨다.
▶ 주절에는 <make+목적어+형용사>의 5형식 구문이 쓰였다.

---

04 정답 ③ 55%

해석 한때 목성의 위성들에는 주목할 만한 가치가 있는 어떤 어려움이 있었다. 이 위성들은 Roemer에 의해 매우 면밀히 연구되었는데, 그는 위성들이 (경로상으로) 때로는 예정보다 앞에 있고 때로는 뒤처지는 것처럼 보였다는 것을 알아차렸다. 그것들은 목성이 지구에 특히 '가까울' 때는 '앞섰고', 목성이 지구에서 '더 멀' 때는 '뒤처졌다'. 이것은 중력의 법칙에 따라 설명하기 매우 어려웠을 것이다. 어떤 법칙이 작용해야 할 '어느 한 곳'에서라도 작용하지 않는다면 그건 그냥 틀린 것이다. 하지만 이 불일치의 이유는 매우 간단하고 아름다웠는데, 빛이 목성에서 지구로 이동하는 데 걸리는 시간으로 인해 목성의 위성들을 '보는' 데 약간의 시간이 걸린다는 것이었다. 목성이 지구에 더 가까울 때는 그 시간이 조금 더 짧으며, 지구에서 더 멀 때는 그 시간이 더 길다. 이 이유로 위성들은 지구에 더 가깝거나 더 먼지에 따라 대체로 조금 앞서거나 조금 뒤처지는 것처럼 보인다.

지문 간단히 보기

> 목성의 위성들: 예상되는 위치와 다른 곳에서 관찰됨
> - 목성-지구 거리↓ = '앞선' 위치
> - 목성-지구 거리↑ = '뒤처진' 위치

↓

> '불일치'의 이유: 빛이 목성부터 지구까지 오는 시간 때문
> - 목성-지구 거리↓ = 빛의 이동 시간↓ = '앞선' 위치
> - 목성-지구 거리↑ = 빛의 이동 시간↑ = '뒤처진' 위치

해설 목성의 위성 위치가 예측과 달랐던 이유를 설명하는 글이다. 'But the reason ~' 이하로 빛이 목성에서 지구까지 도달하는 데 걸리는 시간 때문에 그러한 '불일치'가 발생했다는 핵심 내용이 제시된다. 따라서 제목으로 가장 적절한 것은 이 핵심 내용을 답으로 유도하는 질문인 ③ '왜 목성의 위성들은 마땅히 있어야 할 위치에서 관찰되지 않을까?'이다.

오답풀이

보기 해석	선택률
① 중력의 법칙을 증명하는 것의 어려움	8%
② 달의 그림자로 만들어지는 착각	8%
④ 빛의 속도 측정 시 장애물: 과거 기술의 한계	5%
⑤ 앞으로, 뒤로: 위성은 알아서 자기 위치를 바꾼다	24%

구문 [1행] There was once **a certain difficulty** with the moons of Jupiter **that is worth remarking on**.
▶ that이 이끄는 관계절이 선행사 a certain difficulty를 꾸민다. 전치사구인 밑줄 부분이 선행사 바로 뒤에 먼저 오면서 관계절이 선행사와 분리되었다.
▶ <be worth V-ing>는 '~할 가치가 있다'라는 의미이다.

05 정답 ⑤ 96%

해석 WGHS 지리 사진 대회

올해 내내 기다려주신 행사가 드디어 돌아왔습니다! Wood Gate 고등학교의 제10회 연례 지리 사진 대회에 참가하세요.

지침
- 참가자는 '우리 도시를 가로지르는 강들의 아름다움'이라는 주제를 사용해야 합니다.
- 제출물은 1인당 사진 한 장으로 제한됩니다.
- 파일 용량은 50MB를 넘으면 안 됩니다.

일정

	시간	장소
제출	10/2~10/8	이메일: geography@woodgate.edu
투표	10/11~10/13	학교 웹 사이트: https://www.woodgate.edu
전시	10/16~10/20	메인 로비

참고 사항
- 학생들이 선정한 상위 10개의 사진이 전시될 것입니다.
※ 더 많은 정보를 얻으려면, 지리 교사실을 방문하십시오.

지문 간단히 보기

> WGHS 지리 사진 대회
> ① 제10회 연례 행사
> ② 주제: '우리 도시를 가로지르는 강들의 아름다움'
> ③ 파일 용량 제한: 50MB
> ④ 투표 기간: 10/11~13 (3일)
> ⑤ 학생들이 선정한 상위 10개 사진을 전시

해설 'The top 10 photos selected by students will be exhibited.'에서 학생들이 선정한 상위 10개 사진이 전시될 예정이라고 하므로, 내용과 일치하는 것은 ⑤ '학생들이 선정한 사진들이 전시될 것이다.'이다.

오답풀이

	보기 해설	선택률
①	~ 10th annual Geography Photo Contest.	0%
②	Participants should use the theme ~	0%
③	~ should not be larger than 50 MB.	1%
④	Voting / October 11–October 13	1%

구문 [2행] The event [(that) you've been waiting for all this year] is finally here!
▶ 주어 The event를 꾸미는 관계절 [ ]에서 목적격 관계대명사가 생략되었다. 동사는 is이다.

06 정답 ⑤ 43%

해설 Joseph Bell 박사는 Edinburgh 대학교의 의학 교수였다. 그의 학생들은 그의 놀라운 관찰력에 신기해했다. 그는 그저 환자들 쪽을 흘긋 보고는 환자의 직업이 무엇인지 혹은 그들이 어떤 병을 앓고 있을지 알아낼 수 있는 것처럼 보였다. 한번은 그가 어떤 환자의 신발만 흘긋 보고서 그 환자가 병원에 오는 길에 골프장을 가로질러 걸어왔다는 결론을 내렸다. Bell의 학생 중 한 명은 자기 선생님의 능력에 특히 감명받았다. 그는 자신이 Bell의 '세세한 것을 알아채는 오싹한 기술'이라고 부른 것의 예시로 공책을 채웠다. 그 학생은 마침내 런던 외곽에 자기 병원을 열었다. 일이 한가할 때, 그는 소설을 쓰면서 여유 시간을 채웠다. 그는 Bell 박사의 지각 능력을 취해서 그것을 자신이 만든 등장인물에게 주었는데, (이 등장인물은) 젊은 의사인 Arthur Conan Doyle을 전 세계적으로 유명하게 만든 인물이었다. 그리하여 가장 복잡한 진단조차도 '아주 쉬워' 보이게 했던 그 교수는 소설 속 가장 위대한 탐정인 Sherlock Holmes에 대한 영감이 되었다.

지문 간단히 보기

> 엄청난 관찰력을 지녔던 Joseph Bell 박사
> ↓
> 제자 중 한 명(Arthur Conan Doyle)이 그의 관찰력에 특히 감명받음
> ↓
> 관찰력의 예시를 적어뒀다가 훗날 자신의 소설 캐릭터 구상에 활용
> ↓
> Sherlock Holmes라는 위대한 탐정 캐릭터가 탄생함

해설 마지막 문장에서, 주어 the professor 뒤로 동사가 제시되지 않았다. 따라서 ⑤의 becoming을 became으로 고쳐, 문장의 동사를 채워줘야 한다. 주어를 꾸미는 who절 안에 있는 made와 seem을 동사로 착각하지 않도록 주의한다.

오답풀이

	보기 해설	선택률
①	or 앞의 복수명사 patients를 가리키는 복수대명사이다.	3%
②	'결론 내린' 시점보다 '걸어온' 일이 먼저 일어났으므로 과거완료 시제(had p.p.)를 사용해 표현했다.	12%
③	앞에는 선행사가 없고 뒤에는 5형식 동사 called의 목적어가 없는 불완전한 절이 오므로, 선행사를 포함한 관계대명사 what을 알맞게 썼다.	26%
④	<make+목적어+목적격보어> 구조이므로 형용사를 썼다.	16%

구문 [19행] ~ the professor [who **made** even the most complex diagnosis **seem** "elementary"] ~
▶ the professor를 꾸미는 주격 관계대명사 who절에 <make+목적어+원형부정사> 형태의 5형식 구문이 쓰였다.

07 정답 ① 24%

해석 개념 예술과 컴퓨터 예술의 공통점은 작가의 존재가 감춰진다는 것이었다. 개념 예술가들은 창작의 모든 개인적인 흔적을 완화시켜 예술품과 예술가 사이의 관계를 분리했다. 예술가는 다른 사람이 따라야 하는 일종의 지침인 미리 정해진 시스템을 설치하여 개인화된 제도공의 솜씨라는 개념으로부터 분리되었다. 그런 식으로 Sol LeWitt가 말하듯이 '공예가로서의 예술가의 솜씨에 대한 의존'이 없었다. 사실상 누구나 그 지침을 수행할 수 있었다. 같은 과정이 컴퓨터 예술에서도 이루어졌는데, 예술가는 컴퓨터 자동 장치가 그 지침을 수행하도록 미리 정해진 그리기 알고리즘을 고안했다. 인간 행위자는 개념적 형태를 창안했고, 기계는 이를 작동시켰다. 마찬가지로, 컴퓨터 예술품에는 어떠한 자필의 흔적도, 자발성의 흔적도, 또는 예술적 진정성도 결여되어 있었다. 플로터의 팔이 생산 과정에서 인간의 팔을 대체하곤 했다.

지문 간단히 보기

핵심 소재: 개념 예술과 컴퓨터 예술의 '공통점'

↓

개념 예술: 미리 정해진 시스템 도입
= 창작의 개인적 흔적 약화
= 예술가 개인의 솜씨에 대한 의존 X

↓

컴퓨터 예술: 그리기 알고리즘 도입
= 그 어떤 '자필, 자발성, 예술의 진정성'도 드러나지 X

두 분야 모두, '작가 개인'이 드러나지 않음

해설 글에 따르면, 개념 예술은 미리 정해진 시스템을 도입하여 '예술가 개인의 솜씨'에 대한 의존을 약화시켰고, 컴퓨터 예술은 알고리즘을 통해 아무 '자필이나 자발성의 흔적'도 드러나지 않게 만들었다고 한다. 이를 근거로 볼 때, 두 예술의 '공통점'을 말하는 빈칸에는 ① '작가의 존재가 감춰진다는 것'이 들어가야 한다.

오답풀이

보기 해석	선택률
② 무의미한 반복의 거부	15%
③ 일상적인 대상을 예술로 격상시키는 것	27%
④ 정교함보다 단순함에 대한 선호	17%
⑤ 예술가들이 협력해서 작업하려는 경향	18%

구문 [5행] ~ a type of instruction **for another to follow**.
▶ a type of instruction을 꾸미는 to follow 앞에 <for+목적격> 형태로 의미상 주어가 표시되었다. a type of instruction이 to follow의 의미상 목적어이므로, to follow 뒤에는 목적어가 별도로 나오지 않았다.

08 정답 ① 24%

해석 이상적인 음질은 기술 및 문화적 변화에 발맞춰 많이 달라진다. 예를 들어, MP3와 AAC 등 새로운 디지털 오디오 포맷들의 발달을 생각해 보라. 다양한 매체가 매일 우리에게 압축된 데이터 오디오를 제공하며, 어떤 사람들은 좀처럼 CD 음질(즉, '기술적(준거)' 음질)의 오디오를 경험하지 못한다. 이런 추세는 다른 음질 선호도를 지닌 새로운 청자 세대를 이끌어낼 수도 있다. Stanford 대학교수인 Jonathan Berger의 연구는 이 논지에 불을 지핀다. Berger는 10년간 매년 대학교 1학년 학생들의 MP3 선호도를 측정했다. 그는 매년 점점 더 많은 학생들이 CD 음질 오디오보다 MP3를 선호하게 된다고 말한다. 이러한 발견들은 청자들이 압축된 데이터 포맷에 점차 익숙해지며 그에 맞춰 그들의 듣기 선호도를 바꾼다는 것을 보여준다. 핵심은 기술적 향상이 (가령, 더 높은 해상도와 더 훌륭한 비트 전송률 등) 기술적 의미에서 향상된 음질을 얻으려고 애쓰는 반면, 청자들의 기대는 반드시 같은 길을 따르지는 않는다는 것이다. 결과적으로 어떤 경우에는 '기술적인' 디지털 음질 '향상'이 그 소리의 인지적 가치 저하를 초래할 수도 있다.

지문 간단히 보기

새로운 디지털 오디오 포맷이 발달하는 시대
→ '준거 음질(CD 음질)'을 경험하지 못하는 이들이 생김

↓

그 결과, 새로운 청자 세대 출현: CD보다 MP3 선호

↓

음질 경험에 따라 듣기 선호도 변화
: 기술 향상과 청자의 기대가 같은 길을 가지 '않기도' 함
▶ **기술적으로 우수한 음질이 사람들에게 '낮게' 평가될 수 있음**

해설 여러 디지털 포맷의 발달로 '기술적으로 우수한' 음질을 경험하지 못한 세대가 MP3와 같이 압축된 음질에 대한 선호를 갖게 된다는 내용이다. 그 결과 기술적으로 더 우수한 음질이 반드시 '더 좋게' 느껴지지 않을 수 있다는 의미로 빈칸에 ① '그 소리의 인지적 가치 저하'를 넣어야 한다.

오답풀이

보기 해석	선택률
② 음악 본연의 기능을 이해하지 못하는 것	12%
③ 더 세련된 음악적 영감의 실현	12%
④ 이상적 음질에 관한 여러 세대 간 합의	22%
⑤ CD 음질 오디오에 대한 청취자의 선호 부활	25%

구문 [15행] ~ that listeners gradually **become accustomed to** data-compressed formats and change ~
▶ <be/become/get accustomed to+명사(~에 익숙해지다)> 구문이다.
▶ that절의 동사 become과 change가 <A and B> 형태로 병렬 연결되었다.

09 정답 ③ 43%   2021 10월 35번

해석 한 집단의 학자들, 주로 정치학자들은 인권 조약이 국가들의 행동에 아무런 영향을 미치지 '않는다'고 생각했다. 사실, 보통 자신들을 '현실주의자'라고 부르는 이러한 학자들은 국제법이 일반적으로 국가들의 행동에 영향을 미치지 않는다고 생각했다. 그들은 국제적 활동 무대가 여러 국가들 간의 안보 경쟁, 즉 한 국가의 이득이 다른 국가의 손실인 제로섬 게임이라고 보았다. (국제 변호사들과 인권 옹호자들은 인권 조약이 국가로 하여금 국민들에 대한 처우를 개선하게 만든다고 생각했다.) 이런 상황에서, 국가들이 서로 협력함으로써 얻을 수 있는 이득은 거의 없었는데, 당장에라도 결렬될 수 있는 일시적인 군사 동맹이나 안보 협정을 제외하면 말이다. 국제법은 최소한의 역할만 할 수 있거나 혹은 아무것도 할 수 없었으며, 어쩌면 그저 환상이거나 정교한 선전, 즉 힘의 균형이 달라질 때마다 완전히 없어져 버릴 규칙들의 집합이었다.

지문 간단히 보기

> 인권 조약이 국가의 행동에 영향을 미치지 않는다고 보는 학자들
> = ① '현실주의자'

> '현실주의자들'의 특징
> ② 국제 상황을 '제로섬 게임' 같은 '경쟁'으로 인식
> ④ 국가 간 협력의 이득이 거의 없다고 여김
> ⑤ 국제법은 거의 '환상'에 불과하며 최소의 역할만 수행

해설 정치학의 현실주의자들은 국제 정세가 제로섬 게임과 비슷하다고 여기며 국제법의 영향을 작게 생각한다는 내용의 글이다. 하지만 ③은 (국제법의 일종인) 인권 조약이 각국의 국민 처우 개선에 도움이 된다고 여겨졌다는 내용이므로 주제와 모순된다.

오답풀이

보기 해설 · 선택률

① 첫 문장의 A group of academics를 these academics로 받아 보충 설명하고 있다. — 3%

② 주어인 They가 앞문장의 these academics(= realists)이다. 정치학의 '현실주의자'들은 세계를 '경쟁의 장'으로 본다는 설명이 일관되게 제시된다. — 13%

④ such conditions가 ②의 'the international arena ~, a zero-sum game ~'을 받는다. '현실은 경쟁의 장이다 = 협력으로는 얻을 게 없다'는 설명이 자연스럽게 연결된다. — 31%

⑤ ②, ④에서 제시된 '경쟁' 무대에서는 국제법의 역할이 미미하다는 내용으로 주제를 뒷받침한다. — 6%

구문 [17행] ~ a set of rules [that would be swept away **whenever** the balance of power changed].
▶ 선행사 a set of rules를 수식하는 [ ] 안의 복합관계부사 whenever는 부사절(~할 때마다)을 이끈다.

10 정답 ④ 40%   2022 7월 37번

해석 디지털 세계에서 소극적인 주의 돌리기의 흔한 전략과 사용은 반복을 이용하여 이루어진다. **(C)** 디지털상의 이런 주의 돌리기 전략은 웹 브라우저를 사용해 웹 사이트를 방문하는 온라인 사용자가 가장 기본적이고 어디서든 하는 탐색 동작이 웹 사이트에서 그들에게 제시된 링크나 버튼을 클릭하는 것임을 빠르게 배웠다는 사실에 의존한다. **(A)** 이 동작은 웹 브라우저가 (사용자가) 원하는 웹 페이지 또는 행동으로 향할 수 있도록 여러 번 되풀이해 반복되어, 거의 즉각적이고 반사적인 행동이 되는 지경에 이른다. 악의적인 온라인 행위자들은 이 행동을 이용해서, 웹 사이트에 뭔가 잘못된 것이 있다고 귀띔해줄지도 모르는 웹 페이지의 세부 사항을 사용자가 꼼꼼히 검토하지 못하도록 주의를 분산시킨다. **(B)** 이런 웹 사이트는 악의적인 행위자가 사용자로 하여금 취하길 바라는 행동(가령, 링크 클릭)에 사용자의 관심을 집중시키고, 웹 사이트가 겉보기와 다를 수 있다는 것을 알려줄 수도 있는 어떤 세부 사항에서든 사용자가 주의를 돌리도록 설계된다.

지문 간단히 보기

> 디지털상의 '소극적 주의 돌리기' 전략 → '반복'에 기반

> (C) '이런 주의 돌리기 전략': '클릭' 행위와 관련

> (A) '이 동작(**클릭**)'은 원하는 페이지로 갈 때까지 반사적으로 '반복'
> → 사람들이 웹 사이트의 세부 사항을 놓침

> (B) '이런 웹 사이트': 소극적 주의 돌리기 전략의 적용 사례

해설 '소극적 주의 돌리기 전략'을 소개하는 주어진 글에 이어, (C)는 '이 전략'이 클릭 행위에 바탕을 둔다고 한다. (A)는 '이 클릭'의 반복이 주의 분산으로 이어져 사용자들이 악의적 웹 사이트의 세부 사항을 놓치게 된다는 내용을, (B)는 '이런 웹 사이트'가 곧 주의 돌리기 전략의 적용 사례임을 정리한다. 따라서 ④ '(C)-(A)-(B)'가 정답이다.

오답풀이

보기 해설 · 선택률

①, (A)의 This action과 연결될 내용이 (C) 후반부의 'to click — 4%
② ~' 뿐이므로 (C)-(A)는 고정이다. — 8%

③ (A) 마지막의 the website가 (B) 처음의 The website로 연결되어 '악의적인 행위자의 의도가 담긴' 웹 사이트를 설명하므로 (A)-(B)도 고정이다. — 16%

⑤ (C) 마지막의 a website는 사람들이 클릭을 수행하는 '일반적인 사이트'를, (B) 처음의 The website는 '악의적인 행위자가 고안한 특정한 웹 사이트'를 가리킨다. 따라서 (C)-(B)가 연결되지 않는다. — 32%

구문 [A-4행] ~ **the details** of the web page **that** might tip off the user **that** there is something amiss about the website.
▶ 첫 번째 that은 the details를 꾸미는 주격 관계대명사이다.
▶ 두 번째 that은 동사 tip off의 목적절을 이끄는 접속사이다.

11 정답 ③ 37%

해석 매우 간단한 알고리즘을 넘어선 일부 인공 지능 기반 도구들은 복잡한 영역에서 더 나은 인과 및 확률 추론에 도움이 될 가능성을 보인다. 인간에게는 인과관계 모형을 구축할 수 있는, 즉 어떤 일이 '왜' 생기는지 설명하는 타고난 능력이 있고, 이는 인공 지능 시스템(AI)이 아직 대체로 갖추지 못한 능력이다. 가령, (인간) 의사는 환자에게 어떤 치료가 몸에 미치는 변화를 언급하며 그 치료가 왜 효과적인지 설명할 수 있지만, 현대 머신러닝 체계는 이 치료를 받는 환자들이 평균적으로 더 나아지는 경향이 있다는 것만 알려줄 수 있다. 하지만 정책 개입이 사회 전반에 미칠 영향을 평가하는 상황처럼 인과관계 문제가 충분히 복잡해지면, 인간의 추론은 혼란과 실수에 여전히 악명 높을 정도로 취약하다. 이런 상황에서는 더 체계적인 인공 지능 기반의 도구로 인간의 추론을 돕는 것이 아마 유용할 것이다. 연구자들은 더 정확한 위험 평가를 가능케 하는 등의 의사결정 지원을 위해 Bayesian Networks 사용을 탐구 중인데, 이것은 사건 간 인과관계를 짜고, 다양한 영역에 걸쳐 불확실성 정도를 나타내는 데 쓰일 수 있는 인공 지능 기술이다. 이것들은 테러 공격과 새로운 생태 재앙의 위험성 등, 이용 가능한 역사적 데이터가 거의 없는 새롭거나 드문 위협들의 위험 평가에 특히 유용할 수 있다.

지문 간단히 보기

> 인간은 인과관계 설명에 있어 기계보다 우수
> → (예시) 인간 의사 vs. 머신러닝 체계: 인간은 치료의 영향을 설명해줄 수 있지만, 기계는 확률적 경향만 예측

> 하지만, 인과관계가 복잡해지면 인간이 실수하기 쉬움
> → '이런 상황'에서는 인공 지능 도구가 도움이 될 것

해설 ③ 앞의 문장에서 인간 의사와 머신러닝 체계를 대비하며 인간 의사가 치료의 인과성을 더 잘 설명해줄 수 있다고 하는데, ③ 뒤에서는 '이런 상황'에서 인공 지능이 인간에게 유용할 것이라고 하므로 모순이 발생한다. 따라서 역접어 However로 시작해 글의 흐름을 전환하면서 인간 추론의 '한계'를 언급하는 주어진 문장이 ③에 들어가야 한다.

오답풀이

보기 해설	선택률
① ① 앞의 주제문 뒤로 부연 설명이 시작된다.	6%
② '인간은 머신러닝 체계와 달리 이유를 설명할 수 있다'는 일반론 뒤로 예가 잘 제시된다(For example).	11%
④ 앞에서 말한 '인간 추론을 도와주는 인공 지능 도구'의 예시로 뒤에서 Bayesian Networks를 언급하는 흐름이 자연스럽다.	32%
⑤ 앞의 Bayesian Networks와 같은 more structured AI-based tools를 뒷문장에서 These로 받았다.	14%

구문 [6행] **Going beyond very simple algorithms**, some AI-based tools hold out ~
▶ 분사구문이 문장의 주어 some AI-based tools를 보충 설명한다.

12 정답 ① 53%

해석 체중 감량이 힘들다는 것은 의심의 여지가 없다. 어느 계산법에 따르면, 단 1파운드를 빼기 위해 35마일을 걷거나 7시간 동안 조깅을 해야 한다. 운동과 관련한 한 가지 큰 문제는 우리가 그것을 매우 용의주도하게 추적하지 않는다는 것이다. 미국의 한 연구는 사람들이 운동에서 소모한 칼로리를 4배나 과대평가한다는 것을 발견했다. 그들은 또한 (운동) 이후 평균적으로 자신이 방금 소모했던 칼로리의 약 2배를 섭취했다. Daniel Lieberman이 <The Story of the Human Body>에서 언급했듯이, 공장 작업장의 근로자는 한 해에 사무직 근로자보다 약 175,000칼로리를 더 소비하는데, 이는 60번이 넘는 마라톤에 해당한다. 꽤 인상적이긴 하지만, 여기 타당한 질문이 있다. 얼마나 많은 공장 근로자들이 6일마다 마라톤을 뛰는 것처럼 보이는가? 심히 직설적으로 말해서 많지 않다. 그들 중 대부분이 나머지 우리 대부분과 마찬가지로, 그들이 일하지 않을 때 소모된 칼로리를 전부, 추가로 약간을 더 되돌려놓기 때문이다.
→ 체중 감량은 어려운데, 왜냐하면 사람들이 보통 실제 소모한 것보다 (A)더 많은 칼로리를 소모했다고 생각하고 음식을 많이 먹어 운동(의 효과)을 (B)되돌리기 때문이다.

지문 간단히 보기

> 체중 감량이 어려운 이유: 사람들이 칼로리를 '용의주도하게 추적'하지 않기 때문

> (예시1) 운동하는 사람들: 운동으로 소모한 칼로리를 과대평가
> → 소모된 칼로리의 약 2배를 다시 섭취

> (예시2) 공장 근로자: 사무직 근로자들보다 칼로리 훨씬 더 소모
> → 일하지 않을 때 '그 이상'을 먹어서 체중을 되돌림

해설 체중 감량의 어려움을 설명한 글이다. 사람들은 자신이 소모한 칼로리를 과대평가하는 경향이 있어, 운동 또는 활동 이후 소모한 칼로리 '이상'을 먹어 몸무게를 돌려놓는다는 내용이다. 따라서 요약문의 빈칸에 가장 적절한 것은 ① '더 많은 - 되돌리기'이다.

오답풀이

보기 해설	선택률
② 더 많은 - 강화하기	21%
③ 더 높은 - 보충하기	12%
④ 더 적은 - 지속하기	8%
⑤ 다 적은 - 지연시키기	7%

구문 [8행] They also then consumed, on average, **about twice as many calories as** they had just burned off.
▶ <배수사+as+원급+as(몇 배만큼 더 ~한)> 구문이다. 배수사 twice 앞의 about은 '약, 대략'이라는 의미의 부사이다.

13~14 정답 ① 47% / ④ 38%　2021 3월 41~42번

해석　놀랍게도, 의식은 우리가 생각하고 싶어 하는 것만큼 창의력에 결정적이지 않을 수도 있다. 창의력에는 몇 가지 서로 다른 유형이 있는데, 그중 일부는 의식적이고 일부는 무의식적이다. 창의력은 여러분이 의도적으로 무언가를 창조하려고 시도할 때 일어날 수도 있고, 혹은 여러분이 잠들었을 때 일어날 수도 있다. 어느 경우든, 신경과학자인 Arne Dietrich는 창의적인 두뇌가 소프트웨어와 매우 유사하게 돌아갈 수도 있다고 믿는다. 신경과학자들은 창의력은 본질적으로 뭔가 신비스러운 것보다는 발견에 관한 것으로, 가능성 있는 해결책들을 만들어 내고 이후 체계적으로 그것들을 제거하는 뇌의 기계적인 과정에 의해 주도된다고 믿는다. 그는 컴퓨터의 창의력이 우리 자신의 창의력보다 열등하다고 일축하는 우리의 경향은 인간 문화에 깊이 스며든 이원론에서 비롯된다고 믿는다. "우리는 우리 자신을 과대평가하고, 그것들을(컴퓨터를) 과소평가하고 있다."라고 그는 말한다.
신경과학자로서 Dietrich는 자신은 두뇌를 기계로 취급하며 기계 창의력을 다르다고 보지 않는다고 말한다. 이런 식으로 생각해 보면, 인간의 두뇌만이 유일하게 창의적인 재능을 지니고 있다는 생각은 <u>올바른(→ 한계가 있는)</u> 관점으로 보인다. 다른 이들이 그 생각을 받아들일까? 해법은 컴퓨터 예술가를 인간 예술가와 비교하려는 시도를 멈추는 것이다. 만약 우리가 컴퓨터 창의력을 있는 그대로 받아들이고, 그것을 인간적인 것으로 보이게 하려는 시도를 멈춘다면, 컴퓨터는 우리의 창의적 재능에 관한 새로운 것들을 우리에게 가르쳐 줄 뿐만 아니라, 또한 우리가 상상하기 시작하지도 못할 방식으로 창의적이 될지도 모른다.

지문 간단히 보기

> 인간의 의식: 창의력에 결정적이지 않을 수도 있음

↓

> Dietrich의 견해: '창의력 = (컴퓨터) 소프트웨어'
> = 신비스럽다기보다는, '발견'에 관한 것
> = 가능한 해결책을 만들어내고 소거해가는 '기계적' 과정

↓

> 컴퓨터 창의력을 인간의 창의력보다 열등하게 보는 시각
> = '인간에 대한 과대평가이자, 컴퓨터에 대한 과소평가'
> ▶ **올바르다기보다는, '한계가 있는' 시각**

↓

> 해법: 컴퓨터 예술가와 인간 예술가를 '비교, 구별'하지 말아야 함

구문　[22행] **Considered** in this way, **the idea** [that the human brain has a unique claim to creative talents] **seems** a <u>proper(→ limited)</u> perspective.
▶ 문장의 주어 the idea가 '고려되는' 대상이므로, 분사구문 자리에 수동을 나타내는 과거분사를 썼다.
▶ [ ]은 주어 the idea와 내용상 동격을 이루는 명사절이다. 뒤에 나온 동사 seems가 주어에 맞춰 단수형으로 쓰였다.

13

해설　컴퓨터의 창의력을 인간의 창의력보다 열등한 대상으로 여기지 말고 있는 그대로 받아들이라는 내용이다. 특히 마지막 문장에서 그렇게 해야 컴퓨터가 우리에게 창의력에 관한 새로운 것을 가르쳐 줄 수 있다고 한다. 따라서 ① '창조하는 기계가 창의력을 다시 정의한다'가 제목으로 적절하다.

오답풀이

보기 해석	선택률
② 기계들이 배우고 생각하는 새로운 방식	10%
③ 뇌는 무의식 상태일 때 어떻게 기능하는가	15%
④ 인공 지능의 잠재적 한계	8%
⑤ 첨단 기술은 창의력을 약화시킨다	11%

14

해설　두 번째 문단 첫 문장에서, 기계 창의력이 인간의 창의력과 별로 다르지 않다고 보는 시각이 언급된다. 이에 따르면 인간에게만 창의력이 있다는 사고는 '올바르다'기보다 '한계가 있는' 것이다. 따라서 ④ (d)의 proper를 limited로 고쳐야 문맥상 옳다.

오답풀이

보기 해석	선택률
① deliberately(의도적으로)	8%
② discovery(발견)	9%
③ inferior(열등한)	22%
⑤ embrace(받아들이다)	14%

STEP PLUS+ 수능 기출 마무리 복습

단어 TEST

02 현재 상태　**03** 놀라운, 믿기 힘든　**04** 미리 정해진　**05** 자발성　**06** 정교함, 자세한 설명　**07** ~에 익숙한　**08** 완전히 없애다　**09** 악의적인　**10** ~에 취약한, ~하기 쉬운　**11** 짜다, 설계하다, 배치하다　**12** 직설적인, 무딘

구문 TEST

14 The cat that roams the neighborhood　**15** more extensively than any of us has　**16** let them work from home　**17** will computers teach us new things　**18** have we encountered such a challenging obstacle

01 정답 ⑤ 88% 2023 3월 19번

해석 Mark는 이번 올림픽에서 자유형 수영 경기에 출전하고 있었다. 그에게는 200미터에서 메달을 딸 수 있다는 확고한 믿음이 있었다. 그 당시 수영은 미국 선수들이 장악하고 있어서, Mark는 조국인 영국의 국민 영웅이 되기를 꿈꾸고 있었다. 그날 Mark는 자신의 진짜 마지막 시합인 200미터 결승전에 출전하고 있었다. 그는 훈련을 마쳤고 준비가 되어 있었다. 1분 50초 후에 모든 것이 끝났다. 그는 열심히 노력했고, 최선을 다했지만 4등을 했다. 그는 0.49초 차이로 동메달에 미치지 못했다. 그리고 그것이 Mark의 수영 경력의 끝이었다. 그는 상심했다. 그에게는 아무것도 남지 않았다.

지문 간단히 보기

> 올림픽 결승에서 메달을 딸 수 있다고 확신한 Mark ▶ **자신감**

↓

> 최선을 다했지만, 4등을 기록한 뒤 상심한 Mark ▶ **실망감**

해설 올림픽 결승 수영 경기에서 메달을 따고자 했던 Mark가 아깝게 4등으로 들어와 실망했다는 내용이므로, 심경 변화로 가장 적절한 것은 ⑤ '자신 있는 → 실망한'이다.

오답풀이

보기 해석	선택률
① 걱정하는 → 희망에 찬	3%
② 고마운 → 두려운	3%
③ 기쁜 → 질투하는	2%
④ 무관심한 → 언짢은	2%

구문 [2행] He had a firm belief **that he could get a medal in the 200m.**
▶ a firm belief를 설명하는 동격의 that절이다. 이때 that은 명사절 접속사로, 완전한 문장을 이끈다.

02 정답 ⑤ 85% 2023 6월 22번

해석 인터넷에 관한 한, (많이는 아니어도) 약간 편집적인 것이 이득이 될 따름이다. 인터넷에 있는 모든 것의 익명성 수준을 고려할 때, 여러분이 받을 수도 있는 어떤 자료든 그 타당성에 대해 의문을 제기하는 것이 합리적이다. 일반적으로, 우리가 인도를 따라서 오던 누군가를 만날 때, 특히 너무 놀랍게도 그들이 여러분을 알고 있었다며 자신을 소개할 때, 여러분이 일종의 방어적 자세를 취하는 것은 자연스러운 본능이다. 일부러 우리는 그 사람이 상황, 이름 또는 지인, 혹은 입증해줄 증거(가령 사진)를 제시하여 우리를 어떻게 아는지 증명해야 하는 과제를 설정한다. 일단 우리가 그 정보를 받고 그것이 인지적 검증을 통과하면, 우리는 그 사람이 더 신뢰할 만하다고 받아들인다. 이 모든 것은 몇 분 안에 일어나지만, 우리가 현실 세계에서 수행하는 자연스러운 방어 기제이다. 하지만, 가상 세계에서는 우리의 행복에 물리적인 위협이 없는 것처럼 보이기 때문에, 우리는 덜 방어적인 경향이 있다.

지문 간단히 보기

> 인터넷상에서는 약간 '편집적이어야' 좋음
> = 어떤 자료든 그 타당성에 '의문을 제기하는' 것이 합리적

↓

> 일상의 우리: 처음 마주치는 정보에 '방어 태세(검증 시도)'
> → (예시) 우리를 '안다고' 말하는 사람들을 만났을 때

↓

> 하지만, 가상 세계에서는 이런 '자연스러운' 방어적 경향이 약해짐
> ▶ **정보 검증을 더 시도해야 함**

해설 인터넷상의 어떤 정보든 그 타당성에 의문을 제기하라는 내용이다. 일상에서 우리는 처음 접하는 정보에 방어 태세를 취하며 검증을 시도하지만, 마지막 문장에 따르면 가상 세계에서는 이런 경향이 '약해진다'고 한다. 따라서 ⑤ '방어 기제가 덜 작동하는 가상 세계에서는 신중한 정보 검증이 중요하다.'가 요지로 가장 적절하다.

오답풀이

보기 해석	선택률
① '표현의 자유 남용'에 관해 언급되지 않는다.	5%
② '기술 향상'에 관해 언급되지 않는다.	1%
③ 글에서 현실 세계와 가상 세계는 정보의 '공유'가 아닌 '신뢰성 검증' 측면에서 대비되고 있다.	5%
④ '보안 프로그램'에 관해 언급되지 않는다.	1%

구문 [5행] Typically **it**'s to our natural instinct ~ **to place yourself in some manner of protective position**, especially when they introduce themselves as <u>having known</u> you, ~
▶ 가주어(it)-진주어(to place ~) 구문이다.
▶ 밑줄 친 부분은 완료동명사(having p.p.)로, when절의 동사 introduce보다 having known이 더 과거에 일어났음을 나타낸다. 즉 '소개하는' 시점보다 더 옛날부터 '알고 있었다'는 의미인 것이다.

03 정답 ② 44%

해석 여러분이 일하는 습관에서 이뤄낼 수 있는 가장 중요한 딱 한 가지 변화는 창작 일을 먼저 하고, 대응 업무는 나중에 하도록 바꾸는 것이다. 이것은 전화기와 이메일을 꺼둔 채로 여러분 본인의 우선순위에 있는 창작 일을 위해 매일 많은 시간을 차단한다는 것을 의미한다. 나는 (한때) 좌절감을 느끼는 작가였다. 이런 전환의 실행은 나를 생산적인 작가로 바꾸었다. 하지만 내가 기사나 블로그 게시글 혹은 책 한 챕터를 쓰려고 앉으면 여러 사람이 줄지어서 내가 회신해주기를 기다리지 않던 날이 하루도 없었다. 이것(연락 차단)은 쉽지 않았고 여전히 쉽지 않은데, 특히 "제가 '두 시간' 전에 이메일을 보냈는데요…!"라고 시작하는 전화 메시지를 받을 때면 그렇다. 당연히, 이러한 접근법은 다른 사람들의 기대와 그들이 여러분에게 가하는 압박에 맞지 않는다. 단 한 시간일지라도 세상의 스위치를 끄려면 의지가 필요하다. 그것은 불편하게 느껴지고, 때로는 사람들이 기분 상하기도 한다. 그러나 빈 수신함을 위해 자기 꿈을 포기하는 것보다, 사소한 것으로 몇 사람을 실망시키는 게 더 낫다. 그렇게 하지 않으면, 여러분은 프로 의식이라는 환상을 위해 여러분의 잠재력을 희생하는 것이다.

지문 간단히 보기

> 업무 습관 조언: '창작 작업부터, 대응 업무는 나중에'
> = 전화, 이메일 등 연락 수단을 '차단하고' 창작에 집중

↓

> 물론, 연락을 기다리는 사람들이 있는데 연락을 차단하기란 쉽지 않음 → (예시) 필자 본인

↓

> 하지만, '수신함을 비우려고' 꿈을 포기하느니, 남을 조금 실망시키는 게 나음 ▶ **답장에 매몰되기보다, 진짜 자신이 하고 싶은 창작 일에 몰두하는 것이 중요**

해설 타인을 응대하느라 시간을 빼앗기느니 연락 수단을 일정 시간 차단하고 창조적 작업에 몰두하는 것이 낫다는 내용이다. 이때 '빈 수신함'은 거꾸로 '타인에게 연락해주는 것을 우선순위에 둔' 상황을 가리키므로, ② '타인의 욕구를 충족시키려고 노력하기'가 밑줄 부분의 의미로 적절하다.

오답풀이

보기 해석	선택률
① 혁신적인 행동 방침을 따르기	9%
③ 실수 없이 어려운 일을 마치기	11%
④ 사회적 연결을 제거해 정신적 균형을 유지하기	22%
⑤ 사회적 네트워크를 쌓을 충분한 기회를 확보하기	13%

구문 [15행] **It takes willpower to switch off the world**, even for an hour.
▶ <it takes A to-V(~하는 데 A가 필요하다)> 구문이다. 보통 A 자리에는 시간이나 비용을 나타내는 표현이 온다.

04 정답 ① 55%

해석 환경적 학습은 농부들이 결정의 근거를 '결과' 정보에 관한 관찰에 둘 때 발생한다. 그들은 자신 또는 이웃의 농장을 관찰할 수도 있지만, 그들이 지침으로 삼고 있는 것은 이웃 자체가 아니라 경험적 결과이다. 그들은 농업 활동을 실험으로 보고, 상대적 이점, 기존 자원과의 양립성, 사용의 어려움, 그리고 '시험 가능성', 즉 그것이 얼마나 잘 실험될 수 있는가와 같은 요인을 평가하고 있다. 하지만 그 '시험 가능성'이라는 기준은 정말 문제인 것으로 밝혀지는데, 농부들이 늘 실험하는 것은 맞지만, 작업(경작) 중인 농장이 굉장히 결함 있는 실험실인 까닭이다. 농부들은 연구 시설의 전문적인 실험 토지의 통제된 조건을 마련할 수 없다. 또한 그들이 설령 통제된 실험을 할 수 있다고 해도, 농부들은 다스리기 힘든 복잡하고 관찰하기 어려운 현상들에 자주 직면하기도 한다. 게다가 농부들은 자신이 사용할 수도 있는 몇 가지 생산 방법 그 이상에 관한 이익 정보를 거의 얻을 수 없는데, 이는 '상대적 이점'이라는 기준을 측정하기 어렵게 만든다.

지문 간단히 보기

> 농부들: 자신 또는 이웃의 농장을 '관찰'하여 환경적 학습
> → 농업 활동 = 일종의 '실험'

↓

> 하지만, 작업 중인 농장은 실험실로서 '결함이 있음'
> - 실험실의 통제된 환경을 모방하기 어려움
> - 관찰이나 관리가 어려운 상황도 자주 발생
> - 생산법에 관한 정보에 한계 → 상대성 이점을 측정하기 어려움

해설 농부들은 농장을 일종의 실험실로 삼아 경험적 결과를 관찰하며 환경에 관해 학습하지만, 경작 중인 농지는 실험실로서는 '결함이 있어' 그런 실험에 한계가 따른다는 내용이다. 따라서 ① '농업에서 경험적 관찰을 사용하는 것의 한계점'이 주제로 적절하다.

오답풀이

보기 해석	선택률
② 전통적인 농기구를 현대화할 때의 어려움	9%
③ 농업 혁신에서 시험 가능성을 우선시할 필요성	15%
④ 농업에서 본능적인 결정을 내리는 것의 중요성	13%
⑤ 예측 불가의 농업 현상을 통제하는 방법	9%

구문 [18행] ~ which **makes** the criterion of "relative advantage" **hard to measure**.
▶ <make+목적어+형용사> 형태의 5형식 구문이다. to measure는 목적격보어로 쓰인 형용사 hard를 꾸미는 부사구이다(~하기에 …한).

05 정답 ② 91%

해석 Brushwood 국립 공원 투어 프로그램

자연 속에서 걷는 것은 체력과 건강을 유지하는 훌륭한 방법입니다. 저희 자원봉사 안내자와 함께 무료 공원 산책을 즐기며 숲의 아름다운 풍경과 소리를 감상하세요.

세부 정보
- 3월부터 11월까지 평일에 운영
- 1시간 동안 길을 따라 편안하게 걷기 (3km)
- 가이드당 15명 내지 20명으로 이루어진 그룹

등록
- QR 코드를 스캔하여 투어에 신청하십시오.

참고 사항
- 각 참가자에게 물이 한 병씩 제공될 것입니다.
- 12세 미만 어린이는 어른과 동행해야 합니다.
- 날씨로 인해 투어가 취소될 수도 있습니다.

※ 궁금한 점이 있으시면, brushwoodtour@parks.org로 저희 쪽에 이메일을 보내주세요.

지문 간단히 보기

> Brushwood 국립 공원 투어 프로그램
> ① 자원봉사 안내자와 공원 산책
> ② 3~11월 중 평일에 운영
> ③ 등록: QR코드 스캔하여 신청
> ④ 참가자마다 물 한 병씩 제공
> ⑤ 날씨로 인해 취소 가능

해설 'Open on weekdays from March to November'에서 주말이 아닌 평일에 투어가 진행된다고 하므로, 일치하지 않는 것은 ② '주말에 진행된다.'이다.

오답풀이

보기 해설	선택률
① Enjoy free park walks with our volunteer guides, ~	3%
③ Scan the QR code ~	1%
④ A bottle of water ~ to each participant.	1%
⑤ ~ canceled due to weather conditions.	0%

구문 [3행] Enjoy free park walks with our volunteer guides, **while appreciating** the beautiful sights and sounds of the forest.
▶ <접속사+현재분사(~하면서, ~하는 동안)> 형태의 분사구문이다.

06 정답 ④ 44%

해석 기술의 발달을 미화하는 경향이 있듯이, 모든 새로운 도구나 기계에서 최악을 예상하는 반대 경향도 있다. 플라톤의 <Phaedrus>에서, 소크라테스는 글쓰기의 발전을 한탄했다. 그는 사람들이 머릿속에 넣고 다니던 지식에 대한 대체물로서 글로 쓴 말에 의존하게 됨에 따라, 그들은 그 (책의) 대화 속 등장인물 중 한 명의 말처럼 '기억력을 발휘하기를 그치고 잘 잊어버리게 될 것'이라고 우려했다. 그리고 그들은 '적절한 가르침 없이 많은 양의 정보를 받을' 수 있을 것이기 때문에, '대체로 상당히 무지할 때도 매우 박식하다고 여겨질' 것이었다. 그들은 '진정한 지혜 대신 지혜의 자만심으로 가득 차 있게' 될 것이었다. 소크라테스가 맞지는(→ 틀리지는) 않아서, 이 새로운 기술(글쓰기)은 그가 두려워했던 결과를 실제로 흔히 가져왔지만, 그는 근시안적이었다. 그는 쓰기와 읽기가 정보를 전파하고, 신선한 생각을 촉발하며, (지혜는 아닐지라도) 인간의 지식을 확장하는 데 도움이 되곤 했던 많은 방법을 예견하지 못했다.

지문 간단히 보기

> 기술에서 '최악'을 예상하는 경향 → (예시) 소크라테스

> 글쓰기의 발전에 대한 소크라테스의 '한탄'
> : 글이 인간의 기억 대체 → 인간이 사실은 무지할 때조차 '박식하다'고 여겨질까봐 우려

> 신기술이 실제로 그가 우려한 결과를 초래하기는 했음
> ▶ **소크라테스가 '틀렸던' 것은 아님**

> 하지만, 글의 유용성을 고려하면 그의 우려는 '근시안적'이었음

해설 ④ 뒤는 소크라테스가 글쓰기에 관해 두려워했던 결과가 '실제로 나타났다'는 내용인데, 이는 소크라테스의 부정적 예상이 '틀리지' 않았었다는 의미이다. 따라서 ④에는 right 대신 wrong을 써야 옳다.

오답풀이

보기 해설	선택률
① development(발전)	7%
② substitute(대체물)	14%
③ receive(받다)	20%
⑤ foresee(예견하다)	15%

구문 [5행] He feared that, **as** people came to rely on the written word ~, they would, ~ "**cease** to exercise their memory and **become** forgetful."
▶ feared의 목적어는 밑줄 친 that절이다. 접속사 that과 <주어+동사> 사이에 as가 이끄는 부사절(~함에 따라)이 삽입되었다.
▶ 조동사 would 뒤로 동사원형 cease와 become이 <A and B> 형태로 병렬 연결되었다.

07 정답 ⑤ 20%

해석 생태 건강은 지표면이 동식물의 건강한 삶을 위한 토대를 제공할 수 있도록 그것을 부식토와 광물이 풍부한 상태로 유지하는 데 달려 있다. 토양이 이러한 원료를 잃거나 다량의 오염 물질이 토양에 유입되면, 그 상황은 붕괴한다. 인간이 지표면 아래로 가서 이런 체제의 일부로 변하지 않은 광물이나 다른 화합물을 끄집어내면 문제가 뒤따른다. 납과 카드뮴의 채굴이 그 예시이다. 석유 역시 인간에 의해 지구의 내부에서 채굴되어 지표 생태계에 유입된 물질이다. 비록 식물로부터 형성되기는 해도, 그 결과로 생기는 고도로 환원된 탄소 화합물은 흔히 살아 있는 원형질에 유독하다. 암을 유발할 수 있는 석유 생성 물질인 '폴리염화 바이페닐'의 경우처럼, 어떤 때는 심지어 매우 적은 양일 때도 해당된다(생명체에 유독하다).

지문 간단히 보기

토양에 부식토와 광물이 풍부해야 생태 건강 유지

↓

이런 원료가 부족하거나, 지표가 '오염되면' 상황 붕괴

↓

(예시) 납, 카드뮴, 석유: 생명체에 '유독한' 화합물 포함
→ 채굴해서 지표로 꺼내오면 문제 발생

해설 빈칸 뒤의 예시에서 광물을 지표면 밑에서 채굴해오면 생물에 '유독한' 물질로 인해 문제가 생길 것이라고 한다. 이를 근거로 볼 때, 빈칸 문장은 광물을 캐서 지표로 가져오면 '유독한 물질이 유입될 수 있어' 문제가 된다는 의미여야 한다. 따라서 ⑤ '다량의 오염 물질이 토양에 유입되면'이 답으로 적절하다.

오답풀이

보기 해석	선택률
① 그것 위 식물의 수가 너무 급격히 증가하면	15%
② 그것이 인간에게 충분한 영양 공급을 중단하면	26%
③ 기후 변화가 그것의 화학성분을 변형시키면	19%
④ 외래종이 우세해져 그 주변 자원을 고갈시키면	20%

구문 [1행] ~ keeping the surface of the earth rich in humus and minerals **so that** it can provide a foundation for healthy plant and animal life.
▶ <keep+목적어+형용사(~을 …한 상태로 유지하다)> 형태의 5형식 구문을 확인해 둔다.
▶ 접속사 so that은 목적의 부사절(~하도록, ~하기 위해)을 이끈다.

08 정답 ⑤ 33%

해석 알고리즘 시대의 설계자는 미국 법체계에 위협을 가하는데, 알고리즘이 그 알고리즘의 의도된 용도에 대한 설계자의 이해와 다름없기 때문이다. 알고리즘을 설계하는 사람은 훌륭한 소프트웨어 기술자일 수 있지만, 알고리즘 과정에 들어가야 할 모든 요인에 대한 지식이 없으면, 그 기술자는 자기도 모르게 결정이 좋아봤자 불완전하고 최악의 경우 차별적이며 불공정한 알고리즘을 만들게 될 수 있다. 문제를 악화시키는 것은 알고리즘 설계 회사가, (장기) 이식 대기 중인 환자 중 누가 장기를 받도록 선정될지 결정하는 것부터 형을 선고받은 범죄자 중 누가 집행 유예를 받고 최고형을 받을지 결정하는 것까지 광범위한 용도를 위해 알고리즘을 설계하는 계약을 체결할지도 모른다는 것이다. 그 회사는 각 알고리즘이 어떤 문제를 다뤄야 하는지, 알고리즘이 데이터 수집을 위해 어떤 데이터베이스를 사용할지, 그리고 알고리즘이 잇달아 결정을 내릴 때 어떤 위험을 피해야 할지를 아는 주제별 전문가들을 직원으로 두지는 않을 것이다.

지문 간단히 보기

알고리즘 설계자 = 법체계에 '위협'

↓

모든 요인에 관한 지식이 없다면 알고리즘은 '불완전'

↓

문제 심화 가능성: 알고리즘을 만들 때 늘 모든 분야의 전문가가 갖춰져 있지는 않음
= '좋아봤자 불완전하고, 최악의 경우 차별적이며 불공정한' 알고리즘이 만들어질 수도 있음
▶ **만드는 사람이 얼마나 아는가가 알고리즘에 반영됨**

해설 알고리즘을 설계하는 사람이 알고리즘 과정에 필요한 모든 지식을 알고 있지 않다면 알고리즘 또한 '불완전해질' 수 있다는 내용으로 보아, 결국 알고리즘은 '설계자의 이해 수준'을 반영한다는 것을 추론할 수 있다. 따라서 빈칸에는 ⑤ '그 알고리즘의 의도된 용도에 대한 설계자의 이해'가 들어가야 한다.

오답풀이

보기 해석	선택률
① 대중이 접근할 수 있는 데이터의 양	15%
② 그것이 최선의 결정에 이르고자 혼자 학습하는 능력	20%
③ 알고리즘 사용자에게 지속된 이익을 창출할 잠재력	14%
④ 설계 회사가 운영하는 하드웨어의 기능성	15%

구문 [11행] ~ **from determining** which patients awaiting transplants are chosen ~, **to (determining)** which criminals facing sentencing should be given ~.
▶ <from A to B(A부터 B까지)> 구문이다. 밑줄 친 부분의 which는 둘 다 의문형용사(어떤 ~할지)로, 각각 patients와 criminals를 꾸미면서 동명사 determining의 목적절을 이끈다.

09 정답 ④ 58%

해석 연구에서 시사하기로, 개인들, 특히 특정 체제로부터 이득을 얻어온 사람들은 현재 상태를 지지하고 합리화하는 경향이 있으며, 심지어 (현재 상태에) 분명한 문제가 있을 때도 그러하다. 이런 사람들은 '당신은 충분히 노력하기만 한다면 혼자 힘으로 해낼 수 있다'라는 익숙한 문구로 체제상의 불공평을 정당화한다. '체제 정당화 이론'이라 불리는 심리학의 한 분야는 사람들이 그런 체제들의 결과로 성공했다면 이들이 어떤 식으로 사회적, 경제적, 정치적 체제들이 좋고 공정하고 정당하다고 여기는 경향이 있는지 설명한다. 뉴욕대학교 응용심리학 교수인 Erin Godfrey에 따르면, "정상에 있는 사람들은 능력주의를 믿고 싶어 하는데, 이는 그들이 본인의 성공을 누릴 자격이 있다는 의미이기 때문이다." (실제로, 능력주의의 정의와 결과에 대해 사회 계층에 걸쳐 일반적인 합의가 존재한다는 것은 놀랍지 않다.) 사회에서 유리한 지위에 있는 사람들은 그 체제가 공정하다고 믿으며 그것을 바꿀 이유가 없다고 여길 가능성이 더 크다.

지문 간단히 보기

체제 안에서 이득을 본 사람들: 현재 상태 지지 및 합리화
= ① '노력만 하면 혼자 힘으로 해낼 수 있다'며 체제 정당화

↓

② '체제 정당화 이론' 소개

↓

③⑤ (예시) '정상, 유리한 입지'의 사람들 → 능력주의 지지
= 자신의 성공을 합리화해주는 체제의 정당성 지지

해설 어떤 체제 안에서 성공한 사람들은 그 체제를 지지하고 합리화하는 경향이 있다는 내용으로, '능력주의를 지지하는' 사람들이 예시로 언급된다. 하지만 ④는 예시에 나온 '능력주의'만을 지엽적으로 언급하며 이에 관한 '일반적인 합의'가 있다고 하므로 흐름상 어색하다.

오답풀이

보기 해설 / 선택률

① 앞에 언급된 '체제로 이득을 본 개인들(individuals)'이 주어인 These people로 잘 연결된다. — 5%

② ①까지 언급한 내용을 '체제 정당화 이론'이라는 용어로 잘 설명한다. — 10%

③ 여기서 '능력주의'는 체제 정당화를 보여주기 위한 예시이다. meritocracy가 앞에 나오지 않았다는 이유로 고르지 않도록 한다. — 15%

⑤ ③의 The people who are at the top을 Those who are in an advantaged position으로 재진술하며 비슷한 내용을 전개한다. — 5%

구문 [7행] ~ describes **how** people tend to see social, economic, and political systems as good, fair, and legitimate if they have succeeded as a result of those systems.
▶ <how+주어+동사(어떻게 ~하는지)> 어순의 간접의문문이 문장의 목적어 역할을 한다. <see A as B(A를 B로 여기다)> 구문도 참고한다.

10 정답 ⑤ 32%

해석 고대 농부와 수렵 채집인 모두 계절에 따른 식량 부족을 겪었다. 이 기간에는 어린이도 어른도 며칠 배고픈 채로 잠들곤 했으며, 모두가 지방과 근육을 잃게 마련이었다.
(C) 그러나 더 오랜 기간에 걸쳐 농경 사회는 수렵 채집인보다 심각하고 존재에 위협이 되는 기근에 시달릴 확률이 훨씬 컸다. 수렵 채집이 농업보다 훨씬 덜 생산적이고 훨씬 더 적은 에너지 산출량을 발생시킬지 모르나, 그것은 훨씬 덜 위험하기도 하다.
(B) 이것은 첫째로는 수렵 채집인이 환경에 의해 부과된 자연적 한계 내에서 잘 사는 경향이 있었기 때문이고, 둘째로는 농부들이 보통 주요 작물 한두 가지에 의존하던 상황에서, 수렵 채집인은 가장 혹독한 환경에 있는 이들이라도 수십 가지 다양한 식량 자원에 의존했기에, 대체로 식단을 조절해서 변화하는 환경에 대한 생태계 자체의 역동적인 반응에 맞춰갈 수 있었던 까닭이다.
(A) 보통, 복잡한 생태계에서 한 해 날씨가 한 집단의 식물종에게 적합하지 않다고 판명되면, 이는 거의 반드시 다른 것들에게는 적합하다. 그러나 농업 사회에서 가령 지속적인 가뭄의 결과로 수확이 실패한다면 참사가 일어난다.

지문 간단히 보기

고대 농부도, 수렵 채집인도 계절에 따른 식량 부족 경험
(C) 하지만, 농경 사회가 더 심한 기근 = 수렵 채집이 '덜 위험'

(B) 수렵 채집인들: 1) 환경 속 한계에 잘 적응 2) 식량 자원 다양
(A) 반면, 농경 사회: 한두 작물에 의존 → 수확 실패 시 '참사'

해설 농부도 수렵 채집인도 식량 부족을 겪었다는 주어진 글 뒤로, '그래도' 수렵 채집인들이 덜 위험했음을 말하는 (C)가 연결된다. 이어서 (B)는 '덜 위험했다'를 This로 받아 그 이유를 설명하고, (A)는 농업 사회의 상황을 대비한다. 따라서 ⑤ '(C)-(B)-(A)'가 자연스럽다.

오답풀이 보기 해설

선택률

① 주어진 글은 '식량 부족'을 말하는데 이어서 '날씨, 작물'을 말하는 (A)가 오면 어색하다. — 7%

②, 주어진 글은 수렵 채집인과 농부의 '공통된' 위기를 설명 — 23%
③ 하는데, (B)는 두 집단이 '왜 달랐는지'를 설명하므로 내용이 자연스럽게 연결되지 않는다. — 18%

④ (A)-(B)를 이어서 읽으면 '농부가 수확 실패 시 참사'를 겪는 이유는 '수렵 채집인들이 자연 한계에 더 잘 맞춰 살았기' 때문이라는 어색한 인과 관계가 형성되어 버린다. — 19%

구문 [B-1행] ~ and secondly because **where farmers typically relied on one or two staple crops**, foragers in even the harshest environments relied on ~ and so were usually able to adjust ~
▶ 밑줄 친 부분 중심으로 secondly because절의 구조를 파악한다. 주어는 foragers이고, 동사구 relied on과 were usually able to adjust가 <A and so B> 형태로 병렬구조를 이룬다.
▶ where는 여기서 '~한 상황에서'라는 의미의 부사절을 이끈다.

11 정답 ③ 36%

해석 예술 작품의 제작에 대해 아는 표시를 하는 데는, 가령 화가가 다양한 종류의 물감을 섞는 방법이나 이미지 편집 도구의 작동 방식에 관한 상세한 전문 지식이 필요하지 않다. 필요한 것이라고는 물감 작업과 이미징 앱을 사용한 작업의 중대한 차이에 대한 일반적인 인식일 뿐이다. 이런 인식은 어쩌면 소비자 이미징 앱을 사용하는 방법을 포함해서 컴퓨터 사용법에 대한 기본적인 친숙함뿐 아니라, 물감과 붓에 대한 기본적인 친숙함을 포함할 수도 있다. 예술 비평가와 같은 전문가들의 경우라면, 재료와 기법에 더 친숙한 것이 작품에 관해 잘 알고 내린 판단에 이르는 데 흔히 유용하다. 이것은 모든 종류의 예술 재료나 도구가 예술 창작에 있어 각자의 고유한 도전과 행위유발성을 동반하기 때문이다. 비평가들은 예술가들이 특정한 예술적 효과를 위해 다양한 종류의 재료와 도구를 활용하는 방식에 흔히 관심이 있다. 그들은 또한 예술 작품 자체로 구현된, 특정 재료와 도구로 얻어질 수 있는 것의 한계를 뛰어넘으려는 예술가의 시도가 성공적인지에 관심이 있다.

지문 간단히 보기

예술 작품 제작을 이해할 때 상세한 전문 지식이 필수는 아님
= '일반적 인식', 도구에 관한 '기본적인 친숙함'이면 OK

↓

(반면) 전문가(비평가)들에게는 '상세 지식'이 유용
: 재료/도구마다 고유한 도전과제가 있기 때문
→ 비평가는 다양한 재료/도구 활용과 그 결과물에 관심

해설 ③ 앞은 예술 작품의 제작을 이해하려면 도구에 대한 '일반적, 기초적 지식'이 있으면 된다는 내용인데, ③ 뒤는 각 도구나 재료마다 고유한 과제를 동반한다는 내용이다. 즉 도구나 재료마다 과제가 달라서 '기초적' 인식만 있으면 된다는 인과관계가 어색하다. 이때 주어진 문장을 보면, 도구나 재료에 '더 깊이' 친숙해야 좋은 전문가들을 언급한다. 이 주어진 문장을 ③ 뒤의 This에 대입하면, 도구에 대한 깊은 친숙함이 왜 작품을 잘 알고 판단하게 해주는지 이유를 설명하는 흐름이 잘 완성된다. 따라서 주어진 문장은 ③에 넣어야 한다.

오답풀이

보기 해설	선택률
① '전문 지식이 필요 없다'는 앞 내용을 뒤에서 '일반적 인식만 있으면 된다'고 재진술했다.	3%
② 앞의 'a general sense ~'가 This sense로 잘 연결된다.	10%
④ '비평가'가 갑자기 언급되어 어색해 보인다. 하지만 자세히 보면, 재료나 도구마다 고유한 과제가 있고, '그렇기에' 비평가들이 예술가의 다양한 도구 활용에 관심을 갖는다는 흐름이다.	34%
⑤ 앞문장의 Critics가 뒷문장의 They로 잘 연결된다.	17%

구문 [11행] This sense might involve <u>a basic familiarity with paints and paintbrushes</u> **as well as** <u>a basic familiarity with how we use computers</u>, ~
→ <A as well as B(B뿐만 아니라 A도)> 앞뒤로 명사구인 'a basic familiarity with ~'가 병렬 연결되었다.

12 정답 ① 53%

해석 인간, 그리고 지능이 있는 다른 동물들이 학습하는 방법에는 중요한 차이가 있다. 독일 Max Planck Institute의 진화 심리학자인 Mike Tomasello가 했던 매우 설득력 있는 실험에서, 간식을 담은 퍼즐 상자가 인간 유아와 침팬지에게 주어진다. 둘 다 그 간식을 꺼낼 수 없다. 그다음 그는 간식을 결국 내보내주도록 나무못을 당기고 미는 여러 단계의 동작을 보여준다. 그 동작 중, 그는 명백히 무의미한 단계를 포함시키는데, 마지막 단계 전 자기 머리를 세 번 가볍게 두드리는 것이다. 유아와 침팬지 둘 다 그의 행동들을 모방하고 간식을 얻을 수 있지만, (둘 중) 유아만이 머리를 두드리는 단계를 포함시킨다. 침팬지는 이것이 간식을 얻는 일과 관련이 없음을 알고 절차에서 생략한다. 하지만 인간은 의심 없이 모든 단계들을 따라 한다. 이 상황에서 유아는 자신을 가르쳐준 인간이 각 단계를 이행한 이유가 있을 거라고 믿으며, 그렇기에 과도하게 모방한다. 사실상, 절차의 목표가 덜 명확할수록, 유아는 무관한 단계까지도 더욱 주의 깊고 정확하게 모방할 것이다.
→ 위 실험에 따르면, 간식을 얻기 위한 여러 단계들이 주어질 때, 유아는 침팬지와 달리 그 절차의 모든 단계를 (A)완수하는데, 유아는 각 단계의 (B)적절성을 의심하지 않기 때문이다.

지문 간단히 보기

'인간 vs. 다른 동물'의 학습 방법 차이

실험: 연구자가 먹을 것을 꺼내면서 '무의미한' 행동을 함
(머리를 세 번 두드리기)

↓

결과: 침팬지(무관한 단계 생략) vs. 유아(생략 없이 모방)
→ 유아는 모든 단계에 '이유가 있다'고 믿고 '과도한 모방'

해설 침팬지와 인간 유아에게 간식을 상자에서 꺼내는 방법을 보여줄 때, 침팬지는 명백히 무관해 보이는 단계를 생략하는 반면, 인간은 모든 단계에 '이유'가 있을 것을 믿고 생략 없이 모방한다는 내용이다. 따라서 요약문의 빈칸에는 ① '완수하는데 - 적절성'이 적절하다.

오답풀이

보기 해석	선택률
② 완수하는데 - 복잡성	16%
③ 평가하는데 - 유연성	7%
④ 재배치하는데 - 가변성	10%
⑤ 재배치하는데 - 유용성	9%

구문 [16행] The chimp, **seeing this is not relevant to getting the treat**, omits it from the routine.
▶ <주어+동사> 사이에서 주어를 보충 설명하는 분사구문이다. 분사구문의 의미상 주어인 The chimp가 '아는' 주체이므로 능동을 나타내는 현재분사 seeing을 썼다.

13~14 정답 ② 78% / ④ 51% 2022 3월 41~42번

해석   <What a Plant Knows>에서 생물학자 Daniel Chamovitz는 식물이 자극에 반응하여 움직임을 조절하기 위해 사용하는 정교한 정보 처리 능력을 설명한다. 식물은 자기 줄기를 구부려 '태양을 따라갈' 뿐만 아니라, 빛에 대한 노출을 최대화하고 그렇게 해서 성장을 촉진하는 방식으로 잎을 정렬하기도 한다. 몇몇 식물은 실제로 '기억'해서 일출을 예상하며, 심지어 태양 신호를 받지 못할 때도 이 정보를 며칠 동안 보유한다. <Brilliant Green>에서 Stefano Mancuso와 Alessandra Viola는 식물이 시각, 촉각, 후각, 청각뿐만 아니라, 인간에게는 없는 십여 개 이상의 다른 감각 능력을 갖추고 있다고 주장한다. 예를 들어, 식물의 뿌리는 토양의 미네랄과 수분 함량을 감지하고 그에 따라 성장 방향을 바꾼다.

몇몇 사람은 식물에 신경과 근육이 없다는 이유로 식물의 움직임을 행동이라고 부르기를 꺼린다. 하지만 식물이 폐 없이도 숨을 쉴 수 있고 위 없이도 영양분을 소화할 수 있는 것처럼, 식물은 움직일(행동할) 수 있는 능력도 지니고 있다. 단지 어떤 유기체가 동물에게서 행동을 담당하는 생리학적 메커니즘을 갖고 있지 않다는 이유로, 그 유기체의 행동 능력의 부재(→ 존재)를 일축해서는 안 된다. 식물은 분명히 환경을 감지하고 학습하고 정보를 저장하며, 그 정보를 사용해 움직임을 유도한다. 즉, 식물은 행동한다. 어떤 사람은 식물의 행동에 어느 정도의 '지능'이 있다고 말할지도 모른다. 지능이 정신적인 능력보다도, 환경과의 행동적 상호 작용을 통해 문제를 해결하는 능력 차원에서 정의되는 한, 이것은 사실이다.

지문 간단히 보기

식물: 자극에 반응하여 움직임 조절 가능
- 태양을 '따라서' 움직이고, 태양 관련 정보를 '기억'함
- 뿌리로 환경을 파악해 성장 방향 조절 등등

↓

즉, 식물도 '행동한다'
= 신경이나 근육 등, 동물과 똑같은 신체 메커니즘이 없다는 이유로 행동 능력(의 존재)을 부정할 수 없음
= 식물도 '지능'이 있다

구문   [9행] Some plants actually <u>anticipate</u> sunrise from "memory," and **even when (they are) deprived** of solar signals <u>retain</u> this information for several days.
▶ 문장 전체의 동사는 밑줄 친 anticipate와 retain이다. <A and B> 형태의 병렬구조이다.
▶ even when(심지어 ~할 때)이 이끄는 부사절에서 <대명사 주어+be동사>가 생략되었다. 생략된 they는 문장의 주어인 Some plants를 가리킨다.

13   해설   식물은 비록 동물과 다른 생리적 메커니즘을 지니고 있지만 분명 행동하며, 나름의 지능을 갖고 문제 해결을 해나갈 수 있다는 내용이다. 마지막 세 문장에 답의 근거가 잘 제시된다. 따라서 제목으로 ② '식물은 진정 행동하며 지능도 갖고 있다'가 가장 적절하다.

오답풀이

보기 해석	선택률
① 식물의 성장은 토양 함량에 달려 있다	5%
③ 식물들은 태양 신호의 비밀을 안다	7%
④ 식물과 동물이 생존하는 데 필요한 것	4%
⑤ 자연에서 사는 삶의 이점과 단점	2%

14   해설   식물에게 행동하는 능력이 '있다'는 내용으로 보아, 생리적 메커니즘이 동물과 다르다는 이유로 행동 능력의 '존재'를 부정하면 안 된다는 설명이 흐름상 적합하다. 따라서 ④ (d)에는 absence 대신 presence를 써야 옳다.

오답풀이

보기 해석	선택률
① maximize(최대화하다)	7%
② sensory(감각의)	8%
③ reluctant(꺼리는, 마지못해 하는)	24%
⑤ interactions(상호 작용)	7%

STEP PLUS+ 수능 기출 마무리 복습

단어 TEST
02 증명하다   **03** 포기하다, 버리다   **04** 박식한   **05** 예견하다, 미리 보다   **06** 고갈시키다, 다 써버리다   **07** 차별적인   **08** 부과하다, 가하다   **09** 아는 표시를 하다, 인정하다   **10** 가볍게 두드리다   **11** ~이 박탈된, ~을 빼앗긴   **12** 꺼리는, 마지못해 하는

구문 TEST
14 It is common for people to experience stress   **15** than (to) make a phone call   **16** Those who are in an advantaged position   **17** Those living[who live] in big cities   **18** are likely to get sunburned

01 정답 ① 90% 2024 7월 18번

[해석] 직원 여러분께,
저는 인사 담당자 Laura Miller라고 합니다. 새로 건설된 지역 도로의 교통량을 줄이기 위한 노력의 일환으로, 우리는 자격이 있는 직원들에게 유연 근무 시간 제공을 시작할 예정입니다. 이 계획에 따르면 직원들은 통상 근무 시간의 60~90분 전후로 일을 시작하여, 이에 맞춰 출발 예정 시간을 조정할 수 있습니다. 모든 유연 근무 요청은 부서장에게 제출되어야 하며, 회사의 인력 수요와 상충되지 않는다면 승인될 예정입니다. 추가로, 유연 근무 일정은 회사 목표에 불리하게 영향을 미치지 않는지 확실히 하기 위해 4개월마다 검토될 예정입니다.
Laura Miller 드림

지문 간단히 보기

유연 근무제 도입: 지역 도로 교통량 감소 목적

↓

내용: 통상 근무 시간 60~90분 전후로 출근 시간 조정

↓

신청: 부서장에 제출 후 (사내 인력 여건과 충돌 없으면) 승인
→ 4개월마다 일정 검토

[해설] 유연 근무제 도입을 공지하는 글로, '~ we are starting to offer flextime working hours to eligible employees.'가 답의 결정적 힌트이다. 따라서 목적으로 가장 적절한 것은 ① '유연 근무제 실시 계획을 안내하려고'이다.

[오답풀이]

보기 해설	선택률
② '갈등 조정 기구'는 언급되지 않았다.	1%
③ 아직 유연 근무제가 시행되기 전이므로, '만족도 조사' 역시 실시되지 않은 시점이다.	3%
④ 유연 근무 신청이 부서장을 통해 승인될 예정이라는 내용만 언급되었다. 그 결과를 구체적으로 다루지는 않는다.	4%
⑤ '교통량 감소'는 유연 근무제의 시행 배경으로 언급되었지만, '대중교통'에 관한 내용은 없다.	1%

[구문] [3행] As part of ~, we **are starting to offer** flextime working hours to eligible employees.
▶ 현재진행 시제는 비교적 확실히 일어날 가까운 미래(~할 예정이다)를 나타낼 수 있다.

02 정답 ⑤ 75% 2024학년도 수능 20번

[해석] 가치만으로는 문화가 창조되고 구축되지 않는다. 일부 시간에만 가치에 따라 생활하는 것은 문화의 창조와 유지에 기여하지 않는다. 가치를 행동으로 바꾸는 것은 전투의 절반에 불과하다. 물론, 이것은 올바른 방향으로 나아가는 단계이지만, 그다음에 그러한 행동은 기대되는 바에 대한 명확하고 간결한 설명과 함께 조직 전체에 널리 공유되고 배포되어야 한다. 단순히 그것에 관해 이야기하는 것만으로는 충분하지 않다. 리더와 모든 인력 관리자가 팀 사람들을 지도하는 데 사용할 수 있도록 특정 행동들을 시각적으로 표현해 놓는 것이 중요하다. 스포츠 팀이 경기를 잘하고 승리하는 데 도움이 되도록 고안된, 특정 플레이를 담은 플레이북을 갖고 있듯이, 여러분의 회사는 문화를 행동으로 바꾸고 가치를 승리하는 행동으로 바꾸는 데 필요한 핵심적인 변화를 담은 플레이북을 갖고 있어야 한다.

지문 간단히 보기

문화를 창조하려면 '행동'해야 함 = 가치만으로는 부족

↓

행동하려면, 기대되는 행동에 관한 명확하고 간결한 설명이 조직에 배포되어야 함
= 시각적으로 표현된 자료 필요
= 조직 행동에 관한 '이야기(논의)'만으로는 부족

↓

스포츠 팀과 마찬가지로, 회사에도 '플레이북'이 필요
▶ **가치를 행동으로 바꾸는 지침이 담긴 시각 자료가 필요**

[해설] 조직 문화의 변화를 실제로 이끌어 내려면, 권장되는 행동을 명확하게 시각화한 지침이 필요하다는 내용의 글이다. 따라서 ⑤ '조직의 문화 형성에는 가치를 반영한 행동의 공유를 위한 명시적 지침이 필요하다.'가 주장으로 가장 적절하다.

[오답풀이]

보기 해설	선택률
① 가치 정립만으로는 문화를 만들기 충분치 '않다'는 내용과 모순된다.	7%
② 가치관을 갖는다고 해서 조직적인 행동으로 연결되기는 어렵기에 '설명과 지침'을 마련해줘야 한다는 것이 글의 핵심이다.	8%
③ 행동이 '자발적'이어야 함을 강조하는 글이 아니다.	4%
④ 가치관에 대한 의사소통, 즉 이야기만으로는 충분하지 '않다'는 내용과 모순된다.	3%

[구문] [12행] ~ a playbook with the key shifts **needed to transform your culture into action and turn your values into winning behaviors.**
▶ 과거분사구 'needed to ~'가 the key shifts를 수식한다. 'to transform ~ and (to) turn ~'이 needed에 병렬 연결되어 '~하고 …하는 데 필요한'의 의미를 나타낸다.

03 정답 ① 41%

해석 최근 몇 년간 나는 놀랍게도 거의 모든 문제에 대한 실마리가 '잘못된 스토리텔링'임을 알게 됐는데, 스토리텔링이야말로 우리가 에너지를 모으고 쓰는 방식을 '이끄는' 까닭이다. 나는 이야기, 즉 (다른) 사람들이 우리에게 하는 것 말고 우리가 스스로에게 하는 이야기가 그야말로 개인적, 직업적 운명을 결정짓는다고 믿는다. 그리고 여러분이 자신에 관해 말할 가장 중요한 이야기는 여러분 자신을 '향해서' 하는 이야기다. 그러니 여러분은 '특히' 모든 것 중 아마 가장 친숙하다고 생각할 본인의 이야기를 살펴봐야 한다. "가장 잘못된 이야기는 우리가 가장 잘 안다고 생각해서 절대 면밀히 조사하거나 의심하지 않는 것들이다."라고 고생물학자 Stephen Jay Gould가 말했다. 자신의 이야기를 멀리서 관찰하기보다는, 그 속에 참여하라. 그것이 여러분이 꼭 따르는 이야기가 되게 하라. 스스로에게 올바른 이야기를 하라, 그리고 그 옳음은 '여러분'만이 진정으로 판단할 수 있다. 만일 여러분이 마침내 직접 원하는 이야기를 살고 있다면, 그것은 평범할 필요가 없으며, 그렇게 되어서도 안 되고 되지도 않을 것이다. 그것은 비범해질 수 있고 또 그렇게 될 것이다. 결국, 여러분은 여러분 이야기의 작가일 뿐 아니라 주인공, 곧 영웅이다. 영웅은 절대 평범하지 않다.

지문 간단히 보기

> 세상 거의 모든 문제의 근원 = '잘못된 스토리텔링'
> → 우리가 스스로에게 하는 이야기를 돌아봐야 함

> 이야기를 멀찍이서 관찰하기보다, 그 속에 참여해야 함
> = 자신에게 말한 이야기를 따라서 행동해야 함
> = 이야기 내용을 '옳은 것으로' 만들어야 함
> ▶ **이야기대로 살지 못하면 '잘못된' 것**

해설 스스로 원하고 되뇌이는 이야기를 따라서 살라는 내용으로, 이야기가 현실이 되지 못할 때 '잘못된 스토리텔링'의 문제가 생김을 지적하고 있다. 따라서 밑줄 부분의 의미는 ① '스스로 결정한 삶을 살지 못하는 것'으로 볼 수 있다.

오답풀이

보기 해석	선택률
② 과거에 대한 후회에 사로잡히는 것	6%
③ 우리가 남들과 똑같다고 생각하지 않는 것	23%
④ 다른 누군가의 잘못을 우리 자신의 탓으로 돌리는 것	13%
⑤ 거짓 이야기를 만들어 남을 헐뜯는 것	18%

구문 [7행] And the most important story [**(that)** you will ever tell about yourself] is the story [**(that)** you tell *to* yourself].
▶ 주어 the most important story와 동사 is 뒤의 보어 the story를 각각 꾸미는 관계절에서 목적격 관계대명사가 생략되었다.

04 정답 ① 41%

해석 물건을 고치고 복원하려면 흔히 최초 제작보다 훨씬 더 많은 창의력이 필요하다. 산업화 이전의 대장장이는 바로 자기 인근의 마을 사람들에게 주문에 따라 물건을 만들어 주었기에, 제품을 주문 제작하는 것, 즉 사용자에게 맞게 수정하거나 변형하는 일은 일상이었다. 고객들은 뭔가 잘못되면 물건을 다시 가져다주곤 했고, 따라서 수리는 제작의 연장이었다. 산업화, 그리고 마침내 대량 생산이 이뤄지면서, 물건을 만드는 것은 한정된 지식을 지닌 기계 관리자의 영역이 되었다. 그러나 수리에는 설계와 재료에 대한 더 큰 이해, 즉 전체에 대한 이해와 설계자의 의도에 대한 이해가 계속 요구되었다. 1896년의 <Manual of Mending and Repairing>의 설명에 따르면, "제조업자들은 모두 기계나 방대한 분업으로 일하고, 말하자면 수작업으로 일하지는 않는다. 하지만 모든 수리는 '필히' 손으로 해야 한다. 우리는 기계로 손목시계나 총의 모든 세부사항을 제작할 수 있지만, 기계는 그것이 고장 났을 때 고쳐줄 수 없으며, 시계나 권총은 말할 것도 없다!"

지문 간단히 보기

> 산업화 이전: '수리는 제작의 연장선'
> - 대장장이가 물건을 주문 제작하고, 문제 있으면 수정/변형
> - 제작-수리가 일련의 과정

> 산업화 이후: '제작은 기계, 수리는 사람'
> - 대량 생산이 가능한 기계가 등장하여 제작 전담
> - 수리는 '더 큰 이해'가 필요한 인간의 영역으로 남음

> '제조는 기계나 분업에 맡겨도 되지만, 모든 수리는 손으로'
> ▶ **산업화 이후에도 '수리 = 인간의 작업'**

해설 산업화 이전에는 수리가 제품 제작의 연장선으로 취급되었지만, 산업화 이후로는 제작이 기계에 넘겨진 반면 수리는 계속 인간의 일로 남아 있다는 내용이다. 따라서 글의 제목으로 가장 적절한 것은 ① '현대 대장장이에게 여전히 남은 것: 수리라는 기술'이다.

오답풀이

보기 해석	선택률
② 수리 기술이 어떻게 발전했는가에 관한 역사적 조사	13%
③ 창의적 수리공이 되는 방법: 조언과 아이디어	8%
④ 수리의 과정: 만들고, 수정하고, 변형하라!	23%
⑤ 산업화가 우리의 망가진 과거를 고칠 수 있을까?	13%

구문 [18행] "~ We can make every detail of a watch or of a gun by machinery, but the machine cannot mend it **when (it is) broken**, much less a clock or a pistol!"
▶ 시간의 when절에서 <대명사 주어+be동사>가 생략되고 <접속사+과거분사>의 형태가 되었다. 생략된 it은 앞에 언급된 a watch or a gun을 가리킨다.

05 정답 ③ 94%

해석 Antonia Brico는 1902년에 네덜란드에서 태어나 6살에 미국으로 이주했다. 어렸을 때 한 공원 콘서트에 참석한 후, 그녀는 매우 영감을 받아서 음악을 공부해 지휘자가 되기로 결심했다. 1927년에 그녀는 Berlin State Academy of Music에 입학했고, 그곳의 지휘 (부문) 마스터 클래스를 졸업한 최초의 미국인이 되었다. 1930년에 Brico는 전문 지휘자로 데뷔했고, 이것으로 그녀는 긍정적인 평가를 받았다. 그녀는 유럽 광역 순회 공연을 떠났고, 그 순회 도중 Jean Sibelius에 의해 Helsinki Symphony Orchestra를 지휘해 달라고 초청받았다. Brico는 Denver에 정착했고, 그곳에서 그녀는 후에 Brico Symphony Orchestra로 개명된 Denver Businessmen's Orchestra의 지휘자로 계속 일했다. 1974년에 그녀의 가장 유명한 제자인 포크 가수 Judy Collins가 그녀에 관한 다큐멘터리 영화를 만들었고, 이것은 아카데미상 후보에 올랐다.

지문 간단히 보기

> Antonia Brico의 생애
> ① 네덜란드 출생, 6살에 미국 이주
> ② 어릴 때 공원 콘서트 참석 → 지휘자 되기로 결심
> ③ 1930년 지휘자 데뷔 → 긍정적 평가
> ④ Denver에 정착해 계속 오케스트라 지휘 활동
> ⑤ 제자가 그녀의 생애에 관한 다큐멘터리 제작 → 아카데미상 후보

해설 'In 1930, Brico made her debut as a professional conductor, for which she received positive reviews.'에서 Antonia Brico는 전문 지휘자로 데뷔하여 긍정적 평가를 받았다고 하므로, 일치하지 않는 것은 ③ '전문 지휘자로서의 데뷔에서 부정적인 평가를 받았다.'이다.

오답풀이

보기 해설	선택률
① ~ born in the Netherlands in 1902 and immigrated to the United States at the age of six.	3%
② After attending a park concert ~ made up her mind to study music and become a conductor.	1%
④ Brico settled in Denver, where she continued to work as a conductor ~	1%
⑤ ~ which was nominated for an Academy Award.	0%

구문 [8행] In 1930, Brico made her debut as a professional conductor, **for which** she received positive reviews.
▶ <전치사+관계대명사> 형태의 for which에서 which가 받는 선행사는 her debut이다. for which 뒤에는 완전한 구조가 연결되었다.

06 정답 ⑤ 42%

해석 현대 기술의 경이로움은 우리 조상들이 꿈도 꿔보지 못했을 기회를 사람들에게 제공했지만, 좋은 것들은 늘 그렇듯 부정적인 면에 의해 약화된다. 그 부정적인 면 중 하나는 누구든 그렇게 하기로 선택한 사람이면 자격사항에 상관없이 인터넷이라는 가상의 확성기를 집어 들고 무한히 많은 주제 중 어떤 것에 관해서든 의견을 말할 수 있다는 것이다. 결국 인터넷에는 유치원 교사가 의학 조언을 제공하거나 의사가 여러분 집에 안전하게 구조적 변화를 줄 방법을 제안하지 못하게 막는 규정이 없다. 결과적으로, 잘못된 정보가 정보로 퍼지고, 그 둘을 구별하기가 늘 쉽지는 않다. 이것은 과학자에게 특히 좌절스러울 수 있는데, 그들은 일생에 걸쳐 주변 세상의 복잡성을 이해하는 방법을 배우지만, 결국 이들의 연구는 그 주제에 대한 경험이 분 단위로 측정될 수 있는(경험이 매우 적은) 사람들에게 즉석으로 반박당한다. 이후 이 좌절감은 일반 대중들에게는 과학자와 도전자 둘 다 동등한 신뢰성을 부여받는다는 사실로 인해 줄어든다(→ 증폭된다).

지문 간단히 보기

> 인터넷 발전 → 누구나 원하는 주제에 관해 의견 피력
> ('자격사항에 관계없이')
> ↓
> 그 결과, 잘못된 정보가 정보로 퍼짐 → 과학자들 '좌절'
> ↓
> 일반 대중은 자기 분야에 일생을 바친 전문가와, 해당 경험이 '분 단위'에 불과한 비전문가를 똑같이 신뢰함
> ▶ **과학자들의 좌절이 더 '커질' 상황**

해설 인터넷에서 사람들은 자기 전문 분야가 '아닌' 분야에 관해서도 자유롭게 말할 수 있고, 이 점이 과학자들에게는 더욱 '좌절'이 된다는 내용이다. 일반 대중들의 눈에는 과학자나 다른 비전문가나 신뢰성 면에서 차이가 없기 때문에 과학자들의 좌절감이 '증폭된다'는 의미가 되도록, ⑤의 diminished를 amplified로 고쳐야 옳다.

오답풀이

보기 해설	선택률
① qualifications(자격사항)	6%
② preventing(막는, 방지하는)	13%
③ differentiate(구별하다)	17%
④ challenged(반박당한, 도전받은)	22%

구문 [21행] ~ **the fact** [**that**, to the general public, **both** the scientist **and** the challenger **are** awarded equal credibility].
▶ the fact 뒤의 that은 동격의 명사절 접속사이다. 즉 [ ]이 '사실'의 내용에 해당한다.
▶ [ ]의 주어가 <both A and B> 형태이므로 복수동사를 썼다(are).

07 정답 ② 47%

해석 우리가 정치적 리스크라고 부르는 것의 많은 부분은 사실 불확실성이다. 이것은 사회 갈등에서부터 몰수, 규제상의 변화에 이르기까지 모든 유형의 정치적 리스크에 적용된다. 신용, 시장 또는 운영 리스크와는 달리 정치적 리스크는 비체계적이고, 그렇기에 전형적인 통계적 관점에서 처리하기가 더 어려울 수 있다. 테러리스트들이 미국을 다시 공격할 확률은 얼마나 될까? 지진이나 허리케인과는 달리, 정치 행위자들은 리스크 관리자들이 만든 장벽을 넘어서기 위해 끊임없이 적응한다. 기업들이 몰수의 리스크를 줄이기 위해 국제적 보증이나 법적 계약을 통해 해외 투자를 체계화할 때, (사업) 소재국 정부는 은밀히 진행되는 몰수나 규제상의 차별처럼, 증명하기 굉장히 어렵고 법적으로 비용도 많이 드는 새로운 방해 형태들을 모색한다. 리스크에 대한 관찰은 리스크 자체를 변화시킨다. 충격이 크지만 확률은 낮은 사건들을 줄이는 방법들이 있다. 그러나 이러한 리스크에 대한 분석은 과학인 만큼이나 예술일 수 있다.

지문 간단히 보기

> 정치적 리스크: 비체계적, 통계 처리 어려움
> → (예시) 테러 공격 발생 확률**(예상하기 힘듦)**

> 정치 행위자들은 리스크 방지 대책에 계속 적응**(변화 시도)**
> → (예시) 외국 기업의 투자 시도가 체계화되면, 사업 소재국의 대응도 그에 맞춰 변화

> '리스크를 관찰하면, 리스크 자체가 변하는' 특성
> → 따라서, 정치 리스크 분석 = 과학인 동시에 '예술'
> ▶ **그만큼 예측하기 어렵고 불확실한 요소가 많음**

해설 정치적 리스크는 비체계적인 특성을 지니며, 리스크를 관찰하다 보면 '리스크 자체가 변할' 만큼 변동성이 커서 예측하기 어렵다는 내용이다. 따라서 빈칸에는 ② '불확실성'이 적합하다.

오답풀이

보기 해석	선택률
① 부당함	15%
③ 순환성	16%
④ 모순	17%
⑤ 의사소통 오류	5%

구문 [11행] ~ **new forms of obstruction**, <u>such as creeping expropriation or regulatory discrimination</u>, **that are very hard and legally costly to prove**.
▶ 선행사와 관계절(that ~ prove) 사이에 밑줄 친 부분이 끼어들면서, 선행사와 관계절이 분리되었다.
▶ 주격 관계대명사 that 뒤의 동사가 복수형(are)이라는 점에서 선행사가 복수명사(forms)라는 힌트를 얻을 수 있다.

08 정답 ① 22%

해석 과학자와 예술가의 차이점이 무엇이든, 이들은 '당신과 내가 똑같은 것을 똑같은 방식으로 볼 수 있을까? 만약 그렇다면 어떻게?'라는 똑같은 물음에서 출발한다. 과학적 사고를 하는 사람은 주관성을 제거할 수 있는 사물의 특징, 즉 이상적으로 정량화될 수 있고 그리하여 그 가치가 관찰자에 따라 달라지지 않을 측면을 찾는다. 이런 식으로, 그 사람은 모든 관찰자로부터 독립된 어떤 현실에 도달한다. 반면, 예술가는 자신이 보유한 예술적 기질의 힘에 의지해 자신의 주관성과 독자의 주관성 간 결합을 이룬다. 과학적 사고를 하는 사람에게 이는 분명 마술 같은 생각으로 들릴 것이다. 즉, '당신이 무언가를 열심히 상상한 나머지 그것이 타인의 마음속에도 정확히 당신의 상상대로 갑자기 나타날 거라는 말인가?' 예술가는 관찰자로부터 독립적인 과학자의 현실과 정반대의 것을 추구해 왔다. 예술가는 관찰자에게 의존하는 현실, 즉 실로 그것이 존재할 수라도 있으려면 사람들이 참여해야만 하는 현실을 만들어낸다.

지문 간단히 보기

> 과학자와 예술가의 출발점(공통)
> : '당신과 내가 같은 것을 같은 방식으로 볼 수 있을까?'

> 과학자: 가치가 관찰자에 따라 달라지지 않을 부분 연구
> = 주관성이 제거되고 정량화될 수 있는 면에 관심

> 반면, 예술가: 자신과 관찰자의 주관성을 '결합'하려 함
> = 관찰자에게 '의존하는' 현실 추구
> (과학자가 추구하는 현실과 '정반대')
> ▶ **관찰자가 '함께 참여하는' 현실 창조**

해설 과학자는 관찰자에 따라 가치가 주관적으로 해석되지 않을 부분에 관심을 두지만, 예술가는 이와 '반대되는' 것을 추구한다고 한다. 즉 관찰자에 '좌우되는' 현실을 추구하여 예술가와 관찰자의 주관성을 '결합'시키려 한다는 내용으로 보아, 빈칸에는 ① '사람들이 참여해야만 하는'이 들어가야 한다.

오답풀이

보기 해석	선택률
② 객관성이 유지되어야 하는	24%
③ 과학과 예술이 조화되어야 하는	23%
④ 독자들이 예술로부터 거리를 둔	13%
⑤ 예술가가 자기 자신의 주관성에서 분리된	18%

구문 [12행] ~ you're saying [**(that)** you will imagine something **so** hard **(that)** it'll pop into someone else's head exactly the way you envision it]?
▶ 동사 are saying의 목적어인 [ ]에서 접속사 that이 생략되었다.
▶ [ ] 안은 크게 보아 <so ~ that …(너무 ~해서 …하다)> 구문이다. 결과의 부사절을 이끄는 접속사 that 또한 생략되었다.

09 정답 ④ 40%

해석 비록 우리는 우리가 아이들을 기르는 능력을 지녔다고 믿지만, 실제로는 우리 아이들이야말로 '우리를' 자신이 필요로 하는 부모로 키우는 능력을 지니고 있다. 이러한 이유로, 양육 경험은 부모 '대' 아이의 경험이 아니라, 부모가 아이와 '함께하는' 경험이다. 완전함으로 가는 길은 우리 아이들 무릎에 달렸으며(아이들 몫이며), 우리가 해야 할 일은 자리에 앉아 있는 것뿐이다. 우리 아이들이 우리 자신의 본질로 되돌아가는 길을 알려주기에, 그들은 우리를 가장 잘 일깨우는 사람이 된다. (이는 우리가 우리 아이들의 정신을 일깨우는 데 얼마만큼 관심을 쏟느냐가 그들의 인생을 달라지게 할 수 있다는 뜻이다.) 만일 그들이 증진된 자각의 입구로 우리를 안내할 때 우리가 그들의 손을 잡고 인도를 따라가지 못하면, 깨달음으로 향해 가는 기회를 잃게 된다.

지문 간단히 보기

부모가 아이를 키운다기보다, 아이가 부모를 부모로 만듦

↓

① 그래서 양육은 부모와 아이가 '함께하는' 경험
② 부모는 아이가 이끄는 대로 따르면 됨
③ 아이는 부모를 가장 잘 일깨우는 존재
⑤ 아이의 안내를 따르지 못하면 깨달음에 이르지 못함

해설 부모는 '아이가 이끄는 대로' 양육의 과정을 함께하면 된다는 내용인데, ④는 부모가 아이의 인생에 영향을 미치는 경우를 말하므로 흐름상 어긋난다.

오답풀이

보기 해설   선택률

① 자녀가 부모를 부모답게 만든다는 내용 뒤로, '그렇기 때문에(For this reason)' 부모와 아이가 함께 만들어가는 것이 양육이라는 설명이 자연스럽게 연결된다. — 3%

② in our children's lap과 take a seat가 서로 무관해 보이지만, 속뜻을 파악해야 한다. '아이의 무릎에 완전성이 있다 = 아이들의 역할이 중요하다', '부모는 앉아 있으면 된다 = 아이들의 리드를 따르면 된다'임을 알아야 한다. — 28%

③ ②의 속뜻을 알면 ③도 파악하기 쉽다. our greatest awakeners 또한 '아이들의 역할'을 강조하는 표현이다. — 15%

⑤ they, their가 계속 '아이들'을 나타내며, '이끄는 것은 아이들의 역할'임을 일관성 있게 진술한다. — 11%

구문 [1행] ~ the reality is [that our children hold the power to raise *us* into the parents **they need us to become**].
▶ [ ]이 문장의 주격보어 역할을 한다. 'to raise ~'가 the power를 꾸미고, 'they ~ become'은 the parents를 꾸민다.

10 정답 ④ 29%

해석 결과 기반 가격 책정 중 제일 흔히 알려진 형태는 변호사들이 이용하는 '승소 시 보수 약정'이라는 관행이다.
(C) 승소 시 보수 약정은 개인 상해 및 특정 소비자 소송에 비용이 청구되는 주요 방식이다. 이 방식에서 변호사는 수수료나 지불금을 받지 않다가 소송이 해결된 뒤에 비로소 받는데, 이때 그들은 의뢰인이 받는 금액의 일정 비율을 받는다.
(A) 따라서, 의뢰인에게 유리한 결과만 보수가 지불된다. 의뢰인의 관점에서 보면 이러한 가격 책정은 타당한데, 그 부분적인 이유는 이러한 소송의 의뢰인 대부분이 법률 사무소에 익숙지 않고 어쩌면 겁먹을 수 있기 때문이다. 그들의 가장 큰 두려움은 해결까지 몇 년이 걸릴지도 모르는 소송에 대한 높은 수수료이다.
(B) 승소 시 보수 약정을 사용하여, 의뢰인은 합의금을 받을 때까지 수수료를 지불하지 않도록 보장받는다. 이런 식의 승소 시 보수 약정 사례에서, 서비스의 경제적 가치는 서비스 이전에 결정하기 어렵고, 공급자는 자신이 구매자에게 가치를 전달하는 위험과 보상을 분담할 수 있게 하는 가격을 형성한다.

지문 간단히 보기

'승소 시 보수 약정' 용어 소개 → (C) 용어 설명

↓

(C) 소송 해결 뒤 받을 돈 일부를 변호사에게 주는 방식
(A) 따라서, 재판에서 유리한 결과가 나와야 보수 지급

↓

(A) 보통 의뢰인의 걱정거리: 높은 수수료
(B) 승소 시 보수 약정대로 하면, 합의금 받고 수수료 지불
　　+ 공급자도 수요자와 위험 및 보상을 분담 가능

해설 주어진 글에 언급된 '승소 시 보수 약정'을 (C)에서 변호사와 의뢰인의 관계로 설명한다. (A)는 (C)에서 언급한 대로 의뢰인이 받을 돈을 변호사가 일부 받는다면 의뢰인에게 유리한 결과가 나와야만 변호사가 돈을 받게 된다고 한다. (B)는 (A) 후반부에 언급된 '수수료에 대한 부담'에 이어지는 내용이다. 따라서 ④ '(C)-(A)-(B)'가 적절하다.

오답풀이 보기 해설   선택률

① 주어진 글에 언급된 '승소 시 보수 약정'을 반복하며 개념을 직접 설명하는 단락은 (A)가 아닌 (C)이다. — 2%

②, ③ (B) 후반부의 '서비스 공급자(providers)'와 '구매자(the buyer)'는 각각 변호사와 의뢰인을 경제학적 관점에서 일반화한 표현이므로, 예시가 마무리된 후 제시되는 결론으로 봐야 맞다. — 16% / 14%

⑤ (A)가 (C)에서 설명한 관행을 따른 결과(Therefore)라는 점에서 (C)-(A)는 고정이다. — 40%

구문 [C-3행] In this approach, lawyers do **not** receive fees or payment **until** the case is settled, ~
▶ <not A until B(B하고 나서야 비로소 A하다)> 구문이다. 'B할 때까지 A하지 않는다'라는 직역에서 결국 'B 이후 A'라는 선후 관계를 도출할 수 있다.

해석 나무가 함께 자랄 때는, 각 나무가 가능한 최고의 나무로 성장할 수 있도록 영양분과 물이 모든 나무 사이에 최적으로 분배될 수 있다. 만약 여러분이 경쟁자로 여겨지는 나무를 제거하여 개별 나무를 '도와주면' 나머지 나무를 잃게 된다. 그것들은 이웃 나무들에 메시지를 보내지만 소용이 없는데, 그루터기 외에는 아무것도 안 남아 있기 때문이다. 이제 모든 나무가 각자 자라 생산성에 큰 차이가 생긴다. 어떤 개체들은 당분이 줄기를 따라 확연히 흘러넘칠 때까지 미친 듯이 광합성을 한다. 그 결과, 그것들은 건강하고 더 잘 자라지만 특별히 오래 살지는 못한다. 이는 나무가 자신을 둘러싸고 있는 숲만큼만 튼튼할 수 있기 때문이다. 그리고 지금 숲에는 많은 패자가 있다. 한때는 강한 구성원들의 지원을 받았을 더 약한 구성원들이 갑자기 뒤처진다. 그것들의 쇠락 원인이 위치와 영양분 부족이든, 일시적인 질병이든, 혹은 유전적 구성이든, 이제 그것들은 곤충과 균류의 먹이가 된다.

지문 간단히 보기

함께 자라면 서로 도우며 자라는 숲속 나무들
: 도와준다고 경쟁자를 제거해주면 오히려 나머지를 잃음

↓

(예시) 남은 나무들 중, 광합성을 미친 듯이 하는 경우
→ '그 결과' 잘 자라지만 특별히 오래 살지는 못함
→ 나무는 '자기 주변만큼만' 튼튼하기 때문
  = 주변에 패배자(그루터기)들만 남아 있기 때문
  = 성장을 도와줄 강한 구성원이 주변에 없기 때문

해설 ② 앞에서 경쟁자 나무가 제거된 후 광합성을 많이 한 일부 나무의 예시를 언급하는데, 주어진 문장은 이 나무들을 they로 받아 이들이 건강해 보여도 특별히 오래 살지는 않는다고 설명한다. ② 뒤는 '이들이 오래 살지 못하는 이유'를 언급하므로, 주어진 문장은 ②에 적합하다.

오답풀이

보기 해설	선택률
① 나무마다 성장도가 다르다는 앞문장에 이어 Some individuals의 사례가 적절히 연결된다.	5%
③ And 앞뒤가 모두 주어진 문장의 'they aren't particularly long-lived'를 보충한다. 경쟁자 나무들이 제거된 후 미친 듯이 광합성하는 나무들이 오래 못 사는 것은 '나무가 일반적으로 자기 환경만큼 튼튼한데, 주변에 패배자만 많기 때문'이라는 것이다.	23%
④ 앞문장에서 말한 '패배자들만 남은' 환경에서는 약한 나무들이 강한 나무들의 원조를 받지 못해 성장이 뒤처진다는 흐름이다.	20%
⑤ 뒷문장의 their, they가 앞문장의 Weaker members이다.	21%

구문 [13행] **This is because** a tree can be only as strong as the forest that surrounds it.
▶ <this is because+원인>, <this is why+결과>를 구분해서 기억해 둔다.

해석 경제학의 한 가지 기본 원리는 어떤 것의 공급이 증가하면 그 가격은 내려가야 한다는 것이다. (여기서) 수수께끼는 20세기에는 오랜 기간에 걸쳐 노동의 세계(노동 시장)에서 정반대 상황이 일어나는 것 같았다는 점이었다. 일부 국가에서는 전문학교와 대학으로부터 쏟아져 나오는, 고도로 숙련된 인력 수가 엄청나게 증가했지만, 그들의 임금은 이러한 교육을 받지 않은 사람들과 비교할 때 감소하기보다는 오히려 증가하는 것으로 보였다. 어떻게 이럴 수 있었을까? 고도로 숙련된 노동자의 공급은 실제로 증가해 임금을 낮추었지만, 새로운 기술은 숙련 편향적이어서 고도로 숙련된 노동자에 대한 수요를 급증시켰다. 후자의 효과는 너무 커서 전자를 압도했고, 따라서 일자리를 찾는 교육받는 사람들이 더 많았음에도 그들에 대한 수요가 너무 강해서 그들이 받는 액수는 여전히 증가했다.
→ 20세기에, 고도로 숙련된 노동자들의 공급이 증가한 상황에서 그들의 임금이 (A)올랐던 시기가 있었는데, 이는 새로운 기술이 그들을 (B)선호했기 때문이었다.

지문 간단히 보기

수요-공급 법칙의 반대 사례: 20세기 일자리 상황

↓

고등교육을 받은 인재 공급↑ → 하지만, 이들의 임금↑

↓

이유: '고도의 숙련을 요구하는' 새로운 기술의 등장
      → '교육받은' 노동자에 대한 수요↑
      → 이들의 임금↑

해설 신기술의 도입과 함께 고도로 숙련된 노동자들에 대한 수요가 급증하면서, 이들의 공급 증가로 인해 임금이 낮아지는 효과를 '압도하고' 결국 이들의 임금이 높아지는 결과가 생겼다는 내용이다. 따라서 요약문의 빈칸에는 ① '올랐던 - 선호했기'가 들어가야 한다.

오답풀이

보기 해설	선택률
② 안정화되었던 - 대체했기	14%
③ 증가했던 - 가치를 떨어뜨렸기	19%
④ 감소했던 - 소외시켰기	12%
⑤ 줄어들었던 - 표준화했기	10%

구문 [11행] The supply of high-skilled workers **did grow**, pushing their wages downward, ~
▶ <do/does/did+동사원형>이 동사를 강조한다(실제로 ~하다).

13~14 정답 ④ 40% / ⑤ 50% 2020 10월 41~42번

해석 성격은 여러분의 '개인적 특질'의 가장 안쪽 층이기 때문에, 여러분 (자신)의 성격을 보지 못하기가 쉽(고 또 흔히 그렇)다. 사실, 사람들 대부분은 이른 유년 시절부터 자신의 천성을 완전히 가리는 '맞지 않는 정체성을 취하느라' 대부분의 시간을 보냈기 때문에 자기 성격을 모른다. 대체로 어린 시절의 환경(예를 들어, 부모님이 우리를 양육하는 방식, 사회가 우리와 소통하는 방식, 문화가 우리를 만들어 가는 방식)은 우리가 사실은 다른 유형의 사람인데도 어느 한 유형의 사람이라고 생각하도록 성인이 된 우리를 잘못된 방향으로 이끈다! 어린 시절에, 우리는 우리에게 끊임없이 인상을 심어 주고, 우리가 세상에서 어떤 모습이어야 하는지 피드백을 주고, '옳은' 행동 방식, 지녀야 할 '옳은' 사고와 감정, 참여해야 할 '옳은' 집단을 가르쳐주는 가족과 사회와 문화에 둘러싸여 있다. 비록 우리는 어느 한 모습(우리의 성격)으로 세상에 나오지만, 우리는 이런 외부의 영향으로부터 오랜 시간에 걸쳐 우리의 진짜 자아대로 사는 것에는 불리한 점이 있고 우리의 진짜 자아와 맞지 않는 정체성을 취하면 보상이 있다는 메시지를 자주 받는다. 그러므로 우리는 우리의 진짜 자아를 뒷받침하는 행동, 사고, 관계를 키워나가기보다는, 우리 삶 속의 사람들을 실망시킬(→ 만족시킬) 것들을 키워나간다.

지문 간단히 보기

> 사람들은 (타고난) 자기 성격을 알기 어려움

> 이유: 사람들은 어릴 때부터 진짜 천성 또는 정체성과 '맞지 않는' 정체성을 선택하며 살아감 ← 부모, 사회, 문화(외부)의 영향

> '자아대로' 살면 불리하지만, '맞지 않는' 모습대로 살면 보상이 있다는 것을 학습 → 자기 성격대로 살지 않게 됨
> ▶ 다른 사람들을 '실망시키기'보다는 '만족시킬' 것들을 선택

구문 [3행] ~ from early childhood, they **have spent most of their time** *adopting* out-of-sync identities [that completely mask their natural personalities].
▶ <spend+시간+동명사(~하는 데 …의 시간을 쓰다)> 구문이다.
▶ 주격 관계대명사절의 동사 mask는 선행사인 복수명사 *out-of-sync identities*에 수 일치되었다.

13

해설 사람들이 타고난 자기 성격을 알기 어렵다는 내용의 첫 문장 뒤로 그 이유를 설명하는 글이다. 따라서 제목으로 ④ '왜 우리는 진정한 우리 자신으로부터 멀어질까?'가 가장 적절하다.

오답풀이

보기 해석	선택률
① 당신의 사교성이 당신을 대변하도록 하라	6%
② 성격과 개성을 구축하는 핵심	25%
③ 당신의 충동을 잠재우고 내적 평화를 이루라	7%
⑤ 우리의 자기 가치감은 사회적 성과에 바탕을 둘 수 있을까?	6%

14

해설 자신보다도 가족, 사회, 문화 등 외부에서 원하는 것을 선택하면 보상이 있음을 알게 된다는 내용으로 보아, ⑤ (e)에는 남들을 '만족시킬' 것들을 선택한다는 의미로 disappoint 대신 please를 써야 한다.

오답풀이

보기 해석	선택률
① unaware(모르는)	4%
② mislead(잘못된 방향으로 이끌다)	10%
③ feedback(피드백)	6%
④ outside(외부의)	14%

STEP PLUS+ 수능 기출 마무리 복습

단어 TEST

02 잘못된 **03** ~을 헐뜯다, 나쁘게 말하다 **04** 제작, 날조 **05** 부정적인 면 **06** 즉석으로 **07** ~로부터 독립된, ~와 상관없이 **08** 상상하다, (머릿속에) 그리다 **09** 최적으로 **10** ~의 먹이가 되다 **11** (기간이) 오래 계속되는, 장기적인 **12** ~을 모르다, 놓치다

구문 TEST

14 Not avoiding but facing your fears **15** (to) assess all the data before making[we make] a decision **16** caused the demand for high-skilled workers to soar **17** caused the dog to bark all night **18** operates so quietly that

01 정답 ⑤ 93% 2022학년도 수능 19번

해석 캐나다 전역에서 수많은 공룡 화석으로 유명한 앨버타주의 Badlands를 탐험하는 것이 Evelyn에게는 처음이었다. 젊은 아마추어 뼈 발굴자인 그녀는 기대감으로 가득 차 있었다. 그녀는 흔한 공룡 종의 뼈 때문에 이렇게 멀리까지 이동했던 것이 아니었다. 희귀한 공룡 화석을 발견하고자 하는 평생의 꿈이 막 실현될 참이었다. 그녀는 열심히 그것들을 찾기 시작했다. 하지만 황량한 땅을 여러 시간 배회하고 난 후에도, 그녀는 성과를 얻지 못했다. 이제 해는 지기 시작하고 있었고, 그녀의 목표는 여전히 손 닿지 않는 먼 곳에 있었다. 천천히 어두워지는 눈앞의 땅을 바라보며, 그녀는 혼자 한숨을 쉬었다. "이렇게 멀리 와서 아무 성과도 못 내다니 믿을 수 없어. 이게 무슨 시간 낭비야!"

지문 간단히 보기

공룡 화석을 탐험하러 멀리까지 간 Evelyn ▶ **기대**

↓

아무리 황량한 땅을 뒤져도, 아무 성과도 내지 못함

↓

'시간 낭비'를 했다며 한숨을 쉰 Evelyn ▶ **실망**

해설 공룡 화석을 탐구할 기대로 설레던 Evelyn이 아무 성과도 내지 못하자 실망했다는 내용으로, 글 중간의 however를 기점으로 흐름이 전환된다. 따라서 Evelyn의 심경 변화로 가장 적절한 것은 ⑤ '기대하는 → 실망한'이다.

오답풀이

보기 해석	선택률
① 혼란스러운 → 겁에 질린	1%
② 낙담한 → 자신감에 찬	2%
③ 여유로운 → 짜증 난	1%
④ 무관심한 → 우울한	1%

구문 [6행] **Her life-long dream** to find rare fossils of dinosaurs **was about to come true**.
▶ 밑줄 친 to부정사구는 주어 Her life-long dream을 꾸미는 형용사구로 쓰였다.
▶ <be about to+동사원형(막 ~할 참이다)>을 기억해 둔다.

02 정답 ① 62% 2022 10월 20번

해석 놀랍고 창의적인 프로젝트를 실현하려면 그날그날 아이디어를 실행하는 어려운 상황에서도 많은 노력이 필요하다. 천재는 정말로 '1퍼센트의 영감과 99퍼센트의 노력'이다. 하지만 우리는 그 99%의 이면을 잊어서는 안 되는데, 모든 문제를 순전히 의지력으로 해결하기는 불가능하다는 것이다. 우리는 놀이, 휴식, 탐구를 위한 시간 또한 마련해야 하는데, 이것들은 우리가 기존의 아이디어를 발전시키고 새로운 프로젝트를 진행하도록 돕는 창의적 통찰의 필수 요소이다. 흔히 이것은 루틴을 벗어나기 위한 루틴을 만들거나, 순전히 재미 삼아서 부차적인 탐구 프로젝트를 하거나, 여러분의 뇌가 문제를 바라보는 관점에 시동을 걸 새로운 방법을 찾는 것을 뜻한다. 최적의 창의적 상태를 유지하려면, 정신을 바쁘고 분주하게 해야 하는데, 왜냐하면 창의력의 가장 큰 적은 그야말로 정체해 있는 것이기 때문이다.

지문 간단히 보기

창의적인 프로젝트를 하려면 많은 노력이 필요

순전히 '의지력' 문제가 아니라, 놀이, 휴식, 탐구도 필요

(놀이, 휴식, 탐구로) 정신을 계속 바쁘게 유지할 필요
= 창의력의 가장 큰 적은 '정체해 있는 것'

해설 창의성을 유지하려면 새로운 놀이나 탐구 활동 등으로 뇌를 계속 바쁘게 해야 한다는 내용이므로, 주장으로 가장 적절한 것은 ① '창의성을 유지할 다양한 경험과 활동을 지속해야 한다.'이다.

오답풀이

보기 해설	선택률
② '내적 비판'이나 '성찰'에 관한 글이 아니다.	2%
③ '일상에서의 관찰'보다는 '놀이, 휴식, 탐구'의 중요성을 다루고 있다.	7%
④ 일반적으로 타당해 보이지만, 글의 핵심 내용과는 거리가 있다. '사고의 틀을 버리라'는 것보다는 '놀이, 휴식, 탐구'의 중요성을 말하는 글이기 때문이다.	27%
⑤ '추상적인 생각의 적용'에 관해 언급되지 않았다.	2%

구문 [15행] To stay creatively fit, we must **keep our minds engaged and on the move** ~
▶ 밑줄 친 to부정사구는 목적을 나타내는 부사구이다(~하려면, ~하기 위해).
▶ <keep+목적어+형용사구> 형태의 5형식 구문이다. on the move는 '분주한, (이리저리) 움직이는'이라는 뜻이다.

03 정답 ④ 43%

해석 많은 작가는 독자를 떠올릴 때 너무 모호해지는 흔한 실수를 한다. 대상 독자층을 특정하는 데 있어서, '모두'는 '아무도 아니다'. 만약 여러분이 특별히 한 사람을 위해 글을 쓰고 있다면 다른 사람들이 배제될까 봐 걱정할지도 모른다. 안심하라, 그런 일이 반드시 일어나지는 않는다. 잘 규정된 독자층은 설명과 단어 선택에 대한 결정을 단순화한다. 여러분의 문제는 대상 독자층 너머의 사람들을 끌어들이는 식으로 더 독특해질지도 모른다. 예를 들면, Andy Weir는 자신이 읽는 이야기가 과학적 사실에 확고하게 근거를 두길 바라는 공상 과학 소설 독자들과, 어쩌면 공상 과학 소설을 즐길 수도 있는 로켓 과학자들을 위해 <The Martian>을 썼다. 나는 두 독자층 어디에도 속하지 않지만 그 책을 즐겼다. Weir가 대상 독자층을 만족시키는 데 너무도 성공한 나머지 이들은 이것을 널리, 열정적으로 공유했다. Weir가 모두의 구미를 맞추려 하지 않았기 때문에 그는 핵심 독자층을 즐겁게 해 준 뭔가를 써냈다. 결국 그의 작품은 그 범위를 훨씬 넘어서까지 전해졌다. 직관에 어긋나는 말일 수 있지만, 만약 여러분의 영향력을 넓히고 싶다면 독자에 대한 여러분의 초점을 좁히라.

지문 간단히 보기

독자층을 정할 때 '모두는 아무도 아니다'

↓

독자층을 잘 규정하면 → 설명, 단어 선택 단순화
→ 핵심 독자층 너머에도 어필
→ (예시) <The Martian>

↓

(결론) 독자층을 좁혀야 영향력이 넓어짐 ▶ **너무 모호하거나 넓은 독자군을 공략하면 '실수'**

해설 독자층을 명확하게 좁혀놓고 글을 쓸 때 오히려 다른 독자층까지 매료시킬 수 있다는 내용이다. 특히 '모두의 구미를 맞추려 하지 않았던' 것이 성공적인 글쓰기 전략이었다는 Weir의 사례로 보아, 밑줄 친 부분의 의미로 ④ '모든 독자를 만족시키려 하면 아무도 만족시키지 못한다'가 적절하다.

오답풀이

보기 해석	선택률
① 독자층을 가급적 넓게 생각하는 것이 바람직하다.	11%
② 모든 독자들은 취향에 상관없이 베스트셀러를 사고자 한다.	8%
③ 이야기는 독자에 따라 다양한 반응을 이끌어낼 수 있다.	19%
⑤ 독자를 구체적으로 타겟팅하는 것은 소설가에게 해가 된다.	15%

구문 [15행] Weir was **so** successful at pleasing his target audience **that** they shared it widely and enthusiastically.
▶ <so ~ that …(너무 ~해서 …하다)> 구문이다.

04 정답 ① 46%

해석 가능할 때마다, 우리는 우리가 생각하는 정보를 '재사회화'하기 위한 조치를 취해야 한다. 우리가 머릿속에서 계속하는 지속적인 재잘거림은 사실 일종의 내면화된 대화이다. 마찬가지로, 시험과 평가부터 개요서와 사례 연구, 에세이와 제안서에 이르기까지, 학교와 직장에서 우리가 마주치는 많은 형태의 문서는 사실 종이에 쓰여 어떤 가상의 청자나 대화자에게 건네지는 사회적 대화(질문, 이야기, 논쟁)이다. 조금 거리를 둔 그런 상호 작용을 다시 실제적인 사회적 만남으로 되돌리는 데는 상당한 이점이 있다. 다른 사람들이 관련될 때, 즉 우리가 그들을 모방하고 있든지, 그들과 논쟁하고 있든지, 이야기를 교환하고 있든지, 동조하면서 협력하고 있든지, 또는 그들을 가르치거나 그들에게 배우고 있든지 간에, 뇌가 '똑같은' 정보를 다르게, 그리고 흔히 더 효과적으로 처리한다는 것을 연구에서 입증한다. 우리는 본래 사회적 존재이고, 우리의 생각은 우리가 하는 일련의 생각 안에 다른 사람을 끌어들여서 이득을 본다.

지문 간단히 보기

정보의 '재사회화'는 꾸준히 필요
= 인간의 정보 처리(내면화된 대화)를 '실제적인 사회적 만남'으로 되돌리면 크게 이로움

↓

연구 증거: 사회적 만남 안에서는 같은 정보도 '다르게, 더 효율적으로' 처리 가능
= 타인을 우리 생각에 끌어들이면 이득이 따름

해설 우리의 사고 과정에 '타인을 끌어들이면' 같은 정보도 더 효과적으로 처리되는 등 이득이 있다는 내용이다. 따라서 주제로 가장 적절한 것은 ① '사회적 상호 작용을 통한 정보 처리의 중요성'이다.

오답풀이

보기 해석	선택률
② 신체 활동을 통해 사교 기술을 높이는 방법	8%
③ 인지 기능에 대한 주기적 평가의 필요성	8%
④ 성격 특성이 사회적 상호 작용에 미치는 영향	22%
⑤ 내면화된 사회적 통제의 한 형태인 사회화	16%

구문 [1행] Whenever **(it is)** possible, we should take measures to *re-socialize* the information [**(that)** we think about].
▶ 콤마 앞은 <대명사 주어+be동사>가 생략된 부사절 축약 구문이다. 복합관계부사 Whenever는 여기서 At any time when의 의미이다.
▶ [ ]은 목적격 관계대명사가 생략된 관계절로, the information을 꾸민다.

05 정답 ④ 93%

해석 위 그래프는 연령대별로 낮잠의 길이와 연간 낮잠 일수를 나타낸 것이다. 사람들이 나이가 들수록 낮잠의 길이는 계속해서 줄어들지만, 연간 낮잠 자는 일수는 그렇지 않다. 18~24세 집단은 낮잠 길이가 가장 길어서, 낮잠 길이가 가장 짧은 55세 이상 연령 집단보다 30분 이상 낮잠을 더 잔다. 연간 낮잠 자는 일수로 말하자면, 55세 이상 연령 집단이 135.7일로 가장 많은 반면, 25~34세 집단은 84.8일로 가장 적다. 35~44세 집단은 낮잠 길이에서 3위, 연간 낮잠을 자는 일수에서 2위(→ 3위)를 차지한다. 45~54세 집단의 낮잠 길이와 연간 낮잠 일수는 35~44세 집단보다 적다.

지문 간단히 보기

> 연령대별 낮잠 길이 및 연간 낮잠 일수
> ① 나이 들수록 낮잠 길이는 줄어들지만, 연간 낮잠 일수는 들쭉날쭉
> ② 길이: 18~24세 1위, 55+세 5위 / 격차 30+분
> ③ 일수: 55+세 135.7일(1위), 25~34세 84.8일(5위)
> ④ 35~44세: 길이 55분(3위), 일수 91.3일(**3위**)
> ⑤ 45~55세 길이, 일수 < 35~44세 길이, 일수

해설 도표에 따르면 35~44세 집단의 낮잠 일수는 91.3일인데, 이는 55세 이상 집단(135.7일), 18~24세 집단(93.1일)에 이어 3위이다. 따라서 도표와 일치하지 않는 것은 ④이다.

오답풀이

보기 해설	선택률
① ~ the nap length consistently decreases, but that is not the case with the number of nap days ~	0%
② The 18 to 24 age group, ~ the longest nap length, ~ the 55 and older age group, which has the shortest nap length.	2%
③ ~ the 55 and older age group has the most days, ~ whereas the 25 to 34 age group has the fewest days, ~	1%
⑤ ~ lower than those of the 35 to 44 age group.	1%

구문 [2행] **As** people get older, the nap length consistently decreases, ~
▶ 부사절 접속사 As가 '~함에 따라'라는 의미를 나타낸다.

06 정답 ④ 45%

해석 메타인지는 간단하게는 '생각에 관한 생각'이라는 뜻으로, 이것은 인간 두뇌와 다른 종의 두뇌 간의 주요한 차이점 중 하나이다. 우리가 통상적인 사고 과정 위에 있는 사다리 높은 곳에 서서 왜 우리가 지금 생각하는 대로 생각하는지 평가하는 능력은 진화론적으로 놀라운 일이다. 인간 두뇌에서 가장 최근에 발달한 부분인 전두엽 피질이 자기 성찰적이고 추상적인 사고를 가능하게 하기 때문에 우리는 이 능력을 갖고 있다. 우리는 우리가 우리 자신의 일부가 아닌 것처럼 사고할 수 있다. 영장류의 행동에 대한 연구는 우리의 가장 가까운 사촌인 침팬지조차도, (이들이 거울에 비친 모습을 다른 침팬지라고 생각하지 않고 자기 자신이라는 것을 알아보는 등 약간의 자기 성찰 능력을 지니고 있음에도) 이런 능력이 없다는 것을 보여준다. 그 능력은 양날의 검인데, 왜냐하면 그것은 우리가 지금 생각하는 것을 왜 생각하고 있는지 평가하게 해주는 한편, 쉽게 강박 관념이 될 수 있는 어려운 실존적 질문들 또한 우리가 접하게 하기 때문이다.

지문 간단히 보기

> 메타인지: '생각에 관해 생각하는' 인간만의 능력

> 메타인지의 바탕: 전두엽 피질(자기 성찰적, 추상적 사고 담당)
> → 자신을 '남처럼' 돌아볼 수 있음 (vs. 침팬지)

> (한편으로) 메타인지는 '양날의 검'이기도 함
> → 어려운 실존적 질문을 맞닥뜨리게 하기 때문

해설 ④가 포함된 문장에서 that절의 주어인 even our closest cousins 뒤로 동사가 필요하므로, ④에는 lacking 대신 lack을 써야 한다. 주어 뒤의 the chimpanzees는 주어와 동격을 이루는 삽입구이다.

오답풀이

보기 해설	선택률
① 주어인 Our ability를 꾸미는 to부정사구의 일부로, to stand와 병렬 연결된 것이다(to stand high ~ and (to) evaluate ~).	16%
② 뒤에 'the most recently developed part ~ enables ~'와 같이 <주어+동사>가 나오므로 접속사를 썼다.	10%
③ '우리 자신'이라는 의미의 재귀대명사이다.	10%
⑤ 앞에 선행사가 없고 뒤에 are thinking의 목적어가 없는 불완전한 절이 오므로 what을 적절히 썼다.	19%

구문 [1행] ~ it is one of the main distinctions between the human brain and **that** of other species.
▶ 여기서 that은 brain을 받는 지시대명사이다.

07 정답 ⑤ 24%

해석 문학은 그것이 독자에게 길러 주는 <u>개인적 몰입</u>으로 인해 언어 학습 과정에 유용할 수 있다. 핵심 언어 교육 자료는 언어가 규칙 기반 체계이자 사회의미론적 체계로서 어떻게 작용하는지에 집중해야 한다. 매우 흔히도, 학습 과정은 기본적으로 분석적이고 단편적이며 개성의 수준으로 보면 상당히 피상적이다. 상상력을 발휘해 문학에 몰입하는 것은 학습자들이 외국어 체계의 기계적인 측면 너머로 관심의 초점을 돌리게 해준다. 소설이나 희곡 또는 단편 소설이 일정 기간에 걸쳐 탐구되면, 그 결과로 독자는 텍스트 안에 '살기' 시작한다. (즉) 그 독자는 책에 빠져들게 된다. 개별 단어나 구절이 어떤 의미일 것인지 정확히 파악하는 것은 이야기의 전개를 따라가는 것보다 덜 중요해진다. 그 독자는 사건이 전개되면서 무슨 일이 벌어지는지 몹시 알고 싶어하며, 특정 인물에 친밀함을 느끼고 그들의 감정적 반응을 공유한다. 언어는 '투명해지고', 소설은 그 사람 전체를 그것만의 세계로 끌어들인다.

지문 간단히 보기

> 언어 교육에서 문학의 역할
> : 독자가 상상력을 동원하여 작품에 '몰입'하게 함으로써 언어의 기계적 측면 너머(= 사회의미론적 체계)에 관심을 갖게 함

> 작품을 일정 기간에 걸쳐 읽으며, 독자는 텍스트 안에 '살게' 됨
> - 개별 단어나 구절의 세세한 의미 파악보다는, 사건 흐름을 따라가는 것이 더 중요해짐
> - 특정 인물에 친밀함을 느끼고 감정을 공유함

> (결론) 언어가 '투명해짐' = '소설이 독자를 온전히 그 세계 안으로 끌어들임'
> ▶ **언어보다는, 이야기나 내용에 더 깊이 참여하고 몰입**

해설 문학은 독자가 텍스트 안에 '살게' 만드는, 즉 그 사람 전체를 작품의 세계 안으로 끌어들이는 힘이 있어 언어 학습에 도움이 될 수 있다는 것이 핵심 내용이다. 따라서 빈칸에는 ⑤ '개인적 몰입'이 들어가는 것이 가장 적절하다.

오답풀이

보기 해석	선택률
① 언어적 통찰력	20%
② 예술적 상상력	32%
③ 문학적 감수성	15%
④ 대안적 관점	9%

구문 [9행] Engaging imaginatively with literature **enables learners to shift** the focus of their attention beyond the more mechanical aspects of the foreign language system.
▶ 주어가 동명사구이므로 단수동사(enables)가 쓰였다.
▶ <enable+목적어+to부정사(~이 …할 수 있게 하다)>의 5형식 구조를 기억해 둔다.

08 정답 ② 34%

해석 헤겔의 철학에서는, 비록 보편자와 개별자 사이에 상호 작용과 상호 관계가 있기는 하지만, 보편자가 여전히 개별자보다 더 우위에 있다. 헤겔에게 개인은 '이성'의 관점에서는 구별되지 않는다. 헤겔은 <Philosophy of Right>에서 다음과 같이 특수성과 보편성을 강조한다. '사람은 별나게 행동하여 특수성을 보여준다. 이성적인 것은 모든 사람들이 다니는 고속도로 같은 것으로, 그 누구도 특별하게 두드러지지 않는다.' 여기서 헤겔은 개인이 행동의 관점에서는 서로 구별될 수 있지만 이성의 측면에서는 구별되지 않는다고 주장한다. 특수한 생각들은 존재하지만, 이것들은 결국 보편자로 귀착된다. 혹자는 헤겔이 아리스토텔레스처럼 개별자에만 초점을 둔 것 같다고 말할 수도 있지만 실제로 헤겔은 은근히 보편자가 근본적이라고 보는데, 반면 아리스토텔레스는 개별자를 제1의 실체로, 보편자를 제2의 실체로 여기며, 그렇게 해서 헤겔과는 달리 보편자가 개별자에 종속된다고 강조한다.

지문 간단히 보기

> 헤겔: '인간은 각자 행동을 달리하여 특수성을 드러내지만, 이성의 측면에서는 구별되지 않는다' ▶ **개별자 < 보편자**

> 헤겔 vs. 아리스토텔레스
> - 헤겔: 보편자를 근본으로 봄
> - 아리스토텔레스: 개별자를 근본으로 봄

해설 글에서 헤겔은 인간이 개별 행동의 측면에서는 구별될지라도 이성의 측면에서는 구별되지 않기에, 결국 '개별자가 보편자로 귀착된다'고 주장했다고 한다. '보편자를 근본으로 여겼다'는 마지막 문장의 진술에서 헤겔의 사상이 잘 드러난다. 따라서 빈칸에 들어갈 말로 가장 적절한 것은 ② '보편자가 여전히 개별자보다 더 우위에 있다'이다.

오답풀이

보기 해석	선택률
① 개인은 우주로부터 동떨어져 있다	16%
③ 보편적 진실은 개인 문제의 해결책이 될 수 없다	20%
④ 개인은 실제 그 자체로부터 보편적 원리를 추론할 수 없다	16%
⑤ 모든 개인은 자기만의 특수한 우주를 가져야 한다	14%

구문 [14행] **One might say** that Hegel seems to focus on the individual like Aristotle **but** in reality, **he** subtly **treats** the universal as fundamental whereas Aristotle considers **the individual as primary substance** and **universal as secondary substance** ~
▶ 'One might say ~'와 'he subtly treats ~'가 <A but B> 형태로 병렬 연결되었다.
▶ 밑줄 친 종속절은 <consider A as B(A를 B로 보다)> 구문이다. 2개의 <A as B>가 and 앞뒤로 병렬 연결되었다.

09 정답 ④ 78%

해석 식물은 동물보다 더 빨리 재해로부터 회복하는 경향이 있기 때문에 손상된 환경의 소생에 필수적이다. 왜 식물에게는 재해로부터 회복할 수 있는 이런 특별한 능력이 있을까? 대체로 그것은 식물이 동물과는 달리 생애 주기 내내 새로운 장기와 조직을 생성할 수 있기 때문이다. 이러한 능력은 식물의 분열 조직의 활동 덕분인데, (분열 조직이란) 특정 신호에 반응하여 새로운 세포 조직과 기관으로 분화할 수 있는, 뿌리와 싹에 있는 미분화 세포 조직 부위이다. 재해 시에 분열 조직이 손상되지 않으면, 식물은 회복해서 파괴되거나 척박한 환경을 궁극적으로 변화시킬 수 있다. 번개 맞은 나무가 오래된 상처에서 자라나는 새로운 가지를 형성할 때 비교적 더 작은 규모로 이러한 현상을 볼 수 있다. (식물은 숲과 초원의 형태로 물의 순환을 조절하고 대기의 화학적 구성을 조정한다.) 식물의 재생이나 재발아 외에, 교란된 지역은 재파종을 통해서도 회복할 수 있다.

지문 간단히 보기

식물의 회복 능력: 평생 조직을 생성할 수 있는 능력 덕분에 가능

↓

① 즉, 분열 조직의 활동 덕분
② 분열 조직에 손상 X → 식물의 힘으로 환경 재생 O
③ (예시) 번개 맞은 나무의 가지 재생

↓

⑤ 재생, 재발아 외에도, 재파종으로 환경 재생 O

해설 손상이나 재해로부터 회복해 환경 재생에 기여할 수 있는 식물의 능력에 관한 글인데, ④는 식물의 '회복력'과는 상관없이 물 순환이나 대기 구성 조정과 연관된 역할만을 언급한다. 따라서 전체 흐름과 관계없는 문장은 ④이다.

오답풀이

보기 해설	선택률
① 앞에서 언급한 '평생 새로운 조직 형성'이 '분열 조직 덕분에 가능하다'는 보충 설명이다.	7%
② '분열 조직'에 관한 내용이 이어진다. 분열 조직이 손상되지 않는 한 '재생이 계속된다'는 내용이므로 흐름상 자연스럽다.	4%
③ '나뭇가지'에 대한 언급이 갑작스러울 수도 있지만, 여기서 가지는 '번개로 입은 상처 이후에도 재생하는' 능력을 보여주는 예시이다.	12%
⑤ 재생과 더불어 '재파종'도 있다고 덧붙이며(In addition to) 글을 마무리하는 문장이다.	2%

구문 [14행] ~ when a tree **struck by lightning** forms <u>new branches</u> [that <u>grow</u> from the old scar].
▶ when절의 주어 a tree가 '번개를 맞는' 대상이므로 수동을 나타내는 과거분사로 수식했다. 동사는 forms이다.
▶ [ ]는 new branches를 꾸미는 주격 관계대명사절이다. 선행사가 복수명사이므로 that절의 동사가 복수형(grow)으로 수 일치되었다.

10 정답 ⑤ 30%

해석 과일 숙성 과정은 세포벽의 연화와 감미를 일으키고 색과 맛을 주는 화학 물질의 생산을 유발한다. 그 과정은 에틸렌이라는 식물 호르몬의 생산에 의해 유도된다.
(C) 재배자와 소매업자에게 있어 문제는 숙성 이후에 간혹 아주 빠르게 품질 저하와 부패가 뒤따라서 제품이 무가치해진다는 것이다. 그래서 토마토와 다른 과일은 보통 익지 않았을 때 수확되어 운송된다.
(B) 그러고 나서 일부 국가에서는 소비자에 판매하기 앞서 숙성을 유도할 목적으로 그것들에 에틸렌을 살포한다. 그러나 익기 전에 수확된 과일은 익은 상태로 식물에서 수확된 과일보다 맛이 덜하다. 따라서 생명공학자들은 과일의 숙성 및 연화 과정을 늦출 기회를 보았다.
(A) 만일 에틸렌 생산 혹은 에틸렌에 반응하는 과정을 방해하여 숙성이 늦춰질 수 있다면, 과일은 익어서 맛이 가득 들 때까지 식물에 남아 있어도 되겠지만, 슈퍼마켓 진열대에 도착할 때도 여전히 상태가 좋을 것이다.

지문 간단히 보기

과일 숙성을 유도하는 에틸렌 → (C) 문제 발생(품질 저하 및 부패)

↓

(C) 문제를 막기 위해 과일이 익기 전 수확
(B) '이후' 판매지에서 덜 익은 과일에 에틸렌을 뿌려 숙성 유도

↓

(B) 맛이 덜해지는 문제 발생 → 숙성 자체를 늦추려 함
(A) 에틸렌 작용을 방해하여 숙성이 늦춰지면 문제 해결

해설 과일 숙성 과정에서 에틸렌이 분비된다는 주어진 글 뒤로, (C)는 에틸렌이 작용하면 과일의 판매 가치가 떨어지기 때문에 과일이 익기 '전에' 수확하는 일이 흔하다고 설명한다. (B)는 '그 이후' 판매지에서 과일에 에틸렌을 뿌리기는 하지만, 익고 나서 땄을 때보다 맛이 덜하므로 숙성 자체를 늦출 기회를 보게 된다고 한다. (A)는 (B)에 이어 숙성 지연과 그 기대 효과를 언급하므로, ⑤ '(C)-(B)-(A)'의 순서가 옳다.

오답풀이

보기 해설	선택률
① 에틸렌을 막 소개한 주어진 글 뒤로 숙성 지연의 기대 효과를 말하는 (A)부터 오면 흐름상 어색하다. ripening, ethylene 등 겹치는 단어만 보고 고르지 않도록 한다.	7%
②, 문맥상 (B)의 then은 (C) 뒤에 이어져서 과일이 '수확되고	23%
③ 운송된 이후'를 가리켜야 자연스럽다.	23%
④ (A)에서는 과일이 it인데 (B) 첫 문장은 갑자기 they로 과일을 나타내므로 (A)-(B)의 연결은 자연스럽지 않다. (B)의 they는 문맥상 (C)의 Tomatoes and other fruits이다.	15%

구문 [A-1행] **If** ripening **could be slowed down** ~ fruit **could be left** on the plant ~ but **would still be** in good condition ~
▶ 현재 사실이 '아닌' 내용을 가정하는 가정법 과거 구문이다. 주절과 종속절에 모두 <조동사 과거형+동사원형>이 사용되었다.

11 정답 ④ 52%

해석 책, 또는 글로 된 어떤 메시지에서든 거기서 나온 오타는 일반적으로 내용에 부정적인 영향을 미치며, 때로는 (문자 그대로) 치명적이다. 예를 들어, 쉼표 위치 오류가 생사를 가르는 문제일 수 있다. 마찬가지로 대부분의 돌연변이는 그것이 발생한 유기체에 해로운 결과를 가져오는데, 그것들이 생식 적합성을 감소시킨다는 뜻이다. 하지만, 때때로 유기체의 적합성을 높이는 어떤 돌연변이가 발생할 수 있는데, 이는 초판의 글을 우연히 복사하지 못한 것이 더 정확하거나 최신인 정보를 제공할 수도 있는 것과 꼭 마찬가지이다. 그러나 논거의 다음 단계에서는 그 유사성이 깨진다. 유리한 돌연변이는 다음 세대에 더 많이 나타날 것인데, 그 돌연변이가 발생한 유기체가 더 많은 자손을 낳을 것이고 그 돌연변이가 자손에게 전달되기 때문에 그렇다. 대조적으로, 초판의 오류를 우연히 바로잡은 책이 더 잘 팔리게 될 메커니즘은 존재하지 않는다.

지문 간단히 보기

책이나 글의 오타 = 유기체의 돌연변이 = 적합성에 '해'

하지만, 간혹 적합성을 '높이는' 돌연변이 존재 = 오타도 마찬가지

하지만, '이런 유사성'은 더 나아가면 깨짐
: 적합성을 높이는 돌연변이는 다음 세대로 잘 퍼짐
  vs. 우연히 오류가 바로잡힌 책이 반드시 잘 팔리지는 X

해설 ④ 앞은 책이나 글의 오타가 생체 돌연변이와 '유사성(just as)'을 띤다는 내용인데, ④ 뒤의 두 문장은 오타와 돌연변이의 '차이(By contrast)'를 지적하므로 글의 흐름이 어색하게 끊긴다. 사이에 흐름을 적절히 전환해줄 연결어가 필요하므로, however를 포함한 주어진 문장을 ④에 넣어야 한다.

오답풀이

보기 해설	선택률
① 앞에 언급된 '오타'의 예시(for instance)가 뒤에 이어진다.	2%
② 오타와 돌연변이의 유사성을 중심으로 비교하는 흐름이 Similarly로 자연스럽게 이어진다.	8%
③ however가 흐름 전환을 유도한다. 앞에서 돌연변이와 오타는 '부정적 영향'을 끼친다고 했는데, 뒤에는 '유용할' 수도 있다는 상반된 설명이 잘 연결된다.	11%
⑤ By contrast 앞뒤로 '유용한 돌연변이는 잘 퍼진다 vs. 오류가 우연히 고쳐진 책이 꼭 더 잘 팔리지는 않는다'는 내용이 적절히 대비된다.	27%

구문 [19행] ~ no mechanism **by which** a book [that accidentally corrects the mistakes of the first edition] will tend to sell better.
▶ <전치사+관계대명사> 형태의 by which로 시작하는 관계절이 mechanism을 꾸민다.
▶ [ ]은 by which절의 주어 a book을 꾸미며, 뒤에는 by which절의 동사구가 이어진다.

12 정답 ① 55%

해석 디자인을 통해 개인의 개성을 보여주기 위한 노력은 놀라운 일이 아니다. 디자이너 대부분은 개인으로 일하도록 교육받고, 디자인 문헌은 '(한 명의) 디자이너'에 대한 무수히 많은 언급을 담고 있다. 개인의 재능은 의심의 여지 없이 일부 상품 범주에서 절대적으로 필수인데, 가구, 조명, 소형 가전, 그리고 가정용품 등 기술적 복잡성의 정도가 낮은 비교적 작은 물건들에서 특히 그렇다. 하지만, 더 큰 규모의 프로젝트에서, 심지어 강한 개성이 강력한 힘을 발휘하는 곳에서조차, 상당수의 디자이너가 하나의 콘셉트 실현에 참여한다는 사실이 쉽게 간과될 수 있다. 그러므로 개성에 대한 강조는 문제가 있는데, 많은 성공한 디자이너 '유명 인사들'은 실제로 디자인을 하기보다는 창작 관리자 역할을 더 많이 한다. 진정 혼자 일하는 디자이너와 집단을 이뤄 일하는 디자이너는 구분되어야 한다. 후자의 경우, 관리 조직과 과정들이 디자이너들의 창의성 못지않게 똑같이 유의미할 수 있다.
→ 프로젝트의 (A)크기에 따라 팀 기반 작업 환경을 (B)조직화하는 디자이너의 능력이 개인적 특성 못지않게 중요할 수 있다.

지문 간단히 보기

디자인 작업은 보통 개성, 개인적 작업과 결부됨

하지만, '큰' 프로젝트: 여러 디자이너가 한 작업에 참여
= 성공한 디자이너들은 디자인 실무보다 관리를 더 많이 함

(결론) 개성에 대한 강조가 능사가 아니고, 관리 능력도 중요

해설 흔히 디자이너들은 개성이 중요하고 혼자 일하는 직업으로 여겨지지만, 실상 큰 규모의 프로젝트에서는 디자이너들이 디자인 실무보다도 관리자 역할을 담당해야 할 때가 많다는 내용이다. 따라서 요약문의 빈칸에는 ① '크기 - 조직화하는'이 들어가야 한다.

오답풀이

보기 해석	선택률
② 비용 - 체계화하는	8%
③ 크기 - 확인하는	25%
④ 비용 - 혁신하는	9%
⑤ 목표 - 조사하는	3%

구문 [12행] ~ the fact **that substantial numbers of designers are employed in implementing a concept** can easily be overlooked.
▶ 주어인 the fact의 내용을 동격의 that절이 설명한다. 동사는 can easily be overlooked이다.

13~14 정답 ⑤ 45% / ⑤ 40% 2021 10월 41~42번

 여러 면에서 뉴스 출처의 확산은 놀라운 것이었다. 대중은 이제 사실을 확인하고 다양한 관점을 배울 수 있는 여러 방법을 가지고 있다. 이론적으로, 이러한 접근은 서로 의미 있는 토론을 할 수 있는 능력과 정보에 입각한 의견을 형성하는 능력을 향상시킬 것이다. 하지만 항상 그렇지는 않다.

가장 중요한 발전 중 하나는 미디어가 라스베이거스 뷔페처럼 되어서, 우리는 너무 많은 선택을 가진다는 것이다. 개발자가 알고리즘을 사용하여 이상적인 콘텐츠를 제공하는 틈새 미디어와 개인 맞춤형 소셜 미디어 네트워크를 포함해서 여러분이 온갖 정보의 선택 사항을 검토할 때, 그 모든 것을 탐색하기에는 그야말로 시간이 부족하다. 이런 공간에서는 '반향실'에 갇히기 쉬운데, 여기서는 새롭거나 상반된 내용을 받아들여 섞이게 하지 않아서 여러분의 의견이 남들에 의해 강화되며, 이것은 공론화를 제한하고 극단으로 이어질 수 있다.

이것은 정치 영역에서 아주 뚜렷하다. 전통적으로 대중 매체는 어떤 상황이나 후보자에 대한 사실의 공정한 보도에 (채널을) 맞추고 듣는 곳이었으며, 의견을 형성하고 결정을 내리는 데 필요한 결정적 정보에 대한 동등한 접근 권한을 모두에게 주었다. 케이블 뉴스 네트워크와 편파적인 온라인 출처는 시청자가 정확하고 완전한 정보에 접근할 수 있는 능력을 높일(→ 제한할) 수 있다. 어떤 경우에는, 시청자들이 오로지 자기 이상에 부합하는 콘텐츠에만 관심을 두는 의식적인 결정을 했다.

지문 간단히 보기

> 뉴스 출처 확산에 대한 이론과 실제
> : 토론, 균형 잡힌 여론 촉진 vs. 늘 그렇지는 않음

⬇

> 미디어 = 선택권이 너무 많은 '뷔페'
> → 정보 탐색 시간↓, 새롭고 다른 정보 수용↓
> → 개인의 의견이 타인에 의해 강화되고 극단화되는 경향

⬇

> (예시) 정치 뉴스 출처 확산(케이블 및 기타 편파적 출처)
> ▶ **정확하고 완전한 정보에 대한 접근을 오히려 '제한'**

 [17행] In this space it is easy to become trapped in an *echo chamber*, **where** your own opinions are reinforced by others without introducing new or conflicting content into the mix, **which** restricts public discourse and can lead to extremes.
▶ 관계부사 where는 *echo chamber*를 선행사로 받고, 계속적 용법의 which는 where절의 내용을 선행사로 받는다.

13

 뉴스 출처가 다양해지면서 범람하는 정보를 검토할 시간이 부족한 개인들은 자기 이상에 맞는 정보만 선택적으로 취하며 극단적인 견해에 갇히기 쉬워졌다는 내용이다. 따라서 제목으로 ⑤ '미디어 정보 범람: 균형 잡힌 시각에 대한 장벽'이 가장 적절하다.

오답풀이

보기 해석	선택률
① 온라인 미디어에 이상적인 콘텐츠를 개발하려는 노력	16%
② 케이블 뉴스 네트워크: 공공 담론의 장	14%
③ 미디어 콘텐츠를 정치적 데이터에 활용하는 기법	12%
④ (여러) 미디어 플랫폼 사이의 품질 경쟁 분석	9%

14

 사람들이 자기 이상에 맞는 콘텐츠에만 관심을 둔다는 마지막 문장의 내용으로 보아, ⑤ (e)에는 완전한 정보에 접근하는 능력이 '제한된다'는 설명이 적합하다. 따라서 enhance 대신 limit을 써야 옳다.

오답풀이

보기 해석	선택률
① differing(다양한)	6%
② explore(탐색하다)	7%
③ extremes(극단)	24%
④ equal(동등한)	19%

STEP PLUS+ 수능 기출 마무리 복습

단어 TEST

02 이면, 뒷면 **03** 직관에 어긋나는 **04** 동조하다 **05** 양날의 검 **06** 상상력을 발휘하여, 창의적으로 **07** 전개되다, 펼쳐지다 **08** ~에 종속되는, 부차적인 **09** 재생 **10** ~에 영향을 미치다 **11** 생식의, 재생의 **12** 제한하다

구문 TEST

14 The professor (who[that] is) lecturing today **15** As a boy who[that] grew up in a small town **16** through which we understand differences **17** that[which] increases the fitness of the organism **18** that[which] affects our travel plans

01　정답 ⑤　87%　　　　　　　　　2022 10월 18번

해석　독자 여러분께,
여러분이 제 책에서 보셨듯이, 저는 저에게 이야기와 조언을 보내 주신 분들로부터 많은 것을 배웠습니다. 그 작업을 계속 이어 나갑시다. 재난에 대한 여러분의 경험과, 재난을 피하면서 배우신 점을 제게 이메일로 보내고 싶으시다면, nodisaster@smail.com으로 보내 주십시오. 알려드리고 싶은 것은, 여러분이 이야기를 보내주시면 제가 쓰는 책에 그것을 사용해도 된다고 허락해주시는 거라는 점입니다. 하지만 여러분이 명시적인 허락을 주시지 않는 한, 성함은 사용하지 않겠다고 약속드립니다. 고맙습니다.
Robert Brown 드림

지문 간단히 보기

> 필자 = 작가: 책을 위한 이야기와 조언을 구하며 많이 배움

↓

> 요청: "재난에 대한 경험과 교훈을 이메일로 보내달라"

↓

> 주의사항: 이야기를 보내주면 책에 써도 된다는 '허락'으로 간주
> 　　　　　(단, 이름은 별도 허락 시에만 사용)

해설　재난을 겪었거나 피한 경험에 관해 이메일로 알려달라는 요청의 글이므로, 목적으로 가장 적절한 것은 ⑤ '재난과 관련한 경험담을 보내 줄 것을 요청하려고'이다.

오답풀이

보기 해설	선택률
① '출판 기념회'는 언급되지 않았다.	1%
② 다른 사람의 저작물 사용에 관한 내용이 아니다. '허락'만 보고 고르지 않도록 한다.	9%
③ 'please send it ~'을 항의로 보는 것은 부적절하다.	1%
④ 재난 '대처 요령'에 관해 언급되지 않았다.	0%

구문　[10행] But I promise **not to use** your name **unless** you give me explicit permission.
▶ to부정사의 부정은 <not to+동사원형>으로 나타낸다.
▶ unless는 'if ~ not'으로 바꿀 수 있는 조건 접속사이다. 즉 '~ if you don't give me explicit permission.'으로 바꿀 수 있다.

02　정답 ①　44%　　　　　　　　　2021 3월 22번

해석　매체로 전달되는 안건이 정치에 미치는 영향에 관한 수많은 연구에도 불구하고, 대부분의 연구는 마치 언론이 말만 전달한다는 듯이 글만 검토한다. 이 연구들은 기자들, 분석가들, 논평가들이 어떻게 후보자들을 '말로' 묘사하고 비판하는지를 살펴보았다. 하지만 그것들은 영향력의 또 다른 중대 원천, 즉 시각 자료를 흔히 무시한다. 몇몇 커뮤니케이션 학자들이 말했듯이, "이야기는 흔히 시각적인 내용과 언어적인 내용의 복잡한 결합이며, 매우 흔히도 시각 정보는 너무 강력해서 언어적인 내용을 압도할 정도다." 시각 자료의 영향력을 알아보기 위해 그것들을 다루는 어려움은 다면적이다. 시각 자료를 수집하고 코딩하는 것, 그리고 영향력을 이미지의 특정 부분 탓으로 돌리기 어려운 것은 분명 진정한 학자들로 하여금 주저하게 만들었다. 그러나 시각 자료가 사람들의 인식에 미치는 잠재적인 영향력은 그야말로 너무 중요해 무시할 수 없다. 또한, 시각 자료와 글을 동시에 이해하는 것의 중요성은 과소평가되면 안 된다.

지문 간단히 보기

> 정치 보도 검토 시 '언어 내용'만 살피는 경우가 흔함

↓

> 하지만, 시각 자료도 몹시 중요함
> : '영향력이 너무 강력한 나머지 언어를 압도할 정도'

↓

> 시각 자료를 다루는 데 어려움이 있더라도, 글과 동시에 연구 필요

해설　정치 보도 자료를 분석할 때 언어 내용뿐 아니라 시각 자료가 매우 중요하다는 내용이다. 따라서 요지로 가장 적절한 것은 ① '시각 자료는 정치 관련 보도 자료 연구의 중요한 대상이다.'이다.

오답풀이

보기 해설	선택률
② '의견 검증'이 주된 쟁점이 아니다.	3%
③ '뉴스 편성'에 관해서 언급되지 않았다.	2%
④ 시각 자료는 '무시 못할 정도로 중요하다'는 글의 마지막 두 문장 내용과 상충한다.	40%
⑤ '언론인의 정치 편향'에 관해 언급되지 않았다.	3%

구문　[16행] But the potential impact of visuals on people's perceptions is simply **too important to ignore**.
▶ <too ~ to …(너무 ~해서 …할 수 없다)> 구문이다.

03 정답 ③ 38%

해석 20세기에 접어들면서, 자연 과학에서 훈련받은 인류학자들은 인류에 대한 과학(인류학)이 어떤 모습이어야 하며, 사회 과학자들은 문화 집단 연구를 어떻게 시작해야 하는지를 다시 생각하기 시작했다. 그런 인류학자들 중 일부는 적어도 연구되는 사람들을 실제 관찰하고 이들과 대화하는 데 상당한 시간을 써야 한다고 주장했다. Franz Boas 와 Alfred Cort Haddon 등 초기 민족지학자들은 보통 연구 대상인 사람들이 살던 외딴 지역으로 가서 몇 주에서 몇 달을 거기서 보냈다. 그들은 (식민지 관료, 선교사 혹은 사업가 등) 주민들과 현지에 친숙한 서양인 호스트를 찾아서 이들을 통해 숙박 시설을 구했다. 가끔 그들이 정말이지 가이드 없이 그 지역 사회를 탐험하기도 했지만, 일반적으로 그들은 현지인들과 상당한 시간을 보내지는 않았다. 그리하여 그들의 관찰은 주로 그들의 '베란다'에서 행해졌다.

지문 간단히 보기

> 민족 집단 연구에서 대상들에 관한 '실제 관찰'을 중시해야 한다는 주장이 나오기 시작함

> 초기 민족지학자들: 연구할 지역에 직접 가서 몇 주~몇 달을 보냈으나, 정작 현지인과 많은 시간을 보내지는 않았음

> 즉, 초기 민족지학자들의 연구 방식 = '자기 베란다에서' 연구
> **▶ 연구 대상인 현지인과의 직접 소통이 적었던 연구**

해설 글에 따르면 초기 민속지학자들은 연구 대상이 사는 지역에 직접 가서 수주 또는 수개월을 지내기도 했으나, 막상 현지인과 많은 시간을 보내지는 않았다고 한다. 따라서 이들의 연구 방식을 비유한 밑줄 부분은 ③ '연구 대상인 사람들과 거의 직접 접촉하지 않으면서'의 의미로 볼 수 있다.

오답풀이

보기 해석	선택률
① 원주민과 장기적 관계를 구축하기 위해 노력하면서	15%
② 자연 과학자들과의 공동 연구에 참여하면서	15%
④ 지역 사회에 있는 서양인 호스트와 적극 협력하면서	23%
⑤ 조사 대상인 원주민 문화에 관한 더 넓은 시각을 갖고자 애쓰면서	11%

구문 [1행] ~ anthropologists <u>trained in the natural sciences</u> began to reimagine [**what** a science of humanity should look like] and [**how** social scientists ought to go about studying cultural groups].
▶ 밑줄 부분은 주어 anthropologists를 꾸미는 과거분사구이다. 문장의 동사는 began이다.
▶ what과 how가 각각 이끄는 의문사절이 <A and B> 형태로 연결되어 to reimagine의 목적어 역할을 한다.

04 정답 ⑤ 49%

해석 무급 노동은 '향상된 경제적 가치를 지니는 재화와 서비스를 만들고자 노동을 원료와 결합하는 활동이기' 때문에, 이것은 일이 '맞다'고 주장하려는 시도가 최근에 있었다. Duncan Ironmonger와 같은 경제학자들은 자원봉사의 '경제적' 가치가 계산될 수 있도록 봉사에 금전적 가치를 귀속시키고자 했다. 하지만 그럼에도 불구하고, 무급 노동과 자원봉사는 여전히 우리 자본주의 체제의 규정된 경제적 틀 밖에 있는데, 자본주의가 경쟁과 재정적 보상을 그 초석으로 삼는 데 반해 자원봉사는 그렇지 않기 때문이다. 그렇긴 해도, 자원봉사는 호주 경제에 연간 420억 달러 가량 기여한다고 추정되었다. 비록 우리 경제 구조를 지탱하고 사회적 자본을 증가시키는 데 있어 자원봉사의 재정적 중요성을 정량화하고 기술하려는 시도가 계속 이루어지고 있지만, 이것은 느리게 진행되고 있다. 그리고 자원봉사가 GDP 밖에 (계속) 남아 있는 동안에는 그것의 진정한 가치와 중요성이 무시된다. 정부는 자원봉사의 중요성에 대해 입에 발린 말을 계속 내놓지만, 결국에는 그것을 공식적으로 인정하지 않는다.

지문 간단히 보기

> '무급 노동, 자원봉사 = 일'로 보려는 시도가 이뤄짐

> 하지만, 여전히 경제적 틀 '밖'에 있는 상황
> = 무급 노동과 봉사의 가치와 중요성이 무시되는 중
> = 정부가 공식적으로 (경제적 가치를) 인정하지 않는 중

해설 자원봉사의 경제적 중요성에 주목하려는 시도가 계속 있었으나 아직 별다른 진전이 없다는 내용이므로, ⑤ '자원봉사의 경제적 의의에 대한 인정 부족'이 주제로 가장 적절하다.

오답풀이

보기 해석	선택률
① 자원봉사를 사업 전략으로 이용하려는 노력	9%
② 자원봉사를 노동과 동일시하는 잘못된 견해	15%
③ 자본주의 체제 이해에 대한 장애물	8%
④ 자원봉사자들을 공공 서비스 안에 포함하려는 정부의 노력	16%

구문 [7행] ~ capitalism <u>has competition and financial reward as its cornerstones</u> and volunteering **does not**.
▶ 대동사 does not은 does not have competition and financial reward as its cornerstones의 의미이다.

05 정답 ③ 94% 2021 6월 26번

해석 전직 체코 육상 선수 Emil Zátopek은 역대 가장 위대한 장거리 달리기 선수 중 한 명이라고 여겨진다. 그는 또한 독특한 달리기 스타일로도 유명했다. 신발 공장에서 일하고 있던 시절 그는 1,500미터 경주에 참가해서 2등을 했다. 그 일 이후로 그는 달리기에 더 진지한 흥미를 느끼게 되어 그것에 전념했다. 1952년 헬싱키 올림픽 대회에서 그는 5,000미터, 1만 미터, 마라톤 종목에서 세 개의 금메달을 따고, 각 종목에서 올림픽 기록을 깼다. 그는 Dana Zátopková와 결혼했는데, 그녀 또한 올림픽 금메달리스트였다. Zátopek은 또한 다정한 성격으로 유명했다. 1966년에, Zátopek은 올림픽 금메달을 딴 적이 없었던 호주의 위대한 달리기 선수 Ron Clarke를 프라하에서 열린 체전에 초대했다. 체전 이후 그는 Clarke에게 자신의 금메달 중 하나를 선물로 주었다.

지문 간단히 보기

> Emil Zátopek의 생애
> ① 독특한 달리기 스타일로 유명
> ② 신발 공장 재직 당시 1,500미터 경주에서 2등
> ③ 헬싱키 올림픽에서 3종목 금메달 & 기록 경신
> ④ 올림픽 금메달리스트인 Dana Zátopková와 결혼
> ⑤ 프라하 체전 때 금메달 중 하나를 Ron Clarke에게 선물

해설 '~ breaking Olympic records in each.'에 따르면, Emil Zátopek은 헬싱키 올림픽 당시 3개 종목에서 금메달을 따고 올림픽 기록도 깼다고 하므로, 내용과 일치하지 않는 것은 ③ '1952년 Helsinki 올림픽에서 올림픽 기록을 깨지 못했다.'이다.

오답풀이

	보기 해설	선택률
①	~ famous for his distinctive running style.	1%
②	While working in a shoe factory, ~	1%
④	He was married to Dana Zátopková, ~ an Olympic gold medalist, too.	1%
⑤	~ he gave Clarke one of his gold medals as a gift.	1%

구문 [11행] He was married to Dana Zátopková, **who** was an Olympic gold medalist, too.
▶ who는 Dana Zátopková를 설명하는 계속적 용법의 관계대명사이다.

06 정답 ② 49% 2021 10월 29번

해석 사전적 정의에 따르면, 찬가(讚歌)는 흔히 국가에 대한 충성의 노래이자 '성스러운 음악'인데, 두 가지 정의 모두 스포츠 상황에 적용될 수 있다. 이 장르는 축구에서 독점적이지는 않을지라도 가장 두드러지게 나타나며, 유행가가 구단과 밀접한 연관을 갖게 되고 팬들에 의해 열광적으로 채택되는 많은 사례를 만들어 냈다. 나아가 그것들은 흔히 충성과 정체성의 자발적인 표현으로, Desmond Morris에 따르면 '지역 예술 형태에 근접하는 어떤 것의 수준에 도달했다'. 이런 스포츠 노래들의 강력한 매력 요소는 '팬들이 참여할 수 있는, 기억에 잘 남고 부르기 쉬운 합창'을 특징으로 한다는 것이다. 이것은 팬들의 존재를 더 확실하게 만들기 때문에, 팀의 (경기) 수행에 아주 중요한 부분이다. 이러한 형태의 대중문화는 '품위 있는 미적 거리와 통제'를 유지하는 경향이 있는 지배적인 문화와는 달리, 즐거움과 감정적 과잉을 보여 준다고 말할 수 있다.

지문 간단히 보기

> '찬가': 충성의 노래이자 성스러운 음악 → 스포츠에도 적용(특히 축구)

> 스포츠 찬가의 특성
> - 충성과 정체성의 자발적 표현
> - 외우기 쉽고, 따라 부르기 쉬움
> - 팬들의 존재감을 강화해서 선수들의 경기력에도 영향
> - 즐거움과 감정 과잉을 보여줌

해설 ②가 포함된 문장의 'and,' 뒤를 보면 이미 동사(have reached)가 있으므로 ②는 something을 꾸미는 수식어 자리이다. something은 지역 예술 형태에 '접근하는' 주체이므로, 능동을 나타내는 현재분사로 수식해야 어법상 옳다. 따라서 ②에는 approached 대신 approaching을 써야 한다.

오답풀이

	보기 해설	선택률
①	관계부사 where 뒤에 완전한 절이 왔다.	15%
③	단수 주어(A strong element)에 맞춰 is를 알맞게 썼다.	8%
④	이유를 나타내는 접속사 as이다.	12%
⑤	<be said to-V(~라고 한다)> 구문이다. <be said to have p.p.(~했다고 한다)>와 시점 차이를 구별해 둔다.	13%

구문 [17행] **This form of popular culture can be said to display ~**
▶ 본래 이 문장은 가주어-진주어 구조의 'It can be said that this form of popular culture displays ~'이다. 여기서 진주어인 that절의 주어를 문장 전체의 주어로 올리고, that절의 동사를 to부정사로 바꾸어 문장구조를 간단하게 만들었다.

07 정답 ② 27% 2022학년도 수능 31번

해석 유머는 실제적인 이탈뿐만 아니라 인식의 이탈을 포함한다. 어떤 것이 재미있는 한, 우리는 그것이 진짜인지 허구인지, 진실인지 거짓인지에 관해서는 당장 관심을 두지 않는다. 이것이 우리가 재미있는 이야기를 하는 사람들에게 상당한 여지를 주는 이유이다. 만약 그들이 상황의 어리석음을 과장하거나 심지어 몇 가지 세부 사항을 꾸며서라도 추가적인 웃음을 얻고 있다면, 우리는 그들에게 일종의 시적 허용인 희극적 허용을 기꺼이 허락한다. 실제로, 재미있는 이야기를 듣다가 말하는 사람을 고쳐주려고 하는 사람은—'아냐, 그는 스파게티를 키보드와 모니터에 쏟은 게 아니고 키보드에만 쏟았어.'라면서—아마 다른 청자들로부터 방해하지 말라는 말을 들을 것이다. 유머를 만드는 사람은 생각이 가져올 재미를 위해서 사람들의 머릿속에 그 생각을 집어넣고 있는 것이지, 정확한 정보를 제공하기 위해서가 아니다.

지문 간단히 보기

유머에서 일어나는 '인식의 이탈'
= 어떤 것이 웃기면, 내용의 '진위'는 가리지 않음

↓

즉, 약간의 과장이나 허구가 있어도 OK(=희극적 허용)

↓

사실을 바로잡으려는 노력은 오히려 '방해'로 간주됨

↓

유머의 목적: 재미있는 생각 공유 ▶ **정확한 정보 제공 X**

해설 글에 따르면, 사람들은 유머를 들을 때 정보가 '진실인지 거짓인지'에는 관심을 두지 않으며, 이에 따라 정보를 약간 과장하거나 꾸며내는 것도 허용된다고 한다. 즉, '정확한' 정보를 제공하는 것보다도 재미가 중요하다는 내용이므로, 빈칸에는 ② '정확한'을 넣어야 적절하다. 빈칸이 유머의 목적이 '아닌' 것을 말하므로 주제와 반대되는 키워드가 정답임에 유의한다.

오답풀이

보기 해석	선택률
① 자세한	50%
③ 유용한	10%
④ 부가적인	6%
⑤ 대체의	5%

구문 [10행] Indeed, **someone** listening to a funny story [who tries to correct the teller] ~ will probably **be told** by the other listeners **to stop** interrupting.
▶ 주어 someone은 밑줄 친 현재분사구와 주격 관계대명사절 [ ]의 수식을 받는다. 주어를 꾸미는 현재분사구로 인해 선행사와 관계절의 거리가 멀어졌다.
▶ <be told+to부정사(~하라는 말을 듣다)> 구문이다. <tell+목적어+to부정사(~에게 …하라고 말하다)>의 5형식 구조를 수동태로 바꾼 것이다.

08 정답 ⑤ 17% 2023학년도 수능 34번

해석 우리는 우리의 의식을 현재, 과거, 미래로 분리하는 것이 허구이자 희한하게도 자기 지시적인 틀이기도 하다는 것을 이해한다. 여러분의 현재는 여러분 어머니의 미래의 일부였고, 여러분 자녀의 과거는 여러분의 현재의 일부일 것이다. 시간에 대한 우리의 의식을 이런 전통적인 방식으로 구조화하는 것에는 일반적으로 틀린 게 없고, 이것은 흔히 충분히 효과적이다. 그러나 기후 변화의 경우, 시간을 과거, 현재, 미래로 분명하게 구분하는 것은 심하게 오해의 소지가 있으며, 가장 중요하게는 지금 살아 있는 우리들의 책임 범위를 시야에서 가려왔다. 시간에 대한 우리의 의식을 좁히는 것은 우리 삶이 사실은 깊이 뒤얽혀 있는 과거 및 미래의 발전에 대한 책임에서 우리를 단절시키는 길을 닦는다. 기후의 경우, 우리가 사실을 직면하면서도 책임을 부인한다는 것이 문제가 아니다. (문제는) 시간을 나눔으로써 현실이 시야에서 흐릿해지고, 그리하여 과거와 현재의 책임에 관한 질문들이 자연스럽게 생겨나지 않는다는 것이다.

지문 간단히 보기

시간에 관한 전통적 인식: 과거, 현재, 미래를 나누어 생각

↓

기후 문제에 있어서는, 시간을 나누면 '오해의 소지가 생김'
= 우리의 책임 범위를 '시야에서 가림'
= 우리를 과거, 미래에 대한 책임으로부터 '단절시킴'
▶ **책임을 '보고도 못 본 척'하게 된다기보다는, 아예 보지 못하게 되는 것이 문제**

해설 시간을 과거, 현재, 미래로 나누면 과거나 미래에 대한 책임 의식이 '시야에서 흐려져' 문제라는 내용인데, 빈칸 부분은 문제가 '아닌' 점에 관한 설명이다. 즉 '현실 자체를 모른다기보다도' 현실을 못 보게 되어 문제라는 의미를 완성하는 선택지가 적절하다. 따라서 정답은 ⑤ '우리가 사실을 직면하면서도 책임을 부인한다'이다.

오답풀이

보기 해석	선택률
① 우리의 모든 노력이 효과가 있다고 밝혀지고 그리하여 장려된다	22%
② 충분한 과학적 증거가 우리에게 제공되었다	27%
③ 미래의 우려가 현재의 필요보다 더욱 긴급하다	19%
④ 우리 조상들이 (우리와는) 다른 시간적 틀을 유지했다	16%

구문 [8행] ~ **has,** most importantly, **hidden** from view **the extent of the responsibility of those of us alive now.**
▶ has hidden의 목적어가 길어서 문장 맨 뒤로 보내고, 짧은 전치사구인 from view를 목적어보다 먼저 썼다.

09 정답 ③ 78%

해석 배우, 가수, 정치가, 그리고 수없이 많은 다른 사람들이 사용된 단어의 단순한 해독을 넘어서는 의사소통 수단으로서 사람 목소리의 힘을 인정한다. 따라서 여러분의 목소리를 통제하고 다양한 목적을 위해 사용하는 법을 배우는 것은 경력 초기의 교사로서 개발해야 할 가장 중요한 기술 중 하나이다. 여러분이 더 자신 있게 수업할수록, 더 긍정적인 수업 반응이 나올 확률이 더 크다. (멀리까지 들리도록) 목소리를 크게 낼 수 있는 것이 학교에서 일할 때 매우 유용할 때가 있으며, 시끄러운 교실, 급식실 또는 운동장을 (목소리로) 가를 수 있음을 아는 것은 갖춰두면 매우 좋은 능력이다. (학교 내의 심각한 소음 문제에 대처하려면 학생, 학부모, 그리고 교사가 함께 해결책을 찾아야 한다.) 하지만 항상 나는 가장 큰 목소리는 지극히 드물게 쓰고 소리 치는 것은 최대한 피해야 한다고 조언하고자 한다. 조용하고도 권위 있고 침착한 어조는 약간 당황한 고함보다 훨씬 더 큰 효과를 지닌다.

지문 간단히 보기

> 교사는 자신의 목소리를 목적에 맞게 사용할 수 있어야 함

↓

> ① 수업 때는 자신 있는 목소리가 좋음
> ② 교실, 급식실, 운동장 등 큰 목소리가 유리한 상황들이 있음

↓

> ④ 하지만, 큰 목소리를 가급적 드물게 쓸 것을 권장
> ⑤ 조용하고 침착한 어조가 더 큰 효과를 낼 때도 있음

해설 교사는 자신의 목소리를 상황에 맞게 잘 이용해야 한다는 내용이다. 하지만 ③은 소음 문제 대처를 위해 학생, 학부모, 교사 등 여러 당사자끼리의 협력이 필요하다는 내용이므로 전체 흐름과 무관하다.

오답풀이

보기 해설	선택률
① 교사는 목적에 맞게 목소리를 써야 한다는 주제문 뒤로, '큰 목소리'를 써서 좋을 때(수업)를 예로 들고 있다.	2%
② ①과 마찬가지로 '큰 목소리를 써서 유리한 상황'을 언급하는 문장이다.	4%
④ ②와 ④가 However 앞뒤로 '큰 목소리를 써서 유리할 때가 있다 vs. 큰 목소리는 가급적 덜 써야 좋다'로 적절히 대비된다.	11%
⑤ ④와 같은 맥락의 부연 설명이다. 큰 목소리를 덜 써야 좋다는 말은 곧 '조용한 목소리가 더 효과 있을 때가 있다'는 말과 같다.	2%

구문 [7행] **The more confidently** you give instructions, **the higher** the chance of a positive class response **(is)**.
▶ <the+비교급 ~, the+비교급 …(~할수록 더 …하다)> 구문이다. 문장 마지막에 be동사가 생략되었다.

10 정답 ⑤ 47%

해석 계약 당사자가 계약 위반 시 가치가 떨어질 수 있는 평판 자본을 키워둔 경우라면, 시장 규제 집행 가능성은 더욱 크다. **(C)** 농부와 지주는 높은 수확량을 생산하고 지속적으로 자기 일(역할)을 잘하는 모습을 보여주면서 정직함과 공정함에 대한 평판을 키운다. 작고 긴밀한 농업 공동체에서 평판은 잘 알려져 있다. **(B)** 시간이 흐르며, 지주는 보고된 생산량, 토양의 전반적 품질, 특이하거나 극단적인 행동은 무엇이든 관찰하여 농부를 간접적으로 감시한다. 농부와 지주의 평판은 계약으로 작용한다. 어떤 재배 기간에든 농부는 노력을 줄이거나, 토양을 과도하게 이용하거나, 수확량을 축소 보고할 수 있다. **(A)** 마찬가지로 지주는 울타리, 개천, 관개(물을 댐) 시스템을 과소 관리할 수 있다. 농부와 지주의 행동에 대한 정확한 평가가 시간이 흐르며 이뤄지고, 서로를 희생시켜 이득을 취하려는 농부와 지주들은 향후 남들이 자신들과 거래하지 않으려고 할 수도 있다는 것을 알게 된다.

지문 간단히 보기

> 계약 위반 시 가치가 떨어질 평판 자본이 쌓인 상태에서 시장 규제 집행 가능성이 더욱 커짐 → (C) 예시: 농부와 지주

↓

> (C) 서로 평판 자본을 키워둔 상태
> (B) 시간이 흐르며 서로의 평판이 계약으로 작용

↓

> (B) 농부가 부정직하게 행동
> (A) 마찬가지로, 지주도 부정직하게 행동
> → 시간이 지나며 행위가 정확히 평가되면 남들이 거래를 피하게 됨

해설 평판 자본이 쌓인 경우에는 시장 규제의 가능성이 커진다는 주어진 글 뒤로, (C)는 지주와 농부가 서로 평판을 쌓아둔 상황을 예시로 든다. (B)는 '시간이 흐르며' 농부의 행동이 어떻게 달라질 수 있는지 먼저 언급하고, (A)는 '마찬가지로' 지주도 그렇게 행동할 수 있다고 설명하며 결론을 도출한다. 따라서 ⑤ '(C)-(B)-(A)'가 가장 적절하다.

오답풀이

보기 해설	선택률
① 주어진 글에 '지주'와 '마찬가지로' 볼 만한 대상이 언급되지 않으므로 Similarly로 시작하는 (A)부터 오면 어색하다.	3%
②, 주어진 글에 '지주와 농부'가 언급되지 않으므로, '시간이 흐르며' 이들의 행동이 어떻게 변하는지 설명하는 (B)부터 오면 어색하다.	17% / 13%
④ Similarly를 기준으로 (B)의 underreport와 (A)의 undermaintain이 비슷하게 대응되므로 (B)-(A)가 옳다.	20%

구문 [A-2행] ~ **those farmers and landowners** [**who** attempt to gain at each other's expense] will find that others may refuse to deal with them in the future.
▶ [ ]은 주어를 수식하는 주격 관계대명사절이다.
▶ 밑줄 부분은 will find의 목적어 역할을 하는 명사절이다. that 뒤로 <refuse to-V(~하기를 거부하다)>를 포함한 완전한 구조가 왔다.

11 정답 ⑤ 46%

해석 대부분의 꿈은 렘수면 동안에 발생한다. 렘(REM)은 Rapid Eye Movement(급속 안구 운동)를 의미하는 것으로, (이는) 1958년에 시카고 대학의 Nathaniel Kleitman 교수에 의해 발견된 수면 단계이다. 의대생인 Eugene Aserinsky와 함께, 그는 사람들이 잠을 자고 있을 때 그들이 마치 무엇인가를 '보고' 있는 것처럼 급속 안구 운동을 보인다는 데 주목했다. Kleitman과 Aserinsky의 지속적인 연구는 바로 이 급속 안구 운동 기간 도중에 사람들은 꿈을 꾸지만 정신은 깨어 있는 사람만큼 활발하다는 결론을 내렸다. 흥미롭게도 연구들에서 밝힌 바로는, 급속 안구 운동과 함께 우리의 심장박동이 높아지고 호흡 또한 증가하지만, 몸은 이따금의 씰룩거림과 홱 하는 움직임 외에는 몸을 가만히 유지시키는 뇌 신경 중추 때문에 움직이지 않고 기본적으로 마비되어 있다. 이것은 악몽 중에 깨어나거나 비명을 지르는 것이 어려운 이유이다. 요약하면, 렘 꿈 상태 동안에, 여러분의 정신은 바쁘지만 몸은 움직이지 않는다.

지문 간단히 보기

꿈의 발생: 렘수면(수면 중 급속 안구 운동)

↓

(연구 결과) 렘수면기에 정신 활동은 깨어 있을 때만큼 활발하고, 무언가 보는 것처럼 눈이 빠르게 움직임

(하지만) 흥미롭게도, 몸은 거의 '마비 상태'

'이런 이유로', 악몽에서 깨거나 소리치기 어려움

해설 ⑤ 앞에서 우리는 렘수면기에 정신은 활발해도 몸은 기본적으로 '마비 상태'라고 언급한 데 이어, 주어진 문장은 '이런 이유로(This is why)' 우리가 악몽에서 깨기 어렵다고 설명한다. 즉 주어진 문장의 This가 ⑤ 앞 문장을 가리키므로, 주어진 문장은 ⑤에 들어가야 한다.

오답풀이

보기 해설	선택률
① 앞에 언급된 용어 'REM'을 뒤에서 풀어 설명한다.	2%
② 뒷문장의 he가 앞문장에 언급된 Nathaniel Kleitman이므로 앞뒤 흐름이 자연스럽다.	4%
③ 두 연구자가 계속한 연구를(Ongoing research) 이어서 설명하는 흐름이므로 자연스럽다.	14%
④ Interestingly enough가 글의 흐름을 적절히 전환시킨다. 정신은 깨어 있지만, '흥미롭게도' 몸은 거의 마비되어 있다는 설명이 앞뒤로 자연스럽게 대비된다.	34%

구문 [6행] ~ they exhibit rapid eye movement, **as if** they **were** "looking" at something.
▶ <as if+주어+과거 동사>는 현재 사실과 반대되는 비유를 나타내는 가정법 과거 구문으로, '(실제 ~이지 않지만) 마치 ~인 것처럼'이라는 의미이다.

12 정답 ① 43%

해석 왜 언어와 종교는 적도 주변에서 급증하며, 왜 그것의 빈도가 자민족 중심주의와도 관련되어 있는 것일까? 이 질문들에 대한 답은 병원균의 밀도가 온대 기후나 한랭 기후보다 열대 지방에서 훨씬 더 높다는 사실에 있다. 여러분이 스웨덴에 살면, 500마일 이내의 어떤 집단도 극히 소수인 동일한 병원균에 노출되어 있을 가능성이 크다. 반면에 여러분이 콩고에 산다면, 계곡 반대편에 있는 집단은 아마 여러분이 이전에 접촉한 적이 없는 병원균에 노출되었을지도 모른다. 이런 이유로, 열대 지방의 사람들은 그들이 다른 집단과 교류할 때 병에 잘 걸린다는 것을 알게 되었고, 그래서 그들은 교류를 중단했을 것이다. 과학 이전의 세계에서는 그들의 병을 이웃 탓으로 돌리고 그 결과로 그들(이웃들)을 싫어하는 게 타당했다. 혐오와 두려움이 이웃들을 계속 갈라놓았고, 일단 여러분이 타인과 더는 교류하지 않으면, 언어와 종교 또한 자연스럽게 갈라지게 된다.
→ 적도 주변 지역에서 드러났듯이, 높은 병원균 밀도는 사람들이 이웃 집단과 맺는 상호 작용을 (B)막음으로써 언어와 종교의 (A)다양화를 초래할 수 있다.

지문 간단히 보기

언어와 종교가 적도 쪽에서 급증하는 이유 = 병원균 밀도

(예시) 비적도 지방 vs. 적도 지방
- 스웨덴: 멀리 떨어진(500마일) 집단끼리도 같은 균에 노출
- 콩고: 계곡 건너 사람끼리도 서로 다른 균에 노출
▶ **적도 지방의 병원균 밀도가 더 높기 때문**

다른 집단과 교류 후 아프면 → 이웃, 다른 집단을 탓함
→ 다른 집단과의 교류 중단 → 언어와 종교의 분화 촉진

해설 적도 부근 지방에는 병원균 밀도가 높아서 인구 집단별로 다양한 병원균에 노출되어 있고, 이 때문에 집단 간 교류 이후 아프면 다른 집단을 탓하면서 교류를 줄이게 되어, 결과적으로 언어와 종교의 분화가 이뤄졌다는 내용이다. 따라서 요약문의 빈칸에는 ① '다양화 - 막음'이다.

오답풀이

보기 해설	선택률
② 멸종 - 지연시킴	14%
③ 멸종 - 확장시킴	19%
④ 통일 - 막음	8%
⑤ 다양화 - 확장시킴	15%

구문 [3행] ~ the fact **that** pathogen density is much higher in the tropics than it is in temperate and cold climates.
▶ 접속사 that은 the fact 뒤에서 '사실'의 내용을 설명하는 동격 명사절을 이끈다.
▶ 밑줄 부분은 <비교급+than(~보다 더 …한)> 구문이다. much는 비교급 강조부사(훨씬)이다.

13~14 정답 ② 56% / ⑤ 43% 2023 4월 41~42번

해석 비록 우리 인간이 생존을 위해 반사 반응을 갖추고 있을지라도, 태어날 때 우리는 무력하다. 우리는 대략 1년을 걷지 못하는 상태로 보내고, 완전한 생각을 분명히 말할 수 있기까지 대략 2년을 더 보내며, 자기 자신을 부양할 수 없는 상태로는 더 많은 시간을 보낸다. 우리는 생존을 위해 주변 사람들에게 완전히 의존한다. 이제 이것을 많은 다른 포유동물과 비교해 보라. 예컨대 돌고래는 헤엄치면서 태어난다. 기린은 몇 시간 내에 서는 법을 배운다. 새끼 얼룩말은 태어난 지 45분 내에 달릴 수 있다. 동물의 왕국 전반에 걸쳐 우리 사촌들(다른 동물들)은 그들이 태어난 직후 놀라울 만큼 독립적이다.

겉보기에는 그것이 다른 종들에게 엄청난 이점인 것처럼 보이지만, 이는 사실 한계를 의미한다. 새끼 동물은 대체로 미리 프로그램된 루틴에 따라 뇌가 연결되어 있어서 빠르게 성장한다. 하지만 그러한 준비성은 유연성과 맞바꿔진다. 만약 어떤 불운한 코뿔소가 북극 툰드라, 히말라야 산맥의 산꼭대기, 또는 대도시 한가운데에 있는 자신을 발견했다고 상상해 보라. 그것은 적응할 능력이 없을 것이다(그 이유로 우리는 그런 지역에서 코뿔소를 찾을 수 없다). 미리 준비된 뇌와 동반된 이런 전략은 생태계 속 특정한 적합한 장소 안에서는 잘 작동하지만, 어떤 동물을 그 장소 밖에 둔다면 그것의 번성 가능성은 낮다.

이와 달리, 인간은 얼어붙은 툰드라부터 높은 산맥, 북적거리는 도시 중심지까지 여러 다양한 환경에서 번성할 수 있다. 이는 인간의 뇌가 놀라울 정도로 불완전한 채로 태어나서 가능하다. 모든 것이 연결된 채, 즉 소위 '타고난' 채로 오는 대신, 인간의 뇌는 스스로 인생 경험의 세부 내용에 의해 형성되지 못하게 한다(→ 형성되게 한다). 이것은 오랜 기간의 무력함으로 이어지고 이때 어린 뇌는 천천히 환경에 따라 만들어진다. 그것은 '살아가면서 연결된다'.

지문 간단히 보기

> 인간(태어날 때 무기력) vs. 동물(나면서부터 독립적)

↓

> 동물: 루틴에 따라 뇌가 미리 연결 → 한계(특정 장소 밖에서 번성↓)

↓

> 하지만, 인간: 거의 어디서든 적응 가능
> : 뇌가 살아가면서 인생 경험과 환경에 따라 연결되기 때문
> **▶ 태어날 때 불완전하다는 점이 오히려 '장점'**

구문 [20행] Imagine **if** some unfortunate rhinoceros **found** itself on the Arctic tundra, or on top of a mountain in the Himalayas, or in the middle of a metropolis. It **would have** no capacity to adapt ~.

▶ 가정법 과거 구문이 두 문장으로 나뉘었다. 첫 문장에서 과거시제 동사를 포함한 if절이 '실제로 ~이지 않지만 만일 ~라면 어떨지' 상상해 보라는 의미를 나타내며, <조동사 과거형+동사원형>을 포함한 두 번째 문장이 '(그렇다면) …할 것이다'의 의미를 나타낸다.

13

해설 사람은 동물과 달리 태어날 때 뇌가 불완전하지만, 바로 그 이유로 다양한 환경에 맞춰 적응할 수 있다는 내용이다. 마지막 단락이 글의 핵심을 담고 있다. 따라서 ② '미완성으로 태어나다: 인간에게 주어진 적응력이라는 재능'이 제목으로 적합하다.

오답풀이

	보기 해석	선택률
①	뇌를 다시 연결하여 용기를 향상시키라!	6%
③	인간과 동물의 진화적 경쟁	20%
④	인간 중심적 사고는 어떻게 비극을 가져올까?	6%
⑤	인간의 뇌는 다른 종과의 상호작용을 통해 발달한다	12%

14

해설 인간의 뇌는 '환경에 맞춰 서서히 형성되며' '살아가면서 연결된다'는 마지막 두 문장의 내용으로 보아, 뇌가 인생 경험의 세부 사항으로 다듬어지지 못하게 '금지된다'는 진술은 어색하다. 따라서 ⑤ (e)의 forbids를 allows로 고쳐야 한다.

오답풀이

	보기 해석	선택률
①	helpless(무력한)	10%
②	independent(독립적인)	11%
③	preparedness(준비성)	16%
④	low(낮은)	21%

STEP PLUS+ 수능 기출 마무리 복습

단어 TEST

02 숙박 시설 **03** ~에 전념하다 **04** ~로 유명한 **05** 이탈 **06** 방해하다, 중단시키다 **07** 드물게 **08** 가치를 떨어뜨리다, 평가 절하하다 **09** 적도 **10** 멸종 **11** 분명히 말하다 **12** 의미하다

구문 TEST

14 (should) be respectful to each other **15** devoted himself to it **16** during this period of rapid eye movement that[when] **17** It is her positive personality **18** as good as that of a hybrid vehicle

01 정답 ① 89%

2021 6월 19번

해석 Natalie는 첫 온라인 상담 시간에 접속하면서, "내가 어떻게 컴퓨터 화면을 통해 상담사한테 마음을 열 수 있을까?"라는 의문이 들었다. 상담 센터가 차로 오래 가야 하는 곳에 있었기 때문에, 그녀는 이것이 자신에게 많은 시간을 절약해 줄 것임을 알고 있었다. 다만 Natalie는 그게 상담사를 직접 만나는 것만큼 도움이 될지 확신할 수 없었다. 하지만 일단 (상담) 시간이 시작되자, 그녀의 걱정은 사라졌다. 그녀는 실제로 그것이 예상했던 것보다 훨씬 더 편리하다고 생각하기 시작했다. 그녀는 마치 상담사가 함께 방 안에 있는 듯한 기분을 느꼈다. 상담 시간이 끝날 때, 그녀는 미소를 지으며 그에게 말했다. "온라인에서 꼭 다시 만나요!"

지문 간단히 보기

> 온라인 상담을 앞두고 의문이 든 Natalie
> : 화면 속 상담사에게 어떻게 마음을 열지 확신 X ▶ **의심**

> 하지만 상담이 시작되자 걱정 해소
> → 편리함을 느끼고, 다음 만남도 기약함 ▶ **만족**

해설 온라인 상담이 과연 대면 상담만큼 효과가 있을지 의심하던 Natalie가 막상 상담을 받고 나서는 만족하며 다음 상담을 기약했다는 내용이다. 따라서 심경 변화로 ① '의심하는 → 만족한'이 가장 적절하다.

오답풀이

보기 해석	선택률
② 후회하는 → 혼란스러운	1%
③ 자신감 있는 → 창피한	1%
④ 지루한 → 신난	6%
⑤ 황홀한 → 실망한	0%

구문 [4행] ~ she knew that this would **save her a lot of time**.
▶ <save A B(A에게 B를 절약해주다)>의 4형식 구문이다.

02 정답 ⑤ 81%

2021 10월 22번

해석 시각적 장면은 우리의 감정적인 반응을 불러일으킬 수 있다. 긴장감은 임박한 공포에 대한 예상과 함께 오는 안도감으로 조성된다. 실제로, 예상이나 기대는 우리 감정을 유도하는 데 중요한 역할을 한다. 러시아의 무성 영화 제작자인 Lev Kuleshov는 이런 상황적 영향을 고려했다. 그는 감정이 드러나지 않는 표정을 지은 어느 배우의 장면들 사이에 아이의 관 혹은 수프 한 접시 같은 장면을 배치했다. 똑같이 '감정이 드러나지 않은' 이 표정은 앞에 어떤 이미지가 왔는가에 따라 달리 해석되었다. 그리하여 같은 표정이 맥락에 따라 슬픔 또는 배고픔을 나타내는 것처럼 보였다. 'Kuleshov' 효과에 대한 심리학적 연구들은 사회적 상황이 감정에 미치는 영향을 확증했다. 가령 어떤 사람이 여러분에게 미소를 짓고 나서 감정이 드러나지 않는 표정으로 바뀌면, 이 사람은 언짢거나 실망한 것처럼 보일 것이다. 반대로 어떤 사람이 처음에 화난 것처럼 보이고 나서 감정이 드러나지 않는 표정으로 바뀌면, 그 사람은 약간 기분이 좋거나 긍정적인 것으로 보인다.

지문 간단히 보기

> 시각적 장면: 감정적 반응을 유도함

> Kuleshov 효과: 동일한 무표정도 앞에 제시된 이미지(맥락)에 따라서 다르게 해석됨

> 비슷한 심리학 연구 결과: 앞에 어떤 표정을 지었는지에 따라, 똑같은 무표정도 다른 감정으로 해석됨

해설 앞에 보여준 장면에 따라 동일한 표정에 대한 해석이 달라진다는 내용이므로, 요지로 가장 적절한 것은 ⑤ '선행 장면에 따라서 동일한 시각 정보가 다르게 해석된다.'이다.

오답풀이

보기 해설	선택률
① '장면, 표정' 등 키워드가 빠져 있다.	1%
② 감정의 표현 방식보다는 '해석'이 달라진다는 것이 핵심 내용이다.	12%
③ '시대 상황을 반영한 영화'나 '공감'에 관해서는 언급되지 않았다.	1%
④ '갈등 해결'에 관해서는 언급되지 않았다. 본문의 neutral 만 보고 고르지 않도록 주의한다.	2%

구문 [9행] This same "neutral" expression was interpreted differently depending on **what image preceded it**.
▶ what이 이끄는 명사절이 depending on(~에 따라)의 목적어로 왔다. what은 여기서 image를 꾸미는 의문형용사(어떤)이다.

03 정답 ① 41%

해석 여러분은 여러분이 어쩌면 좋아할 수도 있는 것을 판단하는 알고리즘에 뭔가 무서운 게 있다고 느낄 수도 있다. 그것은 컴퓨터가 여러분이 뭔가를 좋아하지 않을 것이라고 결론 짓는다면 여러분이 그것을 볼 기회가 영영 없을 거라는 의미일 수 있을까? 개인적으로, 나는 어쩌면 혼자서는 발견 못 했을 새로운 음악 쪽으로 안내받는 것을 아주 좋아한다. 나는 같은 노래들을 계속 반복해서 틀어놓는 관습에 빨리 갇힐 때가 있다. 그래서 나는 늘 라디오를 즐겨 듣는다. 하지만 뮤직 라이브러리를 통해 지금 나를 밀고 당기는 알고리즘은 내가 좋아할 보석을 찾는 데 완벽하게 적합하다. 원래 그런 알고리즘에 대한 나의 걱정은 알고리즘이 모든 사람을 라이브러리의 특정 부분으로 몰아넣고, 나머지 부분은 듣는 이가 없는 채로 남겨둘지도 모른다는 것이었다. 알고리즘이 취향의 수렴을 일으킬까? 그러나, 일반적으로 알고리즘 이면의 비선형적이고 불규칙한 수학 덕분에, 이런 일은 발생하지 않는다. 여러분이 좋아하는 것에 비해 내가 좋아하는 것이 작게 갈라져 있다는(조금 차이가 난다는) 점이 우리를 뮤직 라이브러리의 서로 다른 먼 구석으로 보낼 수 있다.

지문 간단히 보기

> 알고리즘에 대한 두려움: '우리가 좋아하지 않는다고 판단된 것은 영원히 접할 기회가 없을까?'

↓

> 두려움 반박: 음악 추천 알고리즘
> - 원래는 필자도 특정 음악에 추천이 '쏠릴까봐' 우려함
> - 하지만, 알고리즘 이면의 '비선형성, 불규칙성'이 이를 방지함

↓

> '우리는 라이브러리의 서로 다른 구석으로 향하게 됨'
> ▶ **각자 조금씩 다른 선호에 맞춰 다양하게 추천받음**

해설 본래 필자는 음악 추천 알고리즘이 청취자를 특정 음악에만 쏠리게 할지도 모른다고 우려했었지만, 사람들의 선호가 조금씩 다르기 때문에 그런 일이 없다는 것을 알게 되었다고 한다. 따라서 밑줄 친 부분은 ① '우리를 각자 취향에 맞게 선택된 음악으로 이끌'의 의미로 볼 수 있다.

오답풀이

보기 해석	선택률
② 우리가 다른 청취자들과 인맥을 쌓을 수 있게 할	15%
③ 우리더러 빈번한 알고리즘 업데이트를 요청하라고 부추길	16%
④ 우리가 재능 있지만 알려지지 않은 음악인들을 발굴하도록 자극할	15%
⑤ 우리가 특정 음악 장르에 대한 우리의 선호를 무시하게 할	14%

구문 [11행] My worry ~ was [**that** they might drive everyone into certain parts of the library, **leaving others lacking listeners**].
▶ [ ]은 문장의 보어 역할을 하는 명사절(~것)이다.
▶ 콤마 뒤 분사구문은 <leave+목적어+현재분사(~을 …한 상태로 두다)> 형태이다.

04 정답 ③ 44%

해석 도덕 철학 교과서는 종종 우리가 'is'와 'ought'라는 단어 사용에 주의를 기울이면 어떤 주장이 윤리적인지 아닌지를 분별할 수 있다고 분명히 말한다. 이런 제언상으로 보면, '너는 약속을 지켜야 한다'는 주장은 'ought'를 사용하므로 윤리에 관한 것이다. '원자는 작다'는 'is'를 사용하므로 윤리에 관한 것이 아니다. 하지만 흔히 예로 인용됨에도 불구하고, 이 is-ought 검사는 심히 불충분하다. 어떤 is 진술은 윤리에 관한 내용을 포함하고, 어떤 ought 진술은 그렇지 않다. 가령 '살인은 옳지 않다'와 '우정은 좋은 것이다'라는 진술을 생각해 보라. 이 주장들은 분명히 윤리적인 내용을 포함한다. is-ought의 검사가 무엇을 탐지하든 간에, 이 주장들은 확실히 그 구분에서 ought 쪽에 해당한다. 하지만 둘 다 'is'를 사용한다. 마찬가지로, '열차가 한 시간 만에 오기로 되어 있다'라는 진술을 생각해 보라. 'ought'의 사용에도 불구하고, 이 진술은 확실히 윤리에 관한 것이 아니다. 윤리에 관한 주장과 윤리에 관한 것이 아닌 주장 사이에는 중대한 차이가 있다. 하지만 우리는 구별을 위해서 단순히 'is'와 'ought'에 의존할 수만은 없다. 대신에 우리는 주장의 핵심에 주의를 기울일 필요가 있다.

지문 간단히 보기

> is와 ought의 사용에 따라 윤리적 진술을 구별하는 것: '불충분'

↓

> is 진술 중에서도 윤리적인 것이 있고, ought 진술 중에서도 윤리적이지 않은 것이 있음

↓

> 단순히 is나 ought의 사용만 살피지 말고, 주장의 핵심을 따져야 함

해설 진술의 '형태(is를 썼는지, ought를 썼는지)'로만 윤리적 여부를 판단하기보다는, 주장의 '핵심'에 주의를 기울여야 한다는 내용이다. 마지막 두 문장에 글의 요지가 있다. 따라서 제목으로 ③ '단어 선택 혹은 내용, 무엇이 주장의 윤리성을 결정 짓는가?'가 가장 적절하다.

오답풀이

보기 해석	선택률
① 'is'와 'ought' 간의 상호 배타적 관계	19%
② 비윤리적으로 들리는가? 당신의 도덕 규범부터 점검하라	4%
④ 언어 형태와 기능의 조화를 어떻게 이룰 것인가	5%
⑤ 'is'를 쓰느냐 'ought'를 쓰느냐, 그것이 윤리적 진술의 핵심이다!	24%

구문 [12행] **Whatever** the is-ought test is tracking, these claims clearly fall on the ought side of that divide.
▶ 복합관계대명사 Whatever가 '무엇이 ~하든 간에'라는 의미의 부사절을 이끈다. 이 Whatever는 No matter what으로 바꿀 수 있다.

해석　거장 피아니스트이자 저명한 작가인 Charles Rosen은 1927년 뉴욕에서 태어났다. Rosen은 어려서부터 피아노에 놀라운 재능을 보였다. 그가 프린스턴 대학교에서 프랑스 문학 박사 학위를 받은 1951년, Rosen은 뉴욕에서 피아노 데뷔와 첫 음반 녹음을 둘 다 해냈다. 열렬한 찬사 속에, 그는 전 세계 수많은 독주회와 오케스트라 연주회에 출연했다. Rosen의 연주는 20세기의 가장 유명한 작곡가들 몇몇에게 감명을 주었고, 그들은 Rosen에게 그들의 곡을 연주해 달라고 요청했다. Rosen은 또한 널리 칭송받는 많은 음악 관련 저서의 저자였다. 그의 가장 유명한 책인 <The Classical Style>은 1971년에 처음 출판되었고, 다음 해에 U.S. National Book Award를 수상했다. 이 작품은 1997년에 증보판으로 재판(再版)되었고, 이 분야에서 획기적인 것으로 남아 있다. 폭넓게 글쓰기를 하는 한편, Rosen은 2012년 사망할 때까지 여생 동안 피아니스트로 계속 공연했다.

지문 간단히 보기

> Charles Rosen의 생애
> ① 어려서부터 피아노에 재능
> ② 1951년 프랑스 문학 박사 취득 → 뉴욕 무대 데뷔 & 음반
> ③ 유명 작곡가들에게 연주를 요청받기도 함
> ④ 1971년 <The Classical Style> 출판
> 　→ 다음 해에 U.S. National Book Award 수상
> ⑤ 2012년 사망 전까지 글쓰기와 연주 병행

해설　'While writing extensively, Rosen continued to perform as a pianist for the rest of his life ~'에서 Rosen은 글쓰기와 피아노 연주 활동을 동시에(While) 했다고 하므로, 내용과 일치하지 않는 것은 ⑤ '피아니스트 활동을 중단하고 글쓰기에 매진하였다.'이다.

오답풀이

보기 해설	선택률
① ~ a remarkable talent for the piano from his early childhood.	0%
② ~ earned his doctoral degree in French literature ~	0%
③ ~ invited him to play their music.	1%
④ ~ won the U.S. National Book Award the next year.	0%

구문　[4행] In 1951, the year **(when)** he earned his doctoral degree in French literature at Princeton University, ~
▶ 시간 선행사 the year 뒤로 관계부사 when이 생략되었다. 관계부사는 일반적인 선행사(the time, the place 등) 뒤에서는 생략되기도 한다.

해석　기술은 음악이 제작되는 방식을 역사적으로 차별화했다. 라이브 재즈 콘서트에서 베이스 연주자는 관객에게 10분간의 즉흥 연주를 해줄 수 있지만, 음반을 만들고 있다면 그렇게 할 수 없다. 초기 디스크가 지닌 시간과 공간의 제약은 이런 자유로운 연주 방식을 불가능하게 했다. 흔히 작품은 많은 디스크로 분리되어 연속성의 결여로 이어지곤 했다. 음악가는 길이뿐만 아니라 기계가 그들의 소리를 녹음하고 흡수하는 방식도 고려해야 했다. 특히 녹음 초창기에는 악기뿐만 아니라 인간의 목소리 또한 녹음되고 나면 흔히 왜곡되었다. 그런 왜곡을 막을 목적으로, 막 생겨나고 있었던 녹음 기술에 맞추고자 소리를 바꾸는 것은 연주자의 몫이었다. 재즈 음악가와 오케스트라는 거의 녹음의 한도에 맞추어 작품을 만들었다. 많은 음악가는 기술의 제약과 이점에 저항했고(→ 받아들였고) 자신의 음반을 그것에 맞게 만들었다. 녹음의 제약은 무대 공연으로 스며들기 시작했다. 음악가는 녹음 스튜디오에서 3분짜리 노래만 하게 제한되었고, 그들은 곧 무대에서도 자신의 노래들을 그 길이로 유지했다.

지문 간단히 보기

> 음악 제작에 기술이 도입되면서 기술의 '제약'도 유입
> - 자유로운 연주 X, 연속성 X
> - 녹음된 소리에 '왜곡' 발생 → 연주자가 소리 조정
> ↓
> 음반 제작, 나아가 무대 연주가 녹음 기술의 한도에 '맞게' 변화
> ▶ **기술의 제약, 이점을 '수용하는' 방향으로 변화**

해설　기술적 한도에 '맞춰서(accordingly)' 음악을 제작하게 되었다는 설명으로 보아, 음악가들이 녹음의 제약과 이점을 '수용했다'는 의미로 ④에 resistant 대신 receptive를 써야 옳다.

오답풀이

보기 해석	선택률
① unable(~할 수 없는)	5%
② lack(결여, 부족)	13%
③ alter(바꾸다)	18%
⑤ kept(유지했다)	12%

구문　[2행] In a live jazz concert **a bass player** can provide the audience with a ten-minute jam session but is unable to do so **if (he or she is) making** a record.
▶ 주어 a bass player 뒤로 동사구인 can provide와 is unable to do so가 <A but B>의 병렬구조로 연결되었다.
▶ 'if making ~'은 조건의 부사절에서 <대명사 주어+be동사>가 생략된 부사절 축약 구문이다. 생략된 he or she는 문장의 주어 a bass player를 가리킨다.

07 정답 ③ 22%

해석 미술사학이나 고생물학과 같은 학과 및 하위(세부) 학과의 성장, 그리고 미술평론가와 같은 특정 인물의 성장은 보관할 가치가 있는 것을 선택하고 정리하기 위한 원칙과 관행을 만드는 데 도움이 되었으나, 그럼에도 불구하고 그것(선택과 정리)은 어려운 일로 남아 있었다. 게다가, 19세기 말엽에 박물관과 대학이 더욱 멀어지고, 세상을 알게 될 매우 가치 있는 경로로서의 대상 개념이 쇠퇴하면서, 수집은 특히 과학에서 가치 있는 지적 활동으로서의 지위를 잃기 시작했다. 과학에서 실로 흥미롭고 중요한 측면은 점점 더 육안으로 보이지 않는 것들이었고, 수집된 것들을 분류하는 것은 더 이상 최첨단의 지식을 생산할 가망이 없었다. '나비 채집'이라는 용어는 '한낱(mere)'이라는 형용사와 함께 쓰여 부차적인 학문적 지위를 갖는 활동을 나타낼 수 있게 되었다.

지문 간단히 보기

> 세상을 파악하는 중대한 경로로서의 '대상' 개념 약화
> + 눈에 보이지 '않는' 것들에 대한 학문적 관심 상승

↓

> '채집, 수집' 활동(의 중요성)에 대한 인식 약화
> = 수집이 최첨단의 지식을 생산할 수 있는 가능성 약화

↓

> (예시) '나비 채집'을 '한낱'이라는 단어와 함께 사용
> ▶ **'부수적' 연구 수단으로 전락하게 됨**

해설 세상을 연구하는 중대 경로로서의 '대상' 개념이 약화되고, 육안으로는 보이지 않는 것들에 대한 관심이 커지면서, 특히 과학 분야에서 '채집, 수집'의 방법론적 중요성이 약화되었다는 내용이다. 따라서 빈칸에는 ③ '부차적인'이 들어가야 한다.

오답풀이

보기 해석	선택률
① 경쟁력 있는	17%
② 참신한	22%
④ 믿을 만한	22%
⑤ 무조건적인	15%

구문 [1행] **The growth** of academic disciplines and sub-disciplines, such as art history or palaeontology, and of particular figures such as the art critic, **helped produce** ~
▶ <A and B>로 연결된 전치사구가 주어 The growth를 꾸민다. <help+원형부정사(~하는 것을 돕다)> 구문도 참고한다.

08 정답 ④ 52%

해석 팬은 감정을 그 자체로 느낀다. 그들은 제공된다고 보이는 것 이상의 의미를 만든다. 그들은 정체성과 경험을 만들고, 다른 사람들과 공유하기 위해 그들만의 예술적 창작물을 만든다. 어떤 사람은 팬 개인으로서 '어떤 스타와 이상적인 관계, 강한 추억과 향수의 감정'을 느끼고 '(자신의) 자아감 발달을 위해 수집하는' 등의 활동을 할 수 있다. 그러나 더 흔히, 개인의 경험은 공통된 애착을 지닌 다른 사람들이 그들의 애정의 대상을 중심으로 교제하는 사회적 상황에 끼워 넣어져 있다. 팬덤의 즐거움 중 많은 부분은 다른 팬들과 관계를 맺는 데서 온다. 1800년대의 보스턴 사람들은 일기에서, 콘서트에 모인 군중의 일부가 되는 것은 (콘서트에) 참석하는 즐거움의 일부라고 묘사했다. 팬들이 사랑하는 것은 팬덤의 대상이라기보다, 그 애정이 제공하는 (팬들 간) 서로에 대한 애착(그리고 서로 간의 차이)이라는 강력한 주장이 제기될 수 있다.

지문 간단히 보기

> 팬들은 여러 팬덤 활동(창작, 수집 등)을 통해 다양한 의미를 만듦

↓

> 하지만, 개인적인 경험은 '다른 팬들과 교제하는 사회적 상황'과 맞물림 ▶ **다른 팬들과의 관계가 핵심**

↓

> (예시) 1800년대 보스턴 사람들: '콘서트 군중의 일부가 되는 것이 콘서트를 가는 즐거움의 일부'라고 기록

↓

> 결국, 팬덤의 대상보다도 팬들끼리의 애착이 중요

해설 팬덤 활동의 핵심은 공통된 애착을 지닌 다른 사람들과 관계를 맺는 사회적 상황에 있다는 내용이므로, 빈칸에는 ④ '다른 팬들과 관계를 맺는 데서 온다'가 들어가야 적절하다.

오답풀이

보기 해석	선택률
① 세계적인 스타들 간의 협업으로 강화된다	13%
② 스타와 사적인 연락을 자주 나누는 데서 비롯된다	19%
③ 팬이 자신의 우상과 함께 나이 들어 가면서 깊어진다	11%
⑤ 스타의 미디어 출연에 의해 고조된다	5%

구문 [12행] **Much of the pleasure of fandom comes** from being connected to other fans.
▶ <부분+of+전체> 주어는 '전체' 명사에 수 일치한다. 여기서 전체 명사는 단수명사인 the pleasure이므로 동사도 단수형인 comes로 썼다.

09 정답 ③ 51%

해석 처음으로 교실에서 실제 음악을 만들어 내는 일에 접근할 때, 악기 사용을 완전히 피하는 것이 좋은 생각이다. 이는 경험이 많지 않은 교사가 감상, 연주 및 작곡을 통해 기본적인 음악 행위 발달에 집중하게 하고, 아이들더러 더 통제 가능한 음원, 즉 목소리와 몸을 두드려 내는 소리(손뼉치기, 딸깍딸깍 소리를 내기, 발 구르기 등)에 집중하게 할 것이다. 음악은 발달 면에서도 역사적으로도 이것들로 시작된다. 가장 표현이 풍부하고 즉각 쓸 수 있는 악기는 인간의 목소리이다. (악기의 음질은 재료, 디자인 및 제작 품질의 직접적인 결과이다.) 몸의 움직임은 음악에 대한 본능적인 반응일 뿐만 아니라 음악을 만들어 내도록 부추긴다. (신체) 조정 능력, 청각적 감수성, 시각 신호와 기호에 대한 반응, 그리고 악기 연주에 필요한 음악적 이해의 많은 부분을 발달시키는 활동은 모두 악기 없이 확립될 수 있다.

지문 간단히 보기

초기 음악 교육에서는 악기 사용을 배제하는 게 좋음

↓

① 악기가 없으면 기본적 음악 행위 발달에 되려 집중 가능
② 본래 가장 기본적인 악기는 인간의 목소리
④ 몸을 움직여보는 것도 도움이 됨

↓

(결론) ⑤ 악기 없이도 음악과 관련된 여러 능력 발달

해설 초기 음악 교육에서 악기 사용을 배제하고, 목소리나 몸을 써서 소리를 내게 하는 것이 도움이 된다는 내용이다. 하지만 ③은 악기 음질에 관해서 언급하므로 글의 흐름에서 벗어난다.

오답풀이

	보기 해설	선택률
①	앞의 avoid using instruments altogether를 This로 받아 부연 설명하는 문장이다.	4%
②	앞에 언급된 voices and body percussion을 these로 가리킨 후, 둘 중 '목소리'의 중요성을 먼저 강조하고 있다.	14%
④	목소리에 이어서 '몸의 움직임'도 중요함을 상기시키는 문장이다. 즉 ①의 voices and body percussion을 ②와 ④에서 하나씩 나누어 강조하는 것이다.	25%
⑤	첫 문장의 재진술이다. '악기 없이' 음악 교육이 이뤄질 수 있다는 논지가 반복된다.	5%

구문 [17행] **Activities** which develop many of the coordination skills, aural sensitivity, responses to visual cues and symbols, and the musical understanding necessary to play an instrument **can all be established** without instruments.
▶ 주어부가 밑줄 친 관계절의 수식을 받아 길어졌다. 동사는 <조동사 +be p.p.> 형태의 수동태이다.

10 정답 ② 31%

해석 두 발 보행, 즉 직립 보행은 엄청난 진화적 조정을 연쇄적으로 일으켰다. 그것은 (호미닌이) 무기를 휴대하고, 음식을 즉석에서 먹는 대신 집단이 있는 장소로 가져갈 수 있도록 호미닌의 팔을 자유롭게 해주었다. 그런데 두 발 보행은 손재주와 도구 사용을 촉발하기 위해 필요했다. **(B)** Hashimoto와 동료들은 도구 사용의 기초가 되는 적응이 인간의 두 발 보행에 필요한 적응과 독립적으로 진화했다고 결론지었는데, 인간과 원숭이 모두에게서 물리적으로 손의 손가락들이 구분되어 있듯이, 1차 감각 운동 피질에서 각 손가락이 구분되어 나타나기 때문이다. **(A)** 이것은 도구 사용에 필요한 복잡한 조작 시 각 손가락을 독립적으로 사용할 수 있는 능력을 만들어 낸다. 그러나 두 발 보행이 없다면 도구 제작 및 도구 사용 중 손(놀림)을 가속화할 때 몸통을 지렛대로 사용하는 게 불가능할 것이다. **(C)** 두 발 보행은 또한 언어의 전제 조건인 더 복잡한 소리 신호 체계를 발전시킬 수 있도록 입과 치아를 자유롭게 해주었다. 이러한 발전으로 에너지 비용이 결국 침팬지의 3배 수준에 이르러, 총 기초 대사율의 최대 6분의 1을 차지하는 더 큰 두뇌가 필요하게 되었다.

지문 간단히 보기

두 발 보행: 손재주와 도구 사용을 위해 필요

↓

(B) '두 발 보행과 도구 사용이 별도로 진화'했다고 본 연구가 있었음
→ 근거: 인간도 원숭이도 뇌 피질에서 손가락이 나뉘어 있음

↓

(A) '이 덕분에' 손가락을 각자 조작 가능
→ (반박) 하지만, 두 발 보행이 가능해야 더 빠른 조작 가능
▶ **직립 보행이 인간의 손재주 발달에 도움이 됐을 것**

↓

(C) 추가로, 두 발 보행으로 입, 치아 발달 → 언어, 뇌 발달

해설 두 발 보행이 인간의 손과 도구 활용에 도움이 되었다는 주어진 글 뒤로, (B)는 두 발 보행과 도구 사용이 따로 발달했다고 주장한 연구가 있었다고 언급한다. (A) 중반부의 But은 (B)의 주장을 반박하며 두 발 보행이 손 사용에 도움이 되었음을 다시 말하고, (C)는 두 발 보행이 추가로(also) 입과 치아, 나아가 언어와 뇌 발달에 기여했다고 설명한다. 따라서 ② '(B)-(A)-(C)'가 적절하다.

오답풀이

	보기 해설	선택률
①	(A)의 This는 (B)의 'each finger ~ cortex'를 가리킨다.	5%
③	(C)에서 화제가 '입, 언어 발달'로 전환되는데 (A)에서 적절한 연결어 없이 다시 '손재주'를 언급하면 어색하다.	17%
④	(A)~(C) 중 (C)만 '손재주'보다 '언어 발달'을 다루므로	31%
⑤	(C)는 마지막으로 고정된다.	17%

구문 [A-3행] But **without bipedalism** it would be impossible ~
▶ <without+명사>는 가정법 과거 구문인 <if it were not for+명사(~이 없다면)>과 같다. 밑줄 친 <조동사 과거형+동사원형>이 가정법 구문이라는 힌트를 준다.

11 정답 ⑤ 28%   2022 9월 39번

해석 새로운 기술의 각 물결은 보안뿐 아니라 사용자 편의성을 향상하려는 의도이지만, 때때로 이것들은 반드시 함께 진행되지는 않는다. 예를 들어 마그네틱 띠에서 내장형 칩으로의 전환은 거래를 약간 느려지게 해서, 바쁜 고객을 간혹 좌절시켰다(방해했다). 서비스를 너무 부담스럽게 만들면, 잠재적 고객은 다른 곳으로 갈 것이다. 이런 장벽은 여러 수준으로 적용된다. 비밀번호, 이중 키 인증, 그리고 지문, 홍채 및 음성 인식 등 생체 인식은 모두 잠재적인 사기꾼으로부터 계정 세부 정보를 숨겨 주는 방법, 즉 여러분의 데이터를 비밀로 유지하는 방법이다. 하지만 그것들은 모두 불가피하게 계좌 사용에 부담을 가중한다. 본인 돈에 접근하는 데 도입된 난관뿐 아니라, 만약 사기로 의심되는 건이 감지되면, 예금주는 본인이 그 의심되는 거래를 했는지 묻는 전화 통화를 응대해야만 한다. 이것은 모두 어느 정도 유용하지만—실제로 여러분의 은행이 여러분을 보호하기 위해 경계를 늦추지 않고 있음을 알게 되면 안심스러울 수 있다—그러한 전화를 너무 많이 받는다면 귀찮아진다.

지문 간단히 보기

신기술 도입으로 보안과 편의가 꼭 함께 향상되지는 X
→ 기술로 서비스 이용 부담이 커져서 고객이 떠날 수도 있음

(예시) 비밀번호, 이중 키 인증, 생체 인식 등: 데이터를 안전하게 보호하지만, 계좌 사용에 '부담' 가중
→ 사기 의심 때마다 '전화': 너무 자주 받으면 '귀찮음'

해설 ⑤ 앞에서 계좌 사용에 '부담이 가중되는' 상황을 말하고, 주어진 문장은 '돈에 접근하기도 어렵고, 확인 전화도 받아야 하는' 구체적인 상황을 들며 '부담'의 내용을 구체화한다. ⑤ 뒤는 주어진 문장에 언급된 '전화'를 such calls로 다시 가리키며, 이 모든 게 유용하고 안심이 될지라도 '귀찮다'는 결론으로 향한다. 따라서 주어진 문장은 ⑤에 들어가야 적절하다.

오답풀이

보기 해설	선택률
① 앞의 예시(For example)로 도출되는 일반적 결론을 뒤에서 자연스럽게 제시한다.	6%
② 뒷문장의 This obstacle은 '고객을 다른 데로 보낼' 장벽을 뜻한다.	13%
③ '장벽이 여러 수준으로 적용되는' 예시로 Passwords, double-key identification, and biometrics를 열거하는 흐름이 자연스럽다.	17%
④ Passwords, double-key identification, and biometrics가 뒷문장의 they로 자연스럽게 연결된다.	35%

구문 [20행] —indeed, **it** can be reassuring **knowing** [that your bank is keeping alert to protect you]— ~
▶ 가주어-진주어 구문으로, 동명사구인 'knowing ~'이 문장의 진짜 주어이다. [ ]은 knowing의 목적절이다.

12 정답 ③ 43%   2021 6월 40번

해석 나무 '심기'가 사회적 또는 정치적인 의미를 가질 수 있다는 생각은 비록 이후에 널리 퍼지긴 했으나 영국인들에 의해 고안된 듯하다. Keith Thomas의 역사서인 <Man and the Natural World>에 따르면, 17세기와 18세기의 귀족들은 자기 재산 범위와 그것에 대한 권리의 영속성을 선언하기 위해 활엽수를 보통 줄지어서 심기 시작했다. 신사들을 대상으로 하는 어느 잡지의 편집자는 독자들에게 묻기를, "그런 살아 있고 성장하는 증인들(나무)의 증언을 통해 여러분의 재산 경계와 한계가 대대로 보존되고 지속되게 하는 것보다 즐거울 게 무엇이겠는가?"라고 했다. 나무 심기는 애국적인 행동으로 여겨진다는 추가적 이점이 있었는데, 왜냐하면 군주가 영국 해군이 의존하는 경재(활엽수에서 얻은 단단한 목재)가 심각하게 부족하다고 선포했기 때문이었다.
→ 영국 귀족들에게, 나무를 심는 것은 자기 땅에 대한 (A)지속적인 소유권을 표시하는 진술 역할을 했고, 이는 또한 국가에 대한 충성심의 (B)표현으로 여겨졌다.

지문 간단히 보기

나무 심기의 의미: 영국에서 기원

의미1: 소유권 범위 및 영속성 선언
→ '살아 있고 성장하는' 나무로 재산 범위를 명확히 표시

의미2: 애국적 행동 → 당시 군주가 해군이 쓸 '목재가 부족'함을 선언(해서 나무를 심는 게 나라를 위한 일이 됨)

해설 나무 심기의 사회정치적 의미를 밝힌 글로, 첫째로 소유권의 범위와 영속성 선언, 두 번째로 애국적 행위라는 의미가 있었다는 내용이다. 따라서 요약문의 빈칸에는 ③ '지속적인 - 표현'이 적합하다.

오답풀이

보기 해설	선택률
① 불안정한 - 확인	18%
② 불안정한 - 과장	12%
④ 지속적인 - 조작	17%
⑤ 공식적인 - 해명	8%

구문 [15행] ~, **for** the Crown had declared a severe shortage of the hardwood on which the Royal Navy depended.
▶ 등위접속사 for가 콤마 앞에 대한 이유를 설명한다. 이유를 설명하는 for는 원칙적으로 문장 맨 앞이 아닌 중간에만 나오는 특징이 있다.
▶ 밑줄 부분은 본래 'which the Royal Navy depended on'인데, 문장 끝의 전치사 on을 관계대명사 앞으로 옮기고 자동사 depended로 문장을 끝맺었다.

13~14 정답 ① 47% / ③ 39% 2022 6월 41~42번

해석 일단 어떤 사건이 목격되면, 구경하는 사람은 그것이 정말로 비상 상황인지 결정해야 한다. 비상 상황은 항상 명확하게 그렇다고 꼬리표가 붙어 있는 것은 아니다. 대기실로 쏟아져 들어오는 '연기'는 화재로 발생할 수도 있고, 혹은 단순히 증기 파이프의 누출을 나타낼 수도 있다. 거리에서의 비명은 공격, 아니면 가족 간의 다툼을 나타낼 수도 있다. 출입구에 누워 있는 한 남자는 관상 동맥증을 앓고 있을 수도 있고, 아니면 그저 술을 깨려고 잠자고 있는 것일 수도 있다.

어떤 한 상황을 해석하려고 하는 사람은 자신이 어떻게 반응해야 할지 알기 위해 흔히 주변 사람들을 본다. 만약 다른 모든 사람이 침착하고 무관심하다면, 그는 그런 상태를 유지하려는 경향이 있을 것이다. 다른 모든 사람이 강하게 반응하고 있다면, 그는 아마 경계하게 될 것이다. 이러한 경향은 단순히 맹목적인 순응이 아닌데, 보통 우리는 우리 주변의 다른 사람들이 어떻게 행동하는지로부터 새로운 상황에 관한 많은 귀중한 정보를 얻는다. 길가의 식당을 고를 때 주차장에 아무 다른 차도 없는 곳에서 멈추는 여행객은 드물다.

그러나 때때로 다른 사람들의 반응은 정확한(→ 틀린) 정보를 제공한다. 연구에 따르면 치과 병원 대기실에 있는 환자들의 무관심(태연함)은 그들 내면의 불안을 제대로 보여주지 않는다. 사람들 앞에서 '냉정을 잃는' 것은 창피한 일로 여겨진다. 그렇다면, 잠재적으로 심각한 상황에서, 그곳에 있는 모든 사람은 실제 그런 것보다 더 태연해 보일 것이다. 따라서 군중은 수동성을 통해 사건이 비상 상황이 아님을 넌지시 비쳐서 구성원들이 아무 행동도 하지 않도록 강요할 수 있다. 그런 군중 속에 있는 사람은 누구라도 그 사건이 비상 상황인 것처럼 행동하면 자신이 바보처럼 보일까 봐 두려워한다.

지문 간단히 보기

> 어떤 사건을 보면 '비상 상황'인지 판단 필요
> : 상황이 '라벨링'되어 있는 것이 아니므로 쉽지 않음

↓

> 흔히 사람들은 '주변 사람들의 반응을 참고해' 상황을 판단
> : 주변 사람들은 새로운 상황에 대한 귀중한 정보를 제공

↓

> 하지만 다른 사람들의 반응이 늘 실제를 '제대로 보여주지 않을' 수도 있음 ▶ '틀린' 정보를 줄 때도 있음

↓

> (예시) 치과 대기실 사람들: 내면에 불안함이 있음에도 태연한 모습

구문 [29행] A crowd can thus force inaction on its members by implying, ~, that <u>an event is not an emergency</u>. Any individual in such a crowd fears that he may appear a fool if he behaves **as though it were**.

▶ <as though+주어+과거 동사 ~>는 '(실제로 ~이지 않지만) 마치 ~인 것처럼'의 의미로, 가정법 과거 구문의 일종이다.

▶ it were는 밑줄 친 부분을 참고하면 'the event were an emergency'의 의미를 나타낸다. 대동사 were의 의미를 정확히 알려면 앞에 나온 정보를 잘 살펴야 한다.

13

해설 사람들은 상황을 판단할 때 주변 사람의 반응을 보고 판단하려 한다는 경향을 설명하는 글이므로, 제목으로 ① '우리는 독립적으로 판단하는 걸까? 군중의 영향'이 적절하다.

오답풀이

보기 해석	선택률
② 승리 전략: 남들에게 속지 않는 방법	9%
③ 비상 상황이 우리의 사고방식에 영향을 끼칠까?	23%
④ 이웃과의 화합을 향해 나아가기	8%
⑤ 비상 상황에서 남들을 도와주는 방법	13%

14

해설 마지막 단락은 속으로는 불안해도 겉으로는 더 태연한 치과 대기실에 있는 사람들을 예로 들어, 사람들의 반응이 실제 상황을 그대로 보여주지 않을 수 있음을 설명하고 있다. 따라서 정보가 늘 정확하지 '않다'는 의미로 ③ (c)에는 accurate 대신 false를 써야 한다.

오답풀이

보기 해석	선택률
① labeled(꼬리표가 붙은, 명명된)	4%
② rare(드문)	16%
④ unconcerned(태연한, 무관심한)	31%
⑤ inaction(행동하지 않음)	11%

STEP PLUS+ 수능 기출 마무리 복습

단어 TEST
02 ~보다 앞서다, 선행하다   **03** 수렴   **04** 상호 배타적인   **05** 열렬한 찬사   **06** 연속성   **07** 부차적인   **08** 애착   **09** 전제 조건   **10** 좌절시키다, 방해하다   **11** 영속성   **12** 순응

구문 TEST
14 as if the counselor were in the room   **15** as if it had been hit by a storm   **16** frustrating customers in a hurry   **17** forcing people to seek alternative routes   **18** and the potential customer will go elsewhere

01   정답 ③   91%   2023학년도 수능 19번

해석   모든 에너지를 경주의 마지막 발걸음에 쏟으면서, Jamie는 결승선을 통과했다. 실망스럽게도 그녀는 자신의 개인 최고 기록을 깨는 데 또 실패했다. Jamie는 기어코 자신의 기록을 깨기 위해 몇 달 동안 스스로를 몰아붙였지만, 그것은 모두 수포로 돌아갔다. 그녀가 실패에 관해 어떤 기분을 느끼는지 알아차린 팀 동료 Ken은 그녀에게 다가와 말했다. "Jamie, 비록 오늘 네가 개인 최고 기록을 세우지 못했지만, 네 경기력은 극적으로 향상됐어. 네 달리기 기량이 아주 많이 발전했는걸! 넌 분명히 다음 경주에서 개인 최고 기록을 깰 거야!" 그의 말을 들은 후, 그녀는 자신감을 느꼈다. 이제 목표를 계속 밀고 나갈 의욕을 갖게 된 Jamie는 미소를 지으며 대답했다. "네 말이 맞아! 다음 경주에서 난 틀림없이 내 최고 기록을 깰 거야!"

지문 간단히 보기

> 최선을 다했으나 개인 기록을 깨지 못한 Jamie
> → 몇 달 간의 노력이 수포로 돌아간 기분 ▶ **좌절**

↓

> 동료 Ken이 다가와 경기력 향상을 칭찬하며 응원해줌
> → Jamie가 자신감과 의욕을 회복 ▶ **용기를 얻음**

해설   개인 경주 기록을 깨지 못해 실망했던 Jamie가 동료 Ken의 격려로 자신감을 회복하고 다음 경주를 기약했다는 내용이다. 따라서 심경의 변화로 ③ '좌절한 → 용기를 얻은'이 가장 적절하다.

오답풀이

보기 해석	선택률
① 무관심한 → 후회하는	1%
② 기쁜 → 지루한	0%
④ 초조한 → 무서워하는	1%
⑤ 차분한 → 신이 난	3%

구문   [13행] Jamie, **now motivated to keep pushing for her goal**, replied with a smile.
▶ <주어+동사> 사이에 주어의 상태를 보충 설명하는 분사구문이 삽입되었다. Jamie가 '동기를 부여받은' 대상임을 나타내기 위해 과거분사인 motivated를 썼다.

02   정답 ④   83%   2023 6월 20번

해석   다면적인 창의적 활동에 대한 특정 방해 요인은 어쩌면 너무 이른 전문화, 즉 인생의 너무 이른 시기에 교육 방향을 선택하거나 한 가지 능력 개발에 집중해야 하는 데 있다. 그러나 한 가지 영역에서의 창의력 개발은 비슷한 기술을 필요로 하는 다른 영역에서 효과를 높일 수 있으며, 일반성과 특수성 사이의 유연한 전환은 많은 영역에서 생산성에 도움이 된다. 지나친 특수성은 그 영역 외부의 정보가 과소평가되고 이용되지 못하는 결과를 낳을 수 있어 사고의 고착으로 이어지는 한편, 지나친 일반성은 혼돈, 모호함, 그리고 얕음으로 이어진다. 두 가지 경향 모두, 영역 간 지식과 기술 이전에 대한 위협이 된다. 그러므로, 영역을 넘나드는 창의력 개발에 응당 최적인 것은, 젊은이들이 특정 영역에서 창의적인 과제를 맡을 때 이를 지원해주고, 지식과 기술을 다른 영역, 분야, 과제 안팎으로 적용하도록 격려도 함께 해주는 것이다.

지문 간단히 보기

> 너무 이른 전문화(한 영역 집중) → 다면적 창의 활동 방해

> 한 영역의 창의력은 다른 영역에서도 효과를 높임
> → '일반성과 특수성 사이의 유연한 전환'이 중요

↓

> 지나친 특수성과 지나친 일반성 모두 문제의 소지가 있음

↓

> 젊은이들이 한 영역의 창의력을 다른 분야 안팎으로 적용해보면서 '영역을 넘나드는' 창의력을 키울 수 있도록 지원과 격려가 필요함

해설   한 영역에서의 창의력이 영역을 넘나들며 활용될 수 있도록 젊은이들을 지원하고 격려해야 한다는 내용이다. 마지막 문장에 should와 함께 주장이 잘 제시된다. 따라서 답으로 가장 적절한 것은 ④ '특정 영역에서 개발된 창의성이 영역 간 활용되도록 장려해야 한다.'이다.

오답풀이

보기 해설	선택률
① '도전과 실패를 두려워 말라'는 내용은 언급되지 않았다.	2%
② '투자가 필요하다'는 내용은 언급되지 않았다.	2%
③ '다양한'이라는 단어만 보고 고르기 쉽지만, 글에서 '교육 과정'은 언급되지 않았다.	7%
⑤ 첫 문장에서 조기에 이뤄지는 전문화는 창의력 개발에 '방해 요인'이 된다고 했다.	3%

구문   [15행] **What** should therefore be optimal for the development of cross-domain creativity **is** [**support** for young people in taking up ~] and [**coupling** it with encouragement ~]
▶ what이 이끄는 명사절이 주어로 나오면 단수 취급한다(is).
▶ 주격보어인 명사구 [ ]가 <A and B> 형태로 병렬 연결되었다. 두 번째 [ ]에서 밑줄 친 it이 support를 받는다.

03 정답 ② 47%

2022 4월 21번

해석 저널리스트들은 '초기 발견' 단계에 있는 연구들, 즉 누군가가 어떤 것을 최초로 발견했다고 주장하는 연구를 보도하기를 매우 좋아하는데, 그것의 새로움에 뉴스 가치가 있기 때문이다. 그러나 '사상 최초의' 발견들은 후속 연구에 의해 약화되기가 아주 쉽다. 이런 일이 생길 때 뉴스 매체들은 흔히 다시 돌아가 청중들에게 그 변화를 알려주지 않는다—그들이 심지어 그것에 관해 듣기는 할지 생각하면서 말이다. CBC News 기자인 Kelly Crowe는 한 전염병학자의 말을 인용하며 쓰기를, "현대 연구에서 게재된 연구의 다수 또는 대다수가 잘못된 결과일 수 있다는 염려가 커지고 있다."라고 한다. 그녀는 이어서 말하기로, 저널리스트들이 이런 경향에 관해 비난받을 만하지만, 이들은 자신이 인용하는 연구의 과학자들에 의해 방조되고 있다고 한다. 그녀는 과학 초록의 '결론' 부분들이 명성 있는 학술지와 무비판적으로 미끼를 무는 매체의 관심을 끌고자 때때로 과장될 수 있다고 쓴다. 그렇기는 해도, Crowe는 뉴스와 과학의 목적과 과정 사이에는 그래도 상반된 점이 있다는 것, 즉 과학은 '진화하지만' 뉴스는 '발생한다'는 점을 강조하며 글을 맺는다.

지문 간단히 보기

뉴스 매체: '초기 발견, 새로움'에 집중
→ 연구 결과가 추후 수정되어도 추가 보도 X

↓

많은 현대 연구 결과는 사실상 '틀렸을' 거라는 우려
: 저널리스트도 문제지만, 과학자들도 상황 방조 중

↓

하지만, '과학은 진화하고 뉴스는 발생한다'
▶ **과학의 목적은 지식을 발전시키는 것이지만, 뉴스는 '그 순간 새로운 것'을 보도하는 것**

해설 초기 단계의 과학 연구는 후속 연구에 의해 내용이 계속 수정되지만, 이를 보도하는 뉴스는 '최초'라는 타이틀과 새로움에 집중할 뿐 그 내용의 변화에는 관심을 두지 않는다는 내용이다. 따라서 밑줄 부분은 ② '뉴스는 연구가 어떻게 변화하는지보다는, 그것의 새로움에 집중한다.'의 의미로 볼 수 있다.

오답풀이

보기 해석	선택률
① 뉴스는 결과보다도 연구의 과정을 추적한다.	12%
③ 뉴스는 잘못된 과학적 발견을 비판하여 눈길을 끈다.	25%
④ 과학자들과 달리, 기자들은 시청자들에게 즉각적인 피드백을 준다.	9%
⑤ 기자들은 과학의 중요성에 대한 신뢰를 만들고 강화한다.	6%

구문 [9행] ~ "There is increasing concern **that** in modern research, false findings may be the majority or even the vast majority of published research claims."
▶ 추상명사 concern 뒤로 '걱정'의 내용을 설명하는 동격의 that절이 연결되었다. 밑줄 부분은 주어, 동사, 보어를 모두 갖춘 완전한 2형식 구조이다.

04 정답 ③ 46%

2021학년도 수능 23번

해석 사람과 기계를 협업 시스템으로 생각하지 않고, 자동화될 수 있는 작업은 무엇이든 기계에 할당하며 그 나머지를 사람들에게 맡기면 어려움이 발생한다. 이것은 결국 사람들에게 기계와 똑같이, 즉 인간의 능력과는 다른 방식으로 행동할 것을 요구하게 된다. 우리는 사람들이 기계를 감독하기를 기대하는데, 이는 오랫동안 정신을 바짝 차려야 한다는 뜻으로, 우리가 잘하지 못하는 것이다. 우리는 사람들더러 기계에 의해 요구되는 수준으로 몹시 정확하고 정밀하게 반복 작업을 할 것을 요구하는데, 이 또한 우리가 잘하지 못하는 것이다. 우리가 이런 식으로 어떤 과제의 기계적 구성요소와 인간적 구성요소를 나눌 때, 우리는 인간의 강점과 능력을 이용하지 못하고, 그 대신 우리가 유전적 및 생물학적으로 부적합한 영역에 의존하게 된다. 하지만, 사람들이 실패하면 그들은 비난받는다.

지문 간단히 보기

'기계와 인간의 작업을 분리하면' 문제 발생
→ 인간이 자기 능력과 다른 방식으로 일하게 됨

↓

인간은 '내내 기계를 바짝 감독하며 반복 작업을 고도로 정밀하게 수행해야' 하는데, 사실 인간은 이런 일에 능하지 않음

↓

그 결과, 인간의 강점과 능력이 발휘되지 못함
= 유전적 및 생물학적으로 부적합한 영역에만 의존

해설 인간과 기계를 협업 관계로 보지 않고 역할을 분리할 때 발생하는 '어려움'을 설명하는 글이다. 첫 문장에 주제가 잘 제시된다. 따라서 정답은 ③ '자동화 시스템에서 인간에게 부적합한 과제를 할당하는 것의 문제'이다.

오답풀이

보기 해석	선택률
① 실패를 피하고자 인간적인 약점을 극복하는 것의 어려움	7%
② 기계와 인간이 함께 일하게 하는 것의 이점	17%
④ 인간이 기계 자동화를 계속 추구하는 이유	16%
⑤ 인간의 행동이 기계의 성능에 미치는 영향	13%

구문 [4행] This **ends up requiring** people to behave in machine-like fashion, ~
▶ <end up V-ing(결국 ~하다)>에 <require+목적어+to부정사(~에게 …하도록 요구하다)>의 5형식 구조가 포함되었다.

05 정답 ③ 90%

해석 위 표는 2009년과 2019년에 상위 6개 출처(국)에서 인구 100만 명당 거주민 특허 출원 건수를 보여준다. 2009년에 상위 3개 출처였던 대한민국과 일본, 스위스는 2019년에도 순위를 유지했다. 인구 100만 명당 891건의 거주민 특허 출원으로 2009년 목록에서 4위를 차지했던 독일은 2019년 목록에서 인구 100만 명당 884건의 거주민 특허 출원으로 5위로 떨어졌다. 미국은 인구 100만 명당 거주민 특허 출원 건수에서 감소(→ 증가)를 보이며, 2009년 목록 5위에서 2019년 목록에서 6위로 떨어졌다. 2009년 목록에 들었던 상위 6개 출처 중, 핀란드는 2019년에 다시 순위에 들지 못한 유일한 출처였다. 반면 2009년에 상위 6개 출처 목록에 오르지 못했던 중국은 2019년 목록에서 인구 100만 명당 890건의 거주민 특허 출원으로 4위를 차지했다.

지문 간단히 보기

> 국가별 인구 100만 명당 특허 건수(2009 vs. 2019)
> ① 한국, 일본, 스위스: 1~3위 유지
> ② 독일: 2009년 4위(891건) → 2019년 5위(884건)
> ③ 미국: 2009년 5위(733건) → 2019년 6위(869건)
>   ▶ **수치는 증가했으나 순위가 하락함**
> ④, ⑤ 2009년 순위 국가 중 핀란드는 2019년 순위에 못 들고,
>   중국은 새로 합류함

해설 도표에 따르면 미국의 순위가 5위에서 6위로 하락한 것은 맞지만, 특허 출원 건수는 733건에서 869건으로 오히려 늘었다. 따라서 도표와 일치하지 않는 것은 ③이다.

오답풀이

보기 해설	선택률
① The Republic of Korea, Japan, and Switzerland, ~, maintained their rankings in 2019.	1%
② Germany, which sat fourth on the 2009 list ~ fell to fifth place on the 2019 list ~	1%
④ ~ Finland was the only origin which did not make it again in 2019.	4%
⑤ ~ China, which did not make the list of the top 6 origins in 2009, sat fourth on the 2019 list ~	1%

구문 [6행] **Germany,** which sat fourth on the 2009 list with 891 resident patent applications per million population, **fell** ~
▶ 주어와 동사 사이에 주어를 보충 설명하는 관계절이 삽입되었다.

06 정답 ⑤ 44%

해석 대부분의 과학 역사가들은 우리가 현재 천문학이라 부르는, 별과 행성에 대한 연구에 관해 배우려는 동기로 농업 활동을 조정하기 위한 신뢰성 있는 달력의 필요성을 지적한다. 초기 천문학은 언제 작물을 심어야 하는지에 대한 정보를 제공했고, 인간에게 시간의 흐름을 기록하는 최초의 공식적인 방법을 제공했다. 영국 남부에 있는, 4,000년 된 고리 모양의 돌들인 스톤헨지는 아마도 우리가 살고 있는 세계의 규칙성과 예측 가능성의 발견에 관하여 가장 잘 알려진 기념비일 것이다. 스톤헨지의 커다란 표식은 지점(하지, 동지)과 분점(춘분, 추분)에 태양이 뜨는 지평선의 장소를 가리키는데, 우리는 계절의 시작을 나타내고자 여전히 이 날짜들을 이용한다. 그 돌들은 심지어 (해·달의) 식(蝕)을 예측하는 데 사용되었을지도 모른다. 글이 없던 시절 사람들이 세운 스톤헨지의 존재는 자연의 규칙성, 그리고 눈앞의 모습 이면을 보고 사건의 더 깊은 의미를 발견할 수 있는 인간의 정신적 능력 둘 다를 말없이 증언해준다.

지문 간단히 보기

> 초기 천문학: 농업에 참고할 '달력'이 필요해서 연구됨
>
> ↓
>
> (예시) 스톤헨지
> - 세계의 '규칙성, 예측 가능성'을 파악하려는 시도
> - 하지/동지, 춘분/추분 등에 태양이 뜨는 위치 표시
> - 눈앞의 현상을 넘어 '더 깊은 의미(**예측 가능성**)'를 알 수 있었던 인간의 능력에 관한 증거

해설 문맥상 ⑤는 the ability를 꾸미는 to see behind와 병렬 연결되어 '눈앞의 모습 이면을 보고 더 깊은 의미를 발견해내는 능력'이라고 해석되어야 자연스럽다. 따라서 bears와 병렬구조를 이루는 discovers 대신 (to) discover를 써야 한다.

오답풀이

보기 해설	선택률
① humans의 소유격을 받는 복수대명사이다.	12%
② 고유명사인 Stonehenge 주어 뒤로 단수동사 is가 왔다.	10%
③ the spots를 꾸미는 관계부사 where 뒤로 자동사 rises를 포함한 완전한 1형식 문장이 올바르게 연결되었다.	15%
④ 주어인 The stones가 '사용되는' 대상이므로 수동태를 썼다.	17%

구문 [11행] ~ **the spots** on the horizon where the sun rises at the solstices and equinoxes ~
▶ where가 이끄는 관계부사절은 the spots를 꾸민다. 선행사를 꾸미는 전치사구 on the horizon이 관계절보다 먼저 오면서 선행사와 관계절이 분리되었다.

07 정답 ⑤ 35%

해석 과학은 자전거 체인의 기어 톱니처럼 기억의 크기와 시간에 대한 우리의 인식이 연결되어 있다는 것을 보여준다. 어린 시절 여름날의 기억과 같은 다채롭고 새로운 경험들은 그와 관련된 여러 새로운 정보를 가지고 있다. 그 뜨거웠던 날 동안 우리는 수영하는 법을 배웠거나, 새로운 장소로 여행을 갔거나, 보조 바퀴가 없는 자전거를 타는 법을 마스터했다. 그 시절은 그런 모험들로 천천히 흘러갔다. 그러나, 성년기의 우리 삶은 참신함과 새로움이 더 적고, 통근하거나 이메일을 보내거나 서류 작업을 하는 등 반복되는 일로 가득하다. 그러한 지루한 일을 위해 보관된 관련 정보는 더 적고, 두뇌의 기억 부분이 이용할 수 있는 새로운 장면이 더 적다. 우리의 두뇌는 지루한 일로 채워진 이런 날들을 더 짧다고 이해하며, 그래서 여름날이 빠르게 지나간다. 더 나은 시계를 향한 바람에도 불구하고, 우리의 시간 측정 잣대는 고정되어 있지 않다. 우리는 시계처럼 시간을 초로 측정하는 것이 아니라, 우리의 경험들로 측정한다. 우리에게 시간은 느려질 수도 있고 빠르게 흘러갈 수도 있다.

지문 간단히 보기

어린 시절: 다채롭고 새로운 경험이 많음 = 시간이 느림

↓

성년기: 새로움이 적고, 반복되는 일이 많음 = 시간이 빠름

↓

우리의 시간 인식은 (새로운) 경험이 얼마나 많은지에 달림
= 시간 잣대가 고정되어 있지 않음
= 같은 시간이 느리게 또는 빠르게 느껴질 수 있음

해설 새로운 정보가 많은 어린 시절에는 시간이 느리게 간다고 느끼지만, 반복되는 일이 더 많아지는 성년기에는 시간이 더 빨리 간다고 느낀다는 내용이다. 마지막 두 문장에서 '우리는 초가 아닌 경험으로 시간을 측정하므로, 시간의 흐름은 주관적'이라는 말로 그 이유를 잘 설명한다. 따라서 빈칸에는 ⑤ '기억의 크기와 시간에 대한 우리의 인식이 연결되어 있다'가 가장 적절하다.

오답풀이

보기 해석	선택률
① 우리 뇌의 기억 기능은 나이가 들면서 약해진다	18%
② 경험의 풍부함은 지적 능력에 좌우된다	15%
③ 우리 머릿속 정보 저장 체계는 쉴새없이 돌아간다	15%
④ 사건의 시간적 맥락은 우리의 감정을 깨어나게 한다	11%

구문 [11행] ~ there is <u>less new footage</u> **for the recall part of the brain to draw upon**.
▶ to draw upon이 less new footage를 꾸민다. <for+목적격>은 to부정사의 의미상 주어를 나타낸다.

---

08 정답 ① 34%

해석 여러분이 만약 우리의 믿음이 우리가 사실을 해석하는 방식에 영향을 미친다는 것을 확신하지 못하고 있다면, '날고 있는 말'의 예시를 생각해보라. 선사 시대부터 1800년대 중반까지 질주하는 말 그림은 질주하는 동안 벌어진 말 다리를, 즉 앞다리가 멀리 앞으로 뻗쳐지고 뒷다리는 뒤로 멀리 펴진 모습을 보통 보여주었다. 사람들은 이게 말이 질주한 방식임을 그냥 '알고 있었고', 이는 (또한) 그들이 말이 질주하는 것을 '보았던' 방식이다. 원시인들은 그것을 이렇게 '보았고', 아리스토텔레스도 그것을 이렇게 '보았으며', 빅토리아 시대의 상류층도 그랬다. 그러나 그 모든 것은 1878년 Eadweard Muybridge가 와이어 트리거에 연결된 열두 대의 카메라를 사용해 0.5초도 안 되는 사이에 찍었던 질주하는 말 사진 열두 장짜리 한 세트를 공개했을 때 끝났다. Muybridge의 사진은 말이 질주의 세 번째 스텝에서 다리가 벌어지지 않고 밑에 '모아진' 상태로 공중에 완전히 뜬 채 가는 것을 분명히 보여주었다. 그것은 부유의 순간이라고 불린다. 지금은 아이들도 질주하는 말을 이런 식으로 그린다.

지문 간단히 보기

과거 그림 속 질주하는 말: 앞뒤로 다리를 '펼친' 모습
= 사람들이 '믿고' 또 '보았던' 모습

↓

하지만, Muybridge의 사진으로 정반대 사실이 드러남
= 말은 질주 도중 다리를 '모음'
▶ **사람들이 생각과 믿음에 영향을 받아 실제와 다른 현실을 '보았던' 것**

해설 빈칸 뒤의 예시를 일반화해 주제문인 빈칸을 완성하는 문제이다. 과거 사람들은 말이 달릴 때 다리를 벌린다고 '믿었고', 그리하여 그 모습을 '보았다'고 한다. 이는 믿음이 현실 인식에 영향을 미친 사례로 볼 수 있으므로, ① '우리의 믿음이 우리가 사실을 해석하는 방식에 영향을 미친다'가 정답으로 가장 적절하다.

오답풀이

보기 해석	선택률
② 우리가 보는 것은 과거 기억의 환상이다	22%
③ 심지어 사진조차 잘못된 시각적 인식을 낳을 수 있다	17%
④ 우리가 좋고 나쁨을 판단할 수 있는 기준은 없다	16%
⑤ 우리는 거부할 수 없는 증거에도 불구하고 우리 직관을 고수한다	11%

구문 [10행] ~ Eadweard Muybridge published a set of twelve pictures [**(that)** he had taken of a galloping horse in the space of less than half a second <u>using</u> twelve cameras <u>hooked</u> to wire triggers].
▶ pictures를 꾸미는 목적격 관계대명사 that이 생략되었다.
▶ 'using ~'은 분사구문으로, '~하면서'라고 해석한다. 'hooked ~ triggers'는 cameras를 꾸미는 과거분사구이다.

09 정답 ③ 55%

해석 몇몇 형태의 에너지는 활용도에 있어 다른 에너지보다 더 다용도이다. 예를 들어, 우리는 전기를 무수히 많은 용도로 사용할 수 있는 반면, 석탄을 태워 얻은 열은 동력을 생산하는 것과 같은 고정된 용도로 현재 주로 사용된다. 우리가 석탄을 태워 나오는 열을 전기로 바꿀 때, 상당한 양의 에너지가 공정의 비효율성 때문에 손실된다. 하지만 우리는 석탄이 상대적으로 저렴하기 때문에 기꺼이 그 손실을 받아들이며, 타는 석탄을 전등과 컴퓨터와 냉장고를 작동시키는 데 바로 사용하는 것은 어렵고 불편할 것이다. (탄소 섬유 생산을 위해 석탄을 이용할 경제적인 방법을 찾으면 석탄 생산 감소로 고생하는 지역사회를 소생시키는 데 도움이 될 것이다.) 사실상, 우리는 각기 다른 에너지 형태에 서로 다른 가치를 부여해서, 가치 사다리의 맨 위에는 전기가, 가운데에는 액체와 기체 연료가, 맨 밑바닥에는 석탄이나 장작이 있다. 태양광 및 풍력 기술은 높은 가치의 전기를 즉시 생산한다는 점에서 장점이 있다.

지문 간단히 보기

> 에너지 형태별로 용도의 다양성 면에서 차이가 있음
> ①, ② (예시) 전기(무수히 많은 용도) vs. 석탄(동력 생산 등 한정된 용도)

> ④ 에너지 형태마다 가치도 다름: 전기 - 액체/기체 - 석탄 순서
> ⑤ (추가 예시) 태양 및 풍력 에너지: 가치가 '높은' 전기 생산

해설 에너지별로 용도와 효율에서 차이가 있고, 그에 따라 가치도 상이하다는 내용이다. 하지만 ③은 갑자기 '탄소 섬유 생산'을 언급하며 석탄을 경제적으로 활용할 방법을 찾으면 도움이 된다고 하므로 흐름상 어색하다.

오답풀이

보기 해설	선택률
①, ② '석탄 열의 한정된 용도'에 관한 보충 설명이다. 석탄 열을 동력 생산에 쓸 때도 에너지 손실이 생기기는 하지만, 비용이 비교적 싸기도 하고 가전 등을 직접 돌리는 것보다는 쉽기 때문에 동력 생산에 쓴다는 것이다.	2% 9%
④ 에너지 형태별로 서로 다른 가치가 부여된다는 설명으로 첫 문장의 논의를 발전시킨다.	21%
⑤ ④에서 언급한 '가치 사다리'에 관한 추가 예시로 태양광과 풍력을 언급한다.	12%

구문 [15행] ~ **with** electricity at the top of the value ladder, liquid and gaseous fuels in the middle, and coal or firewood at the bottom.
▶ with 뒤로 <명사+전치사구>가 <A, B, and C> 형태로 병렬 연결되었다. 전체적으로 '~이 …한 상태인'의 의미이다.

10 정답 ① 23%

해석 공간 기준점은 자기 자신보다 더 크다. 이것은 그다지 모순이 아닌데, 랜드마크는 그 자체이기도 하지만, 또한 자기 주변을 규정짓기도 하기 때문이다.
(A) 많은 대학 캠퍼스에서 반복된 한 전형적인 예에서, 연구원들은 먼저 학생들로부터 캠퍼스 랜드마크의 목록을 수집한다. 그다음, 그들은 또 다른 집단의 학생들에게 쌍으로 이루어진 장소 사이의 거리를 추정해 달라고 요청하는데, 일부는 랜드마크까지, 일부는 캠퍼스의 평범한 건물까지를 추정케 한다.
(C) 주목할 만한 결과는, 평범한 장소에서 랜드마크까지의 거리가 랜드마크에서 평범한 장소까지의 거리보다 더 짧다고 추정된다는 것이다. 그래서 사람들은 Pierre의 집에서 에펠탑까지의 거리가 에펠탑에서 Pierre의 집까지의 거리보다 더 짧다고 추정할 것이다. 마치 블랙홀처럼, 랜드마크는 평범한 장소를 자기 방향으로 끌어들이는 듯 하지만, 평범한 장소들은 그렇지 않다.
(B) 거리 추정에 관한 이러한 비대칭은 A에서부터 B까지의 거리가 B에서부터 A까지의 거리와 같아야 한다는, 가장 기초적인 유클리드 거리 법칙에 위배된다. 그렇다면, 거리에 관한 추정은 반드시 일관적이지는 않다.

지문 간단히 보기

> 공간 기준점: 주변 공간을 규정짓는 특성
> (A) 대학 캠퍼스에서의 연구 사례

> (A) 장소 간 거리를 추정하는 실험 과정
> (C) 실험의 '놀라운 결과'

> (C) 실제로 같은 거리인데도, 시작점이 랜드마크인 경우 시작점이 일반적인 장소일 때보다 '짧게' 추정됨
> (B) 이 '비대칭': 거리 추정이 꼭 일관되지 않음을 시사

해설 공간 기준점이 되는 랜드마크는 자기 자신을 넘어서 주변을 규정짓는다는 일반적 내용 뒤로, 대학 캠퍼스에서 진행된 연구를 처음 언급하는 (A), 연구의 결과를 설명하는 (C), (C)의 결과를 '이러한 비대칭'이라는 키워드로 정리하는 (B)가 차례로 연결되어야 한다. 따라서 ① '(A)-(C)-(B)'가 가장 자연스럽다.

오답풀이

보기 해설	선택률
②, ③ 거리 추정의 '비대칭'으로 볼 만한 내용이 주어진 글에 언급되지 않으므로 (B)가 처음에 나오면 어색하다.	18% 14%
④, ⑤ (C)는 연구 결과(finding)이므로 과정을 다루는 (A)보다 뒤에 위치해야 한다.	24% 19%

구문 [C-7행] ~ landmarks seem to pull ordinary locations toward themselves, but ordinary places **do not**.
▶ 문장 맨 끝의 대동사 do not은 do not pull landmarks toward themselves의 의미이다.

11 정답 ④ 44% 2025학년도 수능 38번

해석 영업비밀법은 혁신 촉진을 목표로 하지만, 특허 보호와는 아주 다른 방식으로 그 목표를 이룬다. 특허 취득의 이점에도 불구하고, 많은 혁신가들은 비밀 유지를 통해 혁신을 보호하기를 선호한다. 그들은 특허를 취득하는 데 드는 비용과 시간 지연이 너무 크다고 믿거나, 비밀주의가 그들의 투자를 더 잘 보호하고 수익을 키워줄 거라고 믿을지도 모른다. 또한 그들은 특허에서 허용되는 것보다 더 오랜 기간에 걸쳐 발명품이 최고로 활용될 수 있다고 믿을지도 모른다. 하지만, 영업비밀에 관한 특별한 법적 보호가 전혀 없다면, 비밀주의 발명가는 직원 또는 계약자가 그 독점적 정보(핵심 정보)를 공개할 위험을 감수하게 된다. 그 아이디어가 공개되면, 자유 시장 경제의 배경 규범에 따라 그것은 '공기처럼 자유로워질' 것이다. 이런 곤경은 비밀 유지에 의존하려는 발명가라면 누구든 자신의 연구 시설 주변에 통과할 수 없는 높은 울타리를 쌓고 핵심 정보에 접근할 수 있는 사람의 수를 크게 제한하는 데 지나친 자원을 지출하게 할 수 있다.

지문 간단히 보기

> 많은 혁신가가 특허보다도 비밀을 통해 혁신을 보호하고 싶어 함 (비용, 수익, 기간 등의 이유)

↓

> 하지만, 비밀에 대한 법적 보호가 없다면 발명가는 비밀이 공개될 위험을 감수하게 됨

↓

> 아이디어가 공개되면 '공기'처럼 자유롭게 유통될 것이므로, 비밀 보호를 위해 과도한 자원이 투입될 수 있음 → 영업비밀법 필요

해설 ④ 앞까지는 혁신가들을 They로 언급하며, 이들이 왜 특허보다 비밀로 혁신을 보호하고자 하는지 설명한다. 하지만 ④ 뒤는 갑자기 '아이디어가 공개되었을 때'를 말하므로 흐름이 연결되지 않는다. 이때 주어진 문장은 역접어 however로 흐름을 전환하며, 비밀에 대한 법적 보호가 없다면 혁신가가 '비밀 폭로'의 위험을 떠안게 된다는 내용을 말하고 있다. 여기서 언급된 '비밀 폭로'가 이뤄지면 어떤 결과가 발생하고, 그 결과를 막기 위해 또 어떤 노력이 있을지 설명하는 것이 곧 ④ 뒤이다. 따라서 ④가 답으로 적절하다.

오답풀이 보기 해설 선택률

① 영업비밀법과 특허를 대비하는 첫 문장 뒤로 많은 혁신가가 특허보다 비밀을 선호한다는 내용이 적절히 연결된다. — 2%

②, 앞의 many innovators가 They로 계속 연결되며 이들 — 7%
③ 이 어떤 생각으로 비밀을 선호하는지 설명하는 흐름이다. — 11%

⑤ '아이디어가 공개되어 자유롭게 유통되는' 상황은 비밀주의의 발명가 입장에서는 '곤경'스러운 것이므로, 뒤에서 Such a predicament라고 표현했다. — 36%

구문 [18행] Such a predicament **would lead** any inventor <u>seeking to rely upon secrecy</u> **to spend** an inordinate amount of resources ~
▶ <lead A to-V(A가 ~하게 하다)> 구문이다. 밑줄 친 분사구가 A에 해당하는 any inventor를 수식하고 있다.

---

12 정답 ④ 30% 2023 3월 40번

해석 거대한 산업 도시의 출현은 흔히 도시화라고 알려진 사회적 결과를 가져왔다. 도시는 마을이나 작은 소도시의 비공식적인 통제를 해체한다. 대부분의 도시 거주자는 서로 알지 못하고, 도시에서의 사회적 상호 작용 대부분은 주차 안내원, 가게 점원, 혹은 고객처럼 서로를 특정한 역할로만 아는 사람들 사이에서 일어난다. 개인들은 더 자유롭게 자기가 원하는 대로, 그리고 사회 규범에서 벗어나는 방식으로 살 수 있게 되었다. 이에 대응하여, 그리고 도시 생활의 높은 밀도가 수천 명의 유순한 조정을 필요로 하는 이유로, 도시 사회는 도시 행동을 통제하기 위한 매우 다양한 방식을 개발했다. 여기에는 토지의 개인적 사용, (화재 위험 최소화를 위한) 건물 건설 및 관리, 오염과 소음 발생을 통제하는 규제 마련이 포함된다.
→ 거대 산업 도시의 사회적 환경은 도시 사회가 마을이나 작은 소도시의 비공식적인 통제를 (A)없애고 조정된 도시 행동을 효과적으로 유도하기 위한 (B)규제적 조치를 도입하게 했다.

지문 간단히 보기

> 도시화 이후, 마을/소도시 단위의 비공식적 통제 해체
> - 개인은 정해진 역할 안에서 교류
> - 각자 개인 생활의 자유도가 높아짐

↓

> 이에 대응해 도시 차원의 규제 조치가 마련됨
> - 밀도 높은 도시 생활의 특성상 행동 통제가 필요해짐
> - 토지 사용, 건물 관리, 소음 통제 등에 관한 규제 ↑

해설 도시화 이후로 소도시의 비공식적 통제가 해체되고 사람들이 특정한 역할로만 서로 교류함에 따라 개인 생활의 자유도가 높아지면서, 역으로 이에 대응해 도시 차원의 질서 유지 조치가 강화됐다는 내용이다. 따라서 요약문의 빈칸에는 ④ '없애고 - 규제적'이 적절하다.

오답풀이 보기 해설 선택률

보기	해석	선택률
①	제한하고 - 허용적	26%
②	유지하고 - 규제적	20%
③	평가하고 - 간접적	10%
⑤	강화하고 - 허용적	14%

구문 [20행] The social conditions in large, industrial cities **made urban societies remove** the informal controls of the village or small town, ~
▶ <make+목적어+원형부정사> 형태의 5형식 구문이다.

13~14 정답 ① 84% / ③ 54%   2023 10월 41~42번

해석 자연에 대한 지배는 환경 윤리와 환경 정치 이론에서 익숙한 수사적 표현이다. 그것의 역사는 근대 과학, 철학, 정치학의 등장과 더 광범위하게 결부되어 있다. Francis Bacon이 말한 것처럼 '인간의 조건을 개선할' 수 있는 방법으로 물리적 세계를 지배하는 인과 관계에 개입하고자 이러한 관계를 이해하려는 노력은 서구에서 근대성의 시작을 알렸다. 오랫동안 '자연에 대한 지배'는 인간 이외의 환경을 이해하고 통제하려는 이러한 노력을 가리켰고, 그것은 명백히 좋은 것으로 여겨졌다. 이러한 노력은 새로운 기술과 경제적 번영 증가를 가능하게 했고, 여러 형태의 인간 고통의 종식을 약속했으며, 무지와 미신에 대한 이성의 승리를 보여주었다. 그것의 대가는 19세기 산업화와 함께 보이지 않기(→ 보이기) 시작했는데, 그것(산업화)은 명백한 환경 파괴를 야기했고, 많은 사람들 사이에서 땅과 땅을 구성하는 인간 너머의 공동체로부터의 소외감을 초래했다. 사람들은 Mary Shelley의 <Frankenstein(1818)>과 같은 당대 소설들, Wordsworth의 'Michael(1800)'과 이후 Whitman의 <Leaves of Grass(1855)>와 같은 시들, 그리고 자연 문학의 초기 작품인 Thoreau의 <Walden(1854)>에서 이러한 대가에 대한 불안감이 커지는 것을 본다. 그러나 자연에 대한 지배를 문제로 삼는 체계적이고 비판적인 분석은 1970년대 환경 연구 운동이 등장하고서야 진가를 발휘했다. 이후 이 수사적 표현은 주로 부정적 의미를 띠게 됐는데, 자연에 대한 지배가 인간의 이익에 위험할 뿐만 아니라 해롭고 부당한 것으로 여겨지면서 그렇게 되었다.

지문 간단히 보기

> 과거 '자연에 대한 지배' = '근대성의 시작'
> : 환경에 대한 인간의 이해와 통제가 '좋게' 여겨짐

↓

> 산업화 이후 문제점 속출(환경 파괴, 인간-자연의 단절)
> ▶ **자연에 대한 지배의 대가가 '드러나고' 불안도 커짐**

↓

> 오늘날 '자연에 대한 지배' = 비판의 대상(부정적 의미)
> : 인간 이익에 위험할 뿐 아니라 '해롭고 부당하게' 여겨짐

구문 [14행] This effort **made possible** new technologies and rising economic prosperity, ~
▶ <make+목적어+형용사>의 5형식 구조에서, 밑줄 친 목적어가 너무 길어서 목적격보어 possible을 목적어보다 먼저 쓴 것이다.

13

해설 '자연에 대한 지배'가 과거에는 미신에 대한 이성의 승리로 여겨지며 근대성의 신호탄이 되었지만, 오늘날은 주로 부정적 의미를 띤다는 내용이다. 글 중반부의 'Its cost ~' 이후로 글의 흐름이 반전된다. 따라서 제목으로 가장 적절한 것은 ① '자연의 지배에 대한 시각의 변화'이다.

오답풀이

보기 해석	선택률
② 과학은 지식을 향한 욕구에서 시작된다	4%
③ 윤리는 모든 학문 분야에 핵심적이다	4%
④ 문학 속의 자연은 실제적이지 않다	3%
⑤ 친환경은 정말 환경에 친화적일까?	2%

14

해설 자연에 대한 지배로 환경 파괴가 초래되고 인간과 인간 너머의 공동체가 단절되었다는 설명으로 보아, 대가가 눈에 '보이지 않았다'는 설명은 부적절하다. 따라서 ③ (c)의 invisible을 visible로 바꾸어야 한다.

오답풀이

보기 해석	선택률
① control(통제하다)	4%
② possible(가능한)	7%
④ unease(불안)	27%
⑤ negative(부정적인)	8%

STEP PLUS+ 수능 기출 마무리 복습

단어 TEST

02 새로움, 참신함   **03** (기반을) 약화시키다   **04** 할당하다   **05** 쉴새 없이   **06** 확신하지 못하는   **07** ~을 고수하다   **08** 거부[저항]할 수 없는   **09** 일관된   **10** 해체하다   **11** 번영   **12** 부당한

구문 TEST

14 Once (it is) received by our office   **15** whose novels explore identity and culture   **16** may have been used to predict eclipses   **17** may have lost the document   **18** To see[In order to see / So as to see] the stars more clearly

01 정답 ② 88%   2023 10월 18번

해석 귀하가 건강하고 기분 좋게 이 통지를 받으시기를 바랍니다. 10월 9일에 Rosehill 아파트 단지로 귀하의 집 주소가 분명하게 적힌 물품이 배달되었다는 것을 알려 드리기 위해 글을 씁니다. 그런데 귀하에게 그 물품을 전달하려고 여러 번 시도했지만, 그것은 저희 프런트에 장기간 찾아가지 않은 채 남아 있습니다. 배달된 모든 물품을 보관하고 그것들이 신속하게 알맞은 입주민에게 전달되도록 돕는 것이 저희의 책임입니다. 그런 까닭에, 귀하가 저희 운영 시간 동안에 관리 사무실을 방문하셔서 귀하의 물품을 찾아가시기를 정중히 요청드립니다. 이 문제와 관련하여 귀하의 협조에 진심으로 감사드립니다.

지문 간단히 보기

편지 수신자 앞으로 배달된 물품이 있음

↓

관리 사무실 데스크에서 장기간 보관중임

↓

관리 사무실 운영 시간 중 와서 수거하기를 요청함

해설 택배가 수거되지 않은 채로 관리 사무실에 보관되어 있으니 가져가기를 청한다는 내용으로, 'Therefore, we kindly request ~'에 글의 목적이 드러난다. 따라서 정답은 ② '배달된 물품을 찾아갈 것을 요청하려고'이다.

오답풀이

보기 해설	선택률
① '공사'에 관해서 언급되지 않았다.	0%
③ 물품을 잘못 가져간 것이 아니라 아직 가져가지 '않은' 것이므로 '반납'을 부탁할 수도 없다.	7%
④ '도난' 상황은 언급되지 않았다.	1%
⑤ 운영 시간 중에 찾아가라는 요청만 제시될 뿐, 운영 시간 '변경'은 언급되지 않았다.	0%

구문 [11행] Therefore, we kindly request that you **(should) visit** the management office ~
▶ 요구의 동사인 request의 목적절이 '~해야 한다'는 의미를 나타낼 때, that절의 동사 자리에는 <(should)+동사원형>이 쓰인다.

02 정답 ① 85%   2024학년도 수능 22번

해석 여러분의 (고객) 응답에 우선순위를 둘 수 있다면, 그것이 특별히 즐겁거나 화가 나는 경험에 대한 일회성 상호 작용이든, 여러분의 고객 기반 내에서 상당히 영향력 있는 개인과의 장기적 관계 발전이든 간에, 여러분이 개별 고객들과 더 깊은 관계를 맺을 수 있게 된다. 만약 여러분이 어떤 브랜드나 제품 또는 서비스에 관해 호의적인 의견 혹은 그 문제에 대해서 어떤 의견이라도 올려본 적이 있다면, 그 결과 예컨대 그 브랜드 관리자로부터 개인적으로 인정받는다면 기분이 어떨지 생각해보라. 일반적으로 사람들은 할 말이 있어서, 그리고 그것을 말한 데 대해 인정받기를 원해서 글을 올린다. 특히, 사람들이 긍정적인 의견을 게시할 때 그것은 그 게시물을 작성하게 만든 경험에 대한 감사의 표현이다. 여러분 옆에 서 있는 사람에 대한 칭찬은 보통 '감사합니다'와 같은 답을 받지만, 슬픈 사실은 대부분의 브랜드 칭찬이 답을 받지 못한다는 것이다. 이것은 무엇이 칭찬을 이끌어냈는지 이해하고 그 칭찬을 바탕으로 확고한 팬을 만들 수 있는 기회를 잃은 것이다.

지문 간단히 보기

고객 응답을 우선순위에 두면 → 고객과의 관계 ↑

↓

(예시) 소비자가 브랜드나 제품에 대해 의견을 줄 때: '인정'해주는 반응을 받으면 기분이 좋음

↓

하지만, 대부분의 브랜드 칭찬이 응답을 받지 못함 ▶ **응답을 해주면, 이들을 '확고한 팬'으로 만들 수 있음**

해설 고객의 코멘트에 응답해주는 일을 우선순위에 두면 고객과의 관계 발전에 도움이 된다는 내용으로, 첫 문장에 주제가 있다. 따라서 주장으로 ① '고객과의 관계 증진을 위해 고객의 브랜드 칭찬에 응답하는 것은 중요하다.'가 가장 적절하다.

오답풀이

보기 해설	선택률
② 고객 피드백을 '분석하라'는 내용은 언급되지 않았다. 핵심 내용은 피드백에 '답하라'이다.	4%
③ 고객이 먼저 의견을 주고 그에 답하는 상황에 관한 글이다. 선후 관계가 잘못되었다.	3%
④ '부정적 의견'을 받는 경우는 언급되지 않았다.	2%
⑤ '새로운 이미지 창출'에 관해 언급되지 않았다.	3%

구문 [12행] ~ because they <u>want</u> to be recognized for **having said it**.
▶ 전치사 for의 목적어로 쓰인 완료동명사 <having p.p.>는 because절의 동사 want보다 과거를 나타낸다. 동명사 또는 to부정사의 시제는 본동사와 같은지, 본동사보다 과거인지를 상대적으로 나타낸다는 점을 기억해 둔다.

03 정답 ③ 47%

해석 변호사들은 때때로 소유권을 '막대 다발'로 묘사한다. 이 비유는 약 1세기 전에 도입되어 법학 교육과 실무를 극적으로 변화시켰다. 그 비유는 유용한데, 우리가 소유권을 분리되고 또 다시 합쳐질 수 있는 대인 관계적인 권리의 모음으로 보는 것을 도와주기 때문이다. 어떤 자원에 관해 '그건 내 거다'라고 말할 때, 흔히 그것은 여러분이 전체 다발을 구성하는 많은 막대, 즉 판매 막대, 임대 막대, 저당잡히고 허가하고 증여하고 심지어 그것을 파괴할 권리를 소유한다는 뜻이다. 그러나 우리는 흔히 그 막대들을 쪼개는데, 토지 한 면에 대해서 보자면, 땅 주인, 저당권을 가진 은행, 임대차 계약을 맺은 임차인, 토지 진입 면허를 가진 배관공, 광물에 대한 권리를 가진 석유 회사가 있을 수 있다. 이 각각의 관계자는 <u>그 다발의 막대 하나</u>를 소유한다.

지문 간단히 보기

소유권에 대한 비유: '막대 다발' = 여러 대인 관계적 권리의 '모음'

어떤 것을 '소유한다' = 이 권리의 '모음'을 지닌다
→ 권리를 '쪼개는' 것도 가능(막대 하나)

(예시) 토지에 대한 권리: 소유자, 저당권자, 임차인 등등 여러 관계자 존재 ▶ **각자가 토지에 대한 부분적 권리를 지님**

해설 소유권은 '막대 다발'과 같아서 판매, 임대, 저당, 허가 등 많은 권리를 포함하며, 토지를 예로 보면 땅 주인, 저당권자, 세입자, 출입자 등등 많은 이가 얽혀 있다고 한다. 이들은 모두 토지를 '부분적으로 사용'할 수 있다는 점에서, 밑줄 부분은 ③ '재산의 한 측면을 사용할 수 있는 권리'의 의미로 볼 수 있다.

오답풀이

보기 해석	선택률
① 자원을 개발해야 한다는 법적 의무	8%
② 법적으로 부동산 소유권을 주장할 우선권	12%
④ 세입자들에 의해 동등하게 공유되는 빌딩	13%
⑤ 누구도 자기 것이라고 주장할 수 없는 토지 한 면	20%

구문 [17행] **Each of these parties owns** a stick in the bundle.
▶ <each of+복수명사> 주어는 단수 취급한다(owns).

04 정답 ① 36%

해석 웹 이전에 신문 기록 보관소는 주로 전문적 연구원과 언론학과 학생의 곰팡내 나는 영역이었다. 저널리즘은 당연히 최신에 관한 것이었다. 자료 보관소의 일반적 접근 가능성은 저널리즘의 유통기한을 크게 연장시켜, 더 오래된 기사가 이제는 자주 더 최신 기사에 맥락을 제공하기 위해 인용되고 있다. 뉴스에서 마주치는 복잡한 이슈에 관해 의미가 어떻게 형성되는가와 관련하여, 이 새로운 출발은 인쇄물 소비자로서는 명백하지 않았거나 가능하지도 않았던, 뉴스의 기저 이슈와 맥락에 관여하기 위한 준비로 온라인 뉴스 소비자에게 이해될 수 있다. 온라인 뉴스의 떠오르는 특성 중 하나는, 부분적으로는 쉽게 접근할 수 있는 온라인 자료 보관소의 깊이로 결정되는데, 뉴스 기사가 수명이 짧고 연결성이 없는 미디어 구경거리가 아니라 더 큰 경제적, 사회적, 문화적 이슈의 분명한 결과로 이해될 가능성인 듯 보인다.

지문 간단히 보기

웹 이전의 저널리즘: 최신 기사 중심,
기록 보관소 접근성↓(연구자, 전공생 위주)

웹 이후의 저널리즘: 자료 보관소 접근성↑
- 옛날 기사 인용↑
- 기사의 유통 기한↑
- 기저 이슈나 맥락에 관한 정보↑

해설 웹의 등장 이후 자료 보관소에 대한 접근성이 향상됨에 따라 오래된 기사 인용이 더 자유로워지면서 기사의 '유통 기한'이 길어지고, 기저 이슈나 맥락을 더 광범위하게 다룰 수 있게 되었다는 내용이다. 따라서 ① '웹 기반 저널리즘: 더 오래 지속되고 맥락상 더 넓다'가 제목으로 가장 적절하다.

오답풀이

보기 해석	선택률
② 온라인 뉴스는 최신 콘텐츠로 일간 신문을 능가한다!	19%
③ 온라인 미디어 저널리스트는 뉴스 뒤 숨겨진 이야기를 어떻게 전하는가	20%
④ 인쇄된 신문으로 과거로의 여행을 시작하자!	13%
⑤ 웹 세계 저널리즘의 현재와 미래	12%

구문 [13행] **One of the emergent qualities of online news**, [determined in part by the depth of readily accessible online archives], **seems** to be the possibility ~
▶ <one of the+복수명사> 주어는 단수 취급한다(seems). [ ]는 주어를 보충 설명하는 분사구문이다.

해석   Dorothy Lavinia Brown은 미국 남부에서 외과 의사가 된 최초의 흑인 여성이었다. 유아일 때 그녀는 보육원에 맡겨졌다. 고등학교를 졸업한 후, 그녀는 장학금을 받고 Bennett College에 들어갔고, 1941년에 그곳을 졸업한 후, Tennessee주 Nashville에 있는 Meharry 의과 대학에 입학하여 1948년에 졸업했다. 그녀의 인턴 과정은 뉴욕의 Harlem 병원에서 수행되었지만, 그곳에서 그녀는 성별에 대한 반대에 부딪혀 외과의 레지던트 과정을 거부당했다. 그 후 그녀는 Meharry로 돌아와 1954년에 외과 레지던트 과정을 마쳤다. 그녀는 그 후에 Nashville에 있는 Riverside-Meharry 병원의 외과 과장 및 교육원장이 되었고, 또한 George W. Hubbard 병원 소속 외과 의사이자 Meharry 의과 대학 외과 교수가 되었다. 1966년에 그녀는 Tennessee 주의회 의원으로 선출된 최초의 흑인 여성이 되었다.

지문 간단히 보기

> Dorothy Lavinia Brown의 생애
> ① 미국 남부 출신 최초의 흑인 여성 외과의
> ② 유아일 때 보육원에 맡겨짐
> ③ Bennett 대학에 장학금 입학 → Meharry 의대 진학
> ④ Harlem 병원에서 인턴 수련 후, 레지던트 수련을 거부당함
>   → Meharry로 복귀해서 마침
> ⑤ 1966년에 Tennessee 주의회 의원 선출(흑인 여성 최초)

해설   '~ there she ~ was denied residency as a surgeon.'에 따르면, Dorothy Lavinia Brown은 뉴욕 Harlem 병원에서 외과 레지던트 과정을 이어 가려 했으나 성별 이슈로 거부당했다고 한다. 따라서 ④ '뉴욕의 Harlem 병원에서 외과 레지던트 과정을 마쳤다.'가 글의 내용과 일치하지 않는다.

오답풀이

보기 해설	선택률
① ~ the first black female in the American South to become a surgeon.	1%
② As an infant she was placed in an orphanage.	1%
③ After high school, she won a scholarship to Bennett College ~	5%
⑤ In 1966 ~ elected to the Tennessee state legislature.	0%

구문   [7행] ~ there she encountered gender resistance and **was denied residency as a surgeon**.
▶ <deny A B(A에게 B를 허락하지 않다, 거부하다)>의 4형식 문장이 수동태로 바뀌어 <A be denied B>의 형태가 되었다. 수동태 동사 뒤에 목적어가 나온다는 것이 포인트이다.

해석   경제 시스템에서는 한 부문에서 일어나는 일이 다른 부문에 영향을 미치며, 한 부문에서의 재화나 서비스에 대한 수요는 다른 부문에서 파생된다. 가령 상점에서 상품을 구매하는 소비자는 아마 이 상품의 (재고) 보충을 촉발할 것이고, 이것은 제조, 자원 추출, 그리고 당연히도 운송 등의 활동에 대한 수요를 창출할 것이다. 운송에서 다른 점은 이것이 혼자서는 존재할 수 없고 이동은 저장될 수 없다는 것이다. 팔리지 않은 상품은 (흔히 할인 인센티브로) 구매될 때까지 매장 진열대에 남아 있을 수 있지만, 항공편의 미판매 좌석이나 동일 항공편의 미사용 화물 적재 용량은 안 팔린 상태로 남고, 이후에 추가 용량으로 되돌릴 수 없다. 이 경우 기회는 포착된(→ 상실된) 것인데, 제공되는 운송량(공급)이 그것에 대한 수요를 초과했기 때문이다. 파생된 운송 수요는 흔히 상응하는 공급과 조화되기 매우 어려워서, 실제로 운송 회사들은 예측하지 못한 수요를 맞출 수 있는 추가 용량을 (흔히 훨씬 더 높은 가격으로) 어느 정도 두기를 선호할 것이다.

지문 간단히 보기

> 경제 시스템에서, 한 부문에서 일어나는 일은 보통 다른 부문에 영향을 미침 → (예시) 상품 구매

↓

> 하지만, 운송에서는 상황이 다름: 항공편의 좌석이나 화물 용량이 다 사용되지 못하고 남으면, 이 초과된 공급을 되돌릴 방법이 없음
> ▶ **기회가 '상실됨'**

해설   진열돼 있으면 언젠가 구매될 수 있는 매대의 제품과는 달리, 항공편의 좌석이나 용량은 팔리지 않으면 나중에 추가 용량으로 '되돌릴' 수도 없이 미판매 상태로 남는다고 한다. 따라서 기회를 '놓친' 것이라는 결론에 맞게, ④에는 seized 대신 missed를 써야 한다.

오답풀이

보기 해석	선택률
① demands(수요)	5%
② stored(저장된)	12%
③ later(이후에)	16%
⑤ unforeseen(예측하지 못한)	28%

구문   [15행] ~ **since** the amount of transport <u>being offered</u> has exceeded the demand for it.
▶ since는 여기서 이유의 접속사(왜냐하면 ~이다)이다.
▶ 밑줄 친 <being p.p.>는 수동의 의미(~되고 있는)로 the amount of transport를 꾸민다.

07 정답 ④ 45%

해석 1945년 이후 제2차 세계대전 이후 유례없는 경제 성장은 건축 붐, 그리고 중심 도시에서 새로운 교외 지역으로의 대규모 이주를 부추겼다. 교외 지역은 자동차에 훨씬 더 많이 의존했고, 이는 주로 대중교통에 의존하던 것에서 자가용으로의 전환을 알렸다. 이것은 곧 더 나은 고속도로와 초고속도로의 건설과 대중교통의 감소, 심지어 쇠퇴까지로 이어졌다. 이러한 모든 변화와 함께 여가의 <u>사유화</u>가 이뤄졌다. 더 많은 사람이 내부 공간이 더 넓어지고 아름다운 외부 정원이 딸린 자기 집을 갖게 됨에 따라, 그들의 휴양과 여가 시간은 점점 더 집, 또는 기껏해야 인근 지역에 집중되었다. 이러한 집 중심의 여가에서 주요한 활동 한 가지는 TV 시청이었다. 사람들은 더 이상 영화를 보러 전차를 타고 극장까지 갈 필요가 없었고, 유사한 오락이 TV를 통해 무료로 더 편리하게 이용 가능해졌다.

지문 간단히 보기

> 2차 대전 이후 경제 성장 → 도시에서 교외로의 이동 촉발

↓

> 자가용에 대한 의존도 ↑, 대중교통 ↓

↓

> 휴양과 여가 시간도 '집과 인근 지역'에 집중되는, '집 중심의 여가' 문화가 나타남 ▶ **여가의 사유화**

해설 경제 성장 이후 사람들이 자가용을 사고 교외에 더 큰 집을 마련하면서, 대중교통을 통해 도시의 여가를 누리러 나오기보다는 '집 중심의' 여가를 선택하게 되었다는 내용이다. 따라서 빈칸에는 ④ '사유화'가 적절하다.

오답풀이

보기 해석	선택률
① 몰락	13%
② 획일성	18%
③ 회복	12%
⑤ 맞춤화	12%

구문 [16행] **No longer did one have to ride** the trolly to the theater to watch a movie; ~

▶ <부정어구 + did + 주어 + 동사원형> 어순의 도치 구문이다. 부정어구가 문장 맨 앞에 나오면 주어와 동사가 의문문 어순으로 도치된다.

08 정답 ① 39%

해석 서로 다른 학문이 자전적 기억을 어떻게 이해하려고 하는지 설명하려고 노력할 때, 문학 평론가 Daniel Albright는 '심리학은 정원, 문학은 황무지'라고 말했다. 내가 믿기로 그가 의미한 것은 심리학은 패턴을 만들고, 규칙성을 찾으며, 궁극적으로 인간의 경험과 행동에 질서를 부여하려 한다는 것이다. 반면에, 작가는 제멋대로이고 길들여지지 않은 인간 경험의 깊이를 파고든다. 기억을 이해하는 것에 관해 그가 말한 것은 어린아이의 마음에 관한 질문으로 확장될 수 있다. 만약 우리 심리학자들이 질서 있는 패턴, 즉 아이 마음의 규칙성을 밝히는 데 너무 열중한다면, 우리는 우리 주제의 본질적이고 널리 퍼져 있는 특성, 즉 아이가 지닌 더 제멋대로이고 상상력이 풍부한 말하기 방식과 사고방식을 놓칠 수도 있다. 다소 거칠고 색다른 사고방식에 끌리는 듯 보이는 것은 비단 성숙한 작가나 문학 연구가뿐만이 아니라, 어린아이도 역시 그렇다. 어린아이에게 관심이 있는 심리학자는 아이의 사고방식을 더 잘 이해하기 위해 <u>위험을 무릅쓰고 좀 더 자주 황무지에 발을 들여야</u> 할지도 모른다.

지문 간단히 보기

> 기억에 관한 '심리학 vs. 문학'의 이해 방식 비교
> - 심리학 = 규칙, 패턴, 질서 중시 = '정원'
> - 문학 = 제멋대로인 경험 중시 = '황무지'

↓

> 아동 심리 = 제멋대로이고 상상력 풍부
> → 규칙 발견에 집중하는 '정원'식 연구 X
> ▶ **길들여지지 않은 특성을 보는 '황무지'식 연구가 적합**

해설 아동 심리를 연구할 때 '황무지'와 같은 문학의 자유로운 세계를 참고하자는 내용이다. 흔히 심리는 규칙과 패턴을 찾아 나서는 '정원 가꾸기'와 같지만, 아동의 심리는 자유로움이 특성이므로 그에 맞는 '문학식' 접근이 필요하다는 것이다. 따라서 ① '위험을 무릅쓰고 좀 더 황무지에 발을 들여야'가 정답이다.

오답풀이

보기 해석	선택률
② 그들이 가장 소중한 기억을 떠올리도록 도와야	18%
③ 부모로서의 의무의 어려움을 더 잘 이해해야	12%
④ 아동 소설의 핵심 특징을 무시해야	19%
⑤ 그들의 심리 발달 경로를 표준화해야	11%

구문 [16행] It is **not only** the developed writer or literary scholar who seems drawn toward a somewhat wild and idiosyncratic way of thinking; young children are **as well**.

▶ <not only A but also B(A뿐 아니라 B도)>의 변형이다. 세미콜론이 접속사 but을, as well(~도)가 also를 대신한다.

해석 논쟁이란 다른 사람들에게 쟁점에 관한 여러분의 입장을 납득시키려고 노력하면서 '이유를 대는 것'이다. 사람들은 주장을 하고, 그것을 뒷받침한다. 논쟁자는 다른 사람들이 자신의 믿음이나 행동의 '정당성을 인정'하게 하기 위해 노력한다. 그렇다면 사람 간의 논쟁은 우리의 일상적인 갈등이나 협상에서 어떤 역할을 수행한다. 사람 간의 논쟁에서 긍정적인 특징 중 한 가지는 그것이 자신들의 믿음에 대한 이유를 제시할 수 있을 만큼 충분히 강하다고 느끼는 두 사람 간의 언쟁으로 구성되어 있다는 것이다. (그것이 한 사람이 우월감을 드러내는 동안 다른 한 사람은 결국 자신의 열등감을 깨닫게 되는 이유이다.) 만일 두 사람이 논쟁하고 있다면, 그것은 그들이 힘에 있어서(혹은 힘의 균형을 다시 설정하려는 욕구에 있어서) 논쟁을 이어나가기 충분하게 균형을 이뤘기 때문이다. 사실, 논쟁의 결여는 당사자 중 한 명이 너무나 무력함을 느껴서 그 사람이 상대방과 직접 상대하기를 피한다는 의미일 수 있다.

지문 간단히 보기

> 논쟁의 개념: 이유를 들어 자기 입장을 납득시킴
> → ① 일상적인 갈등이나 협상에서 수행하는 역할이 있음

> ② 논쟁의 특징: '자기 의견에 충분한 이유가 있다고 믿는' 두 사람 간에 이뤄짐
> = ④ 논쟁이 있다면, 두 사람 간에 '힘의 균형'이 있다는 뜻
> = ⑤ 논쟁이 없다면, '힘의 불균형'을 예상할 수 있음

해설 논쟁은 서로 자기 주장의 이유를 제시하며 힘의 균형을 이루는 과정이라는 내용이다. 하지만 ③은 우월감과 열등감을 느끼는 쪽이 나뉜다는 의미이므로 '균형'과 상반되는 진술이다. 따라서 ③이 흐름상 적합하지 않다.

오답풀이

보기 해설	선택률
① 논쟁은 '주장을 뒷받침하는' 것으로서 '일상에서 수행하는 역할이 있다'는 부연 설명이다.	5%
② 논쟁의 '긍정적 특징'으로 화제가 좁혀지는 문맥이다.	8%
④ ③이 아닌, ②에 대한 부연 설명이다. '힘이 있는 두 당사자' 간에 이뤄지는 것이 논쟁이므로, 논쟁이 있다는 것은 곧 두 사람이 '힘의 균형'을 찾으려는 시도라는 내용이 자연스럽게 연결된다.	23%
⑤ ④와 마찬가지로 ②를 보충 설명한다. ④와 반대로 '논쟁이 없을 때'는 힘의 균형이 '무너진' 상황임을 알 수 있다는 내용이다.	7%

구문 [7행] ~ two people who feel **powerful enough to set forth** reasons for their beliefs.
▶ <형/부+enough+to부정사(~할 만큼 충분히 …한)> 구문이다.

해석 다윈은 얼굴이 붉어지는 것을 인간 특유의 것으로 여겨, 이것이 사회적 환경에서 당혹감과 자의식에 의해 자기도 모르게 일어나는 신체 반응을 나타낸다고 보았다.
(B) 우리가 혼자 있을 때는 어색하거나 부끄럽거나 창피하다고 느끼더라도 얼굴이 붉어지지 않는다. 이것은 우리가 다른 사람들이 우리를 어떻게 생각할지 염려하기 때문인 듯하다. 연구에 따르면 단지 얼굴이 붉어진다는 말을 듣는 것만으로도 그렇게 된다는 것이 확인되었다. 우리는 다른 사람들이 우리 피부를 꿰뚫어 우리 마음을 들여다볼 수 있는 것처럼 느낀다.
(C) 하지만, 우리가 때로 우리도 모르게 얼굴이 새빨개질 때 사라지고 싶어하기는 해도, 심리학자들은 얼굴이 붉어지는 것이 실제로는 긍정적인 사회적 목적에 부합한다고 주장한다. 얼굴이 붉어질 때, 이것은 우리가 사회적 규범을 어겼음을 인정한다는 것을 타인에게 알리는 신호이자 실수에 대한 사과이다.
(A) 아마도 우리가 잠깐 체면을 잃는 것이 집단의 장기적 결속에는 도움이 되는 것 같다. 흥미롭게도 누군가가 사회적 실수를 저지른 후 얼굴을 붉히면, 우리는 그 사람을 얼굴을 붉히지 않는 사람보다 더 호의적으로 바라보게 된다.

지문 간단히 보기

> 얼굴이 붉어지는 것: 사회적 환경에서의 신체 반응
> (B) 혼자 있을 때는 얼굴이 붉어지지 않음

> (B) 얼굴이 붉어지면 우리는 마음을 간파당하는 기분
> (C) 하지만 이는 사회적으로 긍정적 목적 수행

> (C) 붉어진 얼굴 = 실수에 대한 인정과 사과
> (A) 체면은 좀 잃어도, 집단의 결속에는 도움

해설 얼굴이 붉어지는 것이 '사회적 환경'에서의 반응이라는 주어진 글 뒤로, (B)는 '혼자 있을 때'를 대비해 설명한다. 이어서 (C)는 이것이 '긍정적인 사회적 목적'에 부합한다고 하는데, (A)는 그 목적의 예로 '집단 결속'을 제시하므로, ③ '(B)-(C)-(A)'가 정답이다.

오답풀이 보기 해설

	선택률
① 주어진 글에 '집단 결속'에 관한 내용이 없으므로 (A)부터 연결되면 어색하다.	4%
② (B)에서 '사회적 기능'을 말하지 않으므로 '집단 결속'을 말하는 (A)로 연결되지 않는다.	25%
④ (C)-(A)에서 사회적 목적을 말하는데 (B)에서 갑자기 '혼자 있을 때'를 언급하면 어색하다.	13%
⑤ (A)의 '집단의 장기적 결속'은 (C)의 '긍정적 목적'에 대한 예이므로 (C)-(A)는 고정이다.	10%

구문 [1행] Darwin saw blushing as uniquely human, **representing** an involuntary physical reaction ~
▶ representing은 blushing을 보충 설명하는 분사구로, 계속적 용법의 관계절인 which represents로 바꿀 수 있다.

11 정답 ⑤ 25%

해석 인간 노동자의 고용이 줄어드는 가운데 공장에 로봇을 도입하는 것은 걱정과 두려움을 불러일으킨다. 이러한 두려움을 예방하거나 최소한 완화하는 것은 경영진의 책임이다. 예를 들어 로봇은 기존 조립 라인에서 인간을 대체하는 대신, 새로운 공장에만 도입될 수 있다. 새로운 공장을 계획하거나 기존의 공장에 로봇을 도입하는 데 노동자가 포함돼야 하는데, 그렇게 해서 그들은 그 과정에 참여할 수 있다. 로봇은 회사가 경쟁력을 유지하도록 제조 원가를 낮출 목적으로 필요할 수도 있지만, 이러한 원가 절감을 위한 계획은 <u>노사가 함께해야 한다. 또한 회사 내 새로운 직책을 위해 현재 직원을 재교육하면 해고에 대한 두려움도 크게 줄어들 것이다.</u> 로봇은 특히 매우 반복적인 단순 동작을 잘하기 때문에 교체된 인간 노동자는 로봇의 능력을 넘어선 판단과 결정이 필요한 위치로 옮겨져야 한다.

지문 간단히 보기

공장에 로봇 도입: 인간에게 불안 요소
→ 경영진은 노동자의 불안을 낮추기 위해 노력해야 함

방법1: 도입 계획에 노동자를 참여시키기
- 비용 절감의 목적이든 무엇이든, 노사가 '함께' 계획

방법2: 직원 재교육 및 재배치
- 로봇의 능력을 넘어서는 '판단과 결정'을 인간에게 맡김

해설 공장에 로봇을 도입하는 데 대한 노동자의 불안을 낮출 방법으로, ⑤ 앞까지는 '노사 공동의 참여'가 중요하다고 언급하고, 주어진 문장은 추가 방안(also)으로 직원 재교육 및 재배치를 제시하고 있다. ⑤ 뒤 또한 직원 재배치(replaced, should be moved)를 언급하며 주어진 문장을 보충 설명한다. 따라서 주어진 문장은 ⑤에 넣어야 적절하다.

오답풀이

보기 해설	선택률
① 앞의 worry and fear가 뒤에서 these fears로 지칭된다.	6%
② '노동자의 불안을 줄일 수 있는 경영진의 결정'에 대한 예시가 For example 뒤로 자연스럽게 제시된다.	14%
③ 앞문장과 같이 '새로운 공장에 로봇을 도입한다는 결정' 또는 기존 라인에 로봇을 도입한다는 결정에 노동자를 참여시켜야 한다는 주장이 뒤에서 적절하게 제시된다.	19%
④ 앞뒤 모두 '노동자를 계획에 참여시켜야 한다'는 공통된 논의이므로 논리적 공백이 없다.	34%

구문 [18행] ~ positions **where** judgment and decisions beyond the abilities of robots are required.
▶ 선행사 positions를 꾸미는 관계부사 where 뒤로 수동태가 포함된 완전한 문장이 연결되었다.

12 정답 ② 36%

해석 역사 소설을 위한 연구는 문서로 덜 기록된 보통 사람이나 사건 또는 장소에 아마 초점을 맞출 것이다. 소설은 역사적 맥락을 재창조하는 일상 상황, 감정, 분위기를 묘사하는 데 도움이 된다. 역사 소설은 '역사가들이 밝혀낼 수 있는 맨 뼈대에 살을' 붙이고, '그렇게 해서 꼭 사실이 아니더라도 과거의 사건, 상황, 문화를 더 명확히 시사하는 설명을 제공한다'. 소설은 과거의 부분들을 지어낼 뿐 아니라 그에 못지않게 과거에 색채, 소리, 드라마를 더한다. 그리고 Robert Rosenstone은 지어내는 것이 (역사) 영화의 약점이 아닌 강점이라고 주장한다. 소설은 역사 자료가 부족해 표현된 적이 없는 과거의 일부를 독자가 알게 해 준다. 실제로 Gilden Seavey가 설명하기로, 역사 소설 제작자들이 엄격한 학술적 기준을 강력히 고수했었다면, 많은 역사적 주제는 적절한 증거가 부족해서 여전히 탐구되지 못했을 것이라고 한다. 따라서 역사 소설은 전문 역사와 정반대된다고 여겨져서는 안 되며, 대신에 대중 역사학자도 대중 관객도 그것으로부터 배울 수도 있는, 과거에 대한 도전적인 표현으로 여겨져야 한다.
→ 역사 소설은 (A)불충분한 증거를 사용하여 과거를 구성하지만, 그것은 매력적인 설명을 제공하는데, 이는 역사적 사건에 대한 사람들의 이해를 (B)풍부하게 할 수도 있다.

지문 간단히 보기

역사 소설: 문서나 자료가 '부족한' 인물, 사건을 다룸

역사 소설의 강점
- '꼭 사실이 아니어도' 과거 상황을 더 잘 알게 해줌
- 부족한 부분을 '허구로 채울' 수 있음
- 학자와 대중에게 모두 '배울 점'을 줌
  ▶ **과거에 대한 이해가 '풍부해지게' 도와줌**

해설 글에 따르면 역사 소설은 증거가 부족해 표현되지 못했던 사실에 살을 붙여서, 비록 '허구를 포함할지라도' 과거를 더 풍부하게 이해할 수 있도록 도와준다고 한다. 따라서 요약문에 들어갈 말로 가장 적절한 것은 ② '불충분한 - 풍부하게 할'이다.

오답풀이

보기 해설	선택률
① 사소한 - 지연시킬	16%
③ 구체적인 - 강화할	20%
④ 구식인 - 향상할	19%
⑤ 제한된 - 방해할	9%

구문 [5행] ~ <u>an account [that **while (it is) not necessarily true** provides</u> a clearer indication of past events, circumstances and cultures].
▶ 'while ~ true'는 <대명사 주어+be동사>가 생략된 부사절 축약 구문이다. 생략된 주어 it은 앞에 나온 an account를 지칭한다.
▶ 선행사 an account가 단수명사이므로, 주격 관계대명사 that이 이끄는 관계절의 동사 또한 단수형(provides)으로 쓰였다.

13~14 정답 ② 44% / ⑤ 42% 2024학년도 수능 41~42번

해석 이야기를 과대광고하는 데 이바지하지 않는 한 가지 방법은 아무 말도 하지 않는 것이다. 그러나 이것은 대중과 정책 입안자에게 정보를 전하고/전하거나 제안을 줘야 한다는 강한 책임감을 느끼는 과학자들에게는 현실적인 선택안이 아니다. 언론 구성원들과의 대화는 메시지를 알리고 어쩌면 호의적 인정을 받을 수 있다는 장점이 있지만, 오해를 일으키고 반복적인 해명이 필요하며 끝없는 논란에 얽힐 위험을 감수한다. 따라서 언론과 대화할지 말지는 아주 개인적으로 결정되는 경향이 있다. 수십 년 전에 지구과학자들이 언론의 흥미를 끄는 연구 결과를 발표하는 것은 드문 일이었고, 따라서 언론과의 접촉을 기대하거나 권장하는 일은 거의 없었다. 1970년대에는, 언론과 자주 대화하는 소수의 과학자들은 흔히 그렇게 한 데 대해서 동료 과학자들로부터 비난을 받았다. 지금은 상황이 아주 다른데, 많은 과학자가 지구 온난화와 관련 문제의 중요성 때문에 공개적으로 말해야 한다는 책임감을 느끼고 있으며 많은 기자도 이런 감정들을 공유하고 있기 때문이다. 게다가, 많은 과학자는 자신이 언론의 주목과 그에 따른 대중의 인정을 즐기고 있다는 사실을 깨닫고 있다. 동시에, 다른 과학자들은 기자들과의 대화를 계속 물리치며, 그렇게 해서 자신의 과학을 위한 시간을 더 많이 지켜내고, 잘못 인용될 위험, 그리고 언론 보도와 관련된 다른 불쾌한 상황을 감수한다(→ 피한다).

지문 간단히 보기

> 과학자에게 언론과의 대화
> : 연구자로서 연구를 알릴 기회이자 책임 vs. 논란을 부를 위험

> 시간 흐름에 따른 과학자-언론의 대화
> - 수십년 전(1970년대): 권장 X → 대화하는 소수를 비난
> - 오늘날: 다수가 대화에 대한 책임을 느끼는 한편, 대화를 계속 피하는 이들도 있음 ▶ **오해 여지 회피**

구문 [14행] Decades ago, **it** was unusual **for** Earth scientists **to** have results that were of interest to the media, ~
▶ <it ~ for … to> 형태의 가주어-진주어 구문이다. <for+목적격>이 진주어인 to부정사구의 의미상 주어를 표시한다.
▶ 밑줄 친 <of+추상명사>는 형용사 역할을 한다. 즉 여기서 of interest를 interesting이라는 하나의 형용사로 바꿀 수 있다.

13

해설 과학자들이 언론과 대화할지 말지 선택하는 이슈에 관한 내용이므로, ② '과학자의 선택: 언론에 노출될 것인가, 말 것인가?'가 제목으로 가장 적절하다.

오답풀이

보기 해석	선택률
① 과학자와 언론 간의 골치 아픈 관계	22%
③ 과학자들이여! 언론과 대화할 때 주의하라	13%
④ 과학적 진실과 언론의 주목에 대한 딜레마	15%
⑤ 과학자와 언론 중, 누가 기후 변화에 책임이 있나?	7%

14

해설 마지막 두 문장은 언론과의 대화를 즐기는 과학자들과 '그렇지 않은' 다른 과학자들을 대비하고 있다. 이 '다른 과학자들'은 기자와의 접촉을 물리치고 언론과 연관된 불미스러운 일을 '피하려' 한다는 흐름이므로, ⑤ (e)의 running을 avoiding으로 고쳐야 옳다.

오답풀이

보기 해석	선택률
① advantages(장점)	3%
② unusual(드문, 특이한)	16%
③ criticized(비난을 받는)	11%
④ enjoy(즐기다)	29%

STEP PLUS+ 수능 기출 마무리 복습

단어 TEST
02 ~에 관해 **03** ~을 구성하다 **04** 배관공 **05** (권리를) 주장하다 **06** 추출 **07** ~에 열중하는 **08** ~로 구성되다 **09** 자기도 모르게 하는 **10** ~을 해고하다 **11** 문서로 덜 기록된 **12** 논란(의 여지)

구문 TEST
14 If I were a millionaire **15** if you were acknowledged **16** we had addressed the climate crisis earlier **17** our relationship might be better **18** remain unexplored for lack of evidence

01　정답 ①　95%　　　　2024 6월 19번

해석　Timothy는 책상에 앉아 필사적으로 과학책 페이지를 넘겼다. 그의 과학 프로젝트가 며칠 뒤면 마감인데, 그는 어디서부터 시작해야 할지 막막했다. 마침내 그는 책을 덮고 책상을 치며 외쳤다. "이건 불가능해!" 그의 누나 Amelia가 그 소리에 이끌려 그의 방으로 들어왔다. "동생, 누나가 좀 도와줘?" Timothy가 상황을 설명하자 Amelia는 즉시 해결책을 내놓았다. 그녀는 Timothy가 환경 문제에 대해 배워가는 것을 좋아한다는 것을 알고 그에게 기후 변화에 관한 프로젝트를 해보라고 제안했다. Timothy는 그 아이디어를 생각해 본 후 누나의 말이 옳다는 데 동의했다. "오, Amelia 누나, 누나의 아이디어는 정말 환상적이야! 고마워. 누나는 정말 최고의 누나야!"

지문 간단히 보기

> 과학 프로젝트 아이디어가 떠오르지 않던 Timothy

> 책상을 치며 막막해하자(**좌절**), 누나 Amelia가 도와주러 들어옴

> Amelia가 Timothy에게 기후 변화 프로젝트를 해 보라고 제안

> Timothy가 Amelia에게 '최고의 누나'라고 칭찬(**감사**)

해설　과학 프로젝트 마감이 코앞인데 아이디어가 떠오르지 않아 막막해하던 Timothy가 누나 Amelia의 조언으로 프로젝트 방향을 잡게 되어 고마워했다는 내용이다. 따라서 ① '좌절한 → 고마운'이 심경 변화로 적절하다.

오답풀이

보기 해석	선택률
② 실망한 → 부러운	2%
③ 희망 찬 → 짜릿한	0%
④ 용기를 얻은 → 창피한	0%
⑤ 두려운 → 무관심한	0%

구문　[8행] ~ **suggested** he **(should) do** a project about climate change.
▶ '주장, 요구, 명령, 제안' 동사의 목적절이 당위(~해야 한다)의 의미를 나타낼 때, 목적절의 동사 자리에 <(should)+동사원형>을 쓴다.

02　정답 ⑤　85%　　　　2024 5월 20번

해석　여러분이 중년이 되면, 부하를 견디는 힘의 감소가 지속된 높은 활동 수준과 합쳐지면서(힘은 줄어드는데 활동 수준은 높게 유지됨에 따라) 결합 조직 부상 위험이 최고조에 이른다. 가장 무난한 길은 아프게 하는 일들을 그만두는 것, 즉 불편한 움직임들을 피하고 더 쉬운 형태의 운동을 찾는 것이다. 그러나 이는 여러분이 해야 할 일과 정확히 반대된다. 앞으로 나아가는 길이 있다. 하지만 여기에는 휴식, 얼음찜질 및 약물이라는 전형적인 통증 관리 조언을 따르는 것이 포함되지 않는데, 여러 조사가 보여주기로 이것은 나이와 관련된 관절통과 기능 장애를 치료하는 데 효과적이지 않다고 한다. 이런 방법들은 표면적인 증상을 치료하는 것에 지나지 않는다. 유일한 실질적 해결책은 근육 훈련으로 여러분의 신체를 강화하는 것이다. 여러분이 몇 년 또는 몇십 년 간 운동을 해 왔든, 혹은 체력 단련실에 발을 디딘 적이 한 번도 없든 간에, 여러분의 몸을 회복하고, 진짜 힘을 키우고, 신체적인 잠재력을 실현하기에 별로 늦지 않았다.

지문 간단히 보기

> 중년 이후 하중을 견디는 힘은 줄어드는데 활동 수준이 계속 (높게) 유지되면 부상 위험 ↑
> → 무난한 해결책: 아픈 동작을 피하고, 더 쉬운 운동을 찾는 것

> 실상은 이와 '반대되는' 것이 유일한 실질적 해결책
> = 근육 훈련을 통한 신체 강화
> = 몸을 회복하고, 진짜 힘을 키우고, 신체 잠재력을 실현

해설　글이 전체적으로 '문제-해결'의 흐름이므로, 해결을 제시하는 'The only practical solution is ~' 뒤에 핵심이 있다. 중년 이후로 통증 때문에 불편하게 느껴지는 운동을 피하기보다는, 오히려 근육 단련으로 신체를 강화해야 한다는 것이다. 따라서 ⑤ '중년에는 통증이 따르더라도 근력 운동으로 신체를 강화해야 한다.'가 정답이다.

오답풀이

보기 해설	선택률
① '적절한 체중'에 관해 언급되지 않았다.	1%
② 운동의 '다양한 강도'에 관해 언급되지 않았다.	6%
③ '식단 관리'에 관해 언급되지 않았다.	1%
④ '치료'와 '예방'의 경중을 대비하는 글이 아니다.	5%

구문　[8행] ~, **which** multiple reviews have shown **is** not effective for treating age-related joint pain and dysfunction.
▶ <주격 관계대명사 which+be동사> 사이에 밑줄 친 <주어+동사>가 삽입되었다. 이는 '~이 보여주기로 (…하다)'의 의미로 해석한다.

03 정답 ⑤ 31%

해석 조명을 끄고, 작은 손전등 빛줄기가 여러분의 한쪽 눈 안을 향하게 하라. 시선을 위아래로 움직이면서 빛줄기를 이리저리 흔들어보라. 여러분은 미세한 가지처럼 보이는 것을 얼핏 보게 될 것이다. 이 가지들은 여러분의 망막 위에 있는 혈관의 그림자들이다. 그 혈관들은 빛이 눈으로 유입되는 동안 끊임없이 그림자를 드리우지만, 이 그림자는 절대 움직이지 않기 때문에, 뇌는 그것에 반응하기를 멈춘다. 손전등 빛줄기를 이리저리 움직이면 딱 그림자가 잠시 눈에 보이게 될 정도로 그림자를 움직이게 된다. 이제 여러분은 움직이지 않는 것을 단지 쳐다보기만 해서 어떤 이미지가 사라지게 할 수 있는지 궁금할지도 모르겠다. 하지만 이것은 불가능한데, 시각 체계가 끊임없이 눈의 근육을 가볍게 흔들고 있고, 이것이 세상 이미지의 완벽한 고정을 막기 때문이다. 이 근육의 움직임들은 믿을 수 없을 정도로 작지만, 그 효과는 엄청나다. 그것들(움직임)이 없다면 우리는 시선을 고정한 직후 보이는 것을 무시하게 되어 (그것을) 보지 못하게 될 것이다! 흥미로운 개념이다. 근사치의 완벽함이 완벽한 완벽함보다 더 낫다는 것 말이다.

지문 간단히 보기

눈 안에 빛줄기를 비춰 망막 혈관의 그림자를 보는 경우
- 원래는 그림자가 움직이지 않아 뇌가 '반응을 멈춤'
- 빛줄기를 움직이면 그림자도 움직임 → 눈에 보임

우리의 시각 체계도 눈 근육을 계속해서 흔듦
= 우리가 보는 이미지가 완벽하게 고정 X
= 뇌가 이미지를 '무시하지' 않음 → 눈에 보임

(비유) 근사치의 완벽함이 완벽한 완벽함보다 더 낫다
▶ **눈 근육의 흔들림이 이미지 지각에 도움이 된다**

해설 우리 뇌는 움직임이 없는 물체에는 반응하지 않기 때문에, 우리 시각 체계는 눈 근육을 미세하게 계속 흔들어 이미지의 완벽한 '고정'을 막음으로써 이미지가 '무시되지' 않게 한다는 내용이다. 따라서 ⑤ '눈 근육의 떨리는 움직임은 우리더러 뇌가 무시할지도 모르는 것을 볼 수 있게 해준다.'가 정답이다.

오답풀이 보기 해석   선택률

① 여러분의 시야를 흐리게 만드는 것이 사실은 여러분의 눈을 보호한다.   26%

② 어떤 대상이 더 빨리 움직일수록, 눈은 더 민감하게 반응한다.   14%

③ 강한 빛에 노출된 눈은 이미지 왜곡에 취약해진다.   17%

④ 지속적인 초점 조정은 눈 근육을 피로하게 만든다.   13%

구문 [18행] **Without them, we would go blind** by tuning out what we see shortly after fixating our gaze!
▶ <without+명사> 뒤 주절에 <would+동사원형>이 온 가정법 과거 문장으로, '~이 (실제로 있지만 만일) 없다면'의 의미이다. 이 Without them은 If it were not for them으로 바꿀 수 있다.

04 정답 ④ 42%

해석 자연재해와 노화는 (여러) 사회가 전 인류 역사에 걸쳐 다루고 있는 두 가지 문제이다. 정부는 두 가지 모두에 대응해야 하지만, 둘의 역학은 완전히 다르고 이 점이 대응의 본질에 깊은 영향을 끼친다. 단지 노화 기울기를 그려보는 것으로 정책 결정자들은 (노화) 문제 이해에 큰 진척을 보인다. 사람들은 일정하고 일관성 있는 속도로 늙어가기 때문이다. 노화 문제를 해결하는 방법에 대한 이견들이 있을 수 있으나 (이것이 정치적 복잡성이다), 문제의 본질에는 (결코) 논쟁의 여지가 없다. 자연재해로 사망한 사람들의 숫자를 그려보는 것은 자연재해의 무작위성을 강조하는 것 외에는 이 문제에 대한 이해를 거의 진척시키지 않는다. 그러므로, 정책 대응을 준비하는 것은 어떤 (특정) 영역에서 다른 영역에 비해 훨씬 더 쉽다. 입력 정보가 일관성 있고 예측하기 쉬울 때, 그것은 정보 처리가 대단히 용이하게 하고 예측적 문제 해결을 가능하게 한다. 문제가 인과적으로 복잡하고 변수가 많을 때, 적절한 대응을 결정하는 것은 반응적 노력이다.

지문 간단히 보기

인류의 오랜 두 가지 문제: 자연재해와 노화
→ 두 문제의 역학(양상)이 완전히 달라서 대응도 달라짐

(예시) 노화: '노화 기울기'를 그려보면 쉽게 파악O
    vs. 자연재해: '사망자 기울기'를 그려본다고 파악X

(문제의 본질에 따라) 영역별로 대응 마련이 쉽기도, 어렵기도 함
→ 예측적 접근과 반응적 접근 중 적합한 것을 택해야 함

해설 자연재해와 노화는 그 역학과 본질이 서로 달라서 각자에 대한 적절한 대응도 달라진다는 내용이다. 대비 관계가 연결어 등에 의해 명확하게 드러나지는 않지만 내용을 보고 '역학의 차이'를 이해할 수 있어야 한다. 따라서 주제로 가장 적절한 것은 ④ '문제의 본질에 따라 다른 정부의 접근법'이다.

오답풀이 보기 해석   선택률

① 자연재해 도중 성급한 의사결정을 내리는 것의 위험   8%

② 인구 고령화에 대해 정부가 우려하는 이유   10%

③ 정책 결정의 종합적 역사를 연구하는 의의   16%

⑤ 사회 문제 대처 시 예측적 문제 해결의 이점   25%

구문 [1행] Natural disasters and aging are two problems [**that** societies have been dealing with for all of human history].
▶ two problems를 수식하는 [ ]에서 that은 목적격 관계대명사로, 뒤에 현재완료 진행시제 동사구인 have been dealing with의 목적어가 없는 불완전한 절이 연결되었다.

05 정답 ⑤ 96%   2024 6월 26번

해석 Will Rogers(1879~1935)는 미국의 유명한 공인이었다. 그는 여덟 번째 아이로 태어났다. 어렸을 때 그는 영리하고 어른스러웠지만 10학년을 마치고 학교를 중퇴했다. 그는 카우보이와 말에 매우 관심이 많았고, 밧줄로 묘기를 하는 방법까지 배웠다. 1902년에 그는 미국을 떠나 남아프리카 공화국과 호주에서 카우보이이자 로핑 아티스트(동물을 밧줄로 붙잡으며 공연하는 사람)로 일했다. 미국으로 돌아와서, 그는 50편이 넘는 영화에 출연했으며 예능인으로서 (그의 목소리가) 라디오에서 자주 들렸다. 그는 또한 재치와 유머를 겸비한 뛰어난 신문 칼럼니스트로서 4,000편이 넘는 칼럼을 썼다. 그는 안타깝게도 경력의 절정이던 1935년에 세상을 떠났다. Rogers는 너무도 인기가 많아서 그의 사후 U.S. Capitol(미국 국회의사당)에 그의 동상이 설치될 정도였다. 그는 많은 재능을 지녔던 위대한 미국인으로 기억될 것이다.

지문 간단히 보기

> Will Rogers의 생애
> ① 8번째 자녀로 출생
> ② 카우보이와 말에 관심 → 밧줄 묘기 배움
> ③ 남아프리카 공화국과 호주에서 카우보이 & 로핑 아티스트
>   → 미국 복귀 후 50편이 넘는 영화에 출연
> ④ 뛰어난 신문 칼럼니스트 → 4,000편 넘게 집필
> ⑤ 그의 사후 U.S. Capitol에 동상이 세워짐

해설 '~ after his death his statue was installed in the U.S. Capitol.'에서 Rogers의 동상이 설치된 것은 그의 죽음 '이후'라고 하므로, 내용과 일치하지 않는 것은 ⑤ '생전에 그의 동상이 U.S. Capitol에 설치되었다.'이다.

오답풀이

보기 해설	선택률
① He was born as the eighth child.	0%
② He was very interested in cowboys and horses, ~	0%
③ After returning to the U.S., he appeared in more than 50 movies ~	1%
④ He was also an outstanding newspaper columnist ~	1%

구문 [14행] Rogers was **so** popular **that** after his death his statue was installed in the U.S. Capitol.
▶ <so ~ that …(너무 ~해서 …하다)> 구문이다.

06 정답 ⑤ 21%   2024 9월 30번

해석 우리 모두 자신이 신중하고 사려 깊게 생각하며 건전하고 신뢰성 있는 판단을 내릴 수 있는 합리적인 행위자라고 여기고 싶어 한다. 우리는 우리가 일반적으로 다양한 관점을 고려하고 정보에 입각한 결정을 내린다고 믿을지도 모른다. 사실, 우리는 심리학자 Dan Ariely가 이 주제에 관한 자기 책에 붙인 제목처럼 '예측할 수 있게 비합리적'이다. 우리는 모두 자동적이고 반사적인 사고를 하며, 대체로 더 쉬운 길을 택해 정신적 노력을 절약한다. 우리 각자가 자신이 신중하게 생각한다는 주관적인 인상을 가질 수도 있지만, 흔히 우리는 성급한 판단을 내리거나 아예 실질적인 판단을 하지 못한다. 게다가, 수많은 편향이 성찰적이고 신중한 사고를 억제하거나 무시하며, 직관적인 이론 또한 정확한 과학적 설명의 수용을 방해할 수 있다. 우리의 정신이 어떤 식으로 작용하고 편향은 어떤 식으로 작용할 수 있는지 더 많이 이해하면 우리 각자가 잘못된 추론에 덜 빠지고, 더 합리적이 되고, 타인의 사고에 있는 문제를 더 잘 알게 될 수 있다. 우리의 정신 과정에 내재한 합리성(→ 한계)를 이해하는 법을 배우는 것은 또한 우리가 다른 사람들에게 더 효과적으로 정보를 주는 능력을 향상하는 데도 도움이 될 수 있다.

지문 간단히 보기

> 통념: '우리는 신중하게 생각하며 합리적으로 행동함'
>
> ↓
>
> 반박: 실제로 우리는 '예측 가능하게 비합리적'
> = 자동적, 반사적 사고('더 쉬운 길')에 의존
> = 성급한 판단을 내리거나, 실질적 판단을 하지 못함
> = 수많은 편향과 직관적 이론 때문에 성찰적이고 신중한 사고 X
> ▶ **우리 정신 과정에는 '한계'가 있음**

해설 인간의 정신 과정은 '예측 가능하게 비합리적'임을 설명하는 글이다. 마지막 문장 앞까지 자동적 사고, 편향, 직관적 이론 등 여러 요소의 영향으로 인간의 판단이나 정보 수용이 합리성과는 거리가 있다는 내용이 주를 이룬다. 따라서 정신 과정의 특성을 요약하는 ⑤에는 rationality 대신 limitations를 써야 한다.

오답풀이

보기 해설	선택률
① informed(정보에 입각한)	6%
② easier(더 쉬운)	11%
③ acceptance(수용)	14%
④ less(덜)	49%

구문 [1행] We all like to **think of** ourselves **as** rational actors, **(who are)** careful and considered in our thinking, capable of sound and reliable judgments.
▶ <think of A as B(A를 B라고 여기다)> 구문이다.
▶ 선행사 rational actors 뒤로 <주격 관계대명사+be동사> 형태의 who are가 생략되고, are의 보어인 밑줄 친 부분만 남아 선행사를 보충 설명한다.

07 정답 ① 34%　　　　　2024 3월 32번

해석　이타적 행위의 도덕적 상태에 대한 상식적인 이해는 우리 대부분이 다른 사람들에 대한 책임에 관해 어떻게 생각하는가와 일치한다. 우리는 우리가 가진 것 중 얼마나 (타인과) 나눠야 하는가를 우리 대신 다른 사람 또는 사회가 결정하면 이를 불쾌하게 여기곤 한다. 우리는 성인이고, 스스로 그런 결정을 내릴 권리가 있어야 한다. 하지만 인터뷰를 해보면, 가장 큰 희생을 한다고—그래서 수혜자들에게 가장 큰 이득을 준다고—알려진 이타주의자들은 정반대로 주장한다. 그들이 주장하기로, 그들은 전적으로 다른 선택권 없이 자기가 행동한 대로 할 수밖에 없었다. 장기 기증자들, 그리고 자기 목숨을 걸어 치명적인 위험에 처한 타인을 구하는 보통 시민들은 자기 입장에 처한 누구든 정확하게 똑같이 행동했을 거라는 확신뿐 아니라, 자신이 뭔가 찬사받을 만한 일을 하지 않았다는 명백한 부인에 있어서 놀랍도록 일관된다. 확실히, 누군가 '더' 이타적일수록, 그들은 인류에 대한 기본적인 도덕적 의무를 회피하지 않도록 우리 모두가 기대받았을 정도로만 행동한 것이라고 주장할 가능성이 더 크다.

지문 간단히 보기

이타적 행위의 도덕적 상태에 대한 상식적 이해
: 남에게 얼마나 나눠줄지는 우리 자신이 결정하는 것

↓

(대비) 이타주의자들의 생각
= "누구나 내 입장이었다면 나처럼 행동했을 것"
= "나는 찬사받을 만한 일을 하지 않았다"
= "도덕적 의무상 다들 기대받는 정도만 한 것"
▶ **"다른 선택권 없이, 그렇게 할 수밖에 없어서 했다"**

해설　'Yet, when interviewed, ~'부터의 내용에 따르면, 타인을 위해 큰 희생을 한다고 알려진 이타주의자들은 자신이 누구든 할 일을 했을 뿐이라고, 즉 모두가 마땅히 기대받는 정도로만 행동한 것이라고 주장한다고 한다. 따라서 빈칸에는 이타주의자들이 주장하는 행위의 '당위성'을 잘 풀어 설명하는 ① '전적으로 다른 선택권 없이 자기가 행동한 대로 할 수밖에 없었다'가 적절하다.

오답풀이　보기 해석　　　　　　　　　　　　　　　　선택률

	보기 해석	선택률
②	경제적으로 보상받았어야 했다	12%
③	그런 선택을 내린 것을 후회했다	14%
④	보답으로 타인의 감사를 마땅히 받을 만했다	17%
⑤	위험한 상황에서 도덕적 의무가 적용될 수 없음을 깨달았다	24%

구문　[8행] Yet, **when interviewed**, altruists {known for making the largest sacrifices—and bringing about the greatest benefits to their recipients}—assert just the opposite.
▶ 주절 앞은 <접속사+과거분사> 형태의 분사구문이다. 문장의 주어이자 분사구문의 의미상 주어인 altruists가 '인터뷰를 당하는' 것이므로 수동을 나타내는 과거분사를 썼다.
▶ 주어가 복수명사이므로 동사 또한 복수형(assert)으로 쓰였다. { } 부분은 주어를 꾸미는 과거분사구(~로 알려진)이다.

08 정답 ⑤ 26%　　　　　2025학년도 수능 34번

해석　중앙 집중화된 공식적 규칙은 역할과 관행을 확립하여 생산적인 활동을 촉진할 수 있다. 야구 규칙은 단지 선수의 행동을 통제하는 것이 아니라, 경기 수행을 구성하는 행동을 결정한다. 규칙은 사람들이 야구 경기를 하지 못하게 막는 것이 아니라, 사람들이 야구를 할 수 있게 하는 바로 그 관행을 만들어낸다. 악보는 규칙을 부과하지만, 그것은 또한 사람들이 음악을 창작할 수 있게 하는 행동 패턴을 만들기도 한다. 기업 설립을 가능하게 하고, 유언과 신탁금 사용을 가능하게 하며, 양도성 증권을 만들어내고, 계약 관행을 확립하는 법규는 모두 개인에게 새로운 기회를 창출하는 관행을 만들어낸다. 그리고 판사, 신탁자, 파트너, 후견인 등의 개인이 법적 체계 안에서 수행하는 역할을 확립하는 법규도 있다. 물론, 이런 역할들을 설정해 주는 법규는 그 역할을 차지하는 개인의 행동을 속박하지만, 규칙은 또한 직접 역할을 만들어내기도 한다. 이런 규칙들이 없다면 개인은 역할을 차지할 기회를 얻지 못할 것이다.

지문 간단히 보기

공식적 규칙의 기능에 관한 여러 예시
- 야구의 규칙: 경기의 관행을 창출
- 악보의 규칙: 음악 창작의 행동 패턴 창출
- 법규: 기업 설립, 유언/신탁, 계약 관행 등등을 규정하여 새로운 기회를 창출

↓

(결론) 규칙으로 인해 행동에 제한이 생기기도 하지만, 결국에는 역할과 관행이 '만들어짐'
= 규칙이 없다면, 역할을 맡을 기회도 없어짐

해설　규칙은 일정 정도 개인의 행동을 속박하지만, 개인의 역할 또는 역할 수행과 관련된 관행을 창출하여 새로운 기회를 마련해준다는 것이 글의 요지이다. 빈칸 뒤에 제시되는 여러 예시를 통해 이러한 공통된 결론을 추론할 수 있다. '규칙이 역할을 만들기에, 규칙이 없다면 역할을 맡을 기회도 없다'는 내용의 마지막 두 문장 또한 결론 도출에 중요한 단서이다. 따라서 ⑤ '역할과 관행을 확립하여 생산적인 활동을 촉진할'이 빈칸에 적절하다.

오답풀이

	보기 해석	선택률
①	합법적이고 생산적인 방식으로 사람들의 행동 패턴을 분류할	17%
②	사람들이 사회 속 자신의 역할과 관행을 재평가하게 할	32%
③	창의적인 생각을 촉진하는 새로운 사고방식을 장려할	9%
④	합법적이고 정해진 맥락 안에서 사람들의 행동을 강화할	17%

구문　[10행] Legal rules [that enable the formation of corporations], [that enable the use of wills and trusts], [that create negotiable instruments], and [that establish the practice of contracting] all make practices ~
▶ 주어 Legal rules를 꾸미는 주격 관계대명사 that절이 <A, B, C, and D> 형태로 병렬 연결되었다. 본동사는 밑줄 친 make이다.

09 정답 ③ 53%

해석 독특하고 진정한 개인으로서의 자아를 만들어야 한다는 문화적 의무가 이행되기 어려운 상황에서, 자아를 개인화한다는 부담스러운 작업은 점점 더 알고리즘에게로 넘겨진다. 검색, 쇼핑, 건강, 뉴스, 광고, 학습, 음악, 그리고 오락의 영역 등, 모든 전면에서 약속되는 '개인화'는 그 어느 때보다 더 정교한 개성의 알고리즘적 구성에 달려 있다. 우리의 디지털 자아를 고유한 개인으로 만들어내기가 더 어려워지면서, 우리는 점점 더 외부로부터 고유한 개인으로 만들어지고 있다. (인공 지능 알고리즘이 우리 정체성에 관해 더 많이 학습할 때, 이 정보를 보호하고, 개인이 본인에 관해 수집된 데이터에 대해서 통제권과 동의를 갖도록 보장하는 것이 필수가 된다.) 개성은 문화적 관행이자 성찰적 과제로부터 알고리즘적 과정으로 재정의된다. 우리의 고유한 자아는 더 이상 우리가 전적으로 책임지는 것이 아니라, 알고리즘으로 보장되는 것이다.

지문 간단히 보기

> 자아의 개인화(독특한 자아 구축) = 알고리즘의 과업

↓

> ① 개인화: '개인의 알고리즘적 구성'에 좌우됨
> ② 우리는 '외부로부터' 고유한 개인으로 만들어짐
> ④ 개성의 재정의(문화적 관행 → '알고리즘적 과정')
> ⑤ 우리의 고유한 자아는 '알고리즘에 의해' 보장

해설 오늘날 개인의 고유한 자아는 알고리즘에 의해 구성된다는 내용으로, 정답인 ③을 제외한 나머지 문장이 사실상 모두 주제의 재진술이다. 하지만 ③은 개인정보의 보호, 통제, 동의 등을 보장해야 한다는 내용이므로 알고리즘과 개성의 관계를 논하는 전체 흐름상 어색하다.

오답풀이

보기 해설	선택률
① 개인의 자아 구성이 알고리즘의 일로 넘어가고 있다는 첫 문장 내용이 거의 반복된다.	2%
② from the outside가 '알고리즘에 의한' 자아 구성을 설명하므로 흐름상 적합하다.	15%
④ <from A to B>의 to B만 잘 봐도, 개인의 자아 구축이 '알고리즘 과정'으로 바뀌고 있다는 주제가 반복됨을 알 수 있다.	26%
⑤ 개인의 고유한 자아 구성이 알고리즘에 의해 보장된다는 말로 글 전체의 결론을 제시한다.	5%

구문 [1행] In a context [**in which** <u>the cultural obligation</u> to produce the self as a distinctive, authentic individual <u>is</u> difficult to fulfill], ~
▶ <전치사+관계대명사> 형태의 in which가 이끄는 관계절이 a context를 수식한다. 이 in which는 where로 바꿀 수 있다.
▶ 밑줄 친 부분이 각각 [ ]의 주어와 동사이다. 사이의 to부정사구가 주어를 수식한다.

10 정답 ⑤ 33%

해석 오늘날, 자연과 도시/교외 공간의 통합에 대한 역사적인 생각들은 지속 가능한 도시 계획에 대한 여러 해석으로 나타난다.
(C) 그러나 이런 접근 방식들에서 사회 정의의 역할은 여전히 논란의 여지가 크다. 예를 들어, 경관 도시론은 다양한 (생물) 종과 자원 이용도가 매우 낮은 경관을 포함하는 자연 서식지 설계를 옹호하는, 비교적 최근에 나온 계획 접근 방식이다.
(B) 그러나 비판가들은 경관 도시론자들이 인간의 필요보다는 미적 및 생태적 관심사를 우선시한다고 주장한다. 이와 반대로 신도시론은 1980년대에 대중화된 접근법으로, 걷기에 적합한 거리와 고밀도 디자인, 그리고 복합 용도 개발을 장려한다.
(A) 그러나 경관 도시론자들은 이런 설계가 자연환경을 우선시하지 않으며, 흔히 하천 우회와 자연 습지 파괴를 수반한다는 것을 알게 되었다. (한편) 또 다른 이들, 가령 '정당한 지속 가능성'이나 '완전 도로(보행, 자전거, 자동차 등이 모두 안전하도록 통행하도록 설계된 도로)'를 주장하는 이들은 두 접근 방식 모두 지나치게 이상주의적이며 사회적 역학 관계와 구조적 불평등의 현실에 충분한 주의를 기울이지 않는다고 여긴다.

지문 간단히 보기

> 지속 가능한 도시 계획에 대한 해석은 다양하게 나타남
> (C) 하지만, 이런 접근 방식들에서 사회 정의의 역할은 여전히 '논란'

↓

> (C) 경관 도시론: 자연 서식지 설계 중시
> (B) 경관 도시론에 대한 비판: 인간의 필요 고려↓

↓

> (B) 한편, 신도시론: 인간의 편의 중시
> (A) 신도시론에 대한 경관 도시론자들의 비판: 자연환경 고려↓

해설 주어진 글에서 언급된 '지속 가능한 도시 계획에 관한 여러 해석'을 (C)에서 '이런 접근 방식들'로 칭한 후, (C)-(B)에서 Landscape Urbanism, (B)-(A)에서 New Urbanism에 관한 소개와 비판을 각각 전개하는 흐름이다. 따라서 ⑤ '(C)-(B)-(A)'가 가장 적절하다.

오답풀이

보기 해설	선택률
① 주어진 글의 interpretations가 (A)의 these designs로 자연스럽게 연결되지 않는다.	5%
②, ③ (B)의 Landscape Urbanists와 관련된 내용이 주어진 글에 없으므로 이들을 '비판'하는 (B)부터 오면 부자연스럽다.	16% / 16%
④ (C)-(A)가 연이어서 '도시 경관론자들'을 언급하지만 (A)는 이들의 '비판 대상'인 '신도시론'에 관한 서술이다. 겹치는 단어만 보고 순서를 확정하면 안 된다.	31%

구문 [C-2행] ~ a relatively recent planning approach **that advocates for native habitat designs** <u>that include diverse</u> **species and landscapes [that require very low resource use].**
▶ 'a ~ approach'를 꾸미는 that절 안에 native habitat designs를 수식하는 밑줄 부분과 landscapes를 꾸미는 [ ]이 중첩되었다.

 정답 ④　43%　　　　　　　　2024 6월 38번

해석　측정된 배출물에 직접 근거를 둔 환경세는 원칙적으로 그 정책의 환경적 목표를 아주 정확히 겨냥할 수 있다. 어떤 기업이 더 많이 오염시키면, 그 기업은 배출물 증가에 정비례하는 추가 세금을 낸다. 따라서 공해 기업은 잔여 배출물의 단위당 세금보다 감소 단위당 비용이 덜 드는 어떤 식으로든 배출량을 줄일 동기를 갖게 된다. 측정된 배출물에 직접 근거해서 세금을 매기는 것의 매우 큰 매력은 공해 기업이 세금 부담액을 줄이고자 취할 수 있는 조치가 곧 배출물도 줄이는 조치라는 점이다. 지속적인 배출물 측정은 특히 개별 배출원이 많은 경우 비용이 클 수 있으며, 이는 많은 오염 문제에서 배출물에 대한 직접 과세에 주요한 저해 요소가 될 수도 있다. 그렇지만, 폐기물 배출에서 특정 물질의 농도와 흐름을 관찰하기 위해 이용할 수 있는 기술이 빠르게 발전해 오고 있다. 앞으로는 측정된 배출물에 대한 세금 부과를 고려하는 것이 더 광범위한 응용 분야에서 가능할 수도 있다.

지문 간단히 보기

배출물 측정량에 비례해 세금 부과: 환경적 목표와 합치

↓

오염 배출물이 많으면 세금도 더 많이 내게 됨 = 기업 입장에서 배출물을 줄일 동기가 생김 = '세금을 줄이려는 노력으로 배출물도 줄이게 되는' 장점

↓

저해 요인: 개별 배출원이 많을 때 측정 비용↑ → 그래도, 측정 기술이 발전하고 있으므로 긍정적 전망 가능

해설　④ 앞에서 배출물에 대한 직접 과세의 장점을 주로 다룬 데 이어, 주어진 문장은 배출원이 많으면 지속된 배출물 측정에서 비용이 커질 수 있다는 잠재적 '저해 요인'을 언급한다. ④ 뒤의 Nevertheless부터는 '그렇지만' 측정 기술이 발전하고 있어 직접 과세의 광범위 적용을 검토해볼 법하다는 내용으로 주어진 문장을 적절히 반박한다. 따라서 ④가 정답이다.

오답풀이　보기 해설　　　　　　　선택률

① 앞에 언급된 '배출물 측정량에 대한 직접 과세'의 의미를 뒤에서 예시로 보충 설명한다.　5%

② '오염을 더 시킨(= 배출량이 더 많은) 기업이 세금도 더 많이' 내므로 '배출물을 줄일 동기가 생긴다'는 흐름이다.　15%

③ 앞의 '배출물을 줄일 동기'가 뒤에서 드러난다. '세금을 줄이려면 곧 배출물을 줄이면' 되기 때문에 동기 부여가 이뤄진다는 것이다.　28%

⑤ 배출물 측정 기술이 발전하고 있으므로 앞으로는 직접 과세의 광범위한 도입도 생각해볼 수 있다는 인과 흐름이 자연스럽다.　10%

구문　[14행] ~ the actions [(that) the polluter can take to reduce tax liability] are actions [that also reduce emissions].
▶ 첫 번째 [ ]는 목적격 관계대명사가 생략된 관계절이며, 두 번째 [ ]는 주격 관계대명사절이다.

 정답 ①　67%　　　　　　　　2025학년도 수능 40번

해석　사람들은 종종 합성 식재료가 천연 식재료보다 더 해롭다고 생각하지만, 항상 그런 것은 아니다. 일반적으로 합성 식재료는 정밀하게 통제되는 방식으로 만들 수 있고 구성과 특성이 명확하여, 잠재적 유독성을 자세히 평가할 수 있다. 반면에 천연 식재료는 흔히 원산지, 수확된 시기, 일생에 걸쳐 경험한 기후, 토양의 질, 분리되고 저장된 방법에 따라 그 구성과 특성이 눈에 띄게 달라진다. 이러한 차이로 인해 안전성 테스트가 매우 어려워질 수 있고, 매번 다를 수 있는 세세한 성분의 잠재적 유독성에 대해 결코 확신할 수 없다. 어떤 경우에는, 천연 식품 성분이 수백 또는 수천 년 동안 명백한 건강상 문제를 일으키지 않고 섭취되어 왔고 그렇기에 안전하다고 추정될 수 있다. 하지만 그래도 매우 주의해야 한다.
→ 합성 식재료 생산 공정의 (A)통제 가능성과 천연 식재료의 변동성은 사람들이 흔히 지니고 있는, 천연 식재료가 더 안전하다는 가정을 (B)반박할 수 있다.

지문 간단히 보기

통념: 천연 식재료가 합성 식재료보다 안전하다 vs. 반박(항상 그런 것은 아니다)

↓

합성 식재료 - 정밀하게 통제된 제조 방식 - 잠재적 유독성을 평가하기 쉬움

↓

반면, 천연 식재료 - 구성, 특성이 천차만별 - 안전성 테스트가 어려움

해설　첫 문장에서 천연 식재료가 합성 식재료에 비해 더 안전할 것이라는 통념이 있지만 '늘 그렇지는 않다'는 말로 반박을 예고한다. 이어서 두 번째 문장부터 합성 식재료가 정밀하게 통제 가능한 방식으로 제조되어서 잠재적 유독성을 자세히 평가할 수 있는 한편, 천연 식재료는 변동성이 커서 안전성을 추정하기 어렵다는 보충 설명이 제시된다. 따라서 요약문의 빈칸에는 ① '통제 가능성 - 반박할'이 적절하다.

오답풀이　보기 해설　　　　　　　선택률

② 예측 가능성 - 지지할　13%

③ 관리 가능성 - 강화할　7%

④ (가격) 적정성 - 뒤집을　6%

⑤ 접근성 - 의문을 제기할　5%

구문　[8행] On the other hand, natural ingredients often vary ~ depending on their origin, the time of year [(when) they were harvested], the climate [(that) they experienced throughout their lifetime], the soil quality, and how they were isolated and stored.
▶ 밑줄 부분은 depending on의 목적어로, <A, B, C, D, and E>의 병렬 구조이다.
▶ the time of year를 꾸미는 [ ]에서 관계부사 when이 생략되었다.
▶ the climate를 꾸미는 [ ]에서 목적격 관계대명사가 생략되고, experienced의 목적어가 없는 불완전한 절이 나왔다.

13~14 정답 ③ 62% / ⑤ 35% 2024 6월 41~42번

해석 우리가 비판적 사고를 '의사결정을 안내하기 위한 증거의 검증 및 평가'라고 본다면, 윤리적 사고란 윤리적 사안을 식별하고 이러한 사안을 다양한 관점에서 평가하여 어떻게 대응할지를 안내하는 데 관한 것이다. 이런 형태의 윤리는 더 높은 수준의 개념적 윤리나 이론과는 구별된다. 이 관점에서 윤리적 사안이나 문제의 본질은 명백하게 옳거나 그른 대응이 없다는 것이다. 따라서 학생들은 (이미) 규정된 일련의 윤리 규범이나 규칙을 따르기보다는, 윤리적 문제를 충분히 숙고하는 법을 배우는 것이 필수적이다. 비록 윤리적인 행동이 '옳다고 여겨지는 행동 원칙에 따라' 행동하는 것으로 정의된다고 하더라도, 이러한 원칙은 개인끼리, 그리고 한 개인 안에서도 다를 수 있다는 인식을 장려할 필요가 있다. 개인이 중시하는 것은 그들의 공식적 및 비공식적 학습 경험에 영향받은 사회적, 종교적, 혹은 시민으로서의 신념과 관련이 있다. 또한 개인의 관점은 상황에 좌우될 수도 있는데, 이는 다른 환경에서 다른 시점에 다른 감정을 느끼고 있다면 똑같은 개인이 다른 선택을 할 수도 있다는 뜻이다. 따라서 윤리적 사안을 분석하고 윤리적으로 사고하려면 여러분만의 '행동 규범'에 영향을 미치는 개인적 요인들을 이해하고, 이것들이 어떻게 일치할(→ 달라질) 수 있는지 이해하며, 그와 동시에 다른 사람들의 행동 규범과 의사결정을 이끄는 요소들이 다를 수 있다는 점을 인식하고 받아들이는 것이 필요하다.

지문 간단히 보기

> 비판적 사고 개념을 접목한 '윤리적 사고'
> = 다양한 관점에서 윤리적 사안을 평가하고 대처법 파악

↓

> 명백히 '옳고 그른' 대처법이 따로 존재하는 게 아님
> = 개인마다, 한 개인 안에서도 행동 원칙이 다를 수 있음
> = 개인마다 학습 경험과 신념에 따라 가치 있게 여기는 것이 다르며,
>   같은 개인도 상황, 시점, 감정에 따라 영향받을 수 있음

↓

> 윤리적 행동 규범에 영향을 주는 각종 개인적 요인을 잘 파악하는
> 한편, 그것이 서로 '다를' 수 있음도 이해해야 함

구문 [27행] ~ in order to analyse ethical issues and think ethically **it** is necessary **to understand** the personal factors [that influence your own 'code of behaviour'] and how these may coincide(→ vary), ~

▶ 가주어(it)-진주어(to understand ~) 구문으로, 밑줄 친 명사구와 how절이 to understand의 목적어이다.
▶ [ ]은 the personal factors를 꾸민다.
▶ how절의 these는 첫 번째 목적어인 the personal factors를 가리킨다.

13 **해설** 윤리적 사고나 판단은 정해진 일련의 규범보다는 개인마다 옳다고 여기는 바에 맞춰 달라지고, 심지어는 같은 개인 안에서도 상황이나 시점에 따라 달라진다는 내용이다. 따라서 이러한 '개별성'을 강조하는 ③ '윤리적 사고: 개인의 마음을 거니는 여정'이 제목으로 적절하다.

오답풀이

	보기 해석	선택률
①	비판적 추론: 윤리적 의사결정으로 향하는 길	15%
②	윤리가 행동 규범에 미치는 광범위한 영향	10%
④	타인의 눈에 비친 윤리 이론 탐구	8%
⑤	윤리적 선택은 항상 우선일까?	2%

14 **해설** 개인마다, 혹은 한 개인 안에서도 윤리적 사안에 대한 분석이 달라질 수 있다는 내용으로 보아, 윤리적 사고에 관여하는 개인적인 요인끼리도 어떻게 '다를' 수 있는지 파악해야 한다는 결론이 적절하다. 따라서 ⑤ (e)의 coincide를 vary로 고쳐야 옳다.

오답풀이

	보기 해석	선택률
①	essential(필수적인)	5%
②	encourage(장려하다)	9%
③	values(중시하다, 가치 있게 여기다)	11%
④	dependent(좌우되는, 의존하는)	41%

STEP PLUS+ 수능 기출 마무리 복습

단어 TEST
02 기능 장애, 역기능 **03** 고정, 안정(화) **04** 떨리는, 불안정한 **05** 뛰어난 **06** 성급한 판단 **07** 불쾌하게 하다 **08** 진정한 **09** 우선시하다 **10** 저해 요소 **11** 잔여의, 남은 **12** ~에 따라, 맞게

구문 TEST
14 see if[whether] he can join us for dinner **15** by attentively checking your work[by checking your work attentively] **16** The more patiently you wait **17** The quieter the library (is) **18** lest she forget a single word

MEMO